Holistic Mobile Game Development with Unity

Master mobile game design and development in this all-in-one guide to creating iOS and Android games in the cutting-edge game engine, Unity. By using Penny de Byl's holistic method, you will learn about the principles of art, design, and code and gain multidisciplinary skills needed to succeed in the independent mobile games industry. In addition, hands-on exercises will help you throughout the process from design to publication in the Apple App Store and Google Play Store.

- Over 70 practical step-by-step exercises recreating the game mechanics of contemporary mobile games, including *Angry Birds*, *Temple Run*, *Year Walk*, *Minecraft*, *Curiosity Cube*, *Fruit Ninja*, and more.
- Design principles, art, and programming in unison—the one-stop shop for indie developers requiring interdisciplinary skills in their small teams.
- An introduction to essential two- and three-dimensional mathematics, geometry, and physics concepts.
- A portfolio of royalty-free reusable game mechanics and assets.
- Accompanying website, www.holistic3d.com, features project source code, instructional videos, art assets, author blog, and teaching resources.
- Challenge questions and lesson plans are available online for an enhanced learning experience.

Penny de Byl is a professor of games and multimedia in Australia. An awardwinning teacher, Penny has taught computer science, computer graphics and game development at top-ranked universities for nearly 20 years. She is the author of three books on designing and developing artificial intelligence and games including the acclaimed *Holistic Game Development with Unity* and winner of the 2011 Unity Technologies' Unity Mobile Generation Great Education Giveaway.

T0138873

Holistic Mobile Game Development with Unity

An All-In-One Guide to Implementing Mechanics, Art Design, and Programming for iOS and Android Mobile Games

Penny de Byl

Focal Press
Taylor & Francis Group

NEW YORK AND LONDON

First published 2015
by Focal Press
70 Blanchard Road, Suite 402, Burlington, MA 01803

and by Focal Press
2 Park Square, Milton Park, Abingdon, Oxon OX14 4RN

Focal Press is an imprint of the Taylor & Francis Group, an informa business

Library of Congress Cataloging-in-Publication Data

Baillie-de Byl, Penny.
    Holistic mobile game development with Unity : an all-In-one guide to implementing mechanics, art design, and programming for iOS and Android mobile games / Penny de Byl.
        pages cm
    1. Computer games—Programming.   2. Mobile games.   3. Unity (Electronic resource)   I. Title.
    QA76.76.C672B336   2014
    794.8'1526—dc23   2014006126

ISBN: 978-0-415-83923-5 (pbk)
ISBN: 978-0-203-77372-7 (ebk)

Typeset in Myriad Pro
by Apex CoVantage, LLC

Printed and bound in the United States of America by Sheridan Books, Inc. (a Sheridan Group Company).

Contents

Preface

About This Book

This book presents the theory and practice of mobile game development art and code for both Apple and Android mobile devices using the Unity game engine. While the exercises are written exclusively for game design and development in Unity, the theoretical concepts transcend the entire mobile game realm.

Four years ago I started teaching mobile game design and development to designers and artists with little programming knowledge. The precursor to this was my idea for a university-level mobile game development course winning the Unity educational curriculum challenge. Unity kindly provided my university with Google Nexus One phones and licenses for Unity's Android plugin. My passion for developing mobile games grew as I saw the power that the Apple had given small indie development teams to publish their ideas and the ease with which Unity made it possible.

Teaching programming to artists is indeed a challenging task. However, when it is presented in an exciting, relevant, and visual way I find students start to push aside their preconceived ideas about writing code. On the flip side, a lot of programmers don't consider themselves to be designers or artists even though they have more than enough sound skills to produce a mobile game on their own. Through the presentation of the design process as an analytical, rule-based activity, the novice artist can easily achieve many visual elements of a game.

My motivation for writing this book is to demonstrate the strong bond, in games and indeed other interactive multimedia, between programming, art, and design. My aim is to deliver practical and timely lessons to both the programmer and artist that can empower individuals to explore the realm of mobile game creation right up to the point of publishing their very first app.

How This Book is Organized

This book has been written for artists and programmers alike who want to learn how to make their own mobile games for the Apple App Store and Google Play by dissecting contemporary mobile games such as *Angry Birds*, *Temple Run*, *Year Walk*, *Bejeweled*, *Minecraft*, and more. It approaches mobile game development using a unique combination of lessons on programming and design theory in unison.

All chapters are structured with theory and practice. There are more than 70 practical exercises that lead the reader through a wide variety of game mechanics, physics, user interfaces and networking examples:

- Chapter 1, "Mobile Game Design and Development," examines the history of mobile gaming technology, provides an introduction to Unity, and steps the reader through practical exercises to get a simple app built to an iPhone/iPad and Android phone/tablet. Most importantly advice for optimizing game art and code to run smoothly on mobile devices is given.
- Chapter 2, "Procedural Literacy," reveals the intricate relationship that exists between art and code with a step-by-step *Minecraft* landscape recreation. It explains the fundamentals of programming and covers the more important mathematics of game environments that all game developers should know.
- Chapter 3, "Mobile Game Interfaces," presents the principles of mobile game interface design and steps the reader through the creation of apps that demonstrate mobile specific interactivity including touch, pinch to zoom, thumbsticks, tilt, and GPS. In addition, tips and tricks are presented for making game interfaces look good on all screen sizes and resolutions.
- Chapter 4, "Aesthetics and Visual Literacy," provides the flip-side to Chapter 2, examining design theory with respect to mobile game creation. It presents the essential visual and audio aspects required to develop a game including static textures, animated sprites, special effects, and finishing touches.
- Chapter 5, "Learning from the Masters: Part One," closely dissects a multitude of contemporary and successful mobile games including *Bejeweled*, *Year Walk*, *Fruit Ninja*, *Harbor Master*, and *Super Monkey Ball*. The reader is taken, step by step, through recreations of specific elements of each game that makes them unique.
- Chapter 6, "Learning from the Masters: Part Two," examines the use of physics, procedurally generated content, and artificial intelligence through hands-on recreations of *Angry Birds*, *Catapult King*, *Temple Run*, and *Curiosity – What's Inside the Cube?*
- Chapter 7, "Multiplayer Experiences," examines asynchronous and synchronous games through the development of multiplayer games on a single device and over a network. Fundamental computer networking theory is explained to equip the reader with knowledge for sending messages between mobile devices connected to the Internet.
- Chapter 8, "Publishing, Players, and Promotion," reveals the challenges game developers face in getting their game noticed in the app stores. It provides numerous tips for monetizing and publishing games including the deployment of in-game advertising, in-app purchasing, and social networking with Facebook and Twitter. In addition, step-by-step instructions are given for building and distributing games from Unity via the Apple App Store and Google Play.

The Companion Website

The web site accompanying this book is www.holistic3d.com. It contains all the files referred to in the hands-on exercises herein, finished examples, and many other teaching and learning resources including instructional videos and PowerPoint slides.

Acknowledgements

First I would like to thank the reviewers, Mike Daly and Mark Backler. I must say their feedback has been some of the most encouraging and constructive feedback received in the ten years I have been writing. No doubt their thorough revision of my material and advice has made this book all the better.

Next, I acknowledge Unity3d for their fantastic game engine. The types of games developers are making with it is truly inspirational and I hope together with the content of this book and my previous one, *Holistic Game Development*, a new generation of game designers feel empowered to continue providing high quality, unique mobile gaming experiences. I also greatly appreciate all members of the Unity community who regularly contribute to the forums at http://forums.unity3d.com as they are an invaluable knowledge base.

I'd also like to thank my games design students at Bond University who've acted as guinea pigs for all the exercises contained herein. Observing the use of the step-by-step activities in a classroom environment has helped to iron out any issues as well as pick up coding typos.

My friends James, Kayleen, Sian, Mark, and Jeff likewise deserve a big thanks for their continued encouragement and belief in my abilities, acting as shoulders to cry on and providing a touch of reality when required. Special thanks to James for his exception abilities and help with Adobe Illustrator, Photoshop, and Maya, and Kayleen's enthusiasm for contributing the accompanying PowerPoint slides.

Finally, the biggest thanks go to my family, Daniel, Tabytha, and Merlin the Labrador. They have all been so supportive and understanding during the times I've locked myself in the office cursing at code and furiously writing to meet deadlines. Daniel has been a massive support throughout this project. His partnership in editing and testing all the exercises is always invaluable. This book would not have made it to the shelves without him. He is an absolute wiz with Microsoft Word and has an uncanny knack for finding logic errors in code. Tabytha (aged ten) has been perfect at keeping me grounded, bringing me out of my workaholic habits with games of Monopoly, Uno, and getting me to find her cheat codes for *The Sims* or figuring out why her *Minecraft* world has gone missing. There are more important things in life than constantly working and in her own way she is teaching me to relax. As always, Merlin has provided daily emotional support as a foot-warmer evidenced by the dog-shaped silhouette in the carpet under my desk.

As a programmer and artist, nothing excites me more than being about to use code to produce art. To me games are the perfect medium through which one can really express one's creative urges. If you are reading this, I shall assume you feel the same. I sincerely hope you enjoy reading this book and learn something new and useful with each page.

Disclaimer from Unity about the cover

The Unity name, logo, brand, and other trademarks or images featured or referred to within this book are licensed from and are the sole property of Unity Technologies. Neither this book, its author, nor the publisher is affiliated with, endorsed by, or sponsored by Unity Technologies or any of its affiliates.

Mobile Game Design and Development

We don't need to be the first to market. We need to be the best to market.
Zynga CEO Mark Pincus

1.1 In the Beginning…

Taking the first steps into a development project can often seem an overwhelming process; let alone venturing into an entirely new platform: mobile. Developing games for any platform is a highly rewarding experience where the result of combining carefully crafted aesthetics and ingenious programming mechanics produces more than a game, it produces an experience. Creating desktop and console games has evolved beyond that of an amateur hobby, into a multibillion-dollar industry that encompasses and fuels a range of industries outside that of video games and creative media, including sports, finance, shopping, cooking, medicine, and education. For many years, desktop and console-based games were the platform of choice: a joystick, handheld-controller, or keyboard and mouse were the sword and shield of many players as they entered into their chosen game realm. With the turn of the millennium the status quo shifted, and a new player emerged as a viable and fruitful platform for games: the mobile phone.

Since the invention of electronic devices, people have been working to put games on them. We can't help deny our built-in playful instinct to make things interactive and fun. We have been doing so since birth in order to learn more about the world. Scientific experimentation could even be construed as an extension of play, as play is a mental state in pursuance of high-level reasons, problem-solving and creativity.

The first noted electronic game, William Higinbotham's *Tennis for Two*, was created on an oscilloscope (a device for displaying electrical current instantaneously on screen). This lead the way for a plethora of casual games appearing on pretty much any electronic device with buttons, for example, calculators, television sets, and digital watches. Soon games started appearing on mobile phones: *Tetris* was the first made available on the Hagenuk MT-2000 soon followed by *Snake* (illustrated in Figure 1.1) in 1997. Nokia included the game on a selection of mobile phone devices, before joining forces with Motorola, Sony Ericsson (previously Ericsson), Microsoft, and a handful of other technology leaders to form the Wireless Application Protocol (WAP) Forum in 1997; now referred to as the Open Mobile Alliance. The organization is responsible for managing the data specifications and protocols that facilitate wireless network and data interoperability. It is the cornerstone for providing global communications standards and the foundation of all mobile application development. The Open Mobile Alliance is also responsible for technology that allows us to connect with others over a network connection—such as the type used in multiplayer gaming—and ensures mobile software usability.

The portable platform revolution inspired many innovative, independent software developers. As WAP technology matured, the caliber of games began to expand to include mobile versions of classics such as *Prince of Persia*, *JAMDAT Bowling*, and a port of *Space Invaders* in the early 2000s. Up until this point, mobile phones featured a monochromatic screen. In 2003, the industry began to adopt color screens, opening up a slew of visual opportunities for developers.

Potentially the most crucial turning point in mobile history to date was the release of the Apple iPhone in 2007. Featuring an accelerometer (for detecting a change in motion), gyroscope (to record device orientation), and a large, full color, multitouch capacitive screen, it completely redefined the design and function of mobile phones. The Apple App Store, opened at the same time, allowed developers for the first time to directly market their applications to iPhone and iPod Touch owners (for low prices when compared with desktop/console games), and presented an opportunity for independent and small-group developers to gain equal footing in the traditionally AAA environment of video games.

Early Apple mobile games utilized multitouch gestures to create new levels of user experience, completely changing traditional game mechanics. The iOS (originally, the iPhone Operating System) on the Apple iPhone, iPad,

FIG 1.1 *Snake* on a Nokia 6120.

and iPod Touch devices is based on the construction of the widely used Mac OS X platform. Developing applications for the platform has been made considerably easier with the addition of a variety of Software Development Kits (SDKs) provided by Apple, primarily in the form of Xcode; a Mac OS X based development environment that allows for creation and thorough testing of iOS applications, as well as Mac applications. The framework itself uses the popular object-oriented programming language known as Objective C, with the platform providing integrated support for memory management, networking, and rapid code development.

One year after the release of the iPhone, Google joined the playing field with the release of their mobile operating system, Android. As both a competitor and rival to iOS, Android is an open-source platform (built on top of the popular Linux platform). It is easily modified and installed on a variety of mobile devices, and provides a number of similar features to that of iOS including: an integrated multiapplication environment, device orientation and email/message/phone functionality. The Google equivalent to the Apple App Store, originally called the Android Market, is Google Play.

In 2010, Apple released another innovative product that would once again change the industry; the iPad. A large, multitouch capacitive tablet that shared many features of the iPhone, but without the phone. The device itself presented yet another avenue for development and creativity. It provided a larger screen that allowed more advanced, detailed applications and games to be created. This opened the proverbial floodgates for beautiful interactive magazines and high-definition animated eBooks such as Moonbot Studios' *The Fantastic Flying Books of Mr. Morris Lessmore* illustrated in Figure 1.2.

Tablets presented a new opportunity for interactivity. Bigger screens allowed for better gesture/touch-based user interaction, and an overall improved user

FIG 1.2 *The Fantastic Flying Books of Mr. Morris Lessmore* on iPad.

experience. Later that same year following the release of the iPad, Google announced a tablet-specific version of Android for such devices, with key vendors in the space adopting support for the operating system in 2011.

The result of this technological boom meant that these compact phones and tablets could be taken anywhere and be used at any time to entertain. However, the exponential rise in popularity of these devices had been met with a significant boost in the number of developers (beginners, seasoned developers, hobbyists, and everyone in-between) flocking to the platform in an attempt to secure their share of more than 40 billion app sales and downloads. In the final quarter of 2012, it was reported that registered Apple developer numbers had exceeded 275,000;[1] a 540% increase from the estimated 43,000 in 2010.[2]

Throughout the past two decades we have seen the mobile platform transition from being a completely new enterprise into one that has taken the world by storm. Being able to create applications and games in the first instance, is part of the challenge but making successful, high-quality applications is what sets amateur developers and successful professional developers apart. No matter how daunting the development process may appear to be, every seasoned expert developer has to start somewhere.

1.2 A Brief History of Mobile Video Games

The video game became truly mobile with the invention of the liquid crystal display (LCD). It was between 1964 and 1968 that researcher George Heilmeier led a team of scientists and engineers at the RCA David Sarnoff Research Center in developing a method for electronically controlling light reflected from liquid crystals and thus producing the first display.

In 1979 Milton Bradley, a company better known for creating board games, released the first handheld game device with interchangeable cartridges and an LCD screen. The Microvision, shown in Figure 1.3, had a 16 × 16 pixel display. A total of 13 games were created for the device between 1979 and 1982 including *Connect Four*, *Star Trek: Phaser Strike*, and *Alien Raiders*. However, the honor of being the first to deliver a true handheld goes to toy company Mattel who two years earlier (in 1977) released a series of games that configured a screen from LED dots. Each device was capable of playing just one game. Titles included *Football*, *Baseball*, *Basketball*, *Missile Attack*, *Armor Battle*, and *Sub Chase*.

In 1980 Nintendo released the first of its Game & Watch series; its earliest major success in the games market. The first generation of these devices included an

[1] Source: "As Boom Lures App Creators, Tough Part is Making a Living," www.nytimes.com/2012/11/18/business/as-boom-lures-app-creators-tough-part-is-making-a-living.html?partner=rss&emc=rss&_r=0.
[2] Source: "How Many Developers Develop for iOS and Android," http://mashable.com/2010/07/02/ios-android-developer-stats.

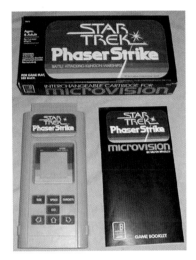

FIG **1.3** *Star Trek: Phaser Strike* on the Microvision.

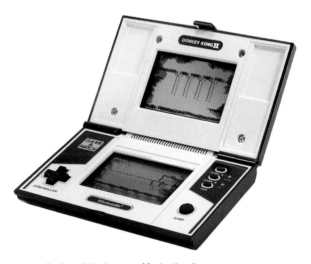

FIG **1.4** The Game & Watch version of *Donkey Kong II*.

LCD screen. The directional navigation pad or control cross, later to become synonymous with Nintendo gaming, was patented during the initial design phase of these devices. The series was produced up until 1991 in a variety of colors, screen size formats, and configurations, including the flip-open dual screen (see Figure 1.4) that later influenced the design of the Nintendo DS. In total, some 60 different Game & Watch games were produced including popular titles such as *Donkey Kong*, *Oil Panic*, *Green House*, *Zelda* and *Super Mario Bros*.

Just before the turn of the decade, in 1989, Nintendo released the handheld gaming device that would rival all competitors for many years to come; the Game Boy. The original device had a monochromatic 160 × 144 pixel

FIG 1.5 Nintendo's Game Boy (photograph courtesy of William Warby).

LCD screen and measured 90 mm (W) × 148 mm (H) × 32 mm (D). In North America it came bundled with *Tetris* and was originally priced at $89.99. During its lifetime more than 800 game titles were released for the device. Other models included the Game Boy Pocket and the Game Boy Light released in 1996 and 1998 respectively.

Around the same time, Atari released the world's first handheld gaming device with a color LCD; the Atari Lynx. However with its $189.95 price tag and up to five hours of life from six AA batteries (compared to the Game Boy's 12 hours on four AA batteries) it could not compete with the Nintendo device.

Another direct competitor to the Game Boy, released in 1990 was Sega's Game Gear. Like the Lynx, it had superior graphics to the Game Boy, but its poor battery performance and high price saw it achieve only a small portion of the market. In addition, both Atari and Sega had failed to attract the cohort of game developers creating for Nintendo, although they did provide some notable titles such as *Sonic the Hedgehog* and Disney's *The Lion King*.

Also in 1990, the NEC Corporation took mobile to a different level by bundling a TV tuner with a portable version of the TurboGrafx-16 video game console. The result was the TurboExpress. The TV tuner included RCA audio and video input, which meant the device could be used as an external monitor. At $249 at launch, the TurboExpress has the honor of being the most expensive handheld video game system ever made.

Although not a commercial success, the Nokia N-Gage (shown in Figure 1.6), released in 2003, was the first serious attempt at integrating game specific hardware with mobile phone capabilities. It also included an MP3 player, PDA and radio. The N-Gage was developed in an attempt to lure gamers away from the Nintendo Game Boy Advance released in 2001. However the button layout of the N-Gage, which was best suited for phone functionality, made the device quite clumsy despite its brilliant graphics and 3D rendering capabilities

FIG 1.6 The Nokia N-Gage (photograph courtesy of J. P. Karna).

of the time. The N-Gage saw only 58 game titles released for it including its premier title *Tony Hawk's Pro Skater*.

The remainder of the 2000s witnessed the release of an advanced range of to-date unrivaled devices including the Nintendo DS and PlayStation Portable (PSP) both released in 2004. The DS is very much reminiscent of the Game & Watch series with its folding dual screens and cross controller. It included more advanced features than its predecessor however, with a touchscreen, wireless connectivity and a microphone. The touchscreen interface introduced a new and novel mechanic into the games market and a series of games for the less seasoned player evolved. This included, most notably, *Dr. Kawashima's Brain Training: How Old Is Your Brain?*, which Nintendo exploited in marketing campaigns to attract people who may not have considered themselves gamers and encourage them to take another look at the device.

While Nintendo stayed with its traditional cartridge style for game delivery, Sony's PSP was the first handheld to use its own proprietary optical disc format. It includes a large 480 × 272 pixel screen measuring in at 97 mm on the diagonal and is WiFi, USB, and Bluetooth enabled. The PSP was succeeded by the PlayStation Vita (PS Vita) in 2011. For this device Sony dispensed with the optical disc for game distribution and instead introduced the PlayStation Vita card; a proprietary flash memory card 30 × 22mm). Interestingly, the PS Vita incorporates the same processor architecture as the iPad 2.

Nintendo's direct market competitor for the PS Vita is the Nintendo 3DS (also released in 2011). Although its central processing unit is a generation behind that of the PS Vita it includes an autostereoscopic screen capable of projecting 3D effects without the need for 3D glasses. To date, the top selling title on this device has been *Super Mario 3D Land*.

As previously mentioned, the biggest disruption to mobile games occurred in 2007 with Apple's launch of the iPhone and App Store. Although the iPhone itself was in no way a direct market competitor with either the Sony or Nintendo platforms, what Apple had done was to revolutionize game development and distribution, and introduce a whole new demographic to handheld gaming. At the same moment, Apple instigated a new era in mobile hardware advances driven by consumer need for bigger, brighter, crisper, and faster gaming and communications portability.

1.3 A Brief History of Mobile Phone Games

Games on mobile devices first became a viable option when the LCD screens and associated processors became capable of displaying more than one line of numerals. Even though early mobile games were based on various incarnations of *Tetris* or *Snake*, the limitation of small shaded square graphics and midi-type *bleeping* audio tracks did not deter developers. While, at the same time, more high quality immersive games, available on desktop computers and consoles, were attracting and defining a generation of hardcore gamers, the mobile market was witnessing the birth of the ubiquitous "casual gamer" in a worldwide marketplace worth more than $5 billion where 33% of gamers play on their smartphones and 25% on handheld devices.[3]

The success of this market on the back of low level graphics, poor sound, and limited user interface emphasizes just how people are driven not to big-budget visual effects but to the actual essence of the game itself; the gameplay. For mobile games within the casual games genre, this includes promising players novel, explorative experiences and unique interactivity. Therefore, while the technical capabilities of mobile devices are indeed improving and becoming more attuned with console capacities what this re-evolution of gaming has shown us is that the ideas are what will carry the games to success.

The inventors of the room-sized ENIAC (Electronic Numerical Integrator and Computer), the world's first electronic general purpose computer, could not have imagined in their wildest dreams the processing power that would be squeezed into the palm of our hands some 50 years later. Without this revolution in technological advancement, the vast array of mobile games available today would not be possible.

1.3.1 The Rise of Mobile Architecture

The primary CPU chip set used in mobile devices is the ARM (Advanced RISC Machine) architecture. Android, iOS, Windows Phone, and BlackBerry OS are just some of the operating systems designed to run on this hardware. In 2011, 95% of the ARM chips produced were used in smartphones. The ARM-based CPUs were first developed for use by Acorn in their computers in the 1980s. By the end of the 1980s Apple and VLSI Technology were working with Acorn on developing newer, more powerful versions. In 1992, Apple-ARM released the ARM6. This chip was first used in the Apple Newton PDA. The specific ARM chipsets are defined in architecture versions. For example, ARMv6 (version 6) included the chipset ARM11 and ARMv7 includes the chipsets named Cortex-A8 and Cortex-A9. At the time of writing, the ARM Cortex-A50 series has just been announced. They will reportedly have 16 times the processing power of the ARM Cortex-8 processors of the first-generation iPhones.

⚫ **On the Web**
If you are interested to learn more about ARM architecture check out the technology at www.arm.com.

---

[3] Source: "2012 Essential Facts about the Computer and Video Game Industry," www. theesa.com/facts/pdfs/ESA_EF_2012.pdf.

For the majority of smartphones the entire system running the device resides on a single chip. These are called Systems on a Chip (SoC). The SoC consists of: a microprocessor; memory; USB, Ethernet, and other external interfaces; and power management circuitry all within a single integrated circuit. They are far more economical to manufacture as a single unit and their compact size make them ideal for mobile devices. Several of the SoCs used in Apple and Samsung devices are shown in Table 1.1.

With reference to Table 1.1, CPU stands for central processing unit. The speed at which it runs is measured in hertz (Hz) or cycles per second. With respect to the CPU, the amount of hertz expresses the clock speed. The clock speed is one factor that determines the speed at which the CPU can process

TABLE 1.1 An Overview of some Apple and Samsung SoCs.

Devices	SoC	CPU Architecture	CPU Clock Speed (GHz) Chipset	GPU Clock Speed (Mhz) Raster Operations (ROPs)
iPhone iPod Touch (1st Gen) iPhone 3G		ARMv6	412 MHz (ARM11)	103 MHz (0.5 ROPs)
Samsung i7500		ARMv6	538 MHz (ARM11)	256 MHz (ROPs NA)
iPad iPhone 4 iPod Touch (4th Gen)	A4	ARMv7	0.8–1.0 GHz single core Cortex-A8	200–250 MHz (2.5 ROPs)
Samsung Galaxy S	Exynos 3 Single*	ARMv7	1 GHz Cortex-A8	200 MHz (5 ROPs)
iPad 2 iPhone 4S	A5	ARMv7	0.8 – 1.0 GHz dual core Cortex-A9	200–250 MHz (dual) (5 ROPs)
Samsung Galaxy SII	Exynos 4 Dual*	ARMv7	1.2 GHz Cortex-A9	240–395 MHz (5 ROPs)
Samsung Galaxy SIII	Exynos 4 Quad*	ARMv7	1.4 GHz Cortex-A9	240–395 MHz (5 ROPs)
iPad 3	A5X	ARMv7	1.0 GHz dual-core Cortex-A9	250MHz (quad) (5 ROPs)
iPhone 5	A6	ARMv7s	1.3 GHz dual core Swift	266 MHz (triple) (5 ROPs)
iPad 4	A6X	ARMv7s	1.4 GHz dual core Swift	300 MHz (quad) (5 ROPs)

* International, AU and KR version only, NA and JP = Qualcom Snapdragon

data. It should be noted that directly comparing the hertz of two CPU is only a good measure of performance difference between the CPUs of the same family.

The graphical processing unit (GPU) is a circuit, not unlike the CPU, but dedicated to the rapid manipulation of data pertaining to the generation of images. A GPU performs operations related to the texturing and display of polygons and accelerates the geometric calculations of translation, rotation, and scaling. Like a CPU, a GPU has a clock speed expressed in hertz. This value is usually much lower for the GPU than a CPU in the same system as the GPU is specialized just for graphics and does not carry the load of a CPU. The hertz of a GPU when multiplied with its raster operation (ROP) value gives the GPU's fillrate. It is the fillrate that you can use to compare one GPU against another. The fillrate tells you how many pixels per second a GPU can process ready for rendering. For example, the GPU in the iPad 3 is capable of drawing 1,250 megapixels/sec.

With both the CPU and GPU, the given clock speeds are best case scenarios reported by the vendors. Actual performance will be affected by the number and complexity of the calculations the chips are required to process. However, while you can't assume the given speeds, they do go some way as to providing the consumer with a comparison by which to judge the capabilities of the mobile devices in which they are installed.

The capacity of the CPU and GPU are fundamental elements taken into consideration when creating a mobile game. This is evident when you examine the types of games that have been available throughout the differing generations of mobile devices.

It's obvious that when you look at the earliest mobile games, such as *Snake*, compared with *The Room* (App Store Game of the Year 2012, illustrated in Figure 1.7) that game aesthetics have come a long way. This is not because the developers have become better at creating them, but that the technology is now such that it affords higher quality images, interfaces, sounds, and other effects. In AAA games, almost 80% of the processing power of the hardware is dedicated to processing and generating the graphics. This is no different in mobile devices. As the chipsets increased in capacity, higher quality games became available.

As previously discussed, however, gaming on mobile phones was also open to a completely different audience than the handheld game devices. Titles not considered of interest to hardcore gamers began to appear on the mobile phones. These included a variety of games, including the everyday classics such as poker, solitaire, and Monopoly, as well as a diverse range of purpose-built mobile games, taking advantage of the devices' novel play mechanics, interface, and market. *Words with Friends*, *Tiny Tower*, *Harbor Master*, *The Room*, *Mini Motor Racing*, *Ski Safari* and *Temple Run* are but a handful of casual games that have found their true calling in the mobile domain.

FIG 1.7 *The Room.*

The advances in networking also affected the available games. Early games were simple, single-player games, but as technology (primarily the capabilities for each of the CPUs in the devices) became more advanced, more detailed games were able to be crafted. Users and players alike would experience devices with vibrant, full color screens, and could interact with games and applications using multiple inputs (including speech and multiple-gesture). Play itself also changed, with gaming becoming both a synchronous and asynchronous activity that could be engaged in by a number of users, located theoretically anywhere in the world.

An often surprising twist on mobile play was the rise of location-based games. As play became portable, users were able to start exploring their physical spaces, and it wasn't long before physically active games and interactive media were created and implemented to provide enchanting experiences that also took players out of their way, and into the real world. Using a combination of Global Positioning Systems (GPS), near-field communication, Bluetooth, and wireless networks to track the position of the player, games like *Shadow Cities* and *Parallel Kingdom* are able to be portable, popular, and support multiple players within a given geographic area. One of the more popular applications of GPS-location based games is the ever-growing concept of geocaching. Originally started in 2010, players play a game of hide and seek using their mobile phones as they search for (and scatter) containers throughout the world. Other popular games like *Tourality* and *SCVNGR* provide a serious component to location-based gaming, by promoting the exploration of a player's local area and wider real world environment by presenting a series of interactive location-based challenges.

1.4 The Mobile Game Developer's Handbook

When it comes down to it, game development is essentially an exercise in software development. Sure there are lots of cool images, sounds, animations, and special effects like you might expect in your favorite film, but it is the underlying code that makes it all work. As such, the game development process should adhere to a tried and true software engineering model, especially if you are working in a team.

1.4.1 Software Development Life Cycle

Software engineering processes and planning may sound like a dry and boring concept if you are ready to jump straight into coding, however some appreciation and knowledge for the process will stand you in good stead as your project progresses. It is critical that you structure your work around time-honored design and development patterns at first and then evolve them to suit your team's work style. The key reason being that a methodology shared by all in the team will assist in your communication, scheduling, project scope, and problem-solving.

The software development life cycle (SDLC) is a software engineering principle that identifies each stage in a project from inception through to delivery. These stages include analysis, design, implementation, testing, and evaluation, as illustrated in Figure 1.8.

During the analysis phase (1), idea-generation, requirements analysis, and feasibility studies are undertaken to identify the project goals and to determine if they are achievable. This is followed by the design phase (2) in which the project is conceptualized and a plan is created in terms of budgets, schedules, and technical requirements. In addition, during the design phase, detailed specifications for the project are realized including screen layouts, program flow, user interfaces, and all other documentation required to fully specify the software before development begins. The third phase is concerned with all elements of building (3) and implementing the project; creating assets, writing scripts, implementing pre-written plugins and modules, and bringing everything together. Following on from development, thorough testing (4) of the finished product is thoroughly completed, where any logical faults or errors that may exist in the system are identified and corrected. It's at this point that the product is released to the world. But the life cycle

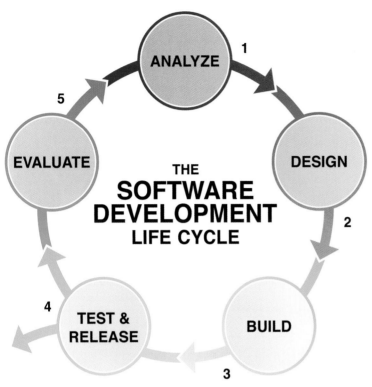

ANALYZE 1

DESIGN 2

BUILD 3

TEST & RELEASE 4

EVALUATE 5

THE
SOFTWARE DEVELOPMENT
LIFE CYCLE

FIG 1.8 The software development life cycle

doesn't stop there. The final phase is evaluation (5). It involves examining not only the quality and completeness of the finished product, but how each module in the software development life cycle was accomplished. The life cycle continues to loop, for each iteration of the project, bugs and other errors may be fixed, and the product may be expanded further and improved, and with each addition more issues and opportunities for expansion (also known as feature creep) may arise. This process will continue until the product is declared finished. There are a variety of SDLC methodologies that can be described along a continuum from agile to sequential illustrated in Figure 1.9.

Sequential methodologies require a big-design-up-front (BDUF) in which the entire project has been planned out according to a comprehensive design document. A sequential project adheres strictly to the phases of the SDLC in that one phase must be completed before the next begins. Essentially, there is no going back. As you might imagine without thorough documentation, a comprehensive design, and well thought-out timeline the strictness of such a methodology can be fraught with danger. Such methodologies work well for very large projects where the final product is clear, the development team large, the clients tend not to be too involved in the development process, and a strict timeframe and budget must be adhered to. Planning the entire

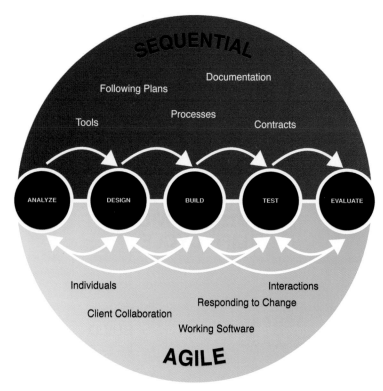

FIG 1.9 Agile versus sequential development.

project up-front also assists in identifying any potential risks and putting in place measures to counteract them should they arise. A very large software engineering project will be destined for failure unless due care has been taken to clearly identify the system's requirements and comprehensive documentation prepared of the project specifications and schedule. Finally, system testing with actual users should not be an afterthought, but something planned ahead of time to fit into the project plan.

At the other end of the SDLC spectrum are the agile methodologies. These are distinguished by frequent meetings, rapid prototyping, and a flexible process that allows for rapid changes in the project specifications as the project progresses. In such methodologies, the complete requirements and solutions evolve throughout the project as collaboration occurs among project stakeholders. They promote a planning process that adapts to the needs of the project as it progresses. This means that sometimes the plan, processes, and goals will change to meet new needs as they become available. Specific methodologies that are classified as agile include Extreme Programming (XP) and Scrum.

During agile development individual team members and their interactions take priority over processes. This means that any predefined plans usually followed during a sequential development are allowed to be modified or discarded at anytime. If a certain way of working is not productive for the team then it is changed to suit individual needs. One software development technique that has evolved from agile processes is pair programming. This practice involves two programmers working together at the one console. This may seem inefficient or a waste of resources, however, the advantages of collaborating on writing code, debugging, problem-solving, and knowledge-sharing far outweigh the cost of having two programmers doing the same task.

Although agile development may sound chaotic, by the end of the project the team will have gone through each of the phases of the SDLC. The difference in the agile approach is that it is far more flexible and iterative, allowing the project schedule to visit and revisit any and all phases at any time as required. For example, the testing phase may be embedded in the building phase along with rapid prototyping. At any point testing may reveal flaws in the initial design and the team is then free to revisit that phase to problem-solve any issues before progressing to building again.

1.4.2 A Game Development Life Cycle

Game development life cycles tend towards the agile end of the continuum and work well for indies and small teams. While mobile game development teams favor no specific methodology from the SDLC literature, many concepts from agile development such as pair programming and regular team meetings are popular. Often notebook sketches, mind maps, and flowcharts are favored over extensive design documents. A technique called "rapid prototyping" is employed in which playable game segments are developed quickly and continually play-tested. For a prototype, the code need not be perfect and the art can merely be represented by placeholders (for example, the boss monster could just be a cube) as long as the game runs and can be played. After testing, the prototype might prove to provide the wrong type of interactions in which case the code is thrown out. This is not a big loss if little effort, other than pure logic, has gone into it.

As mobile game development teams tend to be small, they are often already working closely together and therefore a BDUF is not required. In addition, making a game fun to play and ensuring the user interactive experience is just right are not things necessarily known at the beginning of a project. To assist in illustrating the mobile (or indeed casual) game development process the cycle in Figure 1.10 is presented as a fusion of iterative game design and development techniques taken from the principal author's own development experience and methods referred to by Jesse Schell in *The Art of Game Design* and Tracy Fullerton in *Game Design Workshop*.

The mobile game development cycle in Figure 1.10 is presented as an iterative, spiral life cycle in which the project begins with a game idea and then enters a schedule that rapidly moves through the phases of analysis,

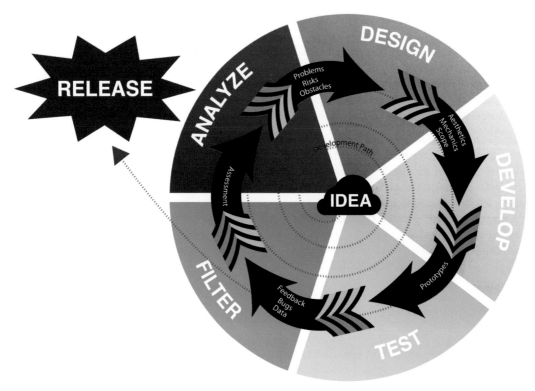

FIG 1.10 An agile game development life cycle.

design, development, testing, and filtering until the game is deemed ready for release. Each of the phases will now be explained in detail.

1.4.2.1 Idea

Every game creation project begins with an idea. Contrary to popular belief, this idea need not be mind-blowingly unique. Not every design team is going to come up with a new idea as novel as birds flinging themselves at green pigs or the honing of ninja skills in making fruit salad. Some of the most successful mobile games are built upon solid visual design, clear interfaces, competent programming, and very simple ideas. Sometimes the ideas aren't even new. For example, the match-three[4] gameplay mechanics of *Bejeweled* are so compelling that they can be found in numerous successful mobile/casual games such as *Puzzle Quest*, *10000000*, and *Fishdom*. Novelty is *a* key to success, but it's not the only one.

1.4.2.2 Filter

The filter phase is the time at which you stand back and take a good look at your game idea, its design, and its development progression from numerous angles.

---

[4] A game mechanic in which a player matches up three or more tiles of the same type to make them disappear from the play area.

Designing and developing a game is a very personal and rewarding experience. In many ways it is like painting to an artist or music to a composer. If you don't have faith in your game, the way it plays, its content, and the way it looks, then it will be very difficult for you to see it through to the end. You must honestly assess your game idea with respect to time-honored and proven ideas on good game-playing experiences, game flow, level-design, aesthetics, interface, and all other visual, auditory, interactive, and mechanical game components.

One way to assess your game on a less subjective level to your gut feeling is to compare it with games targeting the same demographic with the type of content and gameplay you are proposing. Although gamer stereotyping can be a sensitive subject, it actually works to your advantage in aiming right at the hearts of your audience. For example, if your game idea were similar to *Nintendogs*, in which the player trains and plays with a virtual puppy, the most suitable target audience would be children, as opposed to middle-aged men.

In his book *The Art of Game Creation*, Schell asks game designers to filter their ideas through eight key questions.

1. Are you comfortable with the game on an artistic and moral level?
2. Is the game designed in the best way to engage the target audience?
3. Is the game well designed with respect to player experience, engagement, and immersion?
4. Is this game novel enough to attract players?
5. Will players pay to play the game?
6. Can the game be built within the confines of existing software and hardware?
7. Can you see a thriving community of interest evolving around the game?
8. Does the target audience enjoy playing the game?

In summary, what Schell is alluding to are the questions you must ask yourself about the motivations behind developing the game and goals you have set for the game. You may not be making a game for profit and therefore question 5 becomes irrelevant. Rather you might be creating a free game to raise awareness for some cause close to your heart, such as the Royal Society for Prevention of Cruelty to Animals, in which case questions 4, 7, and 8 are more applicable. In the end only you can decide on what these filtering questions will be based on your initial drive to begin the process.

The filter phase is where you decide to continue development, redesign the game, release the game, or ditch the project completely.

1.4.2.3 Analysis
The initial game idea presents your project team with its first problem to solve; "how are we going to make this game?" However, on entering the analysis phase for the first time during a project, the more immediate pressing issues will be whether or not your team has the capacity to develop the game, the risks of beginning the project, and any obstacles standing in the way. The

capacity of your team refers to the members' abilities to produce the art and program code, or work with the technology. For example, if you were to create a 3D game for the Android platform you would require team members with expertise in 3D model creation as well as familiarity with the Android platform in order for your idea to progress into a real project. If you fail to have the required knowledge you could assess the team's ability in gaining these skills within the time and budget constraints of the project. Anything that you can think of that could cause the project to fail needs to be listed. Some of the questions you should ask yourself in this phase include:

- What is our timeline and budget?
- Do we have the necessary skills to address all areas of the game's development?
- Will the game perform well on the target hardware?
- What risks exist that could encumber the projects successful completion?

In the first instance you are performing a strengths, weaknesses, opportunities, and threats (SWOT) analysis on the game idea and your team. This analysis is drawn up in a matrix such as that illustrated in Figure 1.11. The factors coming from the game itself and your project team are your strengths and weaknesses. Strengths are the characteristics that give you an advantage over your competitors and weaknesses are those that will be a disadvantage. You should also consider the external factors influencing your success, including opportunities and threats. The opportunities include ways in which you can exploit your game to its full advantage and threats are factors beyond your control that could disrupt the game's completion. An example of a generic SWOT is given in Figure 1.11. This example is restricted to one item per cell. When you do a SWOT analysis with your team, expect your list to be far more comprehensive.

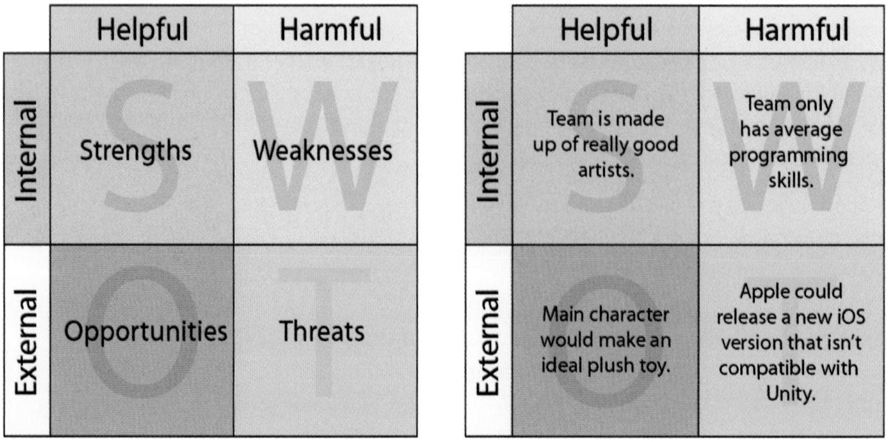

	Helpful	Harmful
Internal	Strengths	Weaknesses
External	Opportunities	Threats

	Helpful	Harmful
Internal	Team is made up of really good artists.	Team only has average programming skills.
External	Main character would make an ideal plush toy.	Apple could release a new iOS version that isn't compatible with Unity.

FIG 1.11 The SWOT analysis matrix and example.

Having completed the analysis phase you will have a list of problems, risks and constraints to take into the next phase in which you can begin problem-solving and planning.

1.4.2.4 Design

Design has been defined as "proactive problem-solving."[5] During this phase you will make your game idea tangible. The problems, risks, and constraints passed from the analysis phase need to be addressed. The details you document in this phase with respect to the game's storyline, player interface, aesthetics, game mechanics, and all other game aspects are what will manifest your idea. In addition, you are not only designing the game but creating the plan for the game development that addresses risk management, budget, timelines, scope, and resources.

The first time the project enters this phase, many of the game's main mechanics and game flow are defined. This does not mean you need to create a comprehensive behemoth of a design document. Readers may even be overjoyed to hear that game designer Jacob Stevens even suggests ditching the game design document as "they are too rigid for iterative development" and "take a long time to write and nobody bothers to read them anyway."[6] Instead use your time to develop mind-maps, concept art, interface designs and gameplay flowcharts. These tools, to be discussed further in the next section, allow you to get at the fundamental core of the workings of your game without all the unnecessary textual fluff.

On future revisits to the design phase, expect the game to evolve and mold according to technological limitations and gameplay testing results. Each time you come back to the design phase is a chance to make your game even better through the continued integration of feedback from play-testers and the experiences of your team.

Moving forward, your team should now have enough information to begin or continue development. This certainly does not mean you need a completed design. In the first instance you might just want to try out a new game mechanic to see if it is technically possible before working on further elements of the design in the next iteration.

1.4.2.5 Develop

Because of the iterative nature of the mobile game development cycle, development may happen in bursts. Programmers will create quick and multiple prototypes just to try things out. Unlike a large software development project where there will be many programmers working on the one version of a large code base, with mobile development you can expect a main code base for

---

[5] Source: Baker, G. E. and Dugger, J. C. (1986). "Helping Students Develop Problem Solving Skills," *The Technology Teacher*, 45(4): 10–13.
[6] Source: www.gamedev.net/page/resources/_/business/practical-tips-for-independent-game-development-r2687.

the actual game surrounded by many other small algorithmic experiments. If you ever want to try something out, don't do it in the main game's code. The complete code for a game is a complex thing. You can never be sure your idea works as cleanly as it should if you are trying to integrate it into the game and then navigate through menu systems and levels just to test it out. In fact, developing in this way is very time-consuming and unnecessary. For example, if you want to test a new multitouch mechanic for navigating the player's character, this can be done in an entirely separate program and ease-of-use tested on players quite rapidly. All this and you don't have to mess with your actual game.

In the first few iterations of the development phase most of the emphasis will be on prototyping game mechanics and building a shell for your game. This shell will include empty game scenes with placeholder art. As most mobile games have a very similar structure scene-wise, you'll be able to put together something quickly that resembles a splash screen, main menu, help screen, main game environment, credits page, etc., even if it doesn't have any content. It could also be that early on in the project the visual aesthetics have not even been fully realized and as they evolve through the continued iterations of the cycle can start to populate the game shell.

Figure 1.12 (a) illustrates the initial prototype for the iPhone game *Dodge Dogs*. The team's game idea included a dog that randomly walked around on the screen

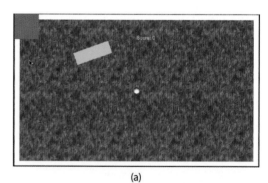

(a)

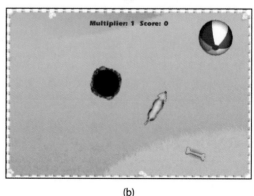

(b)

FIG 1.12 *Dodge Dogs* prototype (a) and completed artwork (b).

turning when it hit the boundary. The final model for the dog was not required to test the algorithm for the dog's movement and therefore a simple rectangular prism acted as the dog until the very late stages of the game's development when an animated model was substituted (shown in Figure 1.12 (b)).

The prototypes developed during this phase are distributed to play testers and team members for thorough evaluation.

1.4.2.6 Test

During the testing phase, runnable prototypes are exhaustively tried and tested for playability. In addition, the software is evaluated against the design specifications to ensure it runs as expected. This includes searching for both logic and programming bugs. Whereas programming bugs actually cause software to crash and exit, logic bugs let the software run, but the behavior is erratic or unexpected.

The testing phase is when you need to become very objective and let go of any preconceived ideas about your game. Giving it over to others to play is a nervous time for all designers and developers and you may find yourself becoming very defensive towards any criticism. However, the hard fact is that once you've released the game, you won't be there when players begin downloading and playing it. You won't be able to offer individual and personal advice to those attempting to interact with it. The game must be able to engage and interact with players by itself. Therefore taking a backseat and observing during the play-testing phase will assist you in creating a far better product.

During the testing phase you will want to observe how play-testers interact with your prototype. Some questions you should ask include:

- Is the interface intuitive?
- Is the interface frustrating to use?
- Is there adequate feedback for player actions?
- Are the play-testers enjoying themselves?
- Are the players able to play the game without me constantly watching over their shoulder and offering suggestions?

At the end of this phase you will have gathered valuable feedback, data, and a list of bugs that can be fed back into the next iteration of the development cycle for further analysis of the original idea and current design. During the entire iteration you will have also collected numerous prototypes and algorithms, art concepts, and solutions for minimizing risks and avoiding obstacles. At this point you are ready to pass the game idea, game design, and this collection of resources through your filtering questions again. Assessing the state of your project with each cycle is imperative to staying on track.

How long each cycle takes will depend on your team and the scope of the project. Agile development is focused on regular meetings and rapid cycling. For a small mobile game project, one iteration of the mobile game development cycle could take a single week, with team meetings the first thing on the agenda to run through the filter and analysis phase before planning out the rest of the week with respect to the other phases. Setting a regular cycle interval will also assist you in breaking up the project into achievable weekly chunks as well as ensuring you are on track to complete and release the game in the timeframe you've set yourself. The more short cycles you perform early on, the better you will be able to determine and plan for future iterations and envisage the release date.

How long does a mobile game take to complete from idea to release? How long is a piece of string? For example, the iPhone game *Dodge Dogs* shown in Figure 1.12 took 13 weeks from idea to a beta release. The iPad game *Flock 'Em!*, soon to be discussed, was in development for more than a year. This is not to say that the later is more complex than the first, but there were different circumstances surrounding the development of each. *Dodge Dogs* was worked on by three team members inputting ten hours per week and *Flock 'Em!* was a solo effort worked on sporadically with an hour here and there in between other projects. In all, it would be quite achievable to produce a high-quality mobile game with a team of two working fulltime, assuming they have the relevant programming and art skills, in less than three months.

1.4.2.7 Release

It is inevitable that at some point you must release your game into the world. This most certainly will not occur after the first iteration. It might take hundreds of turns through the game development cycle before you have a half decent and playable prototype. Deciding when the game is at a release stage may depend on budget and schedules as dictated by others or your own personal confidence in the state of the game. The more cycles the project goes through, the more robust the final game.

1.5 The Mobile Game Designer's Notebook

Planning out your game development process is critical. However sometimes, lengthy design documents are simply not needed, especially in smaller development teams where communication, continuity, and clarity are present throughout everyday. However, larger development teams (and specifically larger development projects) require design documentation to communicate between all team members and ensure that the project stays on course—in terms of the vision for the game, as well as assisting its timely completion.

Design documents come in a variety of shapes and sizes, and the content for the document varies depending on the target market; is it for the development team, or the executives that will decide whether or not to fund it? When design documentation is needed, traditionally a "vision document" is created first. This document is a very short proposal that essentially conveys the core messages, goals, and objectives of the game, consider it very much like an "elevator pitch." The elevator pitch is a short (no more than a couple of minutes) presentation in which you must describe who you are, what you intend to do with the game, when you plan to have it finished, where you foresee releasing it, and also why you feel the game is warranted. During this pitch, you must provide enough details to capture the attention of your audience and maintain their engagement. Throughout the presentation, continue to reinforce the unique selling point (USP). This is what makes your game special, memorable, and successful. If you are hunting for investors, you need to take this one step further and emphasis the potential of your game with respect to the investors' interests. Be clear about what return on investment (ROI) you will deliver.

Thanks to the App Store revolution and rapid development tools for creating high quality mobile games, more than 200 development teams, investor pitching, and complex development pipelines for games are more the exception than the rule. As such, if you're working with a small close-knit team, the types of formal documentation and technical specifications seen in the past are not required. However, less formal sketches, flowcharts, and concept art can be generated during the game's design phase that can just as clearly communicate your ideas and intention just as effectively, if not more, than a 100-page formal design document.

1.5.1 The Paperwork

Flowcharts have been used in software development since there has been software development. They diagrammatically show conceptual and logical flows of the software running or a person interacting with a program. They are very useful in mobile game design to illustrate both gameplay and screen/scene transitions. To illustrate these diagrams, we will examine ones created during the design of the iPad game *Flock 'Em!* shown in Figure 1.13. *Flock 'Em!*

FIG 1.13 *Flock 'Em!*

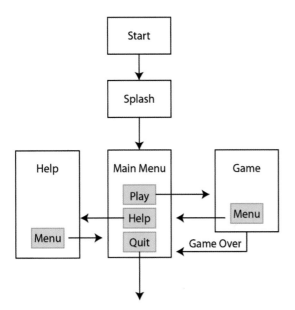
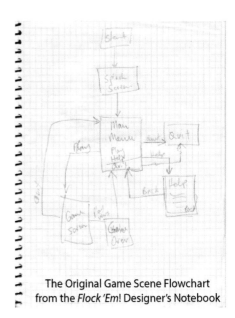

The Original Game Scene Flowchart
from the *Flock 'Em!* Designer's Notebook

FIG 1.14 A generic game scene flowchart and the actual one from *Flock 'Em!*

is a game in which the player must get the sheep from the truck to the barn by enticing them with hay and keeping them out of harm's way. Points are scored for each sheep safely delivered to the barn.

The game scene flowchart illustrates each scene (or screen) that needs to be created for the game and the transitions between them. This is the document that defines the skeleton of your game and is required in the first development phase to create the main game code prototype. As shown in Figure 1.14, each of the scenes you will need to create for the games are shown and the buttons or events that transition between them.

This flowchart clearly assists you in identifying how many scenes you need to create and how the player navigates between them. At this point you'll be able to tell if it's possible for a player to navigate to a particular scene but not get back. The entire game uses the main menu as a central hub. Being able to get from every screen to every other screen in our game is not necessarily a good idea. In Unity, as you will discover soon, scene transitions cause a game lag and therefore the less scenes you have, the better. The more things you can achieve in the one scene, the more robust and playable the game will be.

The gameplay flowchart maps a player's journey through the game. It can become quite complex but will assist the programmers in determining how the game's program will react in response to the player's interactions. It must also demonstrate the behaviors of any objects or characters in the game,

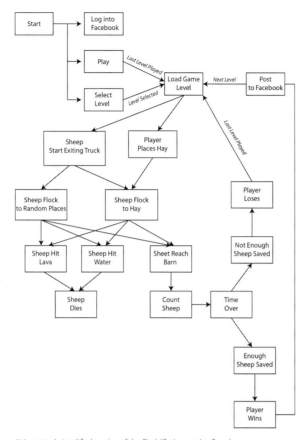

FIG 1.15 A simplified version of the *Flock 'Em!* gameplay flowchart.

how the player's score is determined and when the game is over. Figure 1.15 presents a highly simplified version of the *Flock 'Em!* gameplay flowchart.

Figure 1.15 shows the main game mechanic of playing hay in the game environment in order to attract sheep toward it. It also presents the behavior of the sheep, which is to flock together towards the hay or—if there's no hay present—to flock to a random location. The manner in which the sheep die is also shown.

Note that the flowcharts given here are quite informal. There are several formal flowcharting languages and diagramming standards, however the constraints of such can inhibit the flow of ideas and getting them down on paper during brainstorming sessions. Often what you come up with in team meetings will be sufficient to communicate and record all the game's algorithmic processes.

Last but not least, the design team will make a number of informal and formal sketches of screen mockups and concept art during the

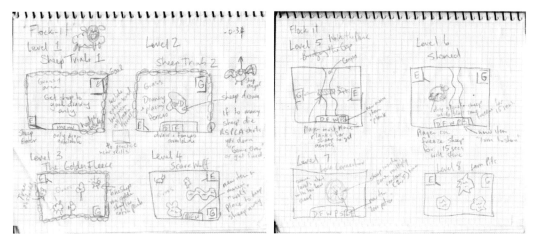

FIG 1.16 Concept sketches for levels from *Flock 'Em!*

project duration. Several of the initial level design ideas for *Flock 'Em!* are given in Figure 1.16.

What you should take away from this section is that game documentation doesn't have to be a laborious process that is usually the last thing to be written up in a game design class the night before the assignment is due. The documentation for the game is the realization of your idea taking shape on paper. If stringent formatting standards get in the way of this process then this will severely hamper your ability to communicate your vision clearly to others. Therefore, ditch the documentation, but get it out of your head and into a medium for others to *ooh* and *aah* at.

1.5.2 Development Checklist

Developing games is fun, exciting, and challenging. More than 40 years ago, the process was excruciatingly time-consuming. For example, the first electronic games (such as *Tennis for Two*) were created by manipulating electronic frequencies by hand. However, today we have access to a variety of software and toolkits that can aid both the design and development process, as well as a slew of hardware configurations that continually push the limits of design and creativity. The act of mobile development can be completed to an extent without having access to a physical device for testing. Software called "emulators" simulate the execution of an application and its interface on a desktop computer. Unfortunately, no matter how well constructed an emulator is, it does not replace the need for testing the application on a real device. For example, without an actual device, the developers cannot test for interactions a user would typically have (such as gestures, tilting, and location services).

Integrated Development Environments (IDEs) are often provided by the manufacturer of a device/operating system. Many of these feature emulators are for testing applications prior to installing the application files onto a device (known as "pushing"), as well as a variety of other packages and code snippets to improve development efficiency.

Apple provides its developers with the IDE Xcode. On registering as a developer with Apple for $99[7] users can download Xcode via the Mac OS App Store for free. It supports a variety of programming languages including C, C++, Objective-C, and Java. With the purchase of an iOS developer license, developers can create applications for desktop machines as well as mobiles. Xcode is exclusive to the Mac platform.

For Android developers, Google provides the Android Software Development Kit (SDK). It provides all the necessary tools for building and deploying apps to android devices. Android SDK is available for a number of platforms including Mac, Windows, and Linux.

The setup and use of both Xcode and the Android SDK will be explored later in the hands-on exercises at the end of this chapter.

Depending on the style of game being produced, the specific requirements for the aesthetics in the game will change. If a three-dimensional game is being produced, then a suitable modelling/animation package—such as Autodesk Maya, Autodesk 3DS Max, or Blender—should be considered. Autodesk products are available from http://usa.autodesk.com. While these products can seem quite expensive for a novice game developer, Autodesk does provide fully functional free student versions. If you are simply learning the craft of making 3D objects for games then these free versions are suitable until you are ready to go commercial. The open free alternative to Autodesk's products is the critically acclaimed modeling software Blender (www. blender.org). Which software you choose to use is purely based on personal preference. Neither one nor the other will serve you any better with respect to creating 3D mobile games. Both Blender and Maya are available for Mac OS and Windows, while 3DS Max is only available for Windows.

For two-dimensional games there is not a need for these types of high-powered 3D modeling packages. Rather, access to software in the Adobe Creative Suite (www.adobe.com/products/creativesuite.html) such as Photoshop or Illustrator is required. If the budget is a little tight, the open source freely available GIMP (www.gimp.org) will provide you with a paint package alternative. All of these software packages are available for both Mac OS and Windows.

This illustrative software is also needed in game production for the creation of 2D assets regardless of whether it is 2D or 3D. Splash screens, menus, user interfaces, and even the textures on 3D models are all flat 2D images. You will require tools to create these in all types of games.

Game worlds must employ sound effects and background music, so investing in sound editing, manipulation, and creation software is a wise

---

[7] Correct at time of writing.

decision. Pro Tools (www.avid.com/US/products/Pro-Tools-Software) is one very popular professional suite as is FLStudio (www.image-line.com/documents/flstudio.html). As with image creation, there is also an excellent free alternative for sound creation and manipulation, Audacity (http://audacity.sourceforge.net).

If you are short on time, software or skills in a particular area then the alternative to making your own game assets is to buy third-party created ones. In fact there is a thriving community of artists and designers on the web with models, sounds, and art to meet almost any purpose. The prices you pay for the assets varies depending on the quality and purpose of use, although there are also many novices willing to give away assets to get their work out there. This is but a short list of some of the more popular places to find assets:

- www.turbosquid.com
- www.freevectors.net
- www.dreamstime.com
- www.istockphoto.com
- www.shutterstock.com
- www.sounddogs.com
- www.3dcafe.com
- www.freesound.org

Once the assets have been created or sourced, a game engine (such as Unity) is required to collect, assemble, and then integrate scripts and other interactive drivers to construct the game world, and the mechanics and rules that govern it. While it is possible to create games directly with Xcode or the Android SDK, a game engine will provide you with a more rapid and smoother path to completion. There are a variety of add-ons and plugins that can be used with Unity to further reduce development time. In addition, Unity provides its own Asset Store with many purpose-build game assets that seamlessly integrate with the environment.

It goes almost without saying that a development computer able to run these programs is also recommended. In addition, external storage and backup of project files and assets is strongly recommended. Cloud services such as Dropbox (www.dropbox.com) or Bitcasa (www.bitcasa.com) should be investigated and used.

For the more programming-savvy and especially in team environments, version control of the project's source should be considered. Subversion (http://subversion.apache.org) is a server/client set of tools that can be used to manage multiple people working on the same code. It also allows developers to roll back to previous working versions of their game. Git (http://git-scm.com) is another version control option.

1.6 Under the Hood

Developing a game from scratch is a mammoth effort. With today's AAA console titles containing upward of 1.5 million lines of code, the task of building a game from the ground up is not one for individuals or small teams. Although it is reported John Carmack (Id Software founder) rewrote *Quake*'s entire rendering code in a weekend, such a commission is beyond the skills of us mere mortals. The expertise required to deliver the level of player experience expected with photo-realistic graphics, believable non-player characters, and responsive environmental physics, to name just a few factors, can only be found in a strong interdisciplinary team. Today, large game development studios hire talent with higher degrees in mathematics and physics to work on their games, thus improving the player experience by delivering truly exceptional immersive virtual environments.

If you are a budding individual game developer or part of a small team, without multiple university qualifications in algebra and Newtonian physics, there is no need to despair. As game development evolved into a process to rival blockbuster Hollywood movie production, game producers got clever with the way they coded the games. Much of the code built for specific purposes, such as rendering the game on the screen and handling physics events, was reusable. This meant hours of programming time could be saved by repurposing sections from previous games. Eventually these reused sections became modularized to the point they were separate sections.

1.6.1 Middleware

A healthy middleware industry arose providing software frameworks to support all the specialized functionality in games. Each of these, a separate product in itself, represents a plug-and-play component for developers to use in their games. Such a module removes the need for many hours of coding effort and—in essence—reinventing the wheel. Middleware, as the name suggests, sits between the hardware, operating system, and the programmer. It takes the pain out of programming for many different types of hardware architectures and configurations allowing the programmer to write much higher level code. For example, what might seem like the simple task of drawing a colored pixel on the screen will differ depending on hardware and operating system. If we assume there are ten different lines of code, each used for drawing a pixel in a different context, that's ten lines of code the programmer must write in addition to other lines that test for the type of device. The use of middleware allows the programmer to concentrate on the one single task of drawing a pixel by using just one line of code. The middleware sorts out which type of device it is dealing with and takes care of the details.

Besides dealing with hardware issues, middleware can also perform complex mathematical and laborious data manipulation tasks, again freeing the programmer to work at a higher level. For example, imagine programming the trajectory of a 3D object through space. Not only would you need a good knowledge of Newtonian physics but also 3D trigonometry and geometry. However, with physics middleware, all you would need to do is define the 3D object, its mass and velocity. The middleware takes the given information and creates the trajectory for you. Examples of middleware used by the games industry include FMOD, OpenGL, and PhysX.

FMOD, a cross-platform audio library developed by Firelight Technologies (www.fmod.com) supports a wide range of audio formats across different platforms including Windows, iOS, Android, Linux, BlackBerry, and Nintendo Wii. The use of FMOD means a programmer does not have to deal with the nuances of integrating sound into a game, which would include handling different formats, playback, and sound effects. It has been used to support the sound requirements of games such as *Guitar Hero*, *Little Big Planet*, *Plants vs. Zombies* and *World of Warcraft*. FMOD is free to use for non-commercial purposes.

OpenGL (www.opengl.org) is a well-known cross-platform, open-source graphics rendering library. It has a version called OpenGL ES for creating 2D and 3D graphics on mobile devices and WebGL for Web-browser based graphics. OpenGL interacts with the graphical processing unit (GPU) of the computer to produce hardware-accelerated rendering on most platforms, with the exception of Windows, where it is currently used for software rendering only. Its major competitor is Microsoft's DirectX built for the same purpose as OpenGL but restricted to Windows-based operating systems and hardware architectures. You can experience OpenGL at work in *Doom 3*, *Hitman*, *RuneScape*, and *Angry Birds*.

PhysX (www.geforce.com/hardware/technology/physx), developed by NVIDIA, performs complex physics calculations. It not only integrates the fundamental mathematical principles of physics and trigonometry but includes algorithms optimized to provide real-time dynamic environments on computers. Without such middleware, games would be very still and lifeless. By integrating such work created by some of the best minds in the domain, today's programmers don't require a university qualification in mathematics and physics to develop exceptionally dynamic and interactive game worlds. PhysX has been used in a wide variety of games from the first-person shooters (FPS) *Borderlands 2* and *Batman: Arkham City* to puzzles such as *Crazy Machines 2*.

Even with the best of middleware, a novice game developer would still struggle to put together an entire game from scratch without the rapid development environments known as "game engines." A game engine is a complete suite of tools with a visual editing environment that integrates a variety of middleware functionality specifically for the purpose of producing computer games. In addition to graphics rendering, sound processing and physics systems, a game engine includes reusable components to handle animation, artificial intelligence, networking, computer memory management, external file access, and scripting languages.

1.6.2 The Generic Game Engine

The structure of a generic game engine is illustrated in Figure 1.17. It is composed of a number of specialist modules working in unison to produce the desired gameplay from configurations given to it by the game developer. At the heart of the engine is a main game loop that cycles continuously while a game is running and monitors inputs and outputs from each of the modules. Any object in the game environment making up its look and feel is a game object. A game object is any item added to the empty game shell provided by the engine such as a sound, the sky, text on the screen, a light, or the player's character. Each object in the game can be assigned a variety of attributes and characteristics that define how it is to behave in the context of the game. For example, the background music track would be a game object that would have a sound attribute specifying the audio file to play. Such an object would not require any physics or AI attributes. On the other hand, an enemy non-player character (NPC) would require AI and physics attributes to assign it believable behaviors. It might also have several sound attributes

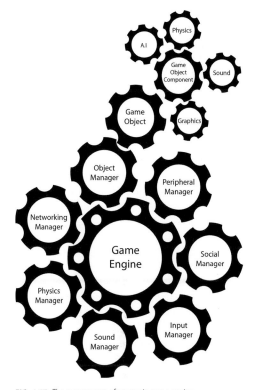

FIG 1.17 The components of a generic game engine.

that specify the sound files to play at different times in the NPC's life (such as a grunt upon getting shot). As some game objects have a visible presence in the game, they will require a graphics component that specifies how they are rendered. In the examples above, the background music track would not require a graphics component as it is not visible, unlike the NPC.

Any game object given a physics component becomes controlled by the physics manager. With each main loop, the physic manager calculates the positions and states of all objects with physics attributes. It takes care of trajectories and collisions, moving game objects within the virtual game world as required.

If networking or multiplayer capability is required in a game, a networking manager handles connection establishment and message passing between game clients in a peer-to-peer (P2P) setting or between client and server in a client-server situation. For example, in a mobile networked car-racing game such as *Mini Motor Racer*, the position and orientation of each car must be communicated to all players and their game-worldview updated accordingly. In this case, the network manager establishes a networked connection between the devices and handles all the nuances of device authentication and handshaking either via Bluetooth or WiFi and ensures messages are passed in the correct order. Without such a manager supplied by middleware, the game programmer would have to write their own complex system to do this, which would take just as much time as creating the game itself.

Any interactions between the player and the game via the controls afforded by the gaming device—be it console, desktop computer, or mobile device—are handled by an input manager. In many cases it can treat a mouse-click in the same way as a finger-touch on a mobile device or a button press on a console controller, making for easier development across platforms. In addition, the input manager ensures both input and output messages are processed by the engine in the correct order.

The sound manager also processes game objects that have a sound attribute assigned. This module mixes the game audio and delivers it to the player as required. It also controls the volume aspects of any special effects or music and allows for individual game objects to have detailed control of their own sounds such as the volume, playing, pausing and also 3D sound effects when required.

In more recent times, the addition of peripheral managers and social managers has been included with game engines. The peripheral manager accesses external devices, other than those of traditional input and output. For example, today's mobile devices include cameras, accelerometers, and GPS locators. More and more games are beginning to use these mechanisms for game input and output. Furthermore, any native functionality afforded by the devices operating system is also fair game for developers and providing a conduit into the game engine to support such integration is crucial (for example, integrating Google Map views into a game interface). In addition, social networking and online gaming communities such as Xbox Live or Apple's Game Center are also popular game inclusions. Today being able to post out to Facebook or Twitter from within a game is not a novelty but a requirement.

Unity is one such game engine built as described here. It integrates the before-mentioned middleware components (FMOD, OpenGL, and PhysX), with others, into a complete game-editing package with an easy-to-master graphical click-and-drag interface. It is a powerful product with a free version that allows developers from novice to AAA to realize their game designs. In the following section we will begin our journey with Unity by presenting a hands-on investigation of the game engines key components and functionalities.

1.7 Up Close and Personal with Unity

In this section we will take you on a guided tour of the fundamental sections in the Unity Editor. The primary illustrations will be taken from Unity 4 with special mention of any specific differences that may be encountered in Unity 3.5.X. Please note the exercises throughout this book take care to ensure they are fully compatible with both versions of Unity. If you are going to start using Unity 4, be aware that your projects will not be backward-compatible.

⊜ **Unity Hands-On**

The Unity Environment: A First Look

Step 1: To begin, download Unity by visiting www.unity3d.com. Unity provides a full version as a 30-day trial with all features unlocked, after which it will revert to the free version. The free version includes the majority of Unity's functionality and the Android or iOS tools. Many great mobile games are built and released with the free version of Unity. All exercises in this book use the free version.

Step 2: When the download is complete install Unity and run the software. On opening you will notice the Unity Editor is comprised of several tabbed windows as shown and explained in Figure 1.18. The major difference between the Unity 3 and 4 editor view is the addition of the Console tab and the assets in the Project tab displayed as folder icons. Besides that you will find they are almost identical.

Step 3: If you didn't create a new project when Unity started create one now by selecting File > New Project from the main menu. The name you give the project will be the same as the folder Unity creates to store the game assets. Unity does not use a single file to save the project as you find in other software such as Word or Photoshop but rather the top level folder. Unity also likes to have everything in its project folders in the correct order, so best not to mess with the structure or add anything manually.

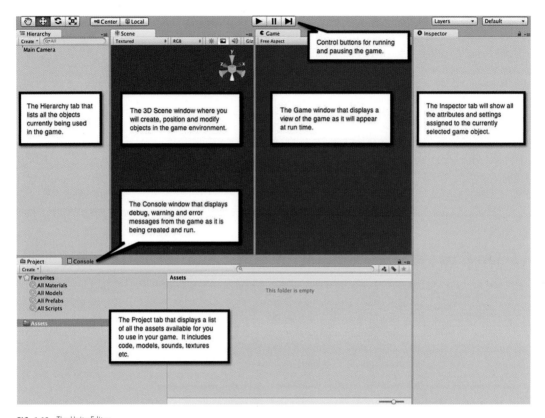

The Hierarchy tab that lists all the objects currently being used in the game.

The 3D Scene window where you will create, position and modify objects in the game environment.

The Game window that displays a view of the game as it will appear at run time.

The Inspector tab will show all the attributes and settings assigned to the currently selected game object.

Control buttons for running and pausing the game.

The Console window that displays debug, warning and error messages from the game as it is being created and run.

The Project tab that displays a list of all the assets available for you to use in your game. It includes code, models, sounds, textures etc.

FIG 1.18 The Unity Editor.

◉ Note

In a game project all the external files brought into your game including code, sounds, models, images etc are referred to as *assets*.

Step 4: We will now create a simple game scene with a sphere. From the main menu select GameObject > Create Other > Sphere. A new game object called *Sphere* will be created and you'll see it in the Hierarchy tab and Scene and Game windows as shown in Figure 1.19. When selected the properties of the *Sphere* are shown in the Inspector tab.

◉ Note

From this point forward the tabs and windows will be referred to only by name. For example, the Hierarchy tab will be called the Hierarchy and the Scene window by its name; Scene. In addition, when asked to select options separated by the > character, assume you can find these in the main menu.

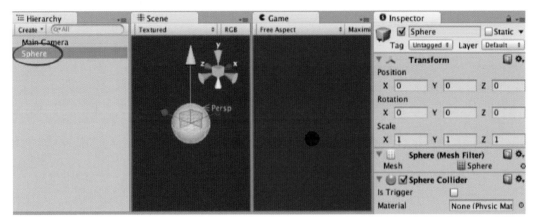

FIG 1.19 Adding a Sphere.

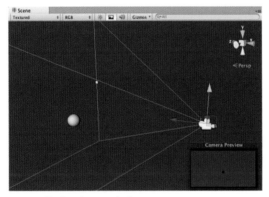

FIG 1.20 The Main Camera in the Scene.

Step 5: If the Sphere appears small in the Scene, place the mouse inside the window and scroll to zoom in. Notice the Sphere in the Game is not affected. The Game is the view of the game from the camera in the scene. The camera is essentially the player's eyes into the game world. You can find the Main Camera as a game object in the Hierarchy. Double-click on it. The Scene will orientate to allow you to see the actual camera as shown in Figure 1.20.

Step 6: Being able to navigate smoothly in the Scene is crucial for positioning and manipulating objects. If you are familiar with other 3D editing tools you'll find the navigation of the Unity Scene familiar. You already know scrolling the mouse will zoom. In addition you can pan by holding down the ALT key and dragging the mouse around in the window or rotate by holding down the Q key and dragging the mouse around. Try this now to move around the scene.

Step 7: To change what you see in the Game the Main Camera needs to be moved. To do this, select the Main Camera in the Hierarchy and press W. A set of green, red, and blue axes will appear in the Scene on the Main Camera. To move the camera, select the tip of one of the axes with the mouse and drag it. Notice how the Game view changes with the camera's view.

To change the camera's orientation, with the Main Camera still selected in the Scene, press E. Green, red, and blue orbital handles will appear around the camera in the Scene. Dragging the mouse over any of these will orient the camera.

The final manipulation you can make to an object in the Scene is to scale it. In this case, scaling the camera won't do anything, so instead, click on the Sphere either in the Hierarchy or the Scene. Press R. Again green, red, and blue axes will appear. This time the axes will have small cubes on the end. There will be a large yellow cube in the centre. Dragging the large yellow cube will evenly resize the Sphere. Dragging the individual cubes at the end of each axis will resize in the same direction. Try this out and observe how the sphere's size changes in the Game.

Each of the transformations you can perform on a game object are shown in Figure 1.21.

● Note
In Unity, when selected, a white framed area can be seen extruding from the camera. This area is called the camera's viewing volume. Only the items inside the viewing volume are visible in the Game.

Step 8: Try pressing the play button at the top centre of the editor. This runs your game. At this time nothing will happen as there's nothing actually going on in your scene. Press the play button again to stop playing.

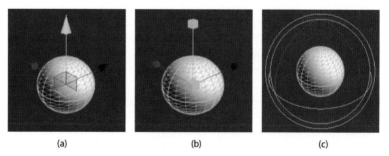

(a) (b) (c)

FIG 1.21 The transformations that can be performed on a game object. When selected (a) press W to move the object, (b) R to resize it, and (c) E to rotate.

Unity will allow you to make live changes to your game when it is in play mode. However, any changes you make (except those made to code) will immediately be reset when you stop playing. This can be a constant annoyance for those new to Unity, especially when you make a lot of changes in play mode. Telling you this now, won't stop you doing it, but hopefully will help you understand what's going on the first time.

Step 9: You may have noticed the sphere looks very flat in the Game. This is because there aren't any lights. When lights are added to a scene 3D objects become shaded and the scene gains depth. To add a light select GameObject > Create Other > Directional Light. The sphere will now be shaded.

Step 10: The components you can add to a game object are found under Component in the main menu. In Unity 4, you can also add a component in the Inspector when an object is selected, as shown in Figure 1.22. These components are synonymous with the game object components discussed in Section 3.1. They allow you to add extra properties and behaviours to game objects such as physics.

For this step we will add physics to the sphere. To do this, with the Sphere selected, choose Component > Physics > Rigidbody. The result will be a Rigidbody component added to the Inspector for the sphere as shown in Figure 1.23. For the Sphere, having a rigidbody simply means it becomes part of the engine's physics system and now will behave as such.

Press play. The Sphere will fall under the influence of gravity.

Step 11: Add a cube to the scene with GameObject > Create Other > Cube. Select the Cube in the Hierarchy and use the W key to set it to move mode and use the mouse to drag the cube beneath the sphere. Add a rigidbody to the cube. Without changing any rigidbody settings, press play. Both the sphere and the cube will fall at the same rate. If you understand basic Newtonian physics there will be no surprises there. For the Cube, in the Inspector, untick the rigidbody's Use Gravity tickbox. The cube will still be influenced by physics events just not gravity.

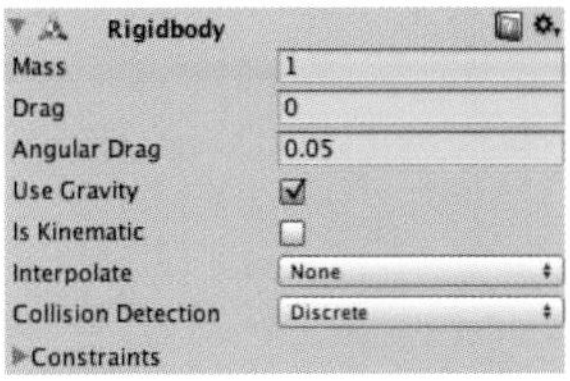

FIG 1.22 Adding a component to a game object in Unity 4.

Play. The Cube will remain stationary until the sphere collides with it, causing it to move under the sphere's influence.

Add more Cubes and place them beneath the Sphere. To add an exact replica of the Cube you've already created, with it selected in the Hierarchy press CMD+D (Mac OS) or CTRL+D (Win) to duplicate it. Right-clicking on the object in the Hierarchy will also give you the option to duplicate. You can then move the new Cube into position. Because it was duplicated it will already have a rigidbody. Depending

FIG 1.23 The Rigidbody Component as it appears in the Inspector.

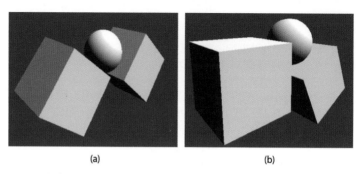

(a)   (b)

FIG 1.24 A sphere and two cubes in the physics system.

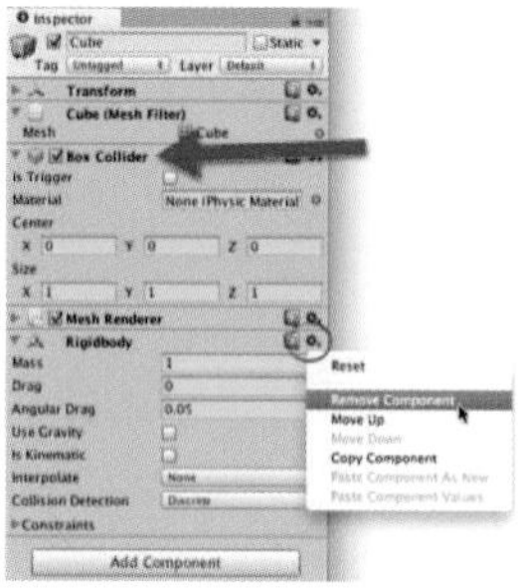

on how you have the cubes positioned, the Sphere will now collide with them and cause them to spin as shown in Figure 1.24 (a). The Sphere will continue falling under the influence of gravity, but the Cubes will only have the Sphere's momentum on collision to carry them and therefore they will not fall in the same way.

Now select one of the cubes and in the Inspector, remove the rigidbody. To do this select the settings icon in the Rigidbody component in the Inspector as shown in Figure 1.25.

FIG 1.25 Removing a component in the Inspector.

More Information: Rigidbodies

For further information on the settings of the Rigidbody component see http://docs.unity3d.com/Documentation/Components/class-Rigidbody.html.

Play. Notice the cube without the rigidbody remains stationary (see Figure 1.23 (b)). Yet it still affects the physics of the other objects in the Scene on collisions. This is because the cube has a box collider component added to it. Most default primitive Unity 3D objects will come with a collider. A collider places the object in the physics system but ensures it isn't affected by physics. For example, if you made a ground plane, you wouldn't want it falling away when something collided with it and therefore it would have a collider, but not a rigidbody. This is not a hard and fast rule, and how you set up your rigidbodies and colliders will depend on different situations.

The physics system will be further elucidated in later chapters, but for now feel free to add more objects and change the rigidbody settings to get a feel for how they will behave.

⬤ **Note**

If you want to set the Main Camera to look at the game world in the same way you are viewing it in the Scene, select the Main Camera and then GameObject > Align with View.

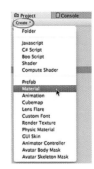

FIG 1.26 Creating a new material in the Project.

Step 12: Another property you can manipulate on a game object is its colour. The colour is defined by a material component. It must be created differently to the physics component. To create a material, go to the Project, select the dropdown menu under Create and choose Material (see Figure 1.26).

When the material is first created it will be called New Material. Click on its name to change it to Green. When it is selected in the Project, the properties of the material will be visible in the Inspector. Click on the Main Color colour box to bring up the colour selection dialogue as shown in Figure 1.27. Set the colour of the material to green.

FIG 1.27 Setting a material to green.

More Information: Materials

For further information on the settings of Unity Materials see http://docs.unity3d.com/Documentation/Components/class-Material.html.

To apply the material to one of the game objects in the Scene simply drag and drop the material from the Project onto the object in the Scene. Alternatively you can drag and drop it onto the game object's name in the Hierarchy or with the game object selected in the Hierarchy, drag and drop the material onto the Inspector.

You can apply this material to any object in the Scene. To change the colour or other properties of the material, select it again in Project and change it in the Inspector. All objects with this material applied will change in response. For example, if you changed the colour of the material to orange, all objects that were green will now appear orange.

Step 13: In the Project, create a new C# script via the dropdown Create menu. It will initially be called NewBehaviourScript. Click on the name in the Project and rename it to spin.

● Note

When you create a new C# script file only specify the name. Do not add .cs on the end. Unity will automatically do that for you. If you look in the Unity project folder the file will appear with a .cs extention. In the editor however, you will only ever see the name.

Step 14: Double-click on the new script file in the Project and it will open up in a code editor. When it does, enter the code below. Note, the code you will need to type in that isn't automatic is shown in bold.

```
using UnityEngine;
using System.Collections;
public class spin : MonoBehaviour {
    // Use this for initialization
    void Start () {
    }
    // Update is called once per frame
    void Update () {
        this.gameObject.transform.Rotate (Vector3.up * 10);
    }
}
```

It is critical to ensure the name specified at the top of the code after public class is exactly the same as the name of the file. This is illustrated in the editor view of the code shown in Figure 1.28. The code must be *exactly* as it appears here. You should always endeavour to check your spelling and capitalization if there is ever a problem.

After you have edited the code, save it and return to the Unity Editor. There is no need to close the code editor as in the normal course of creating a project you'll be back and forth between Unity and it many times.

If you have mistyped the code, Unity will be quick to tell you there is a problem. At the bottom of the editor window a small red, round icon will appear with an error count and across the very bottom an error message.

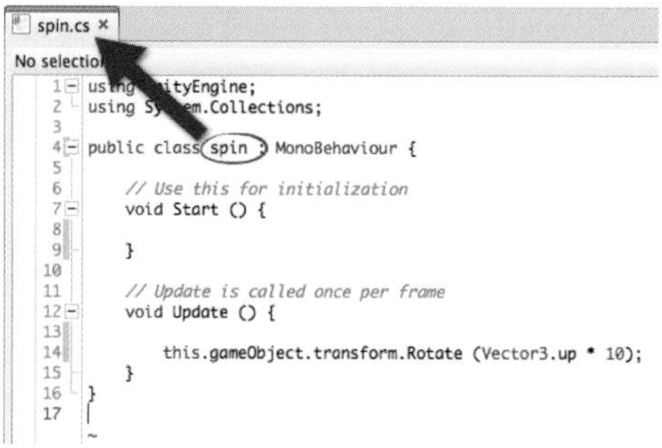

FIG 1.28 The Unity code editor, MonoDevelop displaying spin.cs.

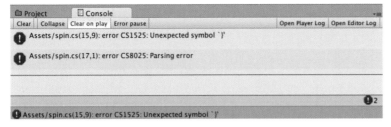

FIG 1.29 Code Errors displayed in the Unity Editor.

The entire list of errors can be found in the Console as shown in Figure 1.29. While the Console is front and center in Unity 4, it can be found under Window > Console in Unity 3.

The errors displayed in Figure 1.29 are typical of what you can expect if you leave a semicolon off the end of a line. In this case the semicolon was removed from line 14 displayed in Figure 1.29. Getting used to coding error messages is something that takes quite a bit of experience. Given the fact that the messages themselves are somewhat *obtuse* doesn't help the matter. More often than not, however, the error messages do give you an idea of the lines on which they are occurring. When you receive one, concentrate your search to these areas. Make certain the code you've used is exactly as it should be. You will learn much more about coding in Chapter 2.

In the Project, take the spin asset and drag and drop it onto a cube from which you removed the rigidbody earlier. You can drop the code onto the object in the Scene, Hierarchy, or Inspector in the same way you added the material component. When a script is attached to a game object, it will appear in its list of components in the Inspector.

Step 15: Code like other components, such as materials, is reusable in Unity. Just as you added the green material to more than one game object, you too can add the spin code to more than one object. Take the same code from the Project and attach it to one of the other cubes in the Scene. If you like, you can also attach it to the camera. When code is written in a generic fashion it can be applied to pretty much any object in your Scene.

This hands-on session has given an overview of the Unity Editor and practical experience with each tab and window. As you proceed through this book you will become more and more familiar with each one. They all work together to expose a different interface into the Unity Game Engine and provide a powerful visual editor when creating your own games.

Whether you are creating desktop, console, or mobile games, the Unity Editor and your use of it does not change. The same game can be created once in the editor and then pushed out to multiple platforms. In the next section we will examine how to get games from the Unity Editor onto iOS and Android mobile devices.

1.8 Platform Development Specifics

Unlike developing for Android, the Apple development platform is locked down tight. Creating a game in Unity and getting it onto a mobile device running Android is a piece of cake compared to getting the same game onto an iPod, iPhone, or iPad. The reason being that Apple have total control over what pieces of software run on their devices. The games you create must have a cryptographic signature before they are allowed to run on an iOS device. This signature is an encoded file provided by Apple giving you permission to push games to iOS devices. The process for obtaining this permission will seem overly complex the first time you do it, however it is necessary for Apple to maintain the quality control they have over the products they allow on their hardware.

1.8.1 Understanding Cryptography

Encryption is a method of taking a message and transforming it so it is incomprehensible. A very simple method is to assign numbers to each of the letters in the alphabet and then rewrite a text message replacing the alphabetical letters with their numerical equivalents. For example if A = 1, B = 2 up to Z = 26 then "holistic" encrypted would be "8 15 12 9 19 20 9 3." Such an encoded string is referred to as "cipher text." Taking the string of numbers and translated them back into the word is the process of decryption. What is known as a "key," is used to encrypt and decrypt the cipher text. To communicate using this method, the first party would use the key to encrypt the original message. On receipt of the encrypted message, the receiver uses the same key to decrypt and reveal the true meaning and content of the original message. This is not the most secure way to transmit sensitive information as anyone in possession of the key—for example, someone intercepting it—could also decipher the message. If the key is used to encrypt the message, when the key itself is being communicated to the recipient it is vulnerable. This particular process is referred to as "symmetric cryptography" and illustrated in Figure 1.30.

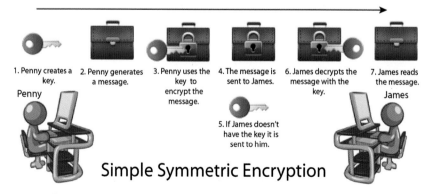

1. Penny creates a key. 2. Penny generates a message. 3. Penny uses the key to encrypt the message. 4. The message is sent to James. 5. If James doesn't have the key it is sent to him. 6. James decrypts the message with the key. 7. James reads the message.

Penny

James

Simple Symmetric Encryption

FIG 1.30 Symmetric cryptography.

A more secure technique for encryption is through the use of an asymmetric key algorithm known as public-key cryptography, in which there are two keys; a public key and a private key. The original sender generates both keys mathematically. The public key can decrypt messages encrypted with the private key and the private key can decrypt messages encrypted with the public key. The private key remains with the original sender and is used to encode messages to be sent. The public key travels with the message and is used to decipher the message at the other end. As with symmetric cryptography, this specific part of the transaction is not secure. However, the recipient can then use the public key they received to then encrypt a message intended for the original sender. Only the original sender can decrypt the message with their private key as it was created with their own public key. This process is illustrated in Figure 1.31. This is what sets public-key cryptography apart from symmetric cryptography.

Because the original message and public key can be intercepted during transmission, it is difficult for the receiver to validate the authenticity of the original message. To partially solve this issue, public-key infrastructures exist in which third parties known as "certificate authorities" validate key pairs.

Public key encryption is used to create digital signatures. A digital signature is not that dissimilar to a handwritten signature or a wax seal on an envelope.

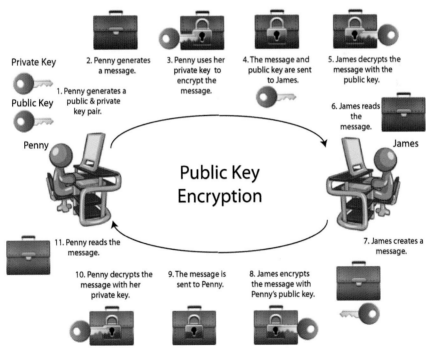

FIG 1.31 Public key cryptography.

In the case of a wax seal analogy, the private key used to sign the document is the sender's seal stamp. It remains the private property of the sender. However, when the document reaches its destination, the wax seal can be used to identify the sender. An actual digital signature goes one step further, ensuring the integrity of the original message has not been altered. This would be like a protective covering on the wax seal document that turned the entire thing purple if someone attempted to modify the contents.

Before a sender can use a digital signature, they must have a digital identity. This identity consists of a public-private key pair and a digital certificate. The digital certificate proves the sender's credentials and is provided by an independent certificate authority. The process is synonymous with having to produce your passport to prove your identity. The passport is a certificate and the certificate authority, in this case, would be your country's government. In the case of the wax sealed letter, the sender who owns the seal would also have to produce an official document provided by, say, the king, to prove that their seal did in fact belong to them.

If you've made it this far in reading this section, you're probably thinking, "On what planet am I going to need to know all this? I just want to make games." In short, if you're going to create games for iOS, then you are about to put this new found knowledge into practice.

1.8.2 Setting up for iOS

As previously mentioned, the games you create need to be signed with a digital signature authorized by Apple. You will need to do this before they can be copied to a device for testing.

In this section, we will take you through the process of getting the Unity application you created in the previous hands-on exercise onto an iOS device.

○ Unity Hands-On
Building from Unity to iOS

Step 1: Visit https://developer.apple.com/programs/ios and enroll in the iOS Developer Program. There is a small fee involved. The process of entering in your details takes about 15 minutes, however Apple's verification procedure can take up to 24 hours. Therefore, be prepared to wait.

Step 2: Once you have your Apple Developer account, you can start creating the public-private keys and setting up the certificates you will need for digitally signing your Unity games. While you are doing this, you should download and install Xcode from the App Store.

Step 3: To create your public-private key pair, open the Keychain app. You can find it on your Mac in Spotlight by typing in Keychain as shown in Figure 1.32.

FIG 1.32 Locating the Keychain application on a Mac.

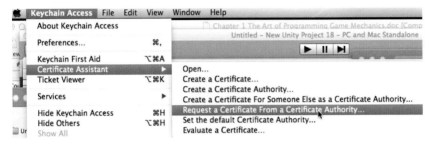

FIG 1.33 Requesting a certificate in Keychain.

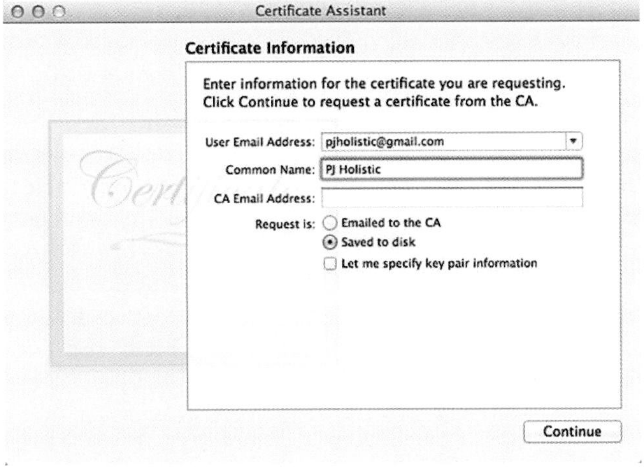

Certificate Assistant

Certificate Information

Enter information for the certificate you are requesting.
Click Continue to request a certificate from the CA.

User Email Address: pjholistic@gmail.com

Common Name: PJ Holistic

CA Email Address:

Request is: ○ Emailed to the CA
⦿ Saved to disk
☐ Let me specify key pair information

Continue

FIG 1.34 The Keychain Certificate Assistant.

Step 4: In Keychain select Keychain Access > Certificate Assistant > Request a Certificate From a Certificate Authority as shown in Figure 1.33.

When the Certificate Assistant, shown in Figure 1.34, opens, type in your Apple ID and Common Name. These must be the same as the ones you used to register for the Apple Developer program. Your common name will be first and last names used during the program registration process. Select the Saved to Disk option. Press the Continue button. Save the certificate request file to your desktop.

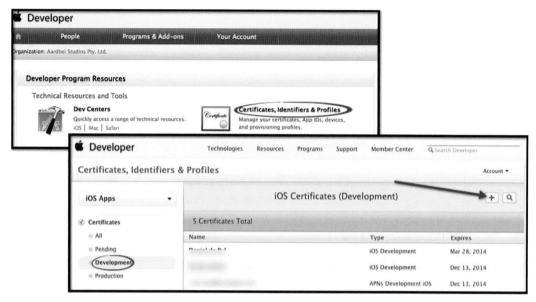

FIG 1.35 Requesting a certificate.

Step 5: Log in to the Apple Developer Center at https://developer.apple.com/membercenter/index.action. Click on iOS Provisioning Portal. On the Provisioning Portal page shown in Figure 1.35, select Certificates & Development from the left hand menu. Select the + button.

On the next page, select iOS App Development and click Continue. The next page will tell you how to make a certificate signing request file. You've already done this. Click Continue. Upload the certificate request file on the next page. You will find your certificate ready to download. Click on Download to retrieve the certificate. Double-click on the file that downloads. Keychain Access will open it. When prompted click Add. In Keychain Access under My Certificates, you will be able to see the new certificate and if you click on it, it will be presented as a valid certificate.

At this point you have a certificate from Apple stating who you are and that you can sign apps for iOS.

Step 6: Next you need to create an App ID. This is the unique ID attributed to every app created. You can also create a wildcard App ID that allows you to use the same App ID over and over while you are developing. However, when you release the app, you will have to make sure you've created a new and unique App ID for it. For now, we will create a wildcard App ID. In the iOS Provisioning Portal click on App IDs in the left-hand menu. Click on the + button. Enter a description and bundle identifier. The description should be the common name for your game. The bundle identifier must have the format *com.x.y* where x is your name or company name and y is the app name. Because we are creating a wildcard, use * for y. In the

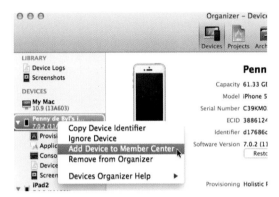

FIG 1.36 Adding a Device to the Member Center.

Wildcard App ID section type in a bundle ID such as *com.holistic.**. Instead of *holistic* you should use your company name or a similar identifier for yourself. Hit the Continue button when you are done.

Step 7: Now that you have a developer certificate and an App ID, you need to be able to authenticate yourself with the device you are putting the game onto. This requires a provisioning profile. When installed on a device it gives the device permission to run the particular app you are sending it. Before you can create a provisioning profile you need to add a device to the Member Center. To do this you need an iOS device plugged into your computer.

Open Xcode. Go to Window > Organizer. In here you will see your device. Ensure the device is selected in the left-hand window. Right-click on it and select Add Device to Member Center, as shown in Figure 1.36.

To create the provisioning profile, click on Provisioning Profiles > Development in the left-hand menu in the Development Center. Select + and then choose the iOS App Development option. Press Continue. Follow the steps selecting the App ID, the certificate, and the device. Give the profile a name and click on Generate. These steps, although on separate pages in the Development Center are illustrated as one in Figure 1.37.

Download the file and double-click on it. The profile will be opened and installed in the Xcode organizer. You can check it is there by returning to the organizer window, selecting the device, and clicking on Provisioning Profiles.

Step 8: Now it's time to build your Unity project to the device. Open the project from the previous hands-on tutorial or create another one. It doesn't have to be anything complicated, even an empty Unity project will do to test your certificates and provisions are setup correctly.

Step 9: In Unity select File > Build Settings. The window shown in Figure 1.38 will open. Select iOS from the Platform box and click on Switch Platform.

Step 10: In the Build Settings window, click on Player Settings. Switch back to the main editor window and notice the Player Settings area in the Inspector.

FIG 1.37 The steps in creating a provisioning profile.

FIG 1.38 Unity's Build Settings Window.

Enter a Company Name. This can be anything you like. The Product Name will be the name as it appears under the icon on the iOS device. Next add the bundle identifier. We created this as a wildcard in the provisioning portal. This means you can type the first two parts in followed by anything you like. It is critical to your app being able to run on the device that the bundle identifier is exactly the same as that you created beforehand. Just replace the * on the end with a word descriptive of your app.

Step 11: Go back to the Build Settings window (File > Build Settings) and click on the Build and Run button. Providing everything is setup correctly, the app will compile in Unity and then Xcode will open. This will be followed by a lot more building and linking and finally the app will be pushed out to the device.

◉ Note

While the process of iOS provisioning presented here has remained unchanged for many years and we expect it to follow the same protocols for some time to come, Apple may change their iOS Developer Center interface. If you find it is different from that presented here, be sure to read through the online iOS workflow guides provided by Apple for updated procedures.

1.8.3 Setting up for Android

After having built a Unity project out to iOS, Android seems like mere child's play. Because Android is an essentially an open-source platform, the regulations for building to Android enabled devices is not as stringent as Apple's iOS procedures. In fact, there are no public-private keys that need to be generated, and there is no need to prove your identity with the devices you are building to. The process for building from Unity to Android is similar on both Mac and Windows machines.

◉ Unity Hands-On
Building from Unity to Android

Step 1: Download the Android SDK (Software Development Kit) for your operating system from http://developer.android.com/sdk/index.html. Unzip the contents and place it in a permanent folder on your computer either in Documents or Applications on a Mac or in Program Files in Windows (i.e., not your desktop).

Step 2: Double-click on the android program in the tools folder of the download to run the SDK manager. The manager screen will look similar to that in Figure 1.39.

Step 3: As shown in Figure 1.39, tick the Android SDK Platform-tools and one of the Android APIs (greater than 2.3). If you are in Windows, check the Android USB drivers as well. Click on the Install button. Depending on your Internet connection this process could take some time.

Step 4: While the Android SDK is installing, check your device has the latest operating system update. To do this, on the device go into Settings > About Device > Software Update > Update. The device will update the operating system if required.

FIG 1.39 The Android SDK Manager.

FIG 1.40 Turning on Android USB Debugging.

Step 5: You will also need to turn on USB debugging to allow Unity to push the game to the device. On the device go to Settings > Developer Options and select USB Debugging as shown in Figure 1.40.

Step 6: Once the Android SDK has installed all the relevant packages you can return to Unity. Using the project from before or a new one, go into the Build Settings (File > Build Settings). Select the Android and click on Switch Platform as shown in Figure 1.41. Ensure you untick the Create Eclipse project box.

Step 7: The only thing you will need to add to the Player Settings at this point is a Bundle ID. It's not important what it is, not like with iOS. In the Build Settings window, click on Player Settings. The settings will appear in the Inspector as shown in Figure 1.42. For the Bundle ID, enter something in the format *com.yourname.appname*.

Step 8: Press Build and Run in the Build Settings window to push the game from Unity to your device. The first time this runs, Unity will ask you

FIG 1.41 Switching to the Android Platform in Unity.

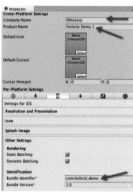

FIG 1.42 Player Settings.

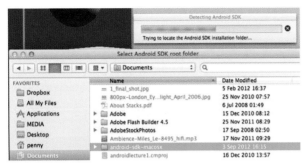

FIG 1.43 Locating the Android SDK.

for the location of the Android SDK as shown in Figure 1.43. Give it the root folder where you unzipped Android previously.

All going to plan your Unity game will appear on the device.

1.9 Optimization

One of the many challenges faced by mobile game developers is the limited processing power of the mobile device central processing unit (CPU) and graphical processing unit (GPU). Although the devices of today are far more powerful than the originals, the muscle in a mobile device will never match that of a desktop machine or console. By employing several optimization techniques, you'll be able to create a top quality game that not only looks good but also runs fast. There are four major performance bottlenecks for which you can cater. These are CPU capacity, vertex processing, fragment processing, and bandwidth. The following discussion of these, while applicable across other game engines, will focus on Unity.

Game characteristics that slow game performance include the number of drawcalls, complex scripts, and complex physics.

1.9.1 Drawcalls

Drawcalls are made to produce the final image that the player sees rendered in a frame. The more drawcalls to produce a single frame, the slower the CPU will be able to generate frames and thus the frame rate drops. Drawcalls are affected by the number of textures and meshes to be processed. The drawcalls can be seen in the Unity Editor in the Game by using the Stats tab as illustrated in Figure 1.44.

Each new material in the scene will induce one drawcall. To reduce this impact, a single texture called a "texture atlas" can be used to replace multiple ones. Several models then share the texture atlas taking their skins from different parts. This technique will be examined in detail in later chapters.

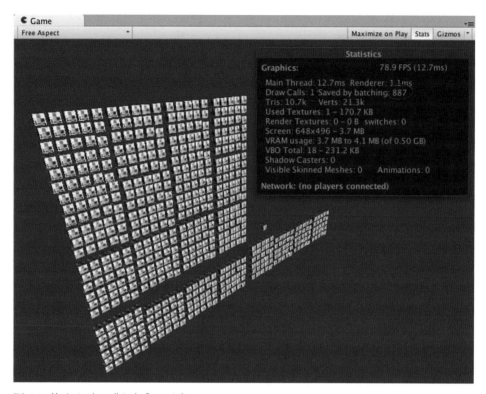

FIG 1.44 Monitoring drawcalls in the Game window.

The number of polygons (triangles) in view of the camera also affects the drawcalls. In the case of Figure 1.44, the camera shows 887 cubes all with the same material. When each individual model has fewer than 900 vertices, Unity will batch it with others of the same material. This means all the cubes are pushed through in just one drawcall. Close to 11,000 polygons sharing the same material can be drawn in one drawcall by paying attention to mesh sizes. Any single mesh can have up to 6,000 polygons before it will require more than one drawcall to render.

Any meshes that fall outside the viewing volume of the camera (frustum) are automatically culled. Their geometry and materials will not affect the number of drawcalls. However, if a large object is only half in the frustum, its entire mesh will be processed and therefore affect the number of drawcalls. Dividing very large meshes up into smaller parts is good practice, especially if only parts of them will ever be visible at any one time.

Another process that reduces drawcalls is occlusion culling. This is the process of not drawing meshes that are hidden by other objects in a scene. This option requires processing of the scene by a hidden camera and is only available in

Unity Pro. For further details on occlusion culling see http://docs.unity3d.com/
Documentation/Manual/OcclusionCulling.html.

One more tip for reducing drawcalls is to limit the number of Unity GUI items being used. Each single one whether it be a button, label, or textbox adds one drawcall.

1.9.2 Simplify Scripts

It's quite easy to create too many unnecessary scripts in Unity when you are trying to put in a whole lot of functionality. As Unity allows scripts to be added to all game objects it's very tempting to give each object its own code. However, eventually the code becomes very messy and you start to lose track of where the functionality is occurring. In addition, the game engine has to process a lot more scripts and you'll never be quite sure which one is executing first. For example, if you have multiple scripts each with an Update() function and something occurring in one is required by another, you've got no control over which one executes first. This of course doesn't slow down processing, but it does make it slower for the engine to interpret all the code.

One thing that will slow down the running of scripts is using enquiry functions that perform searches through the game objects. One that you will soon learn about is GetComponent(). By giving this function the name of an object, you can search through all the objects in the game world. If you know ahead of time the exact object you want to work with in the script, then reference it explicitly. Don't go searching for it at run time.

Also the creation and destruction of game objects after the game has started running also slows down performance dramatically. As you will see in some of the code to follow in this book, the temptation to create an object at run time and then dispose of it when it is no longer needed is great as it's such an easy thing to do. Rather, you want to have a pool of objects that are already created and use them over and over. The process of constantly allocating and deallocating memory is slow. In addition, when you destroy something in Unity script it doesn't instantly get destroyed from memory. This is performed by a cyclic cleanup function. What this means is that if you constantly create objects on the fly you can very quickly fill up memory and crash your program.

1.9.3 Physics

The physics engine is very taxing on the processing of a game. Every item placed in the physics system is processed for movement and collisions. Therefore, if an item does not require physics then don't add physics onto it. Complex collider meshes also require a lot of processing. If you can get away with a box or sphere collider rather than a mesh collider then do. For complex meshes, consider breaking the model up and putting primitive colliders around the individual parts as shown in Figure 1.45.

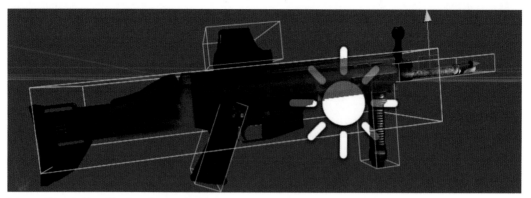

FIG 1.45 Using primitive collider shapes for a complex object.

1.9.4 Vertex Processing

The number of polygons in a mesh—and hence vertices—influences the number of drawcalls. As previously discussed, the more vertices that have to be processed, the slower it is to render them. Ensure your models do not have any superfluous vertices. You should only have points in the mesh that dictate the mesh shape and influence the placement of textures. For example, a cube need only have eight vertices; one for each corner. Any more than this is a waste of processing and computer memory.

Besides the actual number of vertices you'll also want to reduce the number of operations occurring per vertex. Processing that occurs on vertices include transformations, physics, and rendering processes. Limit the number of special texturing effects on meshes. These "shaders," as they are called, perform mathematical functions on vertices to manipulate how they are rendered. Unity has a set of mobile specific shaders you can use when creating mobile games that will reduce this load.

By implementing a Level-of-Detail (LOD) system for meshes you can also greatly reduce the number of vertices being drawn at any one time. Meshes that are far away from the camera do not need to appear in such high quality and therefore can have less detail and hence vertices. Furthermore, reducing the mesh down to a billboard (a 2D plane faking a 3D object) is also an effective way of making a scene look like it is highly detailed when in fact it is not. LOD is a built in feature of Unity Pro, however there are many free scripts available in the community to achieve the same job.

1.9.5 Fragment Processing

A fragment is a candidate pixel that may or may not be rendered, however they are all processed and therefore affect game performance. If a scene suffers from too many overlapping pixels it is called overdraw. Unity has a mode in the Scene in which overdraw can be examined. This is illustrated in Figure 1.46. This shows you the objects being drawn on top of each other and

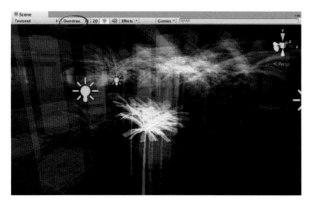

FIG 1.46 The overdraw setting in the Unity Scene Window.

FIG 1.47 Setting the render path options in Unity's Player Settings.

hence multiple drawing of the same pixel. The yellow parts in Figure 1.46 represent the highly processed areas.

The lights in the scene also add processing to fragments. Unity's render path ordains the way in which pixels are lit and drawn to the screen and hence the processing they incur. In Unity, the render path can be set to one of three options; vertex lit, forward, and deferred. Vertex lit renders out each object in one pass, calculating very elementary lighting properties using only the vertices of the meshes in the scene. This gives objects enough depth definition and shading but not shadows or special effects. It is a good choice for low performance mobile devices. The next up in quality is forward rendering. It runs at least two passes per pixel; a base pass to include all lights and effects and additional passes for each extra high quality light in the scene. The highest quality for rendering is deferred lighting (available in Pro only) that performs multiple passes including a bass pass for depth and geometry information, light passes to incorporating lighting effects, and a final pass that combines the first and second passes with colors, texture effects and any other ambient and emissive lighting.

Setting of the render path is done in the Player Settings panel as shown in Figure 1.47. The default is "Forward" and unless you've a serious performance problem, it's the best to use for mobile game development.

As is evident from the types of rendering paths, textures and lighting effects have the most impact on performance. To reduce fragment computations you should endeavor to reduce and, where possible, eliminate transparency, baked textures, the number of lights in a scene, real-time shadows, and post-processing camera effects (for example blur or lens flares).

1.9.6 Consider Bandwidth

Bandwidth in this case, not only refers to the amount of Internet downloads and uploads, but the passing around of data on the mobile devices circuit board. Mobile devices have less bandwidth than other platforms and the

FIG 1.48 The texture compression settings available in Unity.

biggest file sizes passed around between CPU, GPU, and memory are image files. Big, uncompressed textures are a big no-no. Texture files should be kept to resolutions matching a power of 2 size. That means widths and heights of 2, 4, 8, 16, 32, 64, 128, 256 and so on. The images don't have to be square, but a power of 2 size allows them to be more efficiently processed by the device. Unity will automatically compress any textures that are not power of 2 in size and you will notice the difference in image quality. The best mobile texture compression can be achieved with the ETC (Ericsson Texture Compression) or ASTC (Adaptive Scale Texture Compression) standards available in the Unity texture settings panel shown in Figure 1.48. However, be warned that switching between compressions may decrease the texture quality depending on the color profile of the image.

The exercises in this book use Automatic Truecolor to achieve the crispest images in Unity. Although it's worth trying other compressions to see if they don't compromise your image quality but give better performance. Changing the texture compression settings will be dealt with in the next chapter.

Last but not least, you can also better the performance of your mobile game with respect to bandwidth by implementing MIPS in 3D. MIPS for textures is the equivalent of LODs for meshes. If MIPS is selected in the texture settings, Unity will automatically create less detailed images for 3D geometry that is further away from the camera. This way the 3D scene looks more realistic with items that are further away being blurry and less detailed while having the payoff that smaller texture files take up less bandwidth and are therefore more efficient to process. However, if you are creating a 2D game, setting a texture as MIPS will give you blurry, low-quality game environments.

For more detailed information on optimizing a game in Unity see the tips and tricks at http://docs.unity3d.com/Documentation/Manual/ MobileOptimisation.html.

1.10 Summary

In this chapter we've discussed the rise of the mobile phone as a game delivery device. Its unique size and interface affordability poses many challenges for designers and developers. The popularity of games on mobiles has also seen an increase in the availability of rapid development tools. In turn, it has become a more viable option to become successful as an indie developer in solo or small teams.

ne   **C** Game

spect   Maximize on Play   Stats   Gizm

Procedural Literacy

A cloud is made of billows upon billows upon billows that look like clouds. As you come closer to a cloud you don't get something smooth, but irregularities at a smaller scale.

Benoit Mandelbrot

2.1 Introduction

This chapter introduces readers to a critically important skillset for new game designers and practitioners. In it, you will learn the primitive operations and control flow at the level of procedural oratory, design, and creativity encoded in today's highly visual and interactive mobile games and applications. Through the use of computational and visual methods you will explore the patterns and dynamics at the core of computer game code.

If you're more artistically inclined, computer programming may seem like an unnecessary technical skill with no relationship to the theory and aesthetics of design. However, if you are reading this, it is assumed you appreciate the need for such skills in the realm of game development. It is, however, the necessary evil that must be endured so you can fully express your inner game designer. Think of it more as just one toolkit you will require to fully realize your dreams.

Procedural literacy, however, is more than just knowing how to program. Designing and developing any interactive digital media whether it be games or websites requires knowledge beyond code and the ability to comprehend and manipulate processes, integrate human meaning and understanding within a computerized media, and to recognize and compose processes. While computer code is a cornerstone of procedural literacy it is not a knowledge of an exact programming language that is essential, but instead a mastery of the processes, data structures, and algorithms that can be found in all processes that form the foundation of all programming languages.

With this knowledge in your set of game development tools you are far more valuable as a designer and artist in the mobile game industry. Even if you don't fancy yourself as a coder, your knowledge of such will help you bridge the gap between artists and programmers allowing for more effective collaboration. In a small development team, procedural literacy is even more important as all members are required to contribute to all aspects of the game development life cycle.

Without a solid background in procedural literacy as an expressive medium, you will be drastically restricted in the types of games you can create. You will be restricted to developing easy to create games with no ability to design and deliver any new truly novel experiences.

2.1.1 Programming versus Scripting

Today, the terms "program" and "script" are often wrongly interpreted to mean the same thing. For the stalwart computer scientist however, they are very different. If you are to undertake the act of programming there are in fact four levels of programming language from which to choose. With each level the language becomes more abstract.

The lowest level of language is that of *machine code*. This is the type of code in which you speak to the computer on its terms; in 1s and 0s otherwise known as *binary*. Machine code is processed directly by the computer's CPU. It is made up of a set of binary strings. Each string represents a direct command for the CPU to execute. Every CPU has its own set of these strings called the *instruction set*. The Cortex-A9 CPU introduced in Chapter 1—found in the iPad 2, Samsung Galaxy SIII, etc.—implements the Thumb-2 instruction set. This set includes strings of 32 1s and 0s that make up each command.

The second-lowest level language is *assembly language*. This is simply a symbolic representation of machine code. Elementary commands are used to represent the binary instructions of machine code. Assembly language is easier to interpret and debug by a human than staring at a bunch of 1s and 0s. Such code for the Thumb-2 instruction to set memory location R0 to the value 15 looks like this:

```
MOV R0,#15
```

No matter how simple the assembly language is, the CPU still cannot process it. It must be reduced to machine code by the use of a separate program called an *assembler* before it is executed by the CPU.

The third level of language is *compiled language*. This is usually what is referred to most traditionally as a programming language and includes languages such as Pascal, C, and C++. Compiled languages are more intuitive and English-like than assembly languages. Thus, they are easier to understand and modify. For example, the following code will set the value of R0 (a memory location) to 0 if R1 + R2 is 5 otherwise R0 will be set to 10. The assembly code (using Thumb-2) is:

```
ADD R0,R1,R2
CMP R0,#5
BEQ zero
MOV R0,#10
```

whereas the C code is:

```
if ( R1 + R2 = = 5)
{
        R0 = 0;
}
else
{
        R0 = 10;
}
```

Compiled languages are translated into machine code by a *compiler*. This creates a standalone program that can be executed at any time. Once a program is compiled it is almost impossible to get back the original source.[1] If a modification needs to be made to the source code, the original code must be modified before compiling again into a new executable program.

The final and highest level language is the *interpreter language*. This is the level in which scripting languages, such as JavaScript and Lua[2] fall. The language is not compiled as such into a machine readable format, but rather must be accompanied by another program that interprets the code. Scripting is by far the quickest way to develop an application as it can be debugged and reinterpreted quicker than rewriting and compiling a program.

Scripting languages are a popular way to interact with game engines as the engine itself becomes the interpreter. Players who have the game can create

---

[1] Without the use of some sophisticated hacking tools.
[2] A popular scripting language used with a variety of applications including Adobe Photoshop Lightroom, VLC Media Player, Apoxalyx Game Engine and the Silent Storm Game Engine.

mods with such scripts to enhance existing games or create new ones. For example UnRealScript (also known as UScript) is a scripting language for the Unreal Engine. Players with access to the engine, such as the one included with Unreal Tournament are able to program additions such as the Artificial Intelligence (AI) of non-player characters to their liking. One of the earliest scripting interfaces for games was that developed in 1996 by John Carmack for *Quake*. The QuakeC interpreted language allows programmers and players alike to greatly modify the engine and change the behavior of not only NPCs but weapons and the physics system.

Unity allows developers to use three interpreted languages; JavaScript, C#, and Boo. JavaScript in Unity (sometimes referred to as UnityScript) is an elementary scripting language very similar, but not identical, to the JavaScript you can integrate in webpages. C# provides a more optimized and better integrated programming option. The syntax is similar to JavaScript but the affordances of C# are far more powerful. Boo is a simple scripting language also available in Unity. It does not run in Unity for iOS or Android and therefore will not be discussed here.

As previously discussed, there are a set of core processes, data structures, and algorithms that form the basis for all programming languages. Whichever language you decide to master, these fundamentals will carry through to future endeavors with other programming languages. However, as we need to adhere to just one language in this book we've chosen C# first as a follow-on and step up from *Holistic Game Development with Unity* and second because C# forces you to write code in a more optimized way making it the better choice for mobile development. In the next section, a primer for C#, the language to be used throughout this book will be presented.

● On the Web

From this point onward in the text, as hands-on sessions are presented some will require a downloaded Unity project file as a starting point. These files are available on the book's companion website at www.holistic3d.com.

Where possible, the downloadable project files will have been created with Unity 3 and tested for upgradable compatibility with Unity 4 unless otherwise advised.

2.2 Scripting Literacy

The common analogy for learning a programming language, is to compare it to learning any other language—like Japanese, Spanish, or Italian—and this comparison is by all means correct. Every programming language features a specific syntax (the format and style of writing), and provides a variety of prebuilt methods and functions for improving processing abilities and the execution of the game or application.

You will, by no means, read through this section and become an instant programming genius. Learning to program takes time. Years in fact. While you will get an overview of the basics here—and the rest of the book assumes you are new to programming and gives you all the necessary code required to complete the exercises—for a thorough understanding we'd recommend a good C# book such as *Unity 3D Coding Using C#* by Michael L. Croswell.

2.2.1 Anatomy of C#

As with many programming languages, the scripts that are produced using C# can be included in a single file, or dynamically link multiple files together at time of compilation. The skeleton (or minimum structure of a C# file) has been included below. Now, this script is a generic C# file that can be applied to any project. When working with Unity, a slightly modified skeleton script can be used.

```
using System;
namespace myCeeSharpNamespace
{
  class holisticUnityCeeSharp
  {
    public static void Main(string[] args)
    {
      System.Console.WriteLine("Hey!");
    }
  }
}
```

The first line `using System;` is a universally used include statement that allows this script access to a variety of predefined methods and other scripting components which can be used by C#. The `namespace` is an optional (but recommended) component of the script that defines a space for organizing code while also providing a method for creating data types that can be used globally. Namespacing allows for libraries of code to be created. The `class` is a required component in any C# script, and is used to define objects and their specific methods and functions. Within each class, any number of functions `public static void Main` can be included. For every function that is created, we must define the name of the function/ method (`Main`), the public status of the function (and how/where it can be called), and the data type (more on this later on). In this skeleton code, the `Main` function does not return anything (hence `void`). Inside of the `Main` function, a single command has been included; using the System library of code that was included at the start, we are then writing the phrase "Hey!" to the console.

More Information: C# Tutorials from MSDN

The Microsoft Developer Network (MSDN) provides a variety of tutorials spanning all aspects of the C# language. For further information on C#, and additional tutorials, see http://msdn.microsoft.com/en-us/library/aa288436(v=vs.71).aspx.

The next skeleton example is the commonly used starting script that Unity users are presented with when they create a new C# script. The first difference you will notice in comparison to the preceding example is that it doesn't include a `Main()` function. In regular C#, the `Main()` function is the entry point to a program. In Unity, the entry point is handled internally by the engine and therefore you would never include a `Main()` function in your Unity scripts.

```
using UnityEngine;
using System.Collections;
public class holisticUnityCeeSharp : MonoBehaviour {
    // Use this for initialization
    void Start ()
    {

    }
    // Update is called once per frame
    void Update ()
    {

    }
}
```

As in the first example, the `using` keyword includes libraries of code that have already been written, which extend the functionality of our program without needing to write overly complicated methods and functions for processes that already exist. By using the `UnityEngine`, we include a variety of functions, methods, and classes that are necessary for compiling and working with the Unity Engine. Following this, a publically accessible class (`holisticUnityCeeSharp`) is created which inherits the Unity base class of `MonoBehavior`. Within this class, two functions are created for us: `void Start()`, which runs once at the very start of the program, and `void Update()`, which is executed once with each game loop.

To create a C# script in Unity you select the Create menu in the Project and click on C# Script as shown in Figure 2.1. A new file called *NewBehaviourScript* will be created. Rename as you see fit.

FIG 2.1 Creating a new script in Unity.

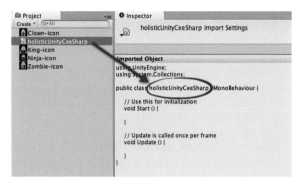

FIG 2.2 C# Script files and class names matching.

Note, it's very important that the name of your script is the name of the class used in the code (see Figure 2.2). If these names do not match you will get an error in Unity.

In Chapter 1 you created a simple script to make a game object spin. Scripts can be related to specific single objects or be used across the entire game project. You will learn more of this later.

2.2.2 Logic

Computers work by running electric currents through a complex series of switches that are either on or off. This is the very reason machine code, discussed in the previous section, exists. A value of ON equates to 1 and OFF equates to 0. Furthermore, the value 1 represents *true* and 0 represents *false*. If there is only one thing you ever learn about programming and computers make sure it is logic. A thorough understanding of this concept will be the crux of all the knowledge and skills to come. This is essentially the language of computers.

When you program you create a lot of logic statements that affect the way a program runs. A program does not necessarily start at the beginning and linearly make its way to the end. Especially in the case of a game, when user input is considered, a program will have to make a series of decisions on what and how to function next. These decisions are made using logic.

Consider the following:

> *if it is raining and cold*
> *take a rain coat*
> *otherwise if it is raining*
> *take an umbrella*
> *otherwise*
> *take nothing*

There are three decision-making statements (or logic) statements in the preceding. A logic statement can be identified as a question with a true or false answer. In the above the decisions to be evaluated are:

is it raining and cold?
is it raining?
are neither of the above statements true?

For the first statement to be true it needs to be both raining and cold. For the second statement to be true it just needs to be raining and the third statement is the default in which neither of the other statements is true. Let's say it is raining and it is cold. If we consider the decisions the first statement would be true and the action would be take *a rain coat*. If it were only raining and not cold the action would be *take an umbrella*.

We make logical decisions every day. Maybe not quite as structured as the one just presented, but the concept of logic should not be foreign to you as it is a part of the human thinking process.

Logic statements themselves are held together with special operators. In our example we use the operator *and* to join *raining* and *cold*. Consider for a moment that the first statement changed to:

if it is raining or cold

We would then choose the action *take a rain coat* if it was either raining or cold or even both. This situation is different from the statement joined with *and* as it required both conditions to be true in order for the entire statement to be true.

A logic statement joined with operatives such as AND and OR is known as Boolean algebra. Besides AND and OR there are five other Boolean algebra operatives; NOT, NAND, NOR, XOR, and XNOR. When all possible combinations of these operatives and 1 and 0 values are written up they form what are known as *truth tables* and are shown in the Quick Reference here.

● Quick Reference

Boolean Algebra

Function	Boolean Algebra Syntax	C#	Truth table		
			INPUT		OUTPUT
AND	A · B	A && B	A	B	A AND B
			0	0	0
			0	1	0
			1	0	0
			1	1	1

Quick Reference

Boolean Algebra—cont'd

OR	A + B	A || B	INPUT		OUTPUT
			A	B	A OR B
			0	0	0
			0	1	1
			1	0	1
			1	1	1

NOT	A	!A	INPUT	OUTPUT
			A	NOT A
			0	1
			1	0

NAND	A · B	!(A && B)	INPUT		OUTPUT
			A	B	A NAND B
			0	0	1
			0	1	1
			1	0	1
			1	1	0

NOR	A + B	!(A || B)	INPUT		OUTPUT
			A	B	A NOR B
			0	0	1
			0	1	0
			1	0	0
			1	1	0

XOR	A Å B	(A && !B) || (!A && B)	INPUT		OUTPUT
			A	B	A XOR B
			0	0	0
			0	1	1
			1	0	1
			1	1	0

XNOR	A ⊙ B	(!A && !B) || (A && B)	INPUT		OUTPUT
			A	B	A XNOR B
			0	0	1
			0	1	0
			1	0	0
			1	1	1

● **On the Web**
Interactive Boolean Algebra Logic Gates
Navigate to the books website at www.holistic3D.com for an interactive
Unity version of Boolean Algebra.

While it's not necessary to know these truth tables off by heart, it is
recommended you familiarize yourself with the ones for AND, OR, and NOT.
Believe it or not, after a while, these statements will start to make a kind
of intellectual sense such that you can conjure up the answers by logical
deduction.

As we explore further into programming the importance of understanding
logic and Boolean algebra will become blatantly clear.

2.2.3 Comments

Comments serve a very useful purpose when writing and developing any
project. Any text contained with a comment is automatically ignored by the
compiler, which allows for code snippets and other notations to be included
in the code without being executed (or even touched) by the program.
Commonly, comments are used to describe the function and actions that
a given snippet of code will perform, or is likely to perform. Although it
takes a couple of extra minutes to write a solid, meaningful comment,
you could be saving yourself (or your team) hours of work decoding the
reason why a particular snippet of code was included in the first place. The
following snippet of code highlights how comments can be used for intrinsic
documentation. As previously mentioned,

```
// This is a single line comment.
/* This is a
   multi-line comment. */
```

2.2.4 Variables

Computer memory is divided up into blocks much like plots of land on a city
map. The smallest plot of computer memory can hold 8 bits or a byte (a string
of eight 1s and 0s). Like the plots on a city map, computer memory blocks
have a unique address. Although instead of 174 Maplehill Drive,
Holistic City, it looks more like 0x5337392F.

Memory stores values used by programs. These values are addressed in the
program as *variables*. A variable is a modifiable block of computer memory
in a program that can be used to store a value. This block of memory can
be overwritten multiple times throughout the execution of a program, or
simply remain at a constant value throughout the duration of the application.
Consider a variable as an empty box; this box can be labeled with any name

that we deem appropriate, and can contain numbers, characters, words or objects. If a value needs to be stored in memory that is larger than a byte, several blocks can be put together.

For example, a byte can store up to eight 1s and 0s (bits) with the biggest value being 11111111. This binary code, equates to 255 decimal. This is because each bit in the byte represents a power of 2 value for the computer. If you write the binary using a layout similar to that shown in Table 2.1 you can add together the decimal values in the same column in which there is a 1 and get the equivalent decimal value for the 8 bit binary.

$$= 128 + 64 + 32 + 16 + 8 + 4 + 2 + 1$$
$$= 255$$

Now if you need to store a value bigger than 255 decimal in computer memory, you will need more than 1 byte.

Different sized blocks of memory are allocated by way of datatypes. These are predefined sizes that store different types of data. Table 2.2 describes some of the most popular data types and examples of the type of data that would be classified as each data type.

Generally, the most commonly used data types are integers, floats, Booleans, and strings. However, depending on the size of the number you are storing, the double data type may be more useful (specifically for when storing much larger numbers of up to 15 digits). The string data type technically isn't a data type. Rather, it is an array of characters that can be "stringed" together to form a word or phrase.

Before a variable can be used in a program it must be declared. Declaring a variable tells the computer to allocate some memory to the program and assign a name to it. The syntax is:

TABLE 2.1 Binary to Decimal Conversion

7^2	6^2	5^2	4^2	3^2	2^2	1^2	0^2
128	64	32	16	8	4	2	1
1	1	1	1	1	1	1	1

TABLE 2.2 Datatypes in C#

Data Type	Declaration	Samples of Data
Integer	int	12, 33, 0, 1, 32654
Character	char	'a', 'b', 'c', 'd', '$'
Floating Point	float	3.11, 4.5, 5.0, 0.1
Boolean	bool	True, False, 0, 1
Double	double	42057.5501, 3.809, 4.3
String	string	"Holistic", "Amazing"

```
datatype name;
```

or

```
datatype name = value;
```

The first allocates a block of memory with a name and the second allocates a block of memory with a name and an initial value. For example, to declare a variable called x and put the value 5 in it, you would write:

```
int x = 5;
```

This allocates an integer sized block of memory, gives it the name x and puts the value of 5 in it.

Note the semicolon on the end of the line. This is of utmost importance. Each statement in C# must end with a semicolon (with the exception of a rare few you will learn about later). This is a kind of marker telling the compiler that you've written a complete line of code. Sometimes a line of code can actually take up more than one physical line on the screen and yet the same code all belongs to the same statement. The semicolon is crucial for identifying the end.

In mathematics, algebra can be used to substitute a number in a formula (or equation) to produce a different result. This same principle applies in programming. Take the following for example:

```
x = 3
```

In this mathematical example x is the name of the variable, and it is assigned a value of 3. This variable could theoretically contain anything, it could contain a whole number, or a decimal, or even another variable. In the following line, we create a new variable (y) and assign it a value using a simple formula. In this line, the value of y would be equal to 14 (the value of x plus 11).

```
y = x + 11
```

Because x and y are both variables, their values can change. At any point in our program, the values of both x and y can be manually set to anything, overwriting the original values for both. In programming, variables can be named anything (not just x or y).

```
mango = 50
width = 300
scale = 1.5
```

The more meaningful you make a variable name the more readable the script will be for yourself and other people. For example if you need to store the player's score in a variable then you would name it score, instead of say, x, because then it is obvious what the value in the variable is for. Although you can name a variable pretty much anything you like there are some limiting factors. First you cannot begin a variable name with a number. For example, *99bottlesofbeer* is not a legal variable name. Second, you cannot have a space or apostrophe in the name. Hence *bottles of beer* would be illegal. You also cannot name a variable after a *reserved word*. A reserved word being a function name or other special word used in the actual programming language. For example, Update or void are not legal variable names.

There are numerous conventions for naming variables; each attempts to make code more readable. One method called Camel Case employs a lowercase at the beginning of the name followed by capitals for each word encapsulated in the variable name. For example, playersScore or numberOfZombiesLeft. Another method uses underscores in-between words in place of a space. The preceding then become players_score and number_Of_Zombies_Left. Which method you employ is up to personal preference, however don't mix the two.

Variables are a crucial component in any program, and must be created (or declared) manually. The computer memory space is not created automatically. Variable declaration is the process of assigning a value, a name and a size to the block that will hold the information or data. Figure 2.3 conceptualizes the variable declarations and initializations in Listing 2.1.

Listing 2.1 Declaring differing variable types

```
int numberOfZombiesLeft = 20;
float goldCoinTotal = 45.67;
bool isDead = true;
char keyPressed = 'p';
string playerName = "Penslayer";
```

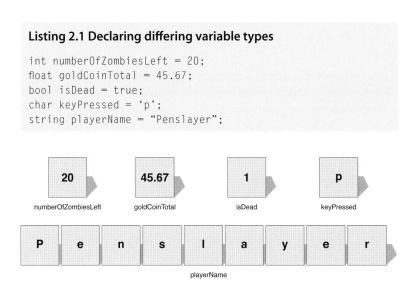

FIG 2.3 Conceptualization of variable declarations in Listing 2.1.

2.2.5 Functions

A block of code that performs a certain specialized operation is called a *function*. Many functions have been pre-written and are contained in the *libraries* previously mentioned. Functions make life easier for the novice coder as they take care of a lot of complex code and bundle it into a single line. For example `Debug.Log()` that prints messages out to the console would contain many lines of code, written by another programmer. Because this type of functionality is required by many other programmers over and over, instead of writing the code to perform this printing operation from scratch, it is placed in a library and all you need to do is make a function call.

You can also write your own functions to perform common tasks as you find yourself repeating code. Let's say, for example, you create some code to reset variables in a game scene thus

```
playerScore = 0;
countDown = 100;
playerPosition = new Vector3(100.0f, 200.0f, 50.0f);
```

This code may be required each time the player respawns from dying, falling off the map or a multitude of other reasons. If you had to repeat these lines of code throughout your entire code base over five times, each time you needed to make a change to the way this code worked, you have to find all five locations in the code and make the changes. For example, the player's starting position might change and you'd have to update the Vector five times. Besides being laborious, your code also becomes unreliable and messy. What happens the time you only remember to make changes to four of the five occurrences? Immediately bugs are introduced. This code would then be better off in a function.

The syntax for writing your own functions is the same as that of the default Unity functions you have already used. For example, the above lines could be consolidated into one function thus

```
void ResetPlayer()
{
    playerScore = 0;
    countDown = 100;
    playerPosition =
    new Vector3(100.0f, 200.0f, 50.0f);
}
```

Now instead of repeating these three lines throughout your code you only need to call the function with

```
ResetPlayer();
```

2.2.6 Operators

The two types of operator that are used in programming are arithmetic and relational. Arithmetic operators are used to perform mathematics and put values into variables. Relational operators are for comparing values in logical decision making statements.

Arithmetic Operators

Operators in programming work the same as they do in mathematics. They are used for addition, subtraction, multiplication, and division. The characters used for each are +, –, * and / respectively and illustrated in Table 2.3.

The order of precedence as applied in mathematics is the same in programming. Parenthesis can be used to force certain operations to occur before others. For example,

```
8 / (2 + 2)
```

equates to 2.

There is also a shorthand for performing operations in which the value of a variable is changed and reassigned to itself such as

```
x = x + 1
```

The second occurrence of the variable is left out and the operation is rewritten as

x+ = 1 or even shorter as x++

In the same way you can do

x– = 1, which is the same as x = x – 1 or shorter as x–,

x* = 1, which is the same as x = x*1, and

x/ = 1 which is x = x/1

In addition, you don't need to just be dealing with a value of 1, any value being used to modify a variable can be employed in this shorthand, for example

x+ = 5

which will add 5 to the existing value of x.

TABLE 2.3 Common mathematical operators used in programming

Operator	Arithmetic Performed	Example in C#	Value of x from example
=	Assignment	x = 7;	7
+	Addition	y = 2; x = y + 8;	10

-	Subtraction	y = 10;
		z = 20;
		x = z – y;
			10

*	Multiplication	y = 2; x = y*6;	12

/	Division	y = 50;
		z = 10;
		x = y/z;
			5

TABLE 2.4 Common relational operators

Operator	Arithmetic Performed	Example in JavaScript	Value of x from example

>	Greater than	y = 10;
		z = 2;
		x = y > z;
			TRUE

<	Less than	y = 15;
		z = 2;
		x = y < z;
			FALSE

>=	Greater than or equal to	y = 42;
		z = 2;
		x = z >= y;
			FALSE

<=	Less than or equal to	y = 5;
		z = 1;
		x = z <= y;
			TRUE

==	Equal to	y = 21;
		z = 18;
		x = y == z
			FALSE

!=	Not equal to	y = 2;
		z = 36;
		x = y != z
			TRUE

Relational Operators

Relational operators are used to make comparisons between values and variables in code. The result of which is a Boolean value. These values are then used in conditional statements to affect the flow of the program. Some examples are shown in Table 2.4.

2.2.7 Conditional Statements

Conditional statements use the results of relational operators or Boolean algebra to divert the flow of the program. We've already discussed condition statements with respect to logic in Section 2.2.2. The most commonly used conditional statement is the if else statement. It is structure like that in Listing 2.2.

Listing 2.2 An if-else Statement

```
if (some test is true)
{
    //do this code
}
else
{
    //do this code
}
```

☉ Unity Hands-On
Conditional Statements
In this short hands-on session we will explore the use of conditional statements.

Step 1: Create a new Unity Project. To the default Scene add a sphere. Position the camera so the sphere is centered in the game. Add a directional light.

Step 2: Create a new C# script called changeSphere and add the following code:

```
using Unity Engine;
using System.Collections;

public class changeSphere : MonoBehaviour {
    // Use this for initialization
    void Start () {
    }

    // Update is called once per frame
    void Update () {
        if(Input.GetKeyDown (KeyCode.A))
        {
            this.transform.localScale + =
new Vector3(-0.1f,-0.1f,-0.1f);
        }
        else if(Input.GetKeyDown (KeyCode.D))
        {
            this.transform.localScale + =
new Vector3(0.1f,0.1f,0.1f);
        }

        if(this.transform.localScale.x > 1.5)
        {
            this.renderer.material.color =
new Color(1.0f,0.0f,0.0f);
        }
        else if(this.transform.localScale.x < 0.5)
        {
            this.renderer.material.color =
new Color(0.0f,1.0f,0.0f);
        }
    }
}
```

Step 3: Save. Attach this code to the sphere. Play. Use the A and D keys to make the sphere get smaller and bigger.

There are two sets of conditional statements in this code. The first tests for certain key presses and then acts on them. The second tests for the x scale of the sphere and sets its color depending on differing values.

2.2.8 Loops

A loop is a special kind of conditional statement that has the potential to execute more than once thus looping around the same block of code several times before continuing. A very common use of loops is to process values in an array where the same operation needs to be applied to each value. No matter how long the array, the loop code stays the same size with respect to the number of lines. For example the code to increase a value by one before printing it each time will be the same no matter if you did it ten or a million times. To do the same operation one line at a time the code would be:

```
int i = 0;
i ++;
Debug.Log(i);
i++;
Debug.Log(i);
i++;
Debug.Log(i);
...etc.
```

To continue printing out values until reaching 100 would take 200 lines of code; one to add a one to the value and another to print the value out. A *for loop* on the other hand makes the process much easier. Its basic syntax is shown in Listing 2.3.

Listing 2.3 A for loop

```
for( initialize; test; update)
{
     //perform some action
}
```

In the *initialize* stage of the loop a variable is declared and initialized. The loop runs the code in between the brackets while the *test* part remains true. This test is written as a conditional statement. The *update* section usually modifies the value of the initial variable for testing the next time the loop executes. If the test does not contain a dynamic value and is therefore always destined to result in a true statement, an endless loop occurs. Such a loop results in program freezes and eventually crashes.

To illustrate a loop in action, the one in Listing 2.4 lists the numbers between 1 and 100.

Listing 2.4 A for loop to print out the numbers between 1 and 100.

```
for(int i = 1; i < = 100; i++)
{
    Debug.Log(i);
}
```

2.2.9 Arrays

An array is not its own datatype but rather the stringing together of the same datatype multiple times. For example, a string is an array of characters, although it is often treated as a special case because it is used so much. To create an array of datatypes other than characters (although you can declare a character array this way instead of using the string datatype) the square brackets are employed thus:

```
int[] numbers = new int[10];
```

This creates an array of ten integer sized blocks in the computer memory physically addressed beside each other. You can then access each block individually with an integer representing the block's location in the array. For example,

```
numbers[2] = 8;
numbers[7] = 4;
numbers[8] = 45;
```

Figure 2.4 illustrates this array and the values assigned to the individual blocks. Note how in programming the first block is always referenced with 0, not 1.

The previous array is considered one dimensional as it stores values in a linear fashion and each box is references with only one integer value. It's possible to have a multidimensional array, the most common of these being two in

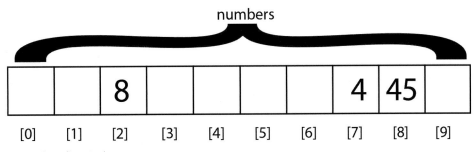

FIG 2.4 A one-dimensional array

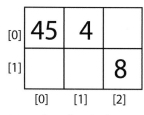

FIG 2.5 A two-dimensional array

which values are referenced by row and column. A two-dimensional array is declared thus

```
int[,] numbers = new int[2, 3];
```

This particular array has two rows each with three columns. Values are assigned to the array using row and column positions for examplenumbers

```
[0,0] = 45;
numbers[0,1] = 4;
numbers[1,2] = 8;
```

This array is illustrated in Figure 2.5.

Of course arrays don't have to hold just integer values, they can store anything from characters to game objects.

For more information on C# arrays visit http://msdn.microsoft.com/en-us/library/aa288453(v=vs.71).aspx.

2.2.10 Classes and Objects

A class is a complex datatype made up of variables called *properties* and functions called *methods*. Imagine a class as a template or recipe that can be used to create many instances of the class, in the same way as a Lego instruction set can be used to produce an identical Lego car over and over. In coding, these instances are called objects.

Figure 2.6 illustrates a simple class called Square. It defines how to draw a square. The variables describe the physical attributes of a square, while the function is an operation that can be performed on or by the square. In this example, it's a function that orients the square and sets the rotation property.

All game objects in Unity are just that . . . objects. Each is defined by its own class. All Unity classes are defined in the online Unity Script Reference. It can be found at http://docs.unity3d.com/Documentation/ScriptReference.

Constructors

Every class has a main function call that brings it into existence. This function is called a constructor and allocates the computing memory required to hold the newly created object. It's not unlike creating a single variable and putting some initial value in it. However instead of

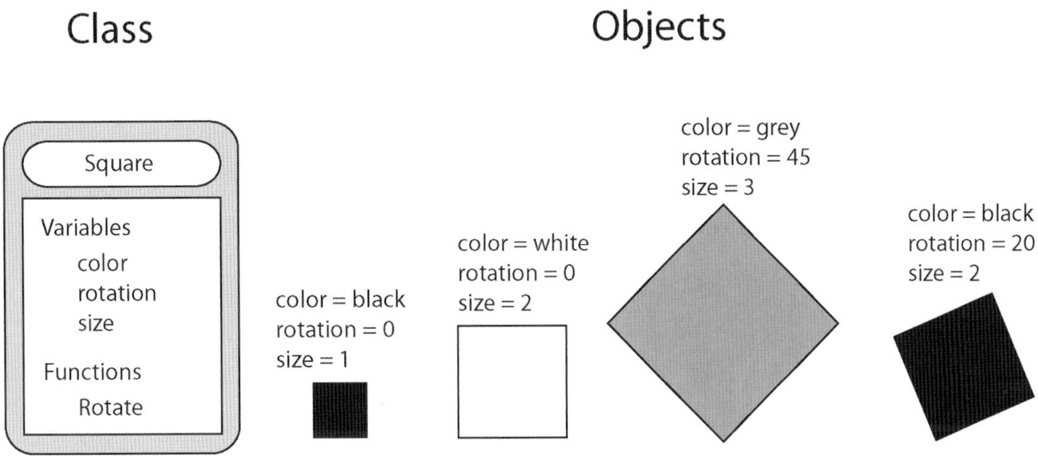

Class

Objects

color = grey
rotation = 45
size = 3

color = black
rotation = 20
size = 2

Square

Variables
   color
   rotation
   size

Functions
   Rotate

color = black
rotation = 0
size = 1

color = white
rotation = 0
size = 2

FIG 2.6 A class called Square and objects created from it.

```
int x = 5;
in the case of a Vector3 it is
Vector3 myPosition = new Vector3(1.0f, 5.0f, 1.5f);
```

The preceding code creates a new Vector3 object called myPosition with the
x, y and z values set to 1, 5 and 1.5 respectively.

Properties/Variables

If you have a look at Unity's script reference for the Vector3 at http://docs.
unity3d.com/Documentation/ScriptReference/Vector3.html you'll see listed
a number of variables and functions. These are accessible via the newly
created object by referencing the names after a full stop. For example,
myPosition.x is the x value set for the vector. To put this value into
another variable we can write:

```
float xPos = myPosition.x;
```

Functions/Methods

A class function performs an operation on an object. You will see numerous
functions listed for Vector3 in the previous link. Functions on objects are
called the same way as to access a variable. For example the Vector3.Set()
function allows you to change the x, y and z values of the vector thus

```
myPosition.Set(5.7,1.2,3.0);
```

2.2.11 Yields and Coroutines

Code executes procedurally in the same order it is written. Sometimes
however you may want the program to pause for a couple of seconds before
continuing or to run two functions at the same time. To do this you need one

function to give up control to another. If you didn't do this the whole program would freeze while the pause was happening.

Each time the main game loops, it runs through all the lines of code in the Update() functions of the scripts attached to the objects in the Scene. The more lines of code involved in this process the slower this operation will be. With each game loop you also get one frame drawn on the screen. Hence the time to execute the code affects the frame update. If you wanted to pause an operation in the code for a couple of seconds, this would add this time to a single game loop and therefore make your game appear to freeze.

To stop this from happening, you can pause the execution of the code and not affect the game loop by putting in a *yield*. The yield halts the function and allows the game loop to get on with other processing and frame drawing, but then returns to the function at the point from which it left to continue the processing.

A yield in Unity cannot be called from the regular Unity specific functions such as Update or Start. If you try you will get an error such as:

```
error CS1624: The body of 'counter.Update()' cannot
be an iterator block because 'void' is not an
iterator interface type
```

A special type of function is required to call a yield. It must have a return type of IEnumerator. Listing 2.5 illustrates the use of a yield inside an appropriate function. Note when this function is called it is started as a coroutine of Update. It is therefore not called in the usual way but instead from inside a StartCoroutine() function.

Listing 2.5 Implementing Yield and Coroutine

```
using UnityEngine;
using System.Collections;
public class counter : MonoBehaviour {
    IEnumerator CountTime()
    {
        Debug.Log("1 second");
        yield return new WaitForSeconds(1);
        Debug.Log("2 seconds");
        yield return new WaitForSeconds(1);
        Debug.Log("3 seconds");
    }
    // Update is called once per frame
    void Update ()
    {
        if(Input.GetKeyDown (KeyCode.A))
        {
            Debug.Log("A Pressed");
```

```
                    StartCoroutine("CountTime");
                    Debug.Log("After Timer");
                }
            }
        }
```

To implement the code in Listing 2.5 in a Unity project, create a C# file called counter, add the code and attach it to the Main Camera. Press the A key to start the timer.

2.2.12 C# versus JavaScript

As previously mentioned, Unity provides support for three primary, interpreted programming languages: JavaScript, C# and Boo. Generally speaking the JavaScript that is supported by Unity, is a modified version commonly referred to as UnityScript, and features a variety of inherited functions and syntax definitions. However, Unity provides full support and integration of C#, without needing any pseudo-definitions, with C# performing better in most instances compared to UnityScript. Syntactically, in other words the structure of the code, there are a number of differences between C# and JavaScript. The following simple programs (provided in both JavaScript and C#) produce the same result, although note the differences in the structure of the program. Firstly, a variable cubeSize is declared as a float data type, and a value of 5.0 is assigned. Then at the start of the program, a cube, with a radius of 5.0, is instantiated in the game world, and an output message is displayed in the console.

Javascript

```
var cubeSize : float = 5.0;
function Start ()
{
    var cube : GameObject =
    GameObject.CreatePrimitive(PrimitiveType.Cube);

    cube.transform.localScale = Vector3 (cubeSize,
    cubeSize, cubeSize);

    Debug.Log("Cube of size " + cubeSize + " has
    been created.");
}
```

C#

```
using UnityEngine;
using System.Collections;
public float cubeSize = 5.0F;
public class holistic : MonoBehaviour
{
    void Start()
```

```
        {
            GameObject cube =
            GameObject.CreatePrimitive(PrimitiveType.Cube);

            cube.transform.localScale = new
            Vector3(cubeSize, cubeSize, cubeSize);

            Debug.Log("Cube of size " + cubeSize + " has
            been created.");
        }
    }
```

The primary differences between JavaScript (or UnityScript) and C# are with respect to how the variables are declared and the functions defined. The specific functions, and syntax, including semi-colons, and parentheses remain consistent.

2.2.13 Common Coding Errors

No matter how much experience you have with coding, there are some errors that will drive you insane and take many minutes if not hours to debug. While logical errors will allow a program to run but function oddly, syntactical errors will stop you dead in your tracks as the program will refuse to compile. The former requires a lot of play testing and code tracing to debug, the later just requires your own understanding of proper coding syntax. If your program will not compile here are the ten most likely common errors.

1. No semicolon at the end of a statement

If you leave a semicolon off the end of a statement, the compiler will consider the next line to be part of the same statement. This will cause compiler errors. Errors will appear in the Console window and at the bottom of the Editor window with a red exclamation mark as shown in Figure 2.7.

When a semicolon is missing the error does not necessarily reflect the exact line where the semicolon is needed. You will need to inspect the code above and around the error to locate the missing statement end marker.

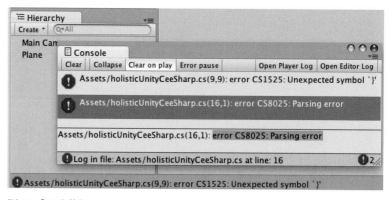

FIG 2.7 Errors in Unity

2. A missing matching parenthesis

Parentheses, brackets, or braces are used to define the start and end of a block of code, the container for logic statements or function variables, or order of precedence in mathematical and Boolean algebra.

A pair of parentheses can actually be used in the middle of many lines of procedural code without consequence, although very few programmers practice this, however whenever you include one opening bracket you must include a closing one. For example,

```
1. void Update()
2.    Debug.Log("Hi There";
3. }
```

is missing a matching brace near the end of line 2 and line 3 has a closing parentheses but no matching opening one.

3. A line break inside a string

A string is data defined inside two double quotes. Putting a new line inside these quotes will cause a compiler error. For example,

```
Debug.Log("Hi
     There");
```

is not legitimate. If the text inside the string actually wraps because of editor formatting, this is fine. However, actually typing a return inside a string will fail. If you must break up a large string into smaller pieces they can be concatenated with a plus sign thus:

```
Debug.Log ("Hi" +
          "There");
```

4. The wrong casing

Programming compilers are very fussy about casing. They consider the variable myScore and MyScore to be two very different values. If a variable name or function has the wrong casing, such as

```
debug.Log("Hi There");
```

then most compiler errors will be similar to

```
error CS0103: The name 'debug' does not exist in the
current context
```

5. The wrong spelling

The wrong spelling of a variable or function name produces the same error as incorrect casing. These two syntactical errors are often very difficult to locate and you need to take note of the compiler error to identify where your typing mistake is.

6. The use of a reserved word for a variable or class name

Sometimes and by complete accident you will choose a reserved word as a variable or function name. A reserved word has special meaning in code and will cause a compiler error if used incorrectly. For example, in C#, interface is a reserved word and hence

```
int interface;
```

produces the error

```
error CS1525: Unexpected symbol 'interface',
expecting '.', '?', '[', '<operator>', or 'identifier'
```

> You'll find a complete set of reserve C# words at http://msdn.microsoft.com/en-us/library/x53a06bb.aspx.
>
>

7. The filename doesn't match the class name

As previously discussed, the filename of a C# script must match that of the code defining the class. If it doesn't then you won't receive an error from Unity until you try and use the script by attaching it to an object. When you do, an error window will open as shown in Figure 2.8, making it clear what you have done wrong.

8. A float has been initialized without an "f" on the end

C# is particularly sensitive to float declaration. If you were to declare

```
float myHeight = 5.687;
```

the error

```
error CS0664: Literal of type double cannot be
implicitly converted to type 'float'. Add suffix 'f'
to create a literal of this type
```

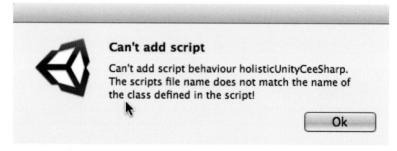

FIG 2.8 Unity error invoked when filename and class name do not match.

would come up. Without a trailing "f" in the initialization, for example,

```
float myHeight = 5.687f;
```

the compiler considers the value 5.687 to be a double. As a double value takes up a larger space in memory than a float, the compiler won't allow this type of operation. However, don't make decimal numbers doubles just to save yourself the errors of forgetting an "f" as this will make your program less efficient to the larger amounts of memory you are manipulating.

9. The wrong type of value is being assigned to a variable

This error is similar to the previous one. If a variable is declared as an integer, then you cannot assign a float value to it. Similarly you can't store a string in a double. If you were to try

```
float characterName = "Deefa Dog";
```

you'd receive the error:

```
error CS0029: Cannot implicitly convert type
'string' to 'float'
```

Implicit conversion means trying to make one datatype directly into another, usually using an equals sign. It won't work.

10. The variables being passed to a function are not the correct datatype

This error is caused by the same issue as the previous one. In passing a value into a function it is being assigned to a variable within that function. If the value the function is expecting is not the same as the value being passed though you will get an implicit conversion error.

For example, if we try and instantiate a new Vector3 and give it the wrong datatypes for the parameters, for example,

```
Vector3 myLocation = new Vector3(6.5, 3.4, "a");
```

two errors occur;

```
error CS1502: The best overloaded method match for
'UnityEngine.Vector3.Vector3(float, float, float)' has
some invalid arguments

error CS1503: Argument '#1' cannot convert 'double'
expression to type 'float'
```

The first informs us we have used the method incorrectly and actually shows us what the usage with the variable types should be and the second is basically an implicit conversion error. In this case we've tried to pass two double values and a string to the Vector3 constructor when it's actually expecting three floats.

For more information on casting and type conversions visit http://msdn.microsoft.com/en-us/library/ms173105.aspx.

● Note

The code in this book has restrictions on the line length due to the page margins. As such you will find single lines wrapped onto multiple lines. For example the code:

```
Vector3 touchPos = Camera.main.ScreenToWorld-
Point(
    new Vector3(Input.mousePosition.x,
        Input.mousePosition.y, 0));
```

can actually be written on one single line in a code editor. When you are typing in the examples, lines like the one above need only be on one line. A line of code ends with a semicolon. When a single line of code wraps, the continuation of the code is preceded with a tab.

2.3 Game Mathematics Literacy

A solid understanding of vector mathematics is critical for developing games. Even with the number of built-in functions that do all the hard calculations for you, having the knowledge is essential in being able to use them and interpret their output. You require this knowledge if you want to position game objects and move them around besides many other things.

2.3.1 Points and Vectors

The fundamental concepts upon which all this mathematics are based are *points* and *vectors*. How each is defined is relative to a coordinate system. Although there are theoretically infinite coordinates systems, in game development we are concerned primarily with two—two- and three-dimensional space (illustrated in Figure 2.9). Space in this sense is defined by a coordinate system comprising the number of axes defining the dimensions. In two-dimensional space there are two axes; x and y. In three-dimensional space there are three axes; x, y, and z. Each axis in the coordinate system is orthogonal with the others. This means the angle between each is equal to 90 degrees. The point at which the axes meet is called the origin or *O*.

To specify the position of a point within the coordinate system a value representing the distance the position is along each of the axes is used. In

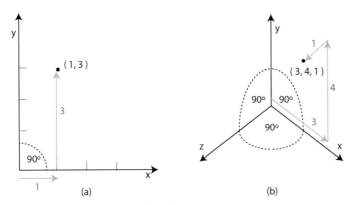

FIG 2.9 The two and three-dimensional coordinate systems.

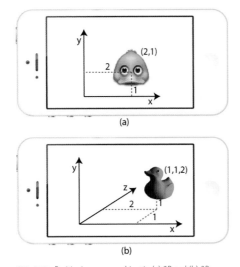

FIG 2.10 Positioning a game object in (a) 2D and (b) 3D.

two-dimensional space, we require two numbers to define the position of a point. As shown in Figure 2.10 (a), a point that is a distance of 2 along the x and 1 along the y is denoted as (2,1). Note, the x distance is always given before the y making all coordinates in two-dimensional space represented by (x, y). In three-dimensional space the z axis is also used. A point 2 along the x, 1 along the y and 2 along the z is denoted (1,1,2) as shown in Figure 2.10 (b). For interest's sake, a point located in six-dimensional space would have a coordinate with six values such as (2,4,1,8,9,–10). Although six-dimensional space is not physical, it is theoretically possible.

All objects in the game world have a position represented by a point. In a 2D game the position is represented by x and y. In 3D it becomes x, y, and z. As illustrated in Figure 2.10, a 2D game environment ignores the z axis and positions everything with just x and y. This means the 2D environment has

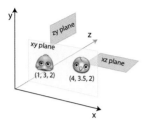

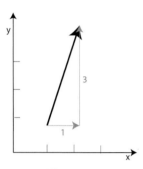

FIG 2.11 Placing objects in an XY plane to fake 2D in 3D.

FIG 2.12 A Vector.

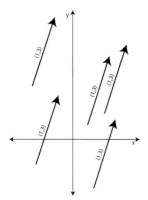

FIG 2.13 The same vector used in multiple positions.

no depth. In a 3D environment, the depth value of z is added to the object's coordinates.

In a 3D game engine such as Unity, a 2D game can be created by ignoring, for the most part, the z axis. As shown in Figure 2.11 when the z value for each game object is the same, the objects are said to reside in the same *plane*. A plane being a flat surface in 3D space. The easiest way to create a plane is to simply restrict the values in either the x, y, or z dimensions. The plane shown in Figure 2.11 is at the fixed z location of 2. Such a plane with fixed z values across the entire surface is called an XY plane, as any object moved around in that plane will only have its x and y values modified; z will always remain constant. An XZ plane will have y values that remain constant and a YZ plane will have x values that remain constant. Examples of XZ and ZY planes are shown in Figure 2.11. Note that while one dimension for each plane remains constant, such as z for the XY plane, its value does not have to be zero.

To complement the concept of a point, which only represents a position in space, we have the vector that indicates direction and length. A vector is denoted in the same way as a point, with a series of n numbers where n is equal to the number of dimensions in the coordinate system. Whereas a point's coordinates are relative to the coordinate system, a vector's values are relative to the origin of the vector. The vector shown in Figure 2.12 is denoted (1,3) as its length in the x direction is 1 and its length in the y is 3. Note these lengths are not measured from the origin of the coordinate system but from the source of the vector.

A vector is drawn as a line with an arrow on the end. The arrow indicates the vector's direction. The length of the vector is calculated using Pythagoras' Theorem using the vector's x and y values as they form the basis of a right-angled triangle of which the vector's length is the hypotenuse (see Equation 1). In the case of the vector in Figure 2.12, the length equates to 3.16.

$$length = \sqrt{x^2 + y^2}$$

Equation 1

```
length = sqrt(x^2 + y^2)                    2D
length = sqrt(x^2 + y^2 + z^2)              3D
```

Because vectors don't have a set starting position, the same vector can appear anywhere in the coordinate system. Figure 2.13 demonstrates the vector (1,3) at a variety of starting locations. Note how the vectors' values are not affected. They all have the same length and direction.

Vectors are used extensively in games to represent distances, velocity, direction, force and others. The distance between two game objects, for example, can be calculated by determining the vector that goes between the objects' positions and then finding the length of that vector. The difference between two points, P and Q is a vector, thus:

$$v = Q - P$$

where v is a vector starting at P and ending at Q.

For example, given the two ducks in Figure 2.14 where the green duck, D1 is at (5,1,1) and the blue duck, D2 is at (5,2,11) the vector between them can be calculated with V = D2 – D1 = (5,2,11) – (5,1,1) = (0,1,10). Note you can also calculate the vector that runs between D2 and D1 (i.e., in the opposite direction) by reversing the equation, thus D1 – D2 = (5,1,1) – (5,2,11) = (0,–1,–10). Both calculated vectors in this example are the same length and parallel. The second just points in the opposite direction. You may have noticed that negating the x, y, and z values of a vector give you this opposite facing vector.

Now that you have the vector between the objects, applying Pythagoras' Theorem to it will give you the distance as:

```
distance = sqrt(0² + 1² + 10²) = 10.05
```

Distance calculations are used in games to determine any number of game world and game object states. For example, the distance between two objects can tell us if they have collided. Distance may also be used in an NPC's artificial intelligence routines to determine if they have seen or heard the player and are able to attack the player. The distance a player moves in the game world during each main game loop establishes their velocity.

Vectors can also be added to points to move them. A vector added to a point gives the coordinates of a second point. This second point is at a position equal to the end of the vector when it is drawn beginning at the first point. In the example given in Figure 2.15 the vector (1,3) is added to the point (–1,1) the resulting point is at (0,4).

If the vector, v, is added to the point, p, the resulting point p^2 can be calculated thus:

```
p² = (p.x + v.x, p.y + v.y)              2D
p² = (p.x + v.x, p.y + v.y, p.z + v.z)   3D
```

In the example given in Figure 2.14, if we wanted to move D1 to the position of D2 we simply add V to D1. In other words, if D1 travels along the path given by V it will end up at the same location as D2. We can mathematically confirm this with D1 + V = (5,1,1) + (0,1,10) = (5,2,11).

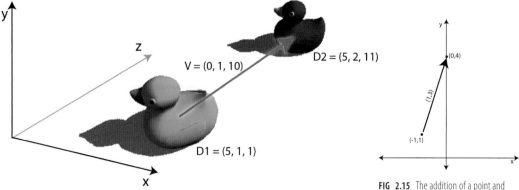

FIG 2.14 Finding the vector between game objects.

FIG 2.15 The addition of a point and a vector.

Now consider we are in a game environment where we would like the green duck to slowly move to the location of the blue duck. If we were to just add the vector between them onto the location of the green duck, the green duck would instantly be on the blue duck. You would not see the green duck slowly moving, it would just hop from its starting position to the blue duck's position. Therefore we need a way to cut the vector up into little pieces and move the duck along one vector at a time.

A useful property of vectors is that they can be easily be divided up into equal sections without affecting their direction. The only property that changes is the length. Say you want the green duck to take ten steps in getting to the blue duck, you just divide the vector by ten. This involves dividing the x, y, and z value by ten. In this case one tenth of V will be $(0/10,1/10,10/10) = (0,0.1,1)$. This new vector, if you draw it will be parallel to the original vector, and if you add it to the position of the green duck 10 times you'll end up at the coordinates of the blue duck thus:

```
Step 1:  (5, 1, 1)    + (0, 0.1, 1) = (5, 1.1, 2)
Step 2:  (5, 1.1, 2)  + (0, 0.1, 1) = (5, 1.2, 3)
Step 3:  (5, 1.2, 3)  + (0, 0.1, 1) = (5, 1.3, 4)
Step 4:  (5, 1.3, 3)  + (0, 0.1, 1) = (5, 1.4, 5)
Step 5:  (5, 1.4, 3)  + (0, 0.1, 1) = (5, 1.5, 6)
Step 6:  (5, 1.5, 3)  + (0, 0.1, 1) = (5, 1.6, 7)
Step 7:  (5, 1.6, 3)  + (0, 0.1, 1) = (5, 1.7, 8)
Step 8:  (5, 1.7, 3)  + (0, 0.1, 1) = (5, 1.8, 9)
Step 9:  (5, 1.8, 3)  + (0, 0.1, 1) = (5, 1.9, 10)
Step 10: (5, 1.9, 3)  + (0, 0.1, 1) = (5, 2, 11)
```

How far is the green duck moving each time? This is easy to determine by calculating the length of the vector $(0,0.1,1)$ which is 1.005. For interest's sake let's assume D1's position changes to $(2,5,15)$ and D2's to $(13,20,30)$. The vector between them would be $D2 - D1 = (13,20,30) - (2,5,15) = (11,15,15)$. If this time we used ten steps to get from D1 to D2 the one-tenth vector would be $(11/10,15/10,15/10) = (1.1,1.5,1.5)$ and the step length would be 2.39. Therefore with each iteration the green duck would be travelling further than it did when the ducks were closer. It would still take ten steps to get from position D1 to D2, but the transition would be faster as more distance is covered with each step. In a game animation this is not a very good way to determine the change in position between one location and another as the speed changes with distance. Rather, we'd prefer our characters to travel at the same speed irrespective of the distance they have to cover. When this is the case, a new type of vector comes in handy; the normalized vector.

The normalized version of a vector is a vector that is parallel with the original vector but always has a length of one. To calculate the normalized vector, the vector is divided by its length. Let's use the previous values between D1 and D2 to demonstrate. The vector between them is $(11,15,15)$. This has a length of

23.9. The normalized vector is then (11/23.9,15/23.9,15/23.9) = (0.46,0.63,0.63). We can prove this is the normalized vector by calculating its length. Allowing for minor rounding off errors, the length is indeed 1.

If you use the normalized vector to move your character you can be guaranteed it will move at a constant speed between destinations irrespective of the distance between them. If you want to speed up the movement of the character, you just multiply the normalized vector by some speed factor.

These properties of vectors will now be explored within Unity.

◉ Unity Hands-On
Exploring Vectors
In this hands-on session we are going to explore vectors in Unity by moving colored ducks around in 3D space. The very concepts you've just read about will be presented in addition to some Unity shortcuts.

Step 1: Download and unzip the project file *VectorDucks1* from the website. Open the main scene by double-clicking on it in the Project. The initial project will look like that in Figure 2.16.

Step 2: Create a new C# file in the Project called *moveduck*. Open it in the editor and modify the code as follows (the new code you are required to add is shown in bold):

```
using UnityEngine;
using System.Collections;
```

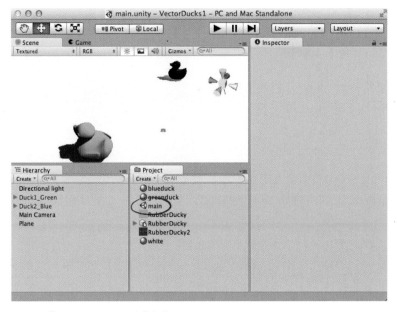

FIG 2.16 The starting project open in Unity 3.

```
public class moveduck : MonoBehaviour {
    public GameObject targetDuck;
    // Use this for initialization
    void Start () {
        Vector3 vectorToTarget =
            targetDuck.transform.position-
            this.transform.position;
        this.transform.position = this.transform.position +
            vectorToTarget;
    }
    // Update is called once per frame
    void Update () {
    }
}
```

Save the file in the editor. Switch back to Unity.

Step 3: Locate the *moveduck* script in the Project. Drag and drop it onto Duck1_Green in the Hierarchy. This will attach the script to the game object. Select the Duck1_Green object in the Hierarchy. You will see the script is now attached in the Inspector. In addition, the variable of Target Duck will be set to None. Drag and drop the Duck2_Blue onto Target Duck in the Inspector for Duck1_Green. This process is illustrated in Figure 2.17.

FIG 2.17 Adding the moveduck script to the green duck and referencing the blue duck.

> **More Information: Vector3**
>
> Unity has its own data structures for vector; Vector2 and Vector3. Vector2 is for vectors in 2D space and Vector3 for 3D space. Vector3 however is the most commonly used and is the underlying storage variable type for all game object transform properties. Even when you make a 2D game in Unity, you'll tend to use Vector3 more often.
>
> For further information on the settings of the Vector3 component see http://docs.unity3d.com/Documentation/ScriptReference/Vector3.html.
>
>

Step 4: Press the play button. Watch how the green duck jumps directly onto the blue duck's position.

So what just happened? The script assigned to the green duck takes the position of the target object and calculates the vector to it. It then adds this vector to the position of the green duck. This sets the green duck's position to the blue duck's position. Vector mathematics in action!

Step 5: Now, let's make the green duck move towards the blue duck in steps rather than one giant leap Modify the code for *moveduck* to this:

```
using UnityEngine;
using System.Collections;

public class moveduck : MonoBehaviour {

    public GameObject targetDuck;
    Vector3 vectorToTarget;

    // Use this for initialization
    void Start () {
        vectorToTarget = targetDuck.transform.position -
            this.transform.position;
        //reduce the target vector to one tenth the size
        vectorToTarget /= 10;
    }
    // Update is called once per frame
    void Update () {
    this.transform.position = this.transform.position +
            vectorToTarget;
    }
}
```

Save and play. The first thing you will notice is that the green duck moves towards the blue duck instead of jumping to its location. The second thing you'll notice is that the green duck doesn't stop once it gets to the blue duck. The reason being that we've moved the code that modifies the duck's position down into the Update. This means the vector is constantly added to the duck's position while the program is playing. It doesn't stop at doing it just ten times.

To make the green duck stop moving when it gets to the blue duck we need to test for the distance between the ducks. If the distance is zero or very small we can assume they are near each other. Modify the code inside the Update to calculate the distance between the ducks and then only continue adding the vector to the green duck if the distance is greater than 1, thus:

```
void Update () {
    float distanceBetweenDucks = Vector3.Distance(
        this.transform.position,
    targetDuck. transform.position);

    if(distanceBetweenDucks > 1)
    {
    this.transform.position = this.transform.
                              position + vectorTo
                              Target;
    }
}
```

Save and play. The green duck will now slide over to the blue duck and stop when it gets near. If you want the duck to stop a little further away, change the 1 in the preceding code to a larger value, such as 5. The reason we are testing if the ducks are further than 1 apart, instead of testing for them being at the exact same location, before updating the green duck's position will become apparent shortly.

Step 6: The current code is designed to move the green duck to the blue duck in ten steps. As previously explained, if the distance between the ducks is made larger the green duck will still need to cover more ground in the same time thus making it move much faster. To witness this, in the Scene, select *Duck2_Blue* and drag it further away from the green duck. Press play and watch how much faster the green duck moves.
Step 7: To make the green duck move at constant speed we will use a normalized vector instead of one that is one tenth the size. Modify the code in the Start thus:

```
void Start () {
    vectorToTarget = targetDuck.transform.position -
                      this.transform.position;
        vectorToTarget = vectorToTarget.normalized;
}
```

Save and play. You'll find that no matter how far away the blue duck is from the green duck, the green duck will always travel at the same speed.

Step 8: Most of the time you won't want a game character to travel at the speed of 1 every game loop. You therefore need to add a multiplier to the normalized vector to speed up or slow down the movement. To add in a speed factor modify the code to the following.

```
... //code above no change
public class moveduck : MonoBehaviour {
    public GameObject targetDuck;
    Vector3 vectorToTarget;
    public float duckSpeed = 0.1f;
    // Use this for initialization
    void Start () {
        vectorToTarget = targetDuck.transform.position
                         - this.transform.position;
        vectorToTarget = vectorToTarget.normalized * duckSpeed;
    }
... //code below no change
```

Save and play. The speed multiplier in this case will move the duck at one tenth of the normalized vector size (i.e., slow the movement down). To speed the duck up you can increase the speed value to a larger value.

2.3.2 Angles

How mean and threatening would Zeus, the final boss in *Gods of War 2*, appear if he could turn and look at you while he was beating the living daylights out of your character? Either, *not very*, or you'd think the AI system in the game was very poorly designed. Being able to programmatically determine the way in which an NPC is facing and where the player character is standing in order to have the NPC turn and face the player is a classic problem in games development that requires angles. If we have the player's position as a point and the NPCs position as a point and the direction it is facing as a vector, we can calculate the angle that the NPC has to turn through in order to face the player. Essentially we want to turn the NPC such that the direction in which it is facing aligns with the vector between it and the character. This is illustrated in Figure 2.18 where *a* is the angle through which the green duck must turn to face the blue duck. Now, if you were the green duck, it would seem fairly obvious how you should turn, but as you are about to see, in vector mathematics there is no intuition allowed and for NPCs the calculations are more complex than mere forward movement.

To find the angle between two vectors the *dot product* of the normalized vectors must be calculated. The dot product is found by multiplying the respective coordinates together and then adding them. This means multiplying

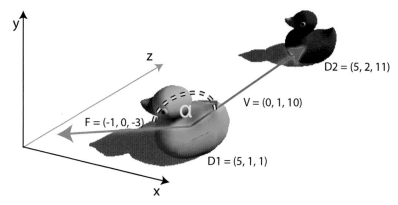

FIG 2.18 The key properties in determining the angle between game objects.

the x values together, the y values together and the z values together and then adding the results of the three multiplications. This is denoted:

```
f . v = fx * vx + fy * vy + fz * vz
```

In the example of the ducks in Figure 2.18, where the normalized version of F, denoted F is (−0.32, 0, −0.95) and V, denoted V, is (0, 0.1, 1), the dot product is:

```
(−0.32, 0, −0.95) · (0, 0.1, 1) = −0.32 x 0 + 0 x 0.1
+ −0.95 x 1 = 0 + 0 + −0.95 = −0.95
```

This value however, is not the angle. The angle is found by calculating the arccosine of the dot product. In this example, the value equates to 161.8 degrees.

Now we know the angle we can turn the green duck around by 161.8 degrees and it will be facing the blue duck, right? Wrong! Because we don't know whether the duck should turn to the left or to the right. Looking at Figure 2.18 it is obvious the green duck should turn clockwise. However for a program to determine this, we need an equation to work it out.

Enter the *cross product*. The cross product of two normalized vectors results in another vector that is perpendicular (at right angles) to both initial vectors and is denoted:

```
F x V = (Fy x Vz − Fz x Vy, Fz x Vx − Fx x Vz,
         Fx x Vy − Fy x Vx)
```

where the facing direction vector is always first.

In our ducks example, the cross product will be:

```
FxV = (−0.32,0,−0.95) x (0,0.1,1)
    = (0x1 − −0.95x0.1, −0.95x0, −0.32x1, −0.32x
      0.1 − 0x0)
    = (0.095, 0.32, −0.032)
```

Now, if we find the cross product and switch the vectors the result will be:

```
VxF = (0,0.1,1) x (−0.32,0, −0.95)
    = (0.1x−0.95 − 1x0, 1x−0.32 − 0x−0.95, 0x0 −
      0.1x −0.32)
    = (−0.095, −0.32, 0.032)
```

The angle found with the dot product $F \cdot V$ relates to the cross product $F \times V$ where the order of the vectors in each equation is critical and must be the same. Therefore it is the first cross product calculated that tells us which way to turn. Here's the trick, if the z value of the cross product is negative it indicates a clockwise turn. If the z value is positive, the turn must be anticlockwise.

● Unity Hands-On
Exploring Angles
Step 1: Download and unzip the project file *VectorDucks2*. This project is the same as you would have completed in the previous hands-on and therefore you can just continue in the same project if you prefer.
Step 2: You may be relieved to find out that Unity takes the hard work out of turning characters and game objects to look at other objects. You do not need to program in dot and cross products. However, it is hoped from the previous section on these concepts that you'll have a better appreciation of what has gone into the Unity functions you're about to implement.

Open the *moveduck* file and modify the Start thus:

```
void Start () {
    vectorToTarget = targetDuck.transform.position -
                     this.transform.position;
    vectorToTarget = vectorToTarget.normalized *
                     duckSpeed;
    this.transform.LookAt (targetDuck.transform.position);
}
```

Save and play. The LookAt function included will turn the green duck to face the blue duck. You can use this function on any game object to orientate it towards any point in the game world. LookAt works by using the game object's forward-facing vector to calculate the angle. The forward-facing vector of a game object is the object's local z axis.

In addition to the game world's coordinate system that specifies where the origin is and how x, y, and z are orientated, each object in the world also has its own local set of axes. The local axes rotate with the game object and help keep track of the direction of the object. When you click on the game object in the Scene, its local axes are highlighted in red for the x axis, green for the y axis and blue for the z axis. Unity assigns the keyword right to the x axis, up to the y and forward to the z. As you can see in Figure 2.19 the green duck model's z or forward axis is aligned with what you would naturally equate to the forward direction of an actual duck. This might

FIG 2.19 The duck model and its local axes.

95

seem like an amusing thing to say until you get some model in which the *z* axis of the model does not face forward. The way in which *z* is aligned with the mesh is critical to the correct functioning of the LookAt function, as it is this *z* or forward axis that is used to orient the model. If the model has the *z* axis sticking straight up with respect to the natural forward of the model's mesh, the LookAt function will tip the model over onto its side when orientating the *z* axis to point directly at the position the function is given.

The way in which the forward axis is facing in a model is a legitimate issue that you will encounter when using third-party assets. To see the effects, download *duckie.fbx*. Drag the file into the Project to add it to Unity. It will appear in the Project with a small blue cube next to it indicating it is a model. Now drag the duckie asset from the Project into the Scene near the green duck. Select the duckie model in the Scene. Notice how the blue z axis points up through the duck's head as shown in Figure 2.20. Unity will consider this the forward facing axis.

Now attach the moveduck script to this new duck in the same way you did for the green duck. Select the duckie object in the Hierarchy, locate the attached script and drag and drop Duck2_Blue into its Target Duck variable. Play. The new duck's forward vector will orient to LookAt the blue duck and as such the duck will slide along with its beak in the ground as shown in Figure 2.21.

Step 3: Short of putting in a model with an incorrect z axis into Maya and reorienting it, a quick fix can be found in Unity. Double-click on the duckie object in the Hierarchy to bring it into view in the Scene. Now select GameObject > Create Other > Cube. Make the duckie a child of the Cube by dragging it in the Hierarchy and dropping it onto the Cube. Notice it will show beneath the Cube in the Hierarchy and slightly indented as shown in Figure 2.22.

In the Scene, the Cube and the duckie may be some distance apart. Now the duckie is a child of the Cube, its transform values in the Inspector are

FIG 2.20 The duck model with the *z* axis facing up through the duck's head.

FIG 2.22 Parenting the Cube to the duckie.

FIG 2.21 The duck model with up facing *z* axis orientated to LookAt the blue duck.

relative to the Cube. This means that as far as the duckie is concerned the Cube represents its world coordinate system and the Cube's position is the duckie's origin. Therefore, if you select the duckie in the Hierarchy and go to the Inspector and set its transform's position to (0, 0, 0), the duckie will move to the same position as the Cube as illustrated in Figure 2.23.

Now take notice of the Cube's z axis. Rotate the duckie model so it faces forward along this axis. That is, you want the duck's beak looking forward. As shown in Figure 2.24, the Cube has become the anchor point for the duck model. After rotating and adjusting the position of the duck, the Cube should sit neatly inside the duck model.

With the Duckie attached to the Cube and facing in the correct direction, it will be the Cube that should now drive the movement of the duck. The duck essentially becomes a passenger along for the ride. With the duckie

FIG 2.23 Zeroing the duckie model position when a child of the cube.

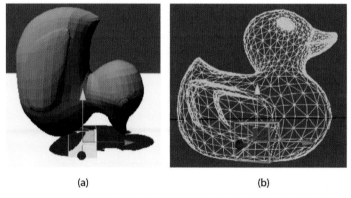

(a)   (b)

FIG 2.24 Rotating the duckie model to align with the Cube orientation; (a) the orientation of the duck after being attached to the Cube, (b) the orientation of the duck after it has been rotated to align with the Cube's z axis.

97

FIG 2.25 Removing a script from a game object.

selected in the Hierarchy, locate the *moveduck* script component select the Settings icon on the right to reveal a small dropdown menu. Select Remove Component to take the script off the duck as shown in Figure 2.25.

Now add the *moveduck* script onto the Cube. With the Cube selected in the Hierarchy be sure you drag and drop Duck2_Blue onto the Target Duck variable.

Play. The script will act on the Cube, not the attached duck and therefore the Cube's z axis will be set to LookAt the blue duck. As the duckie model is attached to the Cube, it will take on all the Cube's transform changes including position and orientation.

Step 4: One final thing to do is to delete the Cube's visual components. We initially used them as a visual reference in positioning the duckie model, but they are no longer needed. Select the Cube in the Hierarchy, in the Inspector locate the Cube (Mesh Filter), Box Collider, and Mesh Renderer components. Remove them using the component's dropdown settings menu as you did when removing the script from the duckie.

2.3.3 Affine Transformations

Affine transformations are the foundation of computer graphics and central to the movement, orientation and sizing of game objects. The mathematics behind them is such that they can manipulate a 2D or 3D object without distorting it. This means proportions of the parts of an object remain the same and parallel edges remain parallel after the transformation has occurred. An affine transformation is any combination of translations (moving), scalings (resizing), and rotations (orienting). An example of an affine transformation is illustrated in Figure 2.26. Figure 2.26 (a) shows the before image of an object being resized, moved, and rotated. Notice how the final object in the after image still represents the initial object. This is the effect of an affine transformation. The initial object is never distorted. Figure 2.26 (b), however, shows a non-affine transformation. The after image still represents a star with a square inside, however both are severely distorted and not recognizable as the first.

In games, when we move objects around in the environment we need to be sure the model or sprite being manipulated is not distorted in anyway. Through the use of affine transformations we can confidently modify objects knowing they will not be structurally damaged. There are four affine transformations; translation, scale, rotation, and skew. With the exception of

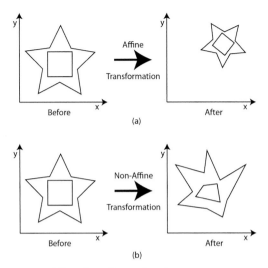

FIG 2.26 Affine and non-affine transformations.

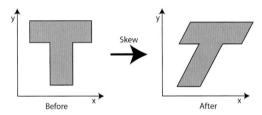

FIG 2.27 Skew.

skew that shears an object by leaning it across in one dimension (as illustrated in Figure 2.27), these affine transformations are the crux of all procedural (code-created) animation in games.

Rotation can be the most difficult transformation to understand as it is performed with more complicated mathematics than translation and scaling. For translation, a point is moved by adding or subtracting a vector. For scaling, an object's points are merely multiplied by a scaling factor. For example if you wanted to make an object half its size you would multiply all its points by 0.5. Rotations require a combination of sine and cosine functions to be used. We will not go into these here. Rather, the interested reader is encouraged to read http://mathworld.wolfram.com/RotationMatrix.html.

How you can rotate an object depends on the number of dimensions in the coordinate system. In 3D, an object can be rotated three ways; around the x axis, around the y axis and around the z axis. Each of these rotations is synonymous with the orientations of aircraft as shown in Figure 2.28. A rotation around the x axis results in a pitch, a rotation around the z axis gives a roll and a rotation around the y axis creates a yaw.

We will now explore affine transformations through three hands-on sessions with examples in Unity.

99

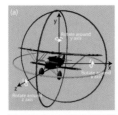

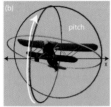

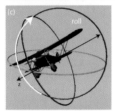

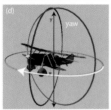

FIG 2.28 The rotation operations: (a) the rotations around each axis, (b) pitch, (c) roll, and (d) yaw.

◉ Unity Hands-On

Translation

Translation means to move an object from one location to another. This is achieved by adding a vector to an object's position. We explored translation in the previous hands-on sessions by moving the green duck towards the blue duck.

Step 1: Download and open the CarDriving project. Open the main scene. In the Scene you will find a large plane and a car model.

Step 2: In the Project create a new C# file called *Drive* and modify the Update function thus:

```
void Update () {
    this.transform.Translate(Vector3.forward);
}
```

Save the code and attach it to the car game object. Do this by dragging the script for *Drive*, onto the car in the Hierarchy. Ensure you don't attach it to the car model in the Project that has the same name. Before playing, select the Camera in the Hierarchy and then GameObject > Align With View to position it in the Game in the same way you are viewing the Scene. Otherwise, when you play, you might find you can't see anything.

Play. The car will move in a forward direction. The code given to it is translating, or moving, the car each update loop. It is using the car's forward vector to do this.

Stop playing. Rotate the car in the Scene to face another direction. Now play again. Notice the car will move again according to its forward *z* axis.

Step 3: As you've noticed the car will continue moving in its forward direction regardless of its orientation. This means we can rotate the car during play in order to steer it. To do this modify your code thus:

```
using UnityEngine;
using System.Collections;
public class Drive : MonoBehaviour {
    float forwardSpeed = 0.1f;
    float rotationSpeed = 1.0f;
    // Use this for initialization
    void Start () {
    }

    // Update is called once per frame
    void Update () {
        float rotation = Input.GetAxis ("Horizontal")
            * rotationSpeed;
        this.transform.Rotate(0, rotation, 0);
        this.transform.Translate(Vector3.forward
            * forwardSpeed);
    }
}
```

Save and play. You'll now be able to steer the car with the left and right arrow keys. In this code, the use of the `Input.GetAxis` function gets readings from the assigned *virtual axes*. These are settings in Unity that map commonly used keyboard, joystick, controller, and mouse controls to navigational and other values. In this case the *horizontal* virtual axes get values from the left and right arrow keys. In the same way you can get the *vertical* axis values from the up and down arrow keys.

In brief we are simply using readings from the left and right arrow keys to adjust the rotation of the car model. The `Translate()` function keeps driving the model forward on its *z* axis. Rotation of an object is applied around one of its three axes. In this case, to turn the car from left to right it needs to rotate around the up, or *y*, axis. This is the reason there are three values given to the `Rotate()` function above. This will be further explained shortly.

The previous code also introduces a multiplier for the forward and rotational speeds. You can use these to adjust how fast the car moves and turns.

More Information: Virtual Axes

For further information on the use of Virtual Axes see http://docs. unity3d.com/Documentation/Manual/Input.html.

Step 4: The current code automatically moves the car forward on each update. Let's change that so the player has control over the forward and backward movement. For this we will implement the vertical GetAxis. Modify the `Update()` function thus:

```
void Update () {
    float rotation = Input.GetAxis ("Horizontal") *
rotationSpeed;
    float direction = Input.GetAxis ("Vertical") *
forwardSpeed;
    this.transform.Rotate(0, rotation, 0);
    this.transform.Translate(Vector3.forward
    * direction);
    }
```

Save and play. The up and down arrow keys will now control the movement of the car in the forward and backward directions. The values for GetAxis are obviously influencing the calculates for rotation and direction, but how? To find out we will employ a quick trick used for debugging. We will print out the values of GetAxis and have a look. To add in this debugging code, modify the Update() function with:

```
void Update () {
    float rotation = Input.GetAxis ("Horizontal") *
    rotationSpeed;
    float direction = Input.GetAxis ("Vertical") *
    forwardSpeed;
    this.transform.Rotate(0, rotation, 0);
    this.transform.Translate(Vector3.forward *
    direction);

    Debug.Log("Horizontal: " + Input.GetAxis ("Horizontal"));
    Debug.Log("Vertical: " + Input.GetAxis ("Vertical"));
}
```

Before playing, open the Console Window. This is the area where errors, warning and debug logs appear. In Unity 4 the Console Window is visible by default. In Unity 3 select Window > Console. Now play. As you press the arrow keys you'll see how the value of GetAxis changes. The vertical value controlled by the up and down keys ranges from 1 to -1. Therefore, the calculation for direction will give a positive value when the up key is pressed and a negative value when the down key is pressed. When the value is negative and multiplied with the forward vector it actually gives a vector that is parallel to the forward vector but rotated 180 degrees to it. Essentially it makes the car move backwards.

Debug.Log() is a great function to remember whenever you aren't quite sure what the value of some variable in your program. If the program isn't running the way you expect, don't ever expect you know what the values of a variable are; print them out to make sure!

○ Unity Hands-On
Rotation
Rotation means to orient an object by turning. An object can be rotated with respect to itself or the world. The rotation is easiest visualized in terms of a rotation around one or more of the axes. In this hands-on session we will explore both types of rotation.

Step 1: Download and open the main scene of the Rotation project. In the Scene you will find a large *x*, *y*, and *z* axes system constructed from cylinders and placed exactly on the origin of the world. In addition there is the car model from the previous exercise. The view is shown in Figure 2.29.

The large constructed axes represents the world axes. If you select the car model in the Scene, you'll notice it has its own set of axes. These are the car's *local* coordinate system.

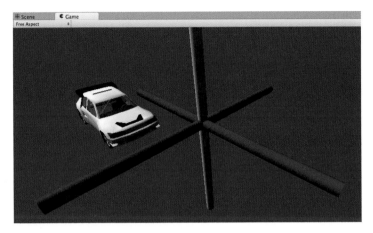

FIG 2.29 The initial Rotation project's main scene.

Step 2: Create a C# script called Rotate. Modify the `Update()` function with:

```
void Update () {
    this.transform.Rotate( 0, 10, 0);
}
```

Save the script and attach it to the car model. Play. The car will be rotated each game loop by 10 degrees around its y axis (the vertical/up axis) resulting in it yawing.

The `transform.Rotate()` function takes three values. Each of these relate to rotations about the x, y, and z axis respectively. To see a rotation of the car about the z axis instead (rolling), change the values of the `Rotation()` function to:

```
    this.transform.Rotate( 0, 0, 10);
```

Step 3: To make the car rotate around the origin of the world instead of itself, modify the `Update()` function with:

```
void Update () {
    this.transform.RotateAround (Vector3.zero, Vector3.up, 10);
}
```

Save and play. The car will now rotate around the origin's (represented by Vector3.zero) y axis by 10 degrees each loop. You can in fact rotate any object around any point in the world, not just the origin. The first variable in the `RotateAround()` function is the world point to revolve around. The second is the axis at that point that determines the direction of the rotation.

● Note

Vector3.zero is just a vector in Unity with the value (0,0,0) you can use it anytime you need a zeroed vector.

Step 4: Both types of rotation can be combined to create a world movement and model rotation effect thus:

```
void Update () {
        this.transform.Rotate (0, 0, 10);
        this.transform.RotateAround (Vector3.zero, Vector3.up, 5);
    }
```

Try this out! The car will roll while spinning around the world's *y* axis. However, you'll notice the car is moving backwards. This is due to the orientation in the world. You could fix this by selecting the car model in the Scene, hitting the E key and rotating the car to face in the opposite direction before playing again.

⊙ Unity Hands-On
Scaling

Scaling is the simple operation of increasing or decreasing the size of an object. To scale a game object its transform is multiplied by a scaling vector that determines the size in the *x*, *y*, and *z* dimensions.

Create a new Unity Project. Add a cube with GameObject > Create Other > Cube. Position the Cube at (0,0,0) by setting the position in the Inspector as shown in Figure 2.30.

Double-click on the Cube in the Hierarchy to center it in the Scene view. Select the Main Camera in the Hierarchy and then GameObject > Align with View to make the Game view match the Scene view. Next add a light into the Scene with GameObject > Create Other > Directional Light. With the light selected in the Hierarchy press the E key and then drag the light's rotation to light the cube as desired.

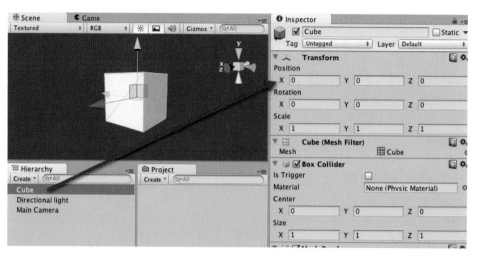

FIG 2.30 Creating and positioning a Cube.

Step 2: Create a C# file called Stretch. Add the following to the `Update()` function:

```
void Update () {
    if( Input.GetKeyDown(KeyCode.A))
    {
        this.transform.localScale - =
            new Vector3(0.1f,0.1f,0.1f);
    }
    else if( Input.GetKeyDown(KeyCode.D))
    {
        this.transform.localScale + =
            new Vector3(0.1f,0.1f,0.1f);
    }
}
```

Save the script and attach it to the Cube. Play. Press the A key to shrink the cube and the D key to grow it. Each time you press a key the scale value of the Cube's transform is being increased or decreased by 0.1 in each dimension. Notice how the scale is affected separately on each dimension. This means you can actually set the Cube to only grow in one direction if you so wish.

This code implements the `Input.GetKeyDown()` function. It checks if a particular key has been pressed and returns true if it is so. Inside the function you can use KeyCode followed by a "." and then the key you desire to monitor. For example if you want to check if the W key has been pressed the code would be KeyCode.W.

More Information: KeyCode

For a list of all the keys that you can monitor see: http://docs.unity3d.com/Documentation/ScriptReference/KeyCode.html.

Step 3: To grow and shrink the Cube along just one axis, modify the values in both new `Vector3()` calls in the preceding code to:

```
new Vector3( 0.1f, 0f, 0f);
```

Save and play. Growth will be restricted to the *x* axis only.

2.4 Procedural Content Generation

While a great deal of the visual elements of a game are created in external applications such as Photoshop and Maya, it seems pertinent at this point to

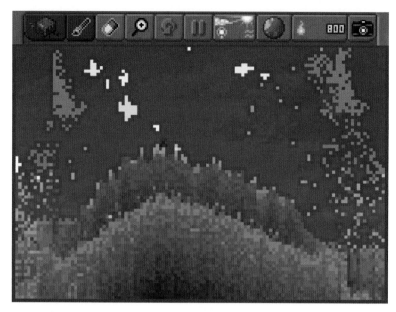

FIG 2.31 The Sandbox (Pixowl Studios, www.pixowl.com).

talk about Procedural Content Generation (PCG). Usually a topic discussed in more advanced chapters, what has already been discussed herein can be used to create interesting and dynamic game content before you learn anything further about textures, models and animations.

In fact many games use PCG to extend their games in limitless and infinite ways that would be beyond the ability of a human artist. For example, *Minecraft* generates new random environments each time you start a new world using a method called Perlin Noise. The iPad game, *The Sandbox* (shown in Figure 2.31), implements algorithms called *cellular automata*, which operate on a grid of cells. This is the exact same fundamental concept driving the underlying simulation in *SimCity*.

PCG is the process by which the artist relinquishes control of their design and allows the computer to algorithmically generate elements of the game. There are multiple techniques that can be used for PCG. The most famous of these is the fractal.

2.4.1 Fractals

Without going into the mathematics behind fractals, they are algorithmically generated patterns that when graphically represented are constructed from self-similar copies of themselves. Although fractals were a known mathematical construct, their true beauty was not accessible to a wider audience until 1975 when mathematician Benoit Mandelbrot used computer graphics to draw them.

Generating a fractal image requires the repetitive use of an algorithm that manipulates as input, output from previous iterations. One of the most famous fractals is Barnsley's fern leaf. It applies four affine transformations to a square as shown in Figure 2.32.

The resulting shape, shown in Figure 2.32, becomes the input for applying the four transformations again. The iterative process can continue for as long as you like. The fern leaf is shown evolving in Figure 2.33 after (a) two iterations, (b) five iterations, and (c) ten iterations.

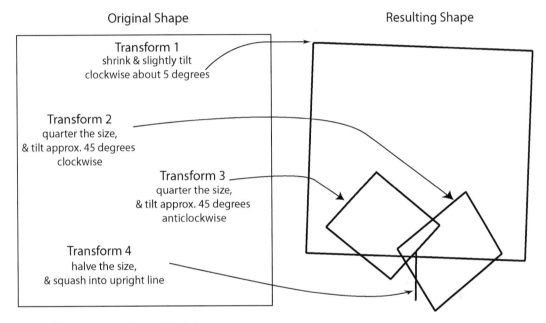

FIG 2.32 The transformations of Barnsley's fern leaf.

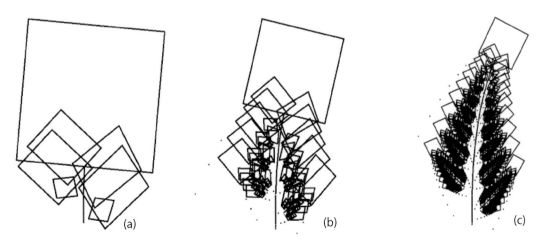

FIG 2.33 Three iterations of Barnsley's fern leaf, after (a) two iterations, (b) five iterations, and (c) ten iterations.

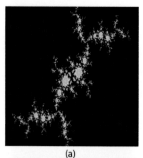

(a)

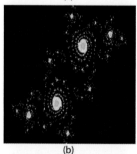

(b)

(c)

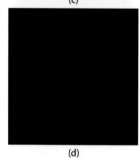

(d)

FIG 2.34 Julia Set examples for (a) −0.189, −0.817; (b) −0.205, −0.658; (c) 0.301, 0.584; (d) 0.295, 0.064.

The image produced by a fractal algorithm is called a *strange attractor*. A good metaphor for the attractor is having a shaped magnet under a piece of paper and throwing iron filings at it. The shape produced where the iron filings stick is the attractor. In the case of Barnsley's fern leaf, the magnet would be the leaf shape. The most fascinating property of fractals is that if the values used by the algorithm are altered slightly, there may be no attractor whatsoever. This is best illustrated with Julia Sets.

In brief, the algorithm for a Julia Set, takes two parameters and runs a number of iterations to see if anything *sticks* to an attractor in order to produce an image. The algorithm uses the exact same formulae each time but just a small change in the value of the parameters can make the difference between an image or no image. While the mathematics involved is too complex to go through here, it is hoped the reader will get an appreciation for the subject by considering the input variables and the images produced in Figure 2.34.

2.4.2 Perlin Noise

While the pure fractal images used in Barnsley's fern leaf and the Julia Sets produces beautiful images, they are too perfect. As they are, they do not give an accurate representation of the real world and game assets created with them are not entirely believable. Consider, for example, using a sine wave to generate a landscape, it would have hills and valleys but they would all be identical. It might go some way to mathematically describing an undulating environment if a random element could be introduced that affected the heights of the hills and the depth of the valleys. Figure 2.35 illustrates a sine wave (a) and a sine wave modified randomly (b). Imagine both these waves as the cross section for a landscape. Figure 2.35 (b) with the random changes would be more realistic.

A PCG method that introduces randomness into values generated from sine and cosine waves is *Perlin Noise*. If you've used the Difference Clouds tool in Photoshop you will have taken advantage of the Perlin Noise algorithm. It produces a seemingly random and yet fluid set of data that can be used for height values on a terrain among other things. Figure 2.35 illustrates the use of a Perlin Noise image (a) and its use in generating a terrain (b). The black areas of the image denote low lying levels with other height levels given by the grey values as they increase to white (the maximum height). An image used in this way to represent the heights of a terrain is called a *height map*. In stark contrast to the believable output from Perlin Noise is a totally random landscape shown in Figure 2.35 (c). If parts of the landscape are allowed to take on random values with no regard to the high values around them, the landscape becomes very jagged and too chaotic. Perlin Noise is calculated in such a way that each height value takes into consideration the heights around it so no sudden sharp inclines occur.

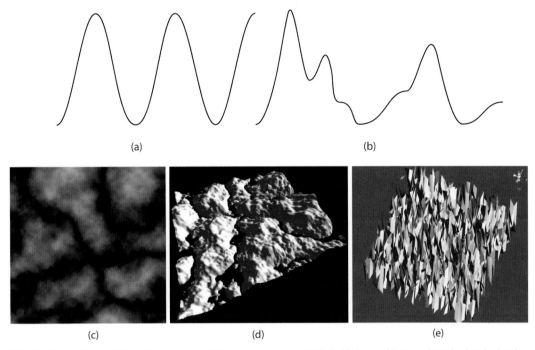

(a)   (b)

(c)   (d)   (e)

FIG 2.35 Illustrates the use of a Perlin Noise image (c) and its use in generating a terrain (d). The black areas of the image denote low lying levels with other height levels given by the grey values as they increase to white (the maximum height). An image used in this way to represent the heights of a terrain is called a height map. In stark contrast to the believable output from Perlin Noise is a totally random landscape shown in Figure 2.35 (e).

More Information: Perlin Noise

If you are interested in the specific of the Perlin Noise algorithm this link provides an easy to understand elucidation and some examples of its use in games: http://devmag.org.za/2009/04/25/perlin-noise.

◉ Unity Hands-On
Minecraft *Landscapes*

When a player starts a new world in *Minecraft*, the default landscape is always different. As part of the game's PCG it uses Perlin Noise. In this hands-on session you will learn how to create a simple *Minecraft*-type landscape using Perlin Noise and add mobile third-person navigation so you can test out the environment on your mobile device.

Step 1: Download and open the main scene of the MinecraftStarter project. In the middle of the Scene you will find a cube reminiscent of a *Minecraft* dirt block. In the Project you will find a Textures folder with images for dirt, grass, snow and water.

Step 2: We already have a dirt block, but now we need ones for grass, snow, and water. To create them, add three new cubes into the Scene with GameObject > Create Other > Cube. It doesn't matter where they are in the Scene but you might like to move them side-by-side so you can see them. Now for each of the three new cubes, drag and drop one each of the grass, snow, and water textures from the Project directly onto the cubes in the Scene. There will now be four cubes in the Scene each with their own texture as shown in Figure 2.36.

Step 3: Because we are going to use a Perlin Noise algorithm to create the landscape, we will need the algorithm to create as many of these blocks as it needs. It will do this dynamically from the template we give it for each block type. In Unity, a template is called a *prefab*. To create a prefab in the Project select Create > Prefab as shown in Figure 2.37. Double-click on the New Prefab in the Project to rename it. Call the first one *dirt*.

Step 4: Select the dirt cube in the Scene or the Hierarchy. Drag and drop this game object onto the newly created dirt prefab in the Project as shown in Figure 2.38. You now have a template or prefab for creating dirt blocks.

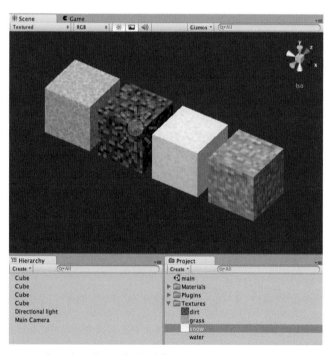

FIG 2.36 Four cubes in Unity each with a different texture.

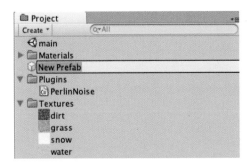

FIG 2.37 Creating a new prefab in the Project.

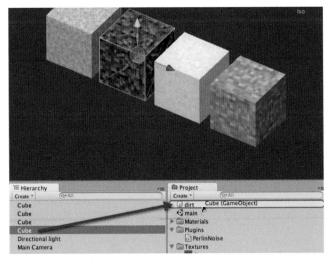

FIG 2.38 Using an existing game object to create a prefab.

Repeat Steps 3 and 4 to create new prefabs for grass, snow, and water. Note, when a game object in the Hierarchy is linked to a prefab in the Project its text will go blue. When you are finished creating the prefabs, select the original cubes in the Hierarchy and delete them. To delete them select them in the Hierarchy and then right-click > Delete. The Scene will now be empty, but you will have prefabs for each of the building blocks of a simple Minecraft landscape.

Step 5: Before we start placing blocks we are first going to generate an image of the Perlin Noise to see it in action. Create a plane in the Scene with GameObject > Create Other > Plane. Orient the camera so you can see it when in the Game.

Step 6: Create a new C# file called *GenerateLandscape* and add the following code:

```
using UnityEngine;
using System.Collections;

public class GenerateLandscape : MonoBehaviour {

    int width = 128;
    int height = 128;
    Texture2D texture;

    // Use this for initialization
    void Start ()
    {
        int octaveCount = 5;
        texture = new Texture2D(width, height,
            TextureFormat.RGB24, false);
        renderer.material.mainTexture = texture;
        renderer.material.shader =
            Shader.Find("Unlit/Texture");
        float[][] perlinNoise =
            PerlinNoise.GeneratePerlinNoise(width,
                height, octaveCount);
        perlinNoise = PerlinNoise.
        AdjustLevels(perlinNoise,
                    0.1f, 0.8f);

        for (int i = 0; i < width; i++)
        {
            for (int j = 0; j < height; j++)
            {
                float col = perlinNoise[i][j];
                texture.SetPixel(i, j,
                    new Color (col, col, col));
                texture.Apply();
            }
        }
    }

    // Update is called once per frame
    void Update ()
    {

    }
}
```

Save the code and attach to the plane. Play. You will get a Perlin Noise pattern appear on the plane as shown in Figure 2.39. Because the algorithm uses a random value, each time you play you'll get a different texture. The code uses a Perlin Noise script that you will find in the Plugins folder of the Project to generate a two dimensional array of values ranging between 0 and 1. By interpreting 0 as black and 1 as white and all other values in between as shades of grey, a pixel in the texture of the plane representing the value in the array at the same location is colored. This process is illustrated in Figure 2.40. For example, if the value in the array

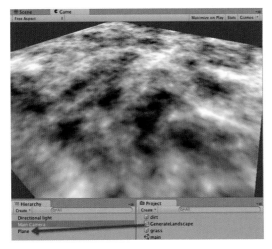

FIG 2.39 A plane in Unity with a Perlin Noise texture.

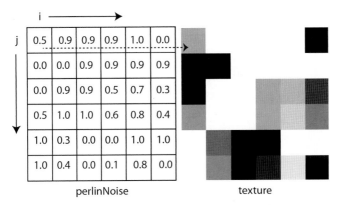

FIG 2.40 A two-dimensional array with Perlin Noise values and corresponding texture.

at perlinNoise[0][0] is 0.5 then the corresponding pixel in the texture, that would be at (0,0) is coloured mid-grey.

As previously discussed the values returned by the Perlin Noise algorithm can be used as a heightmap and that is exactly what we are about to do with it.

Step 7: The plane in the previous example was created for illustrative purposes only so you could see what the Perlin Noise algorithm is generating. It is no longer necessary and can be deleted.

Once the plane is deleted, the GenerateLandscape script can be attached to the Main Camera. The script must be in the Scene in order to run and since the plane it was attached to is gone, it needs to piggyback on another object in the world. You could also create an empty game object with GameObject > Create Empty and attach the script to that.

When you've added the script back into the Scene, modify its code as follows. Note it has been changed considerably and should be checked thoroughly.

```
using UnityEngine;
using System.Collections;

public class GenerateLandscape : MonoBehaviour {
    int width = 64;
    int height = 64;
    public GameObject dirt;
    public GameObject grass;
    public GameObject snow;
    public GameObject water;

    // Use this for initialization
    void Start ()
    {
        int octaveCount = 5;

            float[] [] perlinNoise =
                PerlinNoise.eneratePerlinNoise(width, height,
                    octaveCount);

        perlinNoise = PerlinNoise.AdjustLevels(perlinNoise,
                    0.1f, 0.8f);

        for (int i = 0; i < width; i++)
        {
            for (int j = 0; j < height; j++)
            {
                float h = perlinNoise[i][j];
                Vector3 blockPos = new Vector3(i,
                    Mathf.RoundToInt(h*10), j);

                if(height < 0.2)
                    Instantiate(water, blockPos, Quaternion.
                    identity);
                else if (h < 0.4)
                    Instantiate(dirt, blockPos, Quaternion.
                    identity);
                else if (h < 0.8)
                    Instantiate(grass, blockPos, Quaternion.
                    identity);
                else if (h < = 1.0)
                    Instantiate(snow, blockPos, Quaternion.
                    identity);
            }
        }
    }
}
```

Save the script. Click on the Main Camera and locate the script in the Inspector. It will have four exposed variables ready to be linked with the prefabs created before. Drag and drop the prefabs from the Project onto the corresponding exposed variables in the Inspector as shown in Figure 2.41.

Save and play. Depending on where the camera is located, you may or may not see the landscape generated, shown in Figure 2.42. Don't panic. While the application is still playing switch back to the Scene and you'll be able to navigate around to see your creation. No, it's not perfect, but it's a good start.

The script loops through the perlinNoise array and extracts the value in each cell. The cell's row and column values are used for the blocks' *x* and

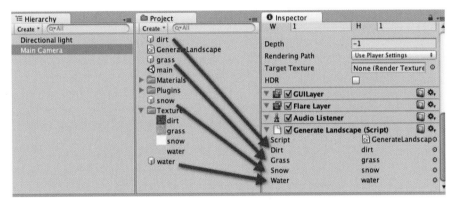

FIG 2.41 Using prefabs as inputs for exposed variables in a script.

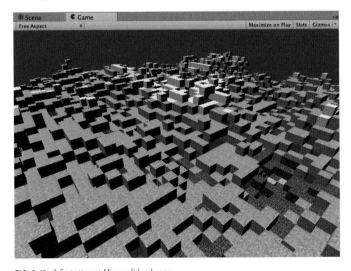

FIG 2.42 A first attempt Minecraft landscape.

z coordinates and the *y* coordinate is determined by the value in the cell (the value between 0 and 1 generated by the Perlin Noise algorithm). In short, the array has become the heightmap for the game environment. The height of the block also determines the type of block that is used at those coordinates.

For example, if the value in the `perlinNoise[5,6] = 0.8` then a block will be created at the coordinates (5, 8, 6) where the cell value is multiplied by ten and made into an integer to represent a *y* value. We are working with strict integer values because each block is 1 unit in size. This makes it easy for calculations. Each column and row number in the array translates directly into the *x* and *z* coordinates for the block position. Because the blocks are positioned at integer values with a gap of 1 between them and the blocks being 1 in size, if you put two next to each other they will neatly meet. In this case, because the block is attributed with a height value of 0.8 the if statement will set it to be snow.

The `Instantiate()` function dynamically creates a new game object from a given prefab. The block prefabs you setup with the exposed variables are used to create the different types of blocks occurring at the different heights, where water is the lowest type of block and snow the highest. The second parameter of `Instantiate()` is the position of the new game object. The third parameter is the orientation of the object as it is created. `Quaternion.identity`, in this case tells the `Instantiate()` function that the rotation of the *x*, *y*, and *z* axes of the object is set to zero.

More Information: Quaternions

Quaternions are a way to represent angles. Euler is another. While Euler angles are easier to understand, Quaternions are more powerful and less susceptible to error encountered in Euler angle manipulation: http://holistic3d.com/?p=592

Step 8: The current algorithm produces a landscape with holes in it. Although each coordinate has a block and if you look at the landscape from above you won't see any gaps, the holes are a result of a block having a height more than 1 in difference of neighboring blocks. This can be seen in Figure 2.43. Block 1 is at (5, 8, 5) and block 2 is at (5, 6, 4). In the

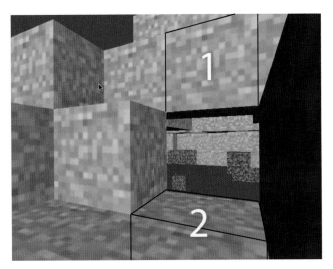

FIG 2.43 Gaps in the *Minecraft* landscape.

XZ plane they are right next to each other, but vertically the distance between them is 2. Because the blocks are only 1 in size, this leaves a gap of 1 block.

Now we could instantiate each block and then backfill downwards by creating more blocks but this creates two issues; 1) how far do you fill downwards, and 2) an awful lot of extra blocks that can't even be seen are created. You could fill downwards until you hit 0 in the *y* direction, however this does enforce the second problem; the creation of a lot of unnecessary blocks. While this might not affect the game running on a desktop computer, it will dramatically affect the performance on a mobile device. Each block you create is a game object Unity needs to remember and process. The current matrix of blocks being created is 64 × 64. If you have just one hidden layer of blocks that is 64 blocks in the computer memory but of absolutely no use.

The solution then is to backfill downwards but only as far as needed to fill any gaps. We can do this by looking at the height values for neighboring cells and if any of them are more than 1 difference in height, another block needs to be added. In fact, the number of blocks to backfill will be equal to the maximum height difference that exists between a block and all its neighbors. As shown in Figure 2.44, any internal block, that is one whose array cell is not around the edge of the perlinNoise matrix will have eight neighbor cells. The cells on the edges have fewer neighbors to compare with.

Instead of comparing each cell with each of its neighbors manually, we can use the existing for loop that is creating the blocks to check the

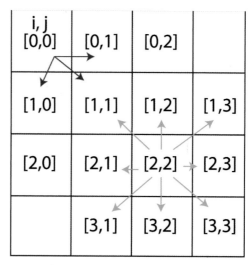

FIG 2.44 Comparing neighboring cell values.

neighbors heights at the same time. To cater for this, modify your script to:

```
using UnityEngine;
using System.Collections;

public class GenerateLandscape : MonoBehaviour {

    int width = 64;
    int height = 64;

    public GameObject dirt;
    public GameObject grass;
    public GameObject snow;
    public GameObject water;

    // Use this for initialization
    void Start ()
    {
        int octaveCount = 5;
        float[][] perlinNoise = PerlinNoise.Generate
            PerlinNoise(width, height, octaveCount);
        perlinNoise = PerlinNoise.AdjustLevels
            (perlinNoise, 0.1f, 0.8f);

        for (int i = 0; i < width; i++)
        {
            for (int j = 0; j < height; j++)
            {
                float h = perlinNoise[i][j];
                Vector3 blockPos = new Vector3(i, Mathf.
                RoundToInt(h*10), j);
                CreateBlock(h, blockPos);
```

```
if(i > 0 && i < width-1 && j > 0 && j < height - 1)
//in the middle
{
    if(((perlinNoise[i][j] - 0.1) >
    perlinNoise[i-1][j-1]) ||
        ((perlinNoise[i][j] - 0.1) >
        perlinNoise[i][j-1]) ||
        ((perlinNoise[i][j] - 0.1) >
        perlinNoise[i+1][j-1]) ||
        ((perlinNoise[i][j] - 0.1) >
        perlinNoise[i-1][j]) ||
        ((perlinNoise[i][j] - 0.1) >
        perlinNoise[i+1][j]) ||
        ((perlinNoise[i][j] - 0.1) >
        perlinNoise[i-1][j+1]) ||
        ((perlinNoise[i][j] - 0.1) >
        perlinNoise[i][j+1]) ||
        ((perlinNoise[i][j] - 0.1) >
        perlinNoise[i+1][j+1]))
        {
            blockPos.y - = 1;
            CreateBlock(h, blockPos);
        }
}
else if(i = = 0 && i < width-1 && j > 0 && j
< height-1)
//along the top edge
{
    if(((perlinNoise[i][j] - 0.1) > perlinNoise[i]
    [j-1]) ||
        ((perlinNoise[i][j] - 0.1) >
        perlinNoise[i+1][j-1]) ||
        ((perlinNoise[i][j] - 0.1) >
        perlinNoise[i+1][j]) ||
        ((perlinNoise[i][j] - 0.1) >
        perlinNoise[i][j+1]) ||
        ((perlinNoise[i][j] - 0.1) >
        perlinNoise[i+1][j+1]))
        {
            blockPos.y - = 1;
            CreateBlock(h, blockPos);
        }
}
else if(i > 0 && i < width-1 && j = = 0 && j
< height-1)
//on the left edge
{
    if(((perlinNoise[i][j] - 0.1) >
    perlinNoise[i-1][j]) ||
```

```
                                ((perlinNoise[i][j] - 0.1) >
                                perlinNoise[i+1][j]) ||
                                ((perlinNoise[i][j] - 0.1) >
                                perlinNoise[i-1][j+1]) ||
                                ((perlinNoise[i][j] - 0.1) >
                                perlinNoise[i][j+1]) ||
                                ((perlinNoise[i][j] - 0.1) >
                                perlinNoise[i+1][j+1]))
                                {
                                    blockPos.y - = 1;
                                    CreateBlock(h, blockPos);
                                }
                        }
                    }
                }
            }
        }

        void CreateBlock(float h, Vector3 blockPos)
        {
            if(h < 0.2)
                Instantiate(water, blockPos, Quaternion.
                identity);
            else if (h < 0.4)
                Instantiate(dirt, blockPos, Quaternion.
                identity);
            else if (h < 0.8)
                Instantiate(grass, blockPos, Quaternion.
                identity);
            else if (h < = 1.0)
                Instantiate(snow, blockPos, Quaternion.
                identity);
        }
    }
```

Note the new function `CreateBlock()`. It has been added to remove the repetitive code that would be needed to create the extra backfill blocks. Whenever you find yourself repeating blocks of code, ask yourself if it would be better as a function.

Save and play. The landscape will be generated without holes.

Step 9: At this stage the landscape will be looking better than before but still requires a few tweaks to get it to a more acceptable stage. First, if you generate a map and have a look at the water level you will notice that it is not flat in places. This is because the `CreateBlock()` function will place water blocks at elevations of 0.1 and 0.0. We need to flatten out the water height so the blocks are always at 0.1. One line of code will fix this. Add the line of code shown in bold in the following snippet

```
        ...
        for (int j = 0; j < height; j++)
        {
```

```
        float h = perlinNoise[i][j];
        Vector3 blockPos = new Vector3(
            i, Mathf.RoundToInt(h*10), j);

        if(blockPos.y < = 2) blockPos.y = 2;
        CreateBlock(h, blockPos);

        if(i > 0 && i < width − 1
            && j > 0 && j < height − 1) //in the middle
    }
    ...
```

This will ensure all blocks at water height are set to a height of 2, not 2 and below, giving you an even water line.

Next, you may want to smooth the terrain so it isn't so jagged. To do this, change the value of the octave variable. Lower numbers will make it more jagged and a value of 10 will flatten it completely. In this case, 6 seems to work well.

Step 10: Finally, we are going to make this map mobile ready and navigable. First select File > Build Settings and switch the platform to iOS or Android as was shown in Chapter 1. Remember to click Add Current to add the current scene to the build. Then ensure you add your Bundle ID into the Player's Settings.

Step 11: Next select Assets > Import Package > Standard Assets (Mobile). A window will open decompressing the package and then ask you to import. Ensure all items from the package are ticked before doing so.

Locate the First Person Controls prefab in the Project under Standard Assets (Mobile) > Prefabs and drag and drop it into the Hierarchy. It will appear as in Figure 2.45. Select the First Person Controls inside the First Person Controls object, note there is one inside the other. Set its position to (20,10,20). The capsule you can see on the screen is your first person collider that will deal with world physics. The dashed boxes on either side of the screen are touch-sensitive pads where you will touch the device to move the character around. If you don't reposition the starting point of the First Person Controls you will simply fall off the edge of the world when the game starts.

Since the First Person Controls has its own camera, you don't need the Main Camera anymore, except that it has your script attached to it. Rather than deleting the camera and adding the script onto another game object, select the Main Camera and, in the Inspector, turn off its Camera and Audio Listener components as shown in Figure 2.46. Because the Main Camera isn't actually a camera anymore you could rename it to something else to avoid confusion later, such as MapGenerator.

Next, find the Player child object of the First Person Controls. Select it and locate the Character Controller as shown in Figure 2.47. Set the Step Offset to 1.2. This controls how high a step can be before the player has to jump up onto it. Setting it to 1.2 now will stop you getting stuck in little divots in your map.

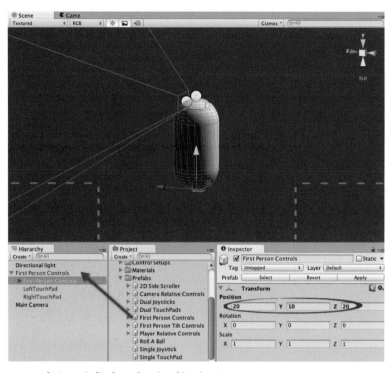

FIG 2.45 Setting up the First Person Controls prefab in the project.

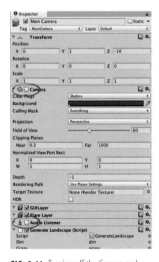

FIG 2.46 Turning off the Camera and Audio Listener components of a game object.

More Information: Character Controller

The Unity Character Controller is used for desktop and mobile use. You can get more information about it from http://docs.unity3d.com/Documentation/Components/class-CharacterController.html.

The default sky color for this First Person Controls prefab is black. Let's change it to blue. The sky color is controlled by the camera. The Main Camera for the Scene is now a child of the First Person Controls as shown in Figure 2.48. Select the Main Camera in the Hierarchy and look for the background color setting. Change it to a desired color.

Finally, you'll probably want to test the game in landscape orientation. To do this, go into the Player Settings on the Build Settings page. In the Inspector, set the Default Orientation to Auto Rotation and untick the Portrait options as shown in Figure 2.49.

FIG 2.47 Setting the maximum size of steps the player character can walk up.

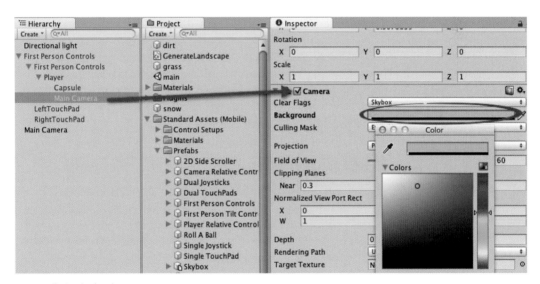

FIG 2.48 Setting the sky color.

Save and build the game to your mobile device. Note, the first person controller we've added only works in iOS or Android mode so you won't be able to move around in the Unity Editor. When the application is running you can move the player by touching and moving your finger in the lower left corner of the device and look around by touching and moving your finger in the lower right corner of the device.

The preceding hands-on session provides you with some experience in developing a procedural algorithm for creating game landscapes. *Minecraft* is just one of a handful of games that uses procedural generation as you will

FIG 2.49 Setting for mobile landscape orientation only.

discover in following chapters. Of course the Perlin Noise algorithm you've just learnt about is only one element of the code used to generate the actual *Minecraft* worlds (of which the rest remain a secret). However with a little creativity and tweaks to the code you could discover some interesting techniques to apply for yourself.

2.5 Summary

In this chapter we've presented a crash course in C# scripting and an examination of the fundamental programming constructs. In addition, some essential mathematics for 3D game programming was offered with practical exercises to reinforce the use of such mathematics in the Unity environment. To demonstrate the power of algorithms and mathematics the *Minecraft* landscape recreation hands-on session was given. It explored further the boundary between visual beauty and logical constructions. Although it is impossible in one chapter to give a reader a full appreciation for the importance of these topics, as you go forward you'll begin to see why and how they are implemented over and over again and why you need a firm grasp of this knowledge if you want to be a games developer.

CHAPTER 3

Mobile Game Interfaces

Do not innovate unnecessarily in UI design. If a standard exists, use it—or as much of it as works with your game.

Ernest Adams

3.1 Introduction

The entry of mobile devices into the gaming world brought with it a variety of challenges with respect to interface development. Not only are the screen sizes non-standard but also there are a variety of novel player–game interface methods to be catered for.

The most challenging aspect is dealing with the differing device screen resolutions. When there was just the original iPhone, developers had 320 × 480 pixels to work with. It made developing interfaces easy, as you knew exactly how it was going to look when the player started up the game. Now, however, there are a multitude of screen sizes to deal with and you can't ever be sure exactly how the player will see the game.

In this chapter we will examine the design of user interfaces with respect to their use in mobile games. Methods used to come up with good looking functional interfaces will be discussed alongside the main rules you should adhere to when coming up with a design. As the quote at the beginning of this chapter says, don't start out trying to be innovative and unique. There are tried and true methods for mobile game interface design that exist and you should use them.

In addition, we will investigate a number of practical ways to get your game to look good on whatever device it is viewed.

3.2 Graphical User Interfaces

In the theatre there exists the term *fourth-wall*. This is the imaginary wall that sits between the actors and the audience. For want of a better metaphor, it is like the one-way mirrored glass windows in police interrogation rooms through which you cannot see out, but observers can see clearly in. As such, this invisible fourth-wall sits there as a one-way mental barrier that seemingly makes the actors oblivious to the audience. When actors address the audience or acknowledge their presence, as occurs in a pantomime, the fourth-wall is declared broken.

Computer games too have a fourth-wall. It is the flat 2D plan, screen, or window through which the game environment is observed. It is also the physical surface onto which the game world is projected and made visible. In addition, it acts as a tactile touch-sensitive surface by which we interact and play via the mechanics of the game itself. Traditionally game interfaces resided on this wall as 2D flat information giving displays behind which the game takes place. Even today many games still employ this type of interface as it is relatively easy to design, the most straightforward way of communicating with the player and easiest to develop. Although there are other interfaces you might consider for your own game.

3.2.1 Interface Types

There are four types of user interface non-diegetic, diegetic, spatial and meta. The defining dimensions of which are whether or not the interface is in the game environment or on the screen and if the interface is a part of the game narrative or not. These types are shown in Figure 3.1.

When an interface resides on the screen and is not actually part of the game world but merely an overlay and not part of the game story it is considered non-diegetic. Non-diegetic interfaces are the most common and easiest to produce. They consist of 2D graphics and text that informs the player of their status and other game information. The example given in Figure 3.1 (a) is from *Mini Motor Racing*. As is typical in many racing games, this non-diegetic interface reports the player's position and lap times. In addition there is a top view of the racing track. Other common elements to find in a non-diegetic

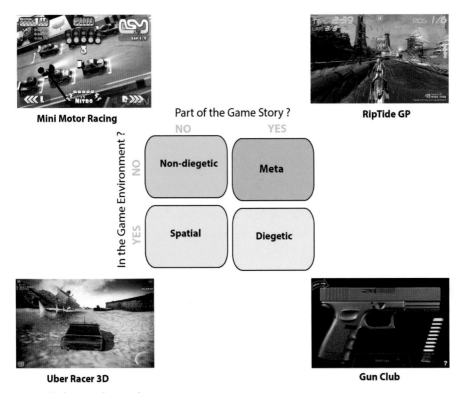

Mini Motor Racing

RipTide GP

Uber Racer 3D

Gun Club

FIG 3.1 The four types of user interfaces.

interface are the player's score, the time, level names and numbers, remaining ammunition count, speed, mini maps, and health.

Figure 3.1 (b) demonstrates a meta representation of an interface. Meta means it is part of the story or narrative but not in the game environment. Like the non-diegetic interface however, a meta interface is displayed on the screen. In a way, the meta interface breaks the fourth-wall by declaring the presence of the screen and the player. The best example is in third-person games when an event occurs to the player's character but the repercussions of this event are made visible on the screen. For example, if a player's character gets shot or harmed, the screen gets splattered with blood. In a racing game in which the car is being viewed externally and from behind, the screen may get cracked or shattered when the car crashes. In the case of *RipTide GP* in Figure 3.1 (b), the player's character is clearly the racer on the jet ski, however the player themselves is given presence in the environment as though following the action in the world with a camera. When water sprays up from the jet ski, it hits the screen and streaks across it. This type of information is meta as the event is not occurring in the game environment yet it is a result of what is happening in the game story.

A diegetic interface is one that is part of the story and part of the environment. These are the most difficult to design, especially in a 3D world, as they have to seamlessly become part of the world but also be obvious and understandable. Some of the best examples are the player's health bar in *Deadspace* that is integrated as a glowing blue strip in the player character's space suit. Another good example is the use of 3D objects such as maps, compasses, and virtual model devices in *Far Cry 2*. The objects are actual game objects required in the game but also give the player necessary information. Figure 3.1 (c) illustrates a diegetic interface in the mobile game *Gun Club*. The amount of ammunition left is actually shown to the player by way of the gun's clip, which is in the game environment rather than a numerical count in 2D displayed at the bottom of the screen.

Finally there is the spatial interface. This is user information and instructions given in the world environment but not an actual part of the story. It's like signals embedded in the world that only the player can see. One example is *The Sims*. When the characters speak with each other they get thought bubbles above their heads. This relays information to the player on what the character is thinking. However these bubbles aren't actually in the game environment, such as a chair or table. They are spatial as their positioning is relative to the world and the location of the Sim in question. Figure 3.1 (d) illustrates a popular spatial interface uses in racing games, in this case the mobile game *Uber Racer 3D*. The green arrows in the image indicate to the player the direction of the track. Similar spatial interfaces are found in *Need for Speed* and *Project Gotham*. Again, these indicators have no presence as such in the game environment, they are purely there for the player's benefit.

However, before you can start building user interfaces of any type you need to know how to program the mobile device to deal with player input.

It Started with a Touch

Until the release of the *Nintendo DS* in 2004 gamers had been restricted to the common computing input devices of the mouse, keyboard, joystick, and gaming console controller. Although *Sega* had experimented with touchscreen controls for their proposed successor to the Game Gear in the early 1990s it was not economically viable, it wasn't until Nintendo put touchscreens in the DS, some ten years later, that the technology started to flourish.

The invention of touchscreens saw a breakthrough in Human Computer Interfaces in which for the first time the intuitive human gesture of pointing and touching with one's finger became a viable method of input. Of course 30 years before the Nintendo DS, light pens—that registered touches on a graphics tablet—provided a similar kind of interface experience, but required specialized hardware and software. It wasn't until the pen could be dispensed with and replaced with a human finger and the technology advanced sufficiently that it became a reality. Now we see touchscreens implemented on a great majority of computer displays from televisions to point-of-sale systems to mobile phones and tablets. There are two main types of touch-sensing technology used in mobile phones; resistive and capacitive.

Resistive touchscreens work through sensing pressure on the surface. They consist of two circuit layers each with an adjoining conductive layer separated by an air gap or spacer dots as shown in Figure 3.2. When a finger pushes into the screen, pushing the conductive layers together, a circuit is completed and a touch thereby registered. This is the same thing that happens when you turn on a light switch. A circuit is completed, electricity flows and the light comes on.

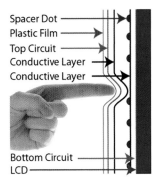

Spacer Dot
Plastic Film
Top Circuit
Conductive Layer
Conductive Layer

Bottom Circuit
LCD

FIG 3.2 The anatomy of a resistive touchscreen.

Capacitive touchscreens, such as those used in mobile devices, consists of a glass or plastic panel coated with a capacitive storing material. This means the screen stores a small electric charge across its surface. When a finger touches the screen it creates a circuit and draws a minute amount of current, to the touch point. Circuit boards in the corners of the screen can calculate the exact location of the touch. The downside of these touchscreens is that they require a capacitive material to touch the surface in order to create the circuit. As such they do not work for gloved fingers or typical pens and pencils.

While resistive screens would seem to make more sense with respect to usability on a mobile device because they can sense pressure from anything tapping on the surface, the capacitive screens have a far lighter touch, meaning you can gently swipe across the surface to interact. This type of interaction is much more difficult on resistive screens. Capacitive screens are also capable of multitouch whereas resistive screens are not. Phones such as the iPhone and Samsung Galaxy have capacitive screens while the Nokia N97 and HTC Tattoo use resistive screens.

In Unity, when a user places a finger on the screen you can capture the tap and movement via the `Input.GetTouch` method. This returns a Touch structure.

From the registered touch you can determine:

- The pixel location of the touch on the screen.
- The number of the finger (this is the order in which fingers have touched the screen starting at 0).

The first finger that touches the screen is recorded as touch 0. If a second finger touches the screen while the first finger is still there, this second finger is registered as touch 1. If the first finger is removed while the second finger is down, the second finger will still be recorded as touch 1. It's a matter of sequence and how many preceding touches there have been that are still in progress. It's not clever enough to determine the difference between fingers (e.g., index versus ring).

The change of location (in pixels) of a finger being dragged across the screen.

The time since the last touch message was received. Touches are picked up in the `Update` loop. If you keep your finger down the time you'll register is the time between `Update` loops and the calling of the `Input.GetTouch` method.

The tap number. This is the order in which the tap occurred with respect to other fingers still registering as down.

The status of the touch. A touch is registered over time as a series of states. When the screen is first touched you trigger a *Began* state. If the finger remains down and stationary it triggers a *Stationary* state. If you drag the finger across the screen you'll get a *Moved* state. When the finger is lifted up an *Ended* state occurs. Finally, if there are five or more simultaneous touches or the device is lifted up to answer a call a *Canceled* state is triggered.

◉ Unity Hands-On
Touch
Lets explore this functionality.

Step 1: Create a new Unity Project and ensure the build settings are for Android or iOS depending on your device.
Step 2: Create a new C# file called *detectTouch* and add the following code:

```csharp
using UnityEngine;
using System.Collections;

public class detectTouch : MonoBehaviour {

    int touchCount = 0;
    Touch lastTouch;

    void OnGUI()
    {
        if(touchCount > 0)
        //if there is a touch print the details
        {
            GUI.Label(new Rect(10,10,200,50),"Position: " +
                lastTouch.position);
            GUI.Label(new Rect(10,30,200,50),"Finger Id: " +
                lastTouch.fingerId);
            GUI.Label(new Rect(10,50,200,50),"Position Change:"
                + lastTouch.deltaPosition);
            GUI.Label(new Rect(10,70,200,50),"Time Passed: " +
                lastTouch.deltaTime);
            GUI.Label(new Rect(10,90,200,50),"Tap Count: " +
                lastTouch.tapCount);
            GUI.Label(new Rect(10,110,200,50),"Phase: " +
                lastTouch.phase);
        }
    }
```

```
// Update is called once per frame
void Update ()
{
    //there has been a touch
    touchCount = Input.touchCount;
    if(touchCount > 0)
    {
        lastTouch = Input.GetTouch(0);
    }
}
```

Save the script. Attach it to the Main Camera.

Build to the device and play. As you touch the screen a GUI will show up giving you details from the Touch structure.

As you will discover in later sections, the screen on which you are playing a game is constituted by a different coordinate system to that in a 3D game world. The screen operates in two dimensions and the game in three. The screen is a moveable window through which you observe the game environment. It can be orientated in any direction, looking at the 3D world from above, below, left, right, or a complex mixture of these.

To touch an object in the game's 3D world is not a simple matter of getting the touchscreen coordinates and determining if the game object is at that position. Because the game object will not be. What you see on the screen is merely a projection of the game world brought forward onto a flat surface. This will be further elucidated in later sections. Suffice it to say a 3D object in the game world is not actually right up against the screen. It could be some distance away.

The method for determining if a 3D object has been touched is to project a vector from the touch-point into the game world. In Unity we do this with a Physics.Raycast function. Its format is

```
Physics.Raycast (ray, hit object, length of ray)
```

A ray, is a vector with a starting position. It is cast from the touch position into the game environment. The *Raycast* function takes three variables; the ray, a hit variable to store information about any game object hit, and the maximum distance to project the ray. The process is illustrated in Figure 3.3. A raycast distance determines how far into the game world the ray should extend while searching for a hit. If there wasn't a distance you could search infinitely never hitting anything.

If an object is hit, the hit variable takes on the value of that object. In the code, we are using this information to destroy the object. This removes it from the game environment.

131

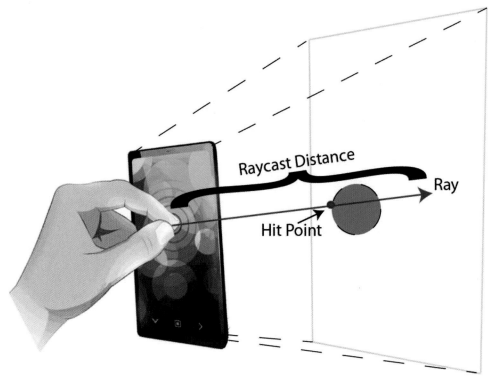

FIG 3.3 Physics raycasting.

> ● **Note**
> The most common problem for the raycast hit process not working is too short a maximum hit distance. If you've written code for processing touch hits and it's just not working, check the distance you've got set. This will be determined by the size of the world, but you shouldn't need a value any bigger than the distance from the camera's near plane to the far plane.

We will now put the *Raycast* function into practice.

● **Unity Hands-On**
Touch 3D Objects
In this hands-on session we are going to spawn apple and android objects that fall down the screen and explode when touched.

Step 1: Download the *Touch3DObject* project and open the main scene. It will be empty with the exception of the camera.

Step 2: First we want to create spawn points to instantiate the android and apple objects. Create a C# script called *spawn* and add the following code:

```
using UnityEngine;
using System.Collections;
public class spawn : MonoBehaviour {
       public GameObject theModel;
       // Use this for initialization
       void Start () {
              //start spawning objects in 5 seconds
              //and then every one second afterwards
              InvokeRepeating("SpawnObjects", 5, 1);
       }

       // Update is called once per frame
       void Update () {
       }
       void SpawnObjects()
       {
              Instantiate(theModel,
                             this.transform.position,
                             theModel.transform.rotation);
       }
}
```

Step 3: Save this script. Now add a cube into the Scene with GameObject > Create Other > Cube. Position the cube so it can be seen by the camera. Drag and drop the spawn script onto the cube. Select the cube in the Hierarchy and locate the attached spawn script in the Inspector. Look for "The Model" exposed variable. Drag and drop the Android prefab from the Project onto this exposed variable. This setup is shown in Figure 3.4. Note in Figure 3.4, the program is playing. You must be in play mode to see the large green android model.

Step 4: Play. In the Hierarchy Android clones will start to appear. When they do, you know the script is working. Depending on the location of the cube and the camera, you may or may not be able to see the android model in the Game. In Figure 3.4, the Android model is actually so large the camera is inside it and therefore it is not visible.

Step 5: To fix this, the Android prefab needs to be resized. Stop playing. Drag the Android prefab into the Hierarchy. Position the Android near the cube. Press R for the resizing axes and then scale the model so it is about the size of the cube or at least visible by the camera as shown in Figure 3.5. Because the Android model in the Scene is linked to a prefab, you can now use the Apply button in the Inspector to update the prefab template.

Step 6: When you pressed play before and the Androids started spawning, you may have noticed they were all on top of each other.

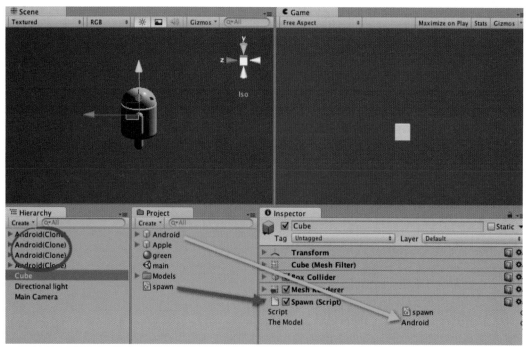

FIG 3.4 Creating a spawn point using prefabs.

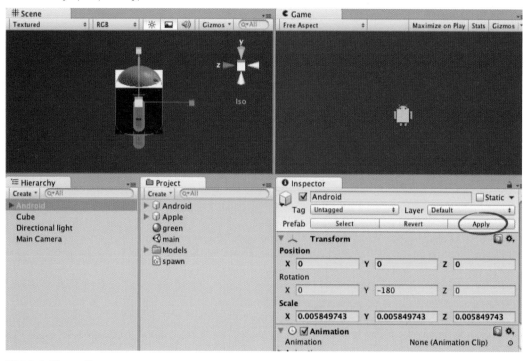

FIG 3.5 Resizing a prefab.

This is because they are not in the physics system and stay in the position they are created. We want them to fall or move down the screen. We could simply add a script to the Android prefab that updates the model's position each Update and moves it down the y axis. The code for this would be something like:

```
this.transform.position.y -= 1;
```

Step 7: However, it would make the game environment we are creating more dynamic if we use gravity and other forces. Not only would it fall down the screen, but it would also bounce off of other physics objects by default. You don't have to write any code as the physics system will do it all for you.

Step 8: To add physics to the Android, select in the Hierarchy and then select Component > Physics > Capsule Collider. A collider specifies the physical boundaries of an object for the physics system. There are different shapes of collider you can use. The collider shows up attached to the model as a green outlined mesh as shown in Figure 3.6.

Step 9: If you can't see the collider mesh it could be way too big or really small. In this example, when it was first added to the Android model it was so small it was not visible. You will need to find the collider

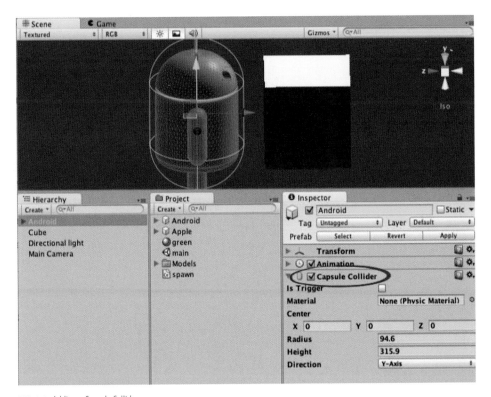

FIG 3.6 Adding a Capsule Collider.

component in the Inspector for the Android and adjust its Radius and Height values until you can see it.

Step 10: The collider by itself does not cause an object to be affected by physical forces. Since we want the Android to fall with gravity, a Rigidbody must also be attached. With the Android in the Hierarchy still selected, select Component > Physics > Rigidbody. Press the Apply button in the Inspector for the Android to apply these changes back onto the template. Delete the Android from the Hierarchy leaving the prefab in the Project.

Step 11: Play. The cube will spawn Androids and they will fall. Because the Androids are also being spawned inside a cube (which by default has a collider on it) the Androids are pushed to the side by the physics system detecting the collision of the objects before they start falling. If you want to prevent this you can remove the collider component from the cube by selecting it in the Hierarchy and then removing the collider in the Inspector.

Step 12: Because everyone loves an explosion we are going to make the Androids blow up when touched. To do this the game must monitor touches on the screen and determine if an object has been hit. On a hit, an explosion is instantiated and the object is removed from the Scene. Let's begin by determining if a touch has hit an object in the world. Create a new C# file called *monitorTouches* and add the following:

```csharp
using UnityEngine;
using System.Collections;

public class monitorTouches : MonoBehaviour {

    // Use this for initialization
    void Start () {

    }

    // Update is called once per frame
    void Update () {
        if (Input.GetMouseButtonDown(0))
        {
            RaycastHit hit;
            Ray ray = Camera.main.ScreenPointToRay
                (Input.mousePosition);
            if (Physics.Raycast (ray, out hit, 10000.0f))
            {
                Destroy(hit.transform.gameObject);
            }
        }
    }
}
```

Step 13: Save and attach to the Main Camera in the Hierarchy. Play. You will be able to touch or click on the Androids and they will disappear.

Step 14: We will now make the Androids blow up when touched. To do this we will employ a Unity asset package. Download *Detonator. unitypackage* to your desktop. In Unity select Assets > Import Package > Custom Package. Select the *Detonator.unitypackage*. Click on Open and when the file is decompressed, with all assets selected click on Import. After import, in the Project, you will find all the detonator files in the Standard Assets folder.

Step 15: We are going to instantiate one of the explosion prefabs from the detonator package at the same time the Android is destroyed. To do this modify the *monitorTouches* script thus:

```
using UnityEngine;
using System.Collections;

public class monitorTouches : MonoBehaviour {
    public GameObject explosion;


    ...


    // Update is called once per frame
    void Update () {

        if (Input.GetMouseButtonDown(0))
        {
            ...

            if (Physics.Raycast (ray, out hit,
            10000.0f))
            {
                Instantiate(explosion,
                    hit.transform.position,
                    Quaternion.identity);
                Destroy(hit.transform.gameObject);
            }

    ...
```

Step 16: Save. Select the Main Camera and find the script in the Inspector as shown in Figure 3.7. The explosion variable will be exposed. Drag and drop one of the explosion prefabs from the Project onto the explosion variable. This explosion will now be instantiated after an object is touched and just before it is destroyed.

Step 17: Move the Cube spawn point up so it is just out of sight of the camera. You want it to spawn Androids above the top of the screen so they stream down.

Step 18: Play. Androids will fall down the screen and you can click on them to cause explosions. This will work on mobile devices too.

Step 19: The last thing that needs to be taken care of in such a game are the game objects that have been created, moved off the screen, and are no longer required. If you play the game as it is, in the Unity Editor, you'll

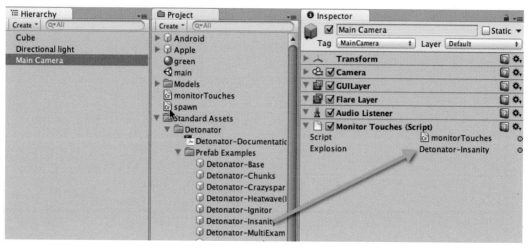

FIG 3.7 Adding an explosion prefab to the script.

notice a build-up of Android clones. If the objects are not destroyed by touching, the list gets longer and longer. These objects are filling up your device's memory. If they've fallen off the screen, you can simply destroy them. To do this create a new C# script called *destroyOnInvisible* and add the following:

```
using UnityEngine;
using System.Collections;

public class destroyOnInvisible : MonoBehaviour {

    void OnBecameInvisible()
    {
        Destroy(this.gameObject);
    }
}
```

Step 20: Save and attach this code to the Android prefab. You can do this by dragging and dropping the script onto the Android prefab in the Project.

Step 21: Play. If you don't touch on an Android, after it falls below the bottom of the screen, it will automatically be destroyed. The above script can be reused on all game objects that you want to ensure are removed from a game when they become invisible.

Step 22: To add more falling Androids and other game objects all you need to do is replicate the process of creating spawning points. You can duplicate the Cube in the Hierarchy and move it to another location to get more Androids. To change the type of model, an Apple prefab has been included you can also use. Don't forget to add a collider and rigid-body onto it. The explosion system on the Main Camera is setup to cause explosions when any 3D object is touched. Therefore you will

FIG 3.8 The final game.

not have to touch this code to add more spawning objects. As the detonation throws out little collision cubes, you'll find you will get some interesting physics dynamics as you play. The final result is shown in Figure 3.8.

More Information: Rigidbodies

Rigidbodies in Unity are components that allow you to set the physics properties of objects. They conform to Newtonian physics, i.e., if you want an object to fall slower, you do not change the mass as mass has nothing to do with falling due to gravity. You could however increase the drag (or friction due to air) to slow the object down. For more information on these settings see http://docs.unity3d.com/Documentation/Components/class-Rigidbody.html.

3.4 Principles of Mobile Game Interface Design

Mobile applications don't necessarily need to be boring. They don't need to be bland, cluttered, and geeky. They can have vibrancy and color and bring together an engaging user interface that will keep users coming back time and time again. Once an understanding for interface design has been acquired, these same skills can be applied to any design-based project. However, there are a number of considerations that need to be addressed when constructing both beautiful as well as functional user interface experiences specifically for smaller screens and touch-based input devices.

There are many facets to interface design ranging from aesthetic visual principles to human–computer interaction considerations. A mobile game interface not only has to look good but it has to be intuitively usable. The small size of the screen makes it challenging to design something that is not only readable but does not clutter the screen. As you can imagine, interfaces such as those of desktop computer games like *Starcraft* need to be totally reinvented in order to work on the mobile screen.

The physical interaction with the device adds to the design challenge. It also opens up a realm of possibilities pushing the designer to rethink traditional interfaces. They must be designed around touch and be as minimalistic as possible. A traditional interface does not necessarily shrink well as artworks can become unrecognizable and text unreadable.

The following principles of mobile game interface design are complementary with other types of game interfaces but considerate of the reduced screen real-estate and sensitive to the fact that the game controls also have to find a place on the screen.

3.4.1 Control

The most important aspect of the interface to a mobile game is its controls. In traditional games, control of moving around the game environment and/or moving the player character or game pieces is provided by means of peripheral equipment be it keyboards, mice, joysticks, or console controllers. While there are numerous peripherals on the market to provide this type of external control of some mobile games, for the majority it's the device itself that must provide the navigation. With the exception of using the device's accelerometer and gyroscope as input, this means screen real-estate must be sacrificed.

In determining how to define the controller interface you must consider how the device is being held. The most common means of navigating 3D spaces on a mobile is to allow manipulation of the game camera with the player's thumbs. When holding the device, this places them near the bottom left and right corners of the screen making this the ideal location for thumbsticks. The use of thumbsticks was illustrated in the *Minecraft* hands-on session in Chapter 2. While many games have fixed thumbsticks, *Final Fantasy 3* on the iPad has a dynamic thumbstick that appears beneath the player's finger wherever they touch on the screen.

When visual navigation controls are not required the entire screen becomes available for the placement of user interface elements. However just placing them anywhere will not simply work.

3.4.2 State Visualization

After being able to get around the game environment or interact with game objects the player needs to know their state. This includes data relevant to their progress in the game such as score, health, ammunition left, laps completed, money, location, time left and many others.

There are numerous ways in which to communicate with the player regarding their status. Text is the first and most obvious. It is necessary to relay to the player what their score is, how much money they have, when time is going to run out, and other numerically related values.

Animations can be used when the player's state changes. One that comes to mind is the death animation in an FPS. However besides something happening in the actual game world, images in the interface can flash or move about to illustrate a change and grab the player's attention. An animated health bar could be employed that shows a change over time or even an analogue clock with a moving dial.

Both text and animations benefit from the use of color. The most commonly used colors to change information from appearing good to bad are green and red respectively. The use of color will be further explored in the next section.

3.4.3 Metaphors

Metaphors are universally recognizable symbols associated with shared meaning. For example the little triangle of the play button is internationally recognized with respect to both audio and video. When used in a game, metaphors embody the saying "a picture is worth a thousand words," with instant communication of a game state, player state, or button purpose. Icons and logos are metaphors.

Iconic metaphors are ideal for games as their simplicity allows them to be recognized in quite small sizes. Quit, play, pause, return, and a variety of other commands can be communicated easily with small simple recognizable images such as those shown in Figure 3.9. The design of such icons should be that they can be reduced to small sizes and still represent the original image. In most cases the icons are used on buttons and therefore the smallest they will become will be the minimum button size, discussed shortly.

Colors are also metaphoric. The UNESCO Vienna Convention on Road Signs and Signals has defined the standard color of traffic lights to be used worldwide. These are green for go, yellow meaning prepare for change, and red for stop. These colors are not only used in traffic lights but transcend different types of media. Green is also a color meaning good. You'll find green used in games on health or power meters when they are at acceptable levels. Red is often used in opposition to green to represent bad. In nature red also signifies bad, as blood and burns are red. The color metaphor used

141

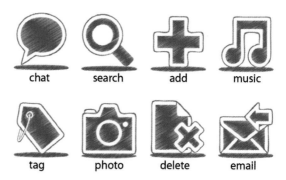

chat   search   add   music

tag   photo   delete   email

Images courtesy of http://www.doublejdesign.co.uk

FIG 3.9 Universally recognized icons.

in games should reflect human instinctual understanding of color as it allows the player to use their world knowledge in the game environment and thus reduces a great deal of effort on the designer and programmer's part. For example, imagine you wanted to use purple for good health and brown for bad health in a game. This would require explanation by way of a tutorial to communicate your intent.

3.4.4 Sound

Whether it be the sound of dropping coins, pouring water, explosions, or button presses, the way in which you integrate sound into your game interface is critical. First, sound provides feedback and alerts for the player. A player knows a button has been activated when they hear the familiar button-press click. They know something is wrong when they hear an alarm sound. They know they've hit the jackpot when they hear the familiar chimes of a poker machine or a bag full of coins dropping onto a hard surface.

Second, sound deepens the game world. Although they might seem like insignificant noises, sound effects such as the player's footsteps, the creaky opening of a door, or wind in the trees provides that little extra touch of realism. It makes the game more tangible to the player as it provides that extra sense by which to perceive the environment.

3.4.5 Consistency and Coherence

Remember back to the early days of the World Wide Web and the dreadful webpage designs with bad layout, clashing outlandish colors, non-uniform fonts, animated gifs, and blinking text? Well you can also achieve this look in your mobile game interfaces by using unaligned different sized and shaped buttons, a variety of font faces and sizes, and colors picked from all over the color wheel.

Good interface design begins with being frugal with the amounts of differing visual elements in your game. At most, two different font faces should suffice

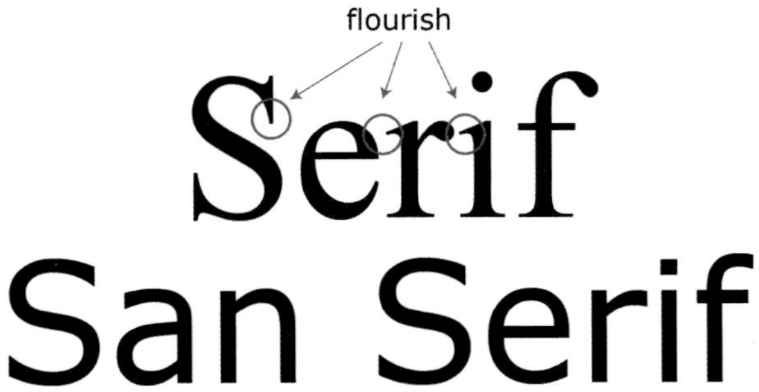

flourish

Serif
San Serif

FIG 3.10 Serif and San Serif font faces.

and, if possible, select just one. You'll also want to use a San Serif face. These are fonts that don't have the flourish on the tips of the letters as shown in Figure 3.10. San Serif fonts are easier to read on digital displays as they appear crisp and clear.

When it comes to buttons, stick with the same shape and finish. If you are using glossy circular buttons then use them everywhere (unless the game itself warrants many different shaped buttons). You may choose to use two different types of button shapes for different functions, for example round buttons on the main interface and square buttons on any pop-up screens. But these should still fit together with respect to coloring and finish. If you have a round green glossy button, then use green glossy square buttons.

3.4.6 Color

Another characteristic that makes for a coherent interface is the color scheme. Picking a color scheme is not just a matter of having a good *eye*, although some people do, but you can also approach it scientifically. Any scheme is selected from the colors on the color wheel. However the selection is not a random one.

Some of the more popular color schemes are shown in Figure 3.11 and are mathematically linked to the color wheel. Complementary colors are opposite each other on the color wheel, such as yellow and purple and communicate energy and vibrancy. Analogous colors are next to each other on the color wheel and promote harmony. They are pleasing to the eye as they depict the way colors appear in nature. Split complementary colors consist of a main color and two other colors picked from either side of the main colors complement. This scheme of three is the best for reducing eye fatigue and maintaining high contrast. It is perfect for use in mobile games in which the player could be looking at the screen for long periods of time. Triadic colors are selected on the corners of an equilateral triangle placed inside the color wheel and tetradic colors by using a square. Both sets produce vibrant combinations. Last, but not least, monochromatic color schemes are made from different tints and shades of a single color. They are very calming and yet authoritative.

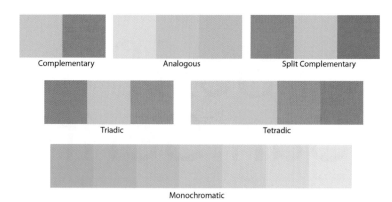

Complementary   Analogous   Split Complementary

Triadic   Tetradic

Monochromatic

FIG 3.11 Color schemes.

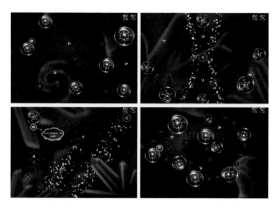

FIG 3.12 *Cyto* by Room 8.

The color scheme you select will depend on the genre and content of your game. If you are creating an *Angry Birds*-type game then you will want a vibrant color scheme that can be provided by complementary, triadic, or tetradic schemes. However for a game such as *Cyto*, as shown in Figure 3.12, analogous colors are used that emphasize the natural flowing world of the microorganism in which the game is set.

More Information: Color Schemes

For automatic color scheme generation try out the interactive website at www.colorhexa.com.

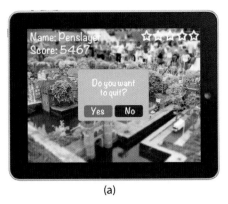
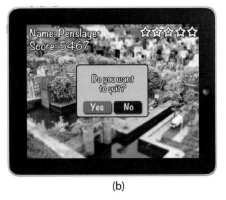

(a)   (b)

FIG 3.13 A simple GUI (a) with white text and no highlights and (b) with strokes and drop shadows employed.

Besides picking the color scheme to determine the colors that will be used for buttons, backgrounds, information boxes, interface controls, and others, you will also need to consider how icons and text will appear and whether or not it will be readable. The best coloring for such on an electronic device is white or light-colored text on a dark background. Because the device is emitting light, white is an active color and therefore easier on the eyes for reading. The dark background provides a contrast that makes the text more vibrant. A common way of putting text in an interface where there is no background behind it, just the game world is to highlight it with a drop shadow or stroke outline. As can be seen in Figure 3.13 (a) the white text looks like its not a suitable choice for the GUI as it gets lost in the colors of the background image. In this case, however, black text would not fare any better. However, as shown in Figure 3.13 (b), the addition of a black stroke around the text makes a world of difference. While the Yes and No buttons shown in Figure 3.13 are dark enough to support the white text without a stroke, they benefit from a slight drop shadow to pick them out from the background.

3.4.7 Usability

In order for a GUI to be usable it must be readable, recognizable, and touchable. According to MIT Touch Lab the average adult human index finger width is between 1.6 and 2 cm.[1] This equates to a touch area that is approximately 45 × 45 pixels. The thumb is an average of 2.5 cm and requires a touch target area of 72 × 72 pixels. Interestingly, the smaller a target area, the longer it takes for someone to touch it. This principle is described in Fitts's Law that states the time to point to a target is a function of the size of the target and the persons distance from it.

[1] Source: http://touchlab.mit.edu/publications/2003_009.pdf

As minimum pixels sizes for touchable areas Apple suggests 44 × 44 on a non-retina display and 88 × 88 on a retina display, Microsoft states a size of 26 × 26 pixels but recommends 34 × 34 pixels to be more usable and Nokia says 28 × 28 pixels. In addition, textboxes and other touchable and editable elements also need to be at least these measurements in height to allow for effective interaction.

Not only must an interface be touchable, but it must be readable. Both Apple and Microsoft suggest a minimum font size of 11 pixels. This becomes 22 on a retina display. There are two types of text in which fonts are used in mobile games. First is dynamic text, which changes throughout the game, such as the player's score. Second there is static text usually pre-rendered onto an image and then used in the game. Although they end up on the mobile game screen in very different ways, the end minimum size should still be adhered to ensure readability.

More Information: Why Icon Design Matters

For more information about making your icons stand out from the crowd, especially in a crowded App Store see http://gedblog.com/2008/12/01/why-icons-matter.

More Information: Interface Design

For more information mobile interface design guidelines see,
Apple: http://developer.apple.com/library/ios/documentation/userexperience/conceptual/mobilehig/MobileHIG.pdf.

More Information: Interface Design (*Continued*)

Microsoft: http://go.microsoft.com/?linkid=9713252.

More Information: Interface Design (*Continued*)

Nokia: http://library.developer.nokia.com/index.jsp?topic=/S60_5th_
Edition_Cpp_Developers_Library/GUID-5486EFD3–4660–4C19-A007–
286DE48F6EEF.html.

3.4.8 Layout

The key principles in graphic design are contrast, repetition, alignment
and proximity. Layout of mobile games covers alignment and proximity.
Alignment positions interface elements to create a visual flow. It forces the
player's eye to look and follow areas of the screen. Proximity groups related
elements together so the player need only look in one location for similar
types of information or types of control interfaces.

When considering the layout it aids to rule the screen design into equal-
sized parts with smaller gutters dividing each area. The number of sections
you require on the screen is up to you, but each should be no smaller than a
touchable button that needs to be no smaller than your fingertip.

But where should the interface elements be located? It depends on the nature
of the game. If thumb control is used extensively, then locating objects at
the bottom or middle sides of the screen will make them difficult to see. In a
racing game controlled by thumbsticks, for example, with the thumbsticks
taking up the bottom corners, the state visualization is best placed at the top
center of the screen as shown in Figure 3.14.

FIG 3.14 An example layout for a racing game.

If the game does not require thumbstick navigation you are free to populate along the bottom of the screen with the user interface as shown in Figure 3.15. In order to keep all information and controls presented on the screen in close proximity, sticking to one edge is a good idea. Players want to be immersed in the game environment not trying to remember where the interface elements are placed.

If you simply cannot get away with a minimalist user interface because of the nature of the game, its mechanics, and the controls don't fit along one side of the screen or in a single corner, the next best option is to push items into the

FIG 3.15 An example layout for a user interface along the bottom of the screen.

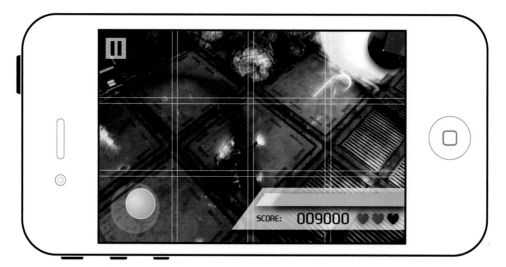

FIG 3.16 An example layout for a game with corner aligned interface elements.

corners. Any non-diegetic interface elements sit best to the sides and corners in order to maximize the screen space for the actual game.

Because screen heights and widths change with different devices pushing things to the corners and sides is easier and looks more consistent than placing them at fixed locations. For example on an original iPhone in landscape with a 480 pixel width, something located in the middle of the screen would be 240 pixels from the left-hand side. However, on an iPhone 5 with the landscape width at 1,136 pixels, the same item would not even sit one-fifth of the way in from the left, shown in Figure 3.17. As a developer you cannot rely on exact pixel locations or sizes for items as they will move and scale depending on the device resolution. Figure 3.17 (a) illustrates a 64 × 64 icon positioned perfectly with pixel coordinates in the center of the screen on an original iPhone. Using the same icon and pixel location on an iPhone 5, as shown in Figure 3.17 (b) produces a much different result.

Interestingly the user interface provides information to the user adding to their cognitive load. This load, in psychology, refers to the amount of pressure placed on an individual's working memory. Too little stimulus leads to an underload and too much to an overload. What this means for your game interface is that all elements presented must be meaningful so as to not add extra load on the player. Any elements that cannot and are not perceived,

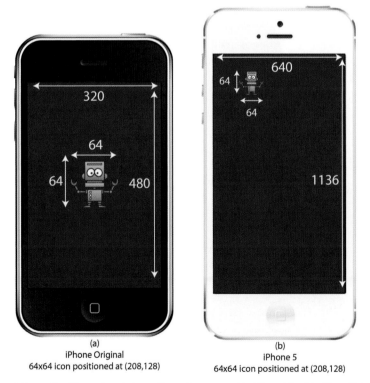

(a)
iPhone Original
64x64 icon positioned at (208,128)

(b)
iPhone 5
64x64 icon positioned at (208,128)

FIG 3.17 The difference in resolutions and layouts between an original iPhone (a) and the iPhone 5 (b).

in effect, become useless. As you will notice in racing or FPS games in which the action occurs in real time, the cognitive load is already high enough. These games tend to have very minimal user interfaces with only extremely relevant state information displayed. It's the same principle as driving a real car and trying to dial a mobile phone by hand. It's dangerous and reduces your cognitive abilities to those of an intoxicated individual. Simulation or role-playing games in which things don't happen in real time, as quickly, or can be paused present the user with a lot more screen present data.

3.5 Unity GUI in a Nutshell

A mobile device screen is the window through which the player sees the game environment. Its surface operates on a different coordinate system to the 3D world. Imagine the screen as a window being held up and moved around by someone viewing the world through it. This window then has an x and y axis drawn on it. Anything on the windowpane has a coordinate relative to the window's coordinate system. It also has a coordinate in the 3D world.

The illustration in Figure 3.18 shows a screen with its own 2D coordinate system in 3D world space. The red star is on the screen at position (3, −3). This is relative to the screen's origin. Because the screen is in the world, the star also has a 3D world coordinate. In this case it is (−13, 12, −2). The relationship between the screen and world will be further explored in the next section.

In Figure 3.18 the coordinate system for the device is shown with the origin in the upper left-hand corner. Although it could be anywhere on the surface it is usually by default on electronic displays to be in the upper left. This is also the case for the coordinate system used by Unity to position GUI objects.

The following hands-on session will introduce you to some of the GUI elements used in Unity and familiarize you with screen layout.

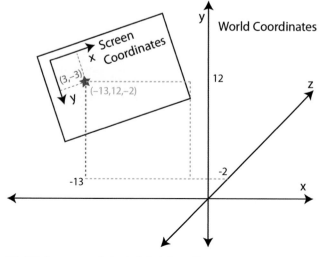

FIG 3.18 The screen coordinates of a device in the world space.

⊙ Unity Hands On

GUI Elements and Exploring the Screen Space

Step 1: Create a new Unity Project for iOS or Android. In the Game change the aspect to a device of your choosing as shown in Figure 3.19.

Step 2: Create a new C# script called *theInterface*. Add the following code:

```
using UnityEngine;
using System.Collections;

public class theInterface : MonoBehaviour
{
    void OnGUI()
    {
        GUI.Button( new Rect(0,0,50,50), "a" );
    }
}
```

Step 3: Save and attach to the Main Camera. Run in the editor. A button will appear in the top left corner of the screen with an "a" on it. You can click on this button. It will also register a touch when on a mobile device. However at this point we haven't programmed it to respond.

Step 4: Each GUI item in Unity is contained in the GUI class. All of these elements must be coded for inside of an OnGUI() function. It is called at least one time each main game loop and on every GUI interface type event such as a touch. As you can see from the code, GUI is used as the prefix to the type of interface element, which in this case is button. All of the possible GUI elements available can be found at http://docs.unity3d.com/Documentation/ScriptReference/GUI.html.

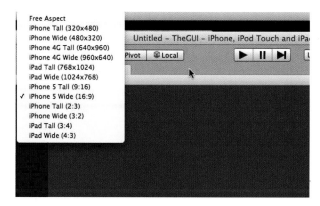

FIG 3.19 Select an aspect ratio for the Game view.

Step 5: Inside the function for each GUI element is a newly constructed rectangle. This rectangle defines the *x, y* position of the element and its width and height as such:

```
new Rect( x position, y position, width, height)
```

Step 6: In this example the button is positioned at (0,0) which places it in the upper left corner of the screen.

Step 7: Update `OnGUI()` in the *theInterface* script with the following lines:

```
...

void OnGUI()
{
    GUI.Button( new Rect(0,0,50,50), "a" );

    GUI.Button( new Rect(Screen.width-50, 0, 50, 50), "b");
    GUI.Button( new Rect(Screen.width-50, Screen.height-50, 50,
    50), "c");
    GUI.Button( new Rect(0, Screen.height-50, 50, 50), "d");
}
```

Step 8: Save and run. You will now have four buttons on the screen; one in each corner. Assuming you don't know the resolution of the device your game is going to run on is a good idea. It means you can code to push the gui elements to the screen extremes using `Screen.width` and `Screen.height`. These values hold the pixel dimensions of the device currently running the program. When in the Unity Editor these values are the same as the aspect ratio and resolution you have the Game window set to.

Step 9: To position a 50 × 50 pixel button in the bottom right hand corner, for example, you need to make the *x* and *y* position of the button 50 to the left and 50 up from the bottom. This leaves a gap 50 × 50 from the starting position of the button which can now cater for the 50 × 50 size of the button itself. If you simply put the button at the screen extremes it would be drawn off the screen. You can see `Screen.width` and `Screen.height` used in the preceding code.

Step 10: The other common placing for a GUI element is in the center; either of the entire screen or the top, bottom or sides. Add the following code to see the positioning of such elements:

```
...

void OnGUI()
{
    GUI.Button( new Rect(0,0,50,50), "a" );

    GUI.Button( new Rect(Screen.width-50, 0, 50, 50),
    "b");
```

```
GUI.Button( new Rect(Screen.width-50, Screen.
height-50, 50, 50), "c");

GUI.Button( new Rect(0, Screen.height-50, 50,
50), "d");

GUI.Box(new Rect(Screen.width/2.0f-50,0,100,30),
    "Top Middle");
GUI.Box(new Rect(Screen.width/2.0f-50,
    Screen.height-30,100,30),"Bottom Middle");
GUI.Box(new Rect(0,Screen.height/2.0f-15,100,30),
    "Left Middle");
GUI.Box(new Rect(Screen.width-100,
    Screen.height/2.0f-15,100,30),"Right Middle");
}
```

FIG 3.20 Positioning GUI elements in the corners and center of the screen sides.

Step 11: Save and play. Each of the elements will be pushed to the extremes of the screen but in the middle of the sides. The center is found by halving the Screen.width and Screen.height values and then taking away half the size of the element. This ensures the GUI element is drawn around the center point rather than starting it at the center point. The result is shown in Figure 3.20.

Step 12: To register the click of a GUI.Button, an if statement is placed around it and the actions to take on a click are placed inside. You can also set variables that in turn make other GUI items visible inside the statements. To see this in action, modify your code to:

```
...

bool labelOn = false;

void OnGUI()
{
    if(GUI.Button( new Rect(0,0,50,50), "a" ))
    {
        labelOn = !labelOn;
    }

    if(labelOn)
        GUI.Box( new Rect(Screen.width/2.0f-50,
        Screen.height/2.0f-50, 100, 100), "Hello");

    GUI.Button( new Rect(Screen.width-50, 0, 50, 50),
    "b");
    ...

}
```

Step 13: Save and try it out. The "a" button will now turn a box that says *Hello* on and off.

> **More Information: Unity GUI Items**
>
> For detailed information on all the Unity GUI items see the Unity manual at http://docs.unity3d.com/Documentation/Manual/GameInterfaceElements.html.
>
>

Step 14: So far we've created all of the elements with the default Unity styling. However you can set your own font faces and colors with a GUIStyle object. These are set and then attached to the GUI elements to change their appearance.

Step 15: Visit www.1001freefonts.com and find a font you'd like to use. Download the file, unzip and place the .ttf file into the Project in Unity. Modify your code thus:

```
bool labelOn = false;
public GUIStyle myStyle;

void OnGUI()
{
    if(GUI.Button( new Rect(0,0,50,50), "a" ))
    {
        labelOn = !labelOn;
    }
    if(labelOn)
        GUI.Box( new Rect(Screen.width/2.0f-50,
            Screen.height/2.0f-50, 100, 100),
            "Hello", myStyle);
    ...
```

Step 16: With the Main Camera selected in the Hierarchy go to the Inspector and find the attached code. A new exposed variable called myStyle will be there. Drag and drop the font you just added to the Project onto the Font element of *myStyle* as shown in Figure 3.21.

Step 17: Play. The popup Hello Box is now styled with the myStyle settings. It will only be this particular element affected by the style as it's the only one you've coded to change. The other GUI items will have the default Unity styling from before. Currently you've only changed the font. It will also be black. To make it white again, select the Normal section of myStyle and set the Text Color value to white as shown in Figure 3.22. Play again to see the font color changed.

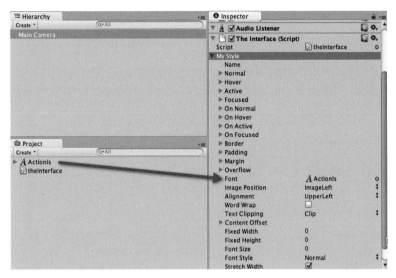

FIG 3.21 Setting up a GUIStyle and setting the font.

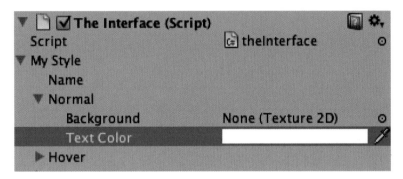

FIG 3.22 Setting the font color for a GUIStyle.

Step 18: The placement of the text will now be aligned to the top left of the GUI.Box rather than in the middle as with the default Unity Style. To fix this set the myStyle Alignment value to *Middle Center*.

Step 19: To increase the size of any font brought into Unity, select it in the Project and in the Inspector modify its size value as shown in Figure 3.23. Once changed click the Apply button.

Step 20: Now when you test the GUI you'll see the size of the font for the Hello Box has changed. To reuse the same font at a different size, duplicate the font in the Project, give it a new name that reflects its size and set the size in the Inspector. Then allocate the new font to another GUI style. For each and every different size you require of a font, you need another font file in the Project. Naming your fonts after their size is a good idea for usability, e.g., *ActionFont_16*, *ActionFont_32* etc.

FIG 3.23 Changing the size of a font.

Note

Some fonts are designed without special characters. For example, they might only contain the alphabet and the numbers 1 through 9. If you are trying to display text with a dollar or percentage sign and they are just not showing up, check the font.

More Information: Unity GUI Styling

For more information on the GUIStyle object and all its settings, see http://docs.unity3d.com/Documentation/Components/class-GUIStyle.html.

3.6 An Alternative to Unity GUI Buttons

While the GUI elements supplied by Unity are effective at achieving many interface requirements they are processor-heavy. If you have a lot of buttons or other GUI elements, the entire interface can impact dramatically on the performance of the game due to the number of drawcalls required to draw it. Drawcalls are discussed in depth in Chapter 4, however know that for each GUI item you use it takes up one drawcall and the more drawcalls, the slower the game will run. A much lighter method is to use images on planes in the game environment as buttons.

⊚ Unity Hands-On

A One Drawcall Button Menu

Step 1: Create a new Unity iOS or Android project. Select the Main Camera and change its Projection from Perspective to Orthographic.

Step 2: Create a png image with three buttons as shown in Figure 3.24. The background should be transparent. This image is also available from the website. Place the image into your Project.

Step 3: In the Scene add a plane and apply the png to it. The default plane will be in the XZ plane therefore if you click on the *y* axis of the widget in the Scene view it will reorient your view to look down. With the plane and buttons visible in the Scene, select the Main Camera and then GameObject | Align with View from the main menu. You may also have to change the size of the camera to bring the buttons into view. In this example, the relevant settings for the plane and the camera are shown in Figure 3.25.

Step 4: At this point your button image may look quite unremarkable. To fix it you need to do two things. First set the material on the plane's shader to Unlit/Transparent as shown in Figure 3.26.

FIG 3.24 A simple menu.

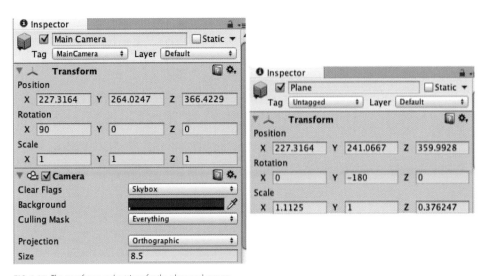

FIG 3.25 The transforms and settings for the plane and camera.

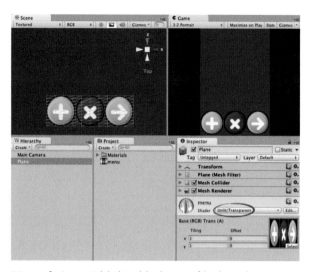

FIG 3.26 Setting material shader and the alignment of the plane and camera.

Step 5: Next, the image on the plane needs its settings tweaked. Select the image file in the Project. The settings for the image will be revealed in the Inspector. Modify the settings in your project to the ones shown in Figure 3.27. First change the Texture Type to Advanced to expose the other options. Next, if the texture's size is not a power of 2 (e.g. the pixel width and height values are not 2, 4, 8, 16, 32, 64, 128 etc.—it doesn't matter if it is square or not), set the value to none to avoid stretching. Turn off Generate Mip Maps by unticking the box. A mip map is like level of detail for images. Depending on how far away the image is from the camera, the blurrier it becomes. In the case of a menu, you always want it nice and crisp no matter where it is. Finally, set the color format to Automatic Truecolor

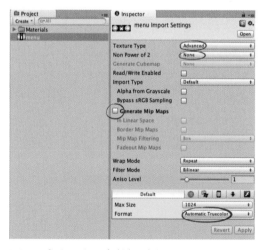

FIG 3.27 Setting an image for highest clarity.

(unless you know for sure your image is something else!) then click on Apply.

Step 6: To determine if a button has been hit or not, they will need colliders. To create these add three cubes into the scene. Resize and position the cubes around each button. Select each cube and one by one remove the attached Mesh Filter and Mesh Renderer via the Inspector. You will be left with the colliders that you can only see, in green, when selected as shown in Figure 3.28.

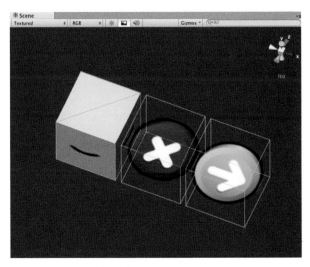

FIG 3.28 Adding touchable colliders to the button image.

Step 7: Rename each of the collider cubes with a unique name such as ArrowButton, CrossButton, and PlusButton as shown in Figure 3.29.

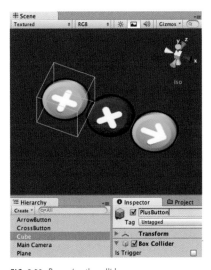

FIG 3.29 Renaming the colliders.

Step 8: Create a C# file named *ginterface*. Add the following code:

```
using UnityEngine;
using System.Collections;

public class ginterface : MonoBehaviour {

    string lastButtonPressed = "none";
    void OnGUI()
    {
        GUI.Box (new Rect(Screen.width/2.0f-50, 0, 100, 20),
    lastButtonPressed);
    }

    void Update ()
    {
        if(Input.GetMouseButtonDown(0) || (Input.touchCount
        > 0 &&
            Input.GetTouch(0).phase == TouchPhase.Began))
        {
            RaycastHit hit;
            Ray ray = Camera.main.ScreenPointToRay
                (Input.mousePosition);

            if (!Physics.Raycast (ray, out hit, 10000))
                return;

            if(hit.transform.gameObject.name == "ArrowButton")
            {
                lastButtonPressed = "Arrow Pressed";
            }
            else if (hit.transform.gameObject.name ==
            "CrossButton")
            {
                lastButtonPressed = "Cross Pressed";
            }
            else if (hit.transform.gameObject.name ==
            "PlusButton")
            {
                lastButtonPressed = "Plus Pressed";
            }
            else
            {
                lastButtonPressed = "none";
            }
        }
    }
}
```

Step 9: Save and attach the script to the Main Camera. In order for this to work the names of each collider cube must be exactly the same as

FIG 3.30 The buttons in action.

the strings given in the conditional statements in the preceding code. If everything is in order, when you run the game and click on the boxes, the label at the top of the screen will change to display the button that was clicked as shown in Figure 3.30.

Step 10: Any function you require each button to execute can now be placed inside the if statements for each.

3.7 Screen to World Space

As we've discovered the screen of the device is a window into the game environment. It is defined by its pixel resolution and is a 2D plane with x and y coordinates starting at (0,0) and increasing positively along both axes out to the sides of the screen. While the screen is flat, the game environment is 3D. On many occasions when you are handling input from screen touches or mouse-clicks, you'll receive the touch location in screen coordinates. These then need to be translated into world coordinates for further processing. This is a common issue, for example, when touching the screen to pick up a 3D object. Before understanding the conversion of screen space into world space, you first need to understand how the world space is structured. We've already investigated the world origin and x, y, and z axes but now we also need to investigate perspective.

3.7.1 Camera Projections

Perspective, as a word, means a cognitive view or outlook. In gaming it refers to the way in which the camera views the world. After all, the camera is the eyes of the player. The camera view can be set to either perspective or orthographic. Perspective reflects the way in which the human eye perceives the real world. Parallel lines project back into the view to a vanishing point and objects tend to

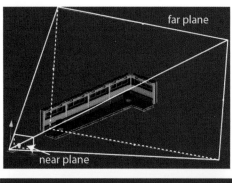
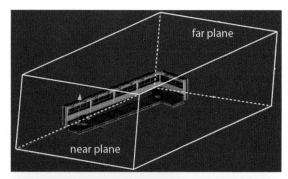
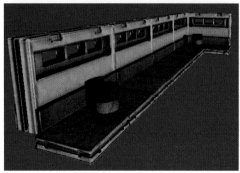
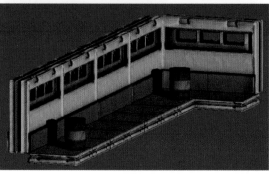

| (a) Perspective | (b) Orthographic |

FIG 3.31 Camera views: (a) perspective, (b) orthographic.

look smaller the further away they are. These properties give a 3D scene depth. Orthographic views have no depth. Instead parallel lines remain parallel, there is no vanishing point and objects of the same size, remain the same size no matter how far away they are. Both camera views are shown in Figure 3.31.

In Figure 3.31 (a) a perspective camera is shown. Each camera has an enclosed space that defines the part of the game environment that is visible. This space is called the viewing volume. The shape of a perspective camera's viewing volume is a pyramid with the top cut off, otherwise known as a frustum. The smaller end is always closest to the actual camera. This flat plane is called the near clipping plane. The bottom of the frustum is called the far plane. In the perspective view, you can clearly see how objects further away from the camera appear smaller such is the case with the barrel.

In Figure 3.31 (b) the orthographic camera's viewing volume can be seen to be rectangular prism in shape. It too has a near plane and a far plane. The barrels in the orthographic view remain the same number of pixels in size and although the same corridor scene is shown for both cameras, the depth of the orthographic view has been completely lost.

In Unity, the camera has a projection setting that you can set to perspective or orthographic depending on the look you want for your game. First-person games tend to use a perspective camera as there is an environment that the player is experiencing as though immersed in it. For platformers, orthographic is more suitable, especially if the camera is on rails and following the action in 2D. Because Unity is a 3D game engine, when you create a 2D game you need to almost forget about the *z* axis (or depth) in the scene and an orthographic camera setting for this case is usually preferred. You'll find this setting in the Inspector when the camera is selected as shown in Figure 3.32.

The size of the camera's viewing volume is determined by the positions of the near and far plane and the field of view (FOV) for the perspective camera and the size for the orthographic camera. In Unity, these settings are found in the Camera component below the Projection setting. The way in which these settings affect the camera and hence the player's view of the game environment is shown in Figure 3.33. For a perspective camera the bigger the FOV the wider the viewing angle. A wider angle allows more of a scene in the

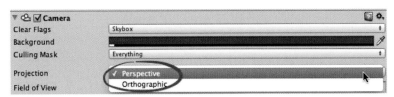

FIG 3.32 Setting Unity's Camera Projection.

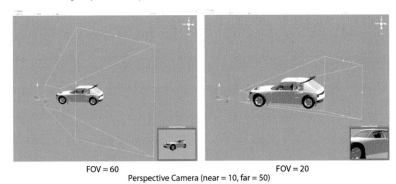

FOV = 60   FOV = 20

Perspective Camera (near = 10, far = 50)

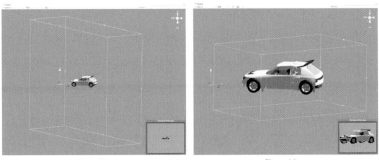

Size = 50   Size = 10

Orthographic Camera (near = 10, far = 50)

FIG 3.33 Effects of FOV and Size settings on camera view.

163

view. A narrow FOV gives the illusion of zooming in. The most common FOV setting in 3D games is 60 degrees as it gives a perspective view similar to that experienced by the human eye in the real world.

Size is the equivalent of FOV for the orthographic camera. The larger the size, the larger the viewing volume and therefore the smaller objects in the same game environment will appear.

Regardless how the camera is set up, as previously discussed, the screen and world coordinate systems will be different. Sometimes you will require a value in one coordinate system to be translated into another. This most frequently occurs in the case of screen-touches where you require that touch to reach out into the game world.

3.7.2 Exploring Screen and World Space by Touch

To better understand the process of switching from 2D screen coordinates to 3D world coordinates we are going to explore an example in Unity that creates spheres in the game environment each time a player touches the screen. This script implements some touch-capturing commands that will be fully explained in the next section.

◉ Unity Hands-On
Screen and World Space

Step 1: Create a new Unity Project and set it for iOS or Android. Add a Directional Light into the Scene to give the environment some depth.
Step 2: Create a new C# script called *createTouchSpheres* and enter the following code:

```
using UnityEngine;
using System.Collections;

public class createTouchSpheres : MonoBehaviour {

    // Use this for initialization
    void Start () {

    }

    // Update is called once per frame
    void Update () {

        if (Input.GetMouseButtonDown(0))
        {
            Vector3 touchPosition = Input.mousePosition;
            Vector3 touchWorld = camera.ScreenToWorldPoint (new
            Vector3 (touchPosition.x, touchPosition.
            y,camera.nearClipPlane + 10));
```

```
GameObject sphere = GameObject.CreatePrimitive(
PrimitiveType.Sphere);
sphere.transform.position = touchWorld;
}

}

}
```

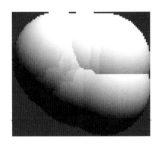

Save the script and attach it to the camera in the Scene. Note, this script will work in the Unity Editor and on a mobile device. The `GetMouseButtonDown(0)` function registers a left mouse-click or a touch. The Input.mousePosition variable will have the coordinates of the mouse-click or the touch when required.

Play. Touch or click on the screen. Spheres will begin to appear under each touch.

Step 3: They are instantiated in the world at the position of the screen touch. The `mousePosition` gives an (*x,y*) coordinate of the touch relative to the screen's XY plane. Remember this is independent of the world environment. The function `camera.ScreenToWorldPoint()` takes the screen position and translates it into a 3D coordinate relative to the world's origin. The screen being touched is essentially the camera's near plane plus ten units. The reason we aren't calculating the touch on the near plane is because any spheres positioned that close to the camera will not be visible as they will be cut in half by the near plane itself. Try this out if you want to see the effect. The greater the units you add to the near plane to calculate the world position, the further away the sphere will be from the camera.

3.8 Swipe, Shout, and Shake it All About!

There are numerous ways in which you can interact with a game environment on a mobile device. This makes designing games with unique player experiences challenging—and developing them even more so. Unlike a desktop computer or game console and television, the screen of a mobile device, in addition to being touched, can be orientated in one of six directions, shaken, tilted, and geographically relocated. In this section we will explore other common gestures, tilting, orientation, and geolocation.

3.8.1 Pinch

When two or more fingers touch the surface and then move together it is considered a pinch gesture. The most common pinch is performed with two fingers as shown in Figure 3.35.

A pinch consists of an initial touch at two different coordinates on the screen. As the fingers are dragged across the screen, usually in a gesture that brings

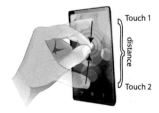

FIG 3.35 A pinch gesture.

the touch positions closer, the distance between the touches decreases. A reverse touch is also possible in which fingers are dragged apart on the surface. The change in the distance between the touches is used as a degree of measure for the touch. For example, a common use of the pinch gesture is for zooming in and out. The greater the change in distance between the starting touch position and the distance between the final touch positions becomes the zoom amount.

In the next hands-on session, the pinch gesture will be explored for zooming in and out on a map.

⊙ Unity Hands-On
Pinch and Zoom

In this hands-on session we will examine the movement of the camera on a mobile device using pinching, zooming, and moving actions. The script employs multitouch techniques and therefore you will require an iOS or Android device for testing.

Step 1: Create a new iOS or Android Unity Project. Position the camera so it is looking straight down the *y* axis. You can do this by selecting the small axes gizmo in the upper right of the Scene window and clicking on the green *y* axis. The Scene will orientate to look directly down. The gizmo will display as in Top View shown in Figure 3.36. Select the Main Camera in the Hierarchy and then GameObject > Align with View to reposition the camera to be looking into the game environment in the same way you are looking into the Scene.

Step 2: Create a plane by selecting GameObject > Create Other > Plane. By default you will be looking directly at the plane as it is created in the XZ plane.

Step 3: Search online for a large satellite image. Save it to your desktop. Drag and drop it into the Project. Once imported drag and drop it onto the plane in the Scene. Your project should look similar to that shown in Figure 3.37.

Step 4: Although the settings for materials will be fully explained in Chapter 4 it seems pertinent at this point to show the setting that will make a material appear fully lit without the aid of a light. Select the material you are using for the map in the Project. In the Inspector there will be a *Shader* setting as shown in Figure 3.38. Select Unlit/Texture. The material will not be affected by lighting conditions in the scene.

Step 5: Create a new C# file called *pinchZoom* and add the following code:

```
using UnityEngine;
using System.Collections;

public class pinchZoom : MonoBehaviour {

    float previousDistance;
    float zoomSpeed = 0.05f;
```

FIG 3.36 The Scene axes gizmo showing Top View.

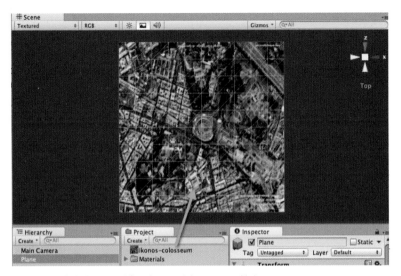

FIG 3.37 A default plane viewed from the top with large texture added.

FIG 3.38 Setting a material's shader.

```
// Use this for initialization
void Start () {
}

// Update is called once per frame
void Update () {

    if(Input.touchCount == 2 && (Input.GetTouch(0).phase ==
```

```
                TouchPhase.Began || Input.GetTouch(1).phase ==
                TouchPhase.Began) )
        {
        //calibrate previous distance
        previousDistance =
                Vector2.Distance(Input.GetTouch(0).position,
                        Input.GetTouch(1).position);
        }
        else if (Input.touchCount == 2 &&
                (Input.GetTouch(0).phase == TouchPhase.Moved ||
                Input.GetTouch(1).phase == TouchPhase.Moved) ) {

                float distance;
                Vector2 touch1 = Input.GetTouch(0).position;
                Vector2 touch2 = Input.GetTouch(1).position;
                distance = Vector2.Distance(touch1, touch2);

                //move camera on the y based on the
                //distance of the pinch
                float yChange = this.transform.position.y +
                        (previousDistance–distance) * zoomSpeed;

                this.transform.position =
                new Vector3(this.transform.position.x,yChange,
                                this.transform.position.z);
                previousDistance = distance;
        }
    }
  }
```

Step 6: Save and attach to the Main Camera. It will determine when two touches happens and record the distance between them. Then when the fingers move, the distance is recalculated and compared with the last distance. The change in this distance will determine if the camera needs to move closer or further away from the plane.

Step 7: Go to the Game view. In the upper left corner is a dropdown box that allows you to set the resolution as shown in Figure 3.39. Set it to the size of your device. This will not affect how the game appears on the device. It is only a guide when viewing in the editor. In addition, move the camera down in the y position so the map fills the view.

Step 8: Save your project and build out to a device. Using two fingers you'll be able to pinch the screen and zoom the camera. Note in the code that it is only the camera's y coordinate that is affected by the pinch. You are therefore just moving the camera up and down on the y axis to simulate zooming.

Step 9: The next thing we will do is clamp the camera so it can't zoom too far out or too far in. First, you need to determine manually the two camera extremes. With the Game view visible, move the camera on its y axis until it is as far zoomed out as you would like. This will probably be the point at which the edges of the plane become visible. Record this y value. Now

FIG 3.39 Viewing the game in the editor as it will appear on the device.

move the camera as close to the plane as you want to allow a user to go. Record this *y* value.

Replace the code:

```
this.transform.position = new
    Vector3(this.transform.position.x, yChange,
        this.transform.position.z);
```

with

```
this.transform.position = new
    Vector3(this.transform.position.x,
        Mathf.Clamp (yChange, 0.8f, 8.5f),
            this.transform.position.z);
```

where 0.8 and 8.5 are substituted by your own zoom in and out values. What the `Mathf.Clamp()` function does is to set a value as long as it falls within a certain range. Otherwise the minimum and maximum values are used. In this case, the *y* position will change according to a pinch change; however, if that value makes the camera go to a *y* value less than 0.8, it will be stopped at 0.8 and if it goes beyond 8.5 it will be fixed at 8.5.

Save and build out to a device for testing.

Step 10: To move the camera across the map while dragging a finger, we first need to consider the camera axis with respect to the screen axis. The screen has *x* and *y* axes only, where *y* is up and down. In our case, these would map directly to the *x* of the screen being equivalent to the *x* of the camera and the *y* of the screen being aligned with the camera's *z*. Therefore we are going to move the camera based on the change in the *x* and *y* of a finger drag, by adding the change in these values to the camera's *x* and *z* respectively.

Step 11: Add a new variable to the top of the script thus:

```
float previousDistance;
float zoomSpeed = 0.05f;
float dragSpeed = 0.05f;
```

Step 12: Then add a new `else if` clause to the existing statement inside the `Update()` function as follows:

```
if(Input.touchCount == 2 &&
    (Input.GetTouch(0).phase == TouchPhase.Began ||
    Input.GetTouch(1).phase == TouchPhase.Began) )
{
    ...
}
else if (Input.touchCount == 2 &&
    (Input.GetTouch(0).phase == TouchPhase.Moved ||
    Input.GetTouch(1).phase == TouchPhase.Moved) )
{
    ...
```

```
        }
        else if(Input.touchCount == 1 &&
                Input.GetTouch(0).phase == TouchPhase.Moved)
        {
            float zDragChange = this.transform.position.z -
                    Input.GetTouch(0).deltaPosition.y * dragSpeed;
            float xDragChange = this.transform.position.x -
                    Input.GetTouch(0).deltaPosition.x * dragSpeed;

            this.transform.position = new Vector3( xDragChange,
                    this.transform.position.y, zDragChange);

        }
```

Step 13: Save and play. If the zooming and dragging is too fast you can modify the sensitivity by changing the `zoomSpeed` and `dragSpeed` variables. Smaller values will make the camera move slower.

3.8.2 Swiping

A swipe is a gesture usually involving one finger registering a touch and then a drag. Of course, there is no reason why multiple fingers could not perform a swipe and you may find benefits and ways to extend an interface by programming for one-figure swipes or multiple-finger swipes. In fact iOS implements four-finger swipes to switch between running applications and five finger swipes to get back to the home screen.

◉ Unity Hands On
Swipe

In this hands-on session you will create a swiping program that draws a ribbon beneath your finger.

Step 1: Create a Unity iOS or Android project. Set the Main Camera to Orthographic with a size of 5.

Step 2: Create an empty game object with GameObject > Create Empty. Rename it Ribbon. While it is selected in the Hierarchy select Component > Effects > Trail Renderer. The resulting project is shown in Figure 3.40.

Step 3: For the Trail Renderer set the *Time* to 0.5. This is how long the ribbon will display. Set the *Start Width* to 0.5 and the *End Width* to 0.1. This will give the ribbon a tapered look.

Step 4: Create a C# program called *swipeTrail* and add the following script:

```
using UnityEngine;
using System.Collections;

public class swipeTrail : MonoBehaviour {
```

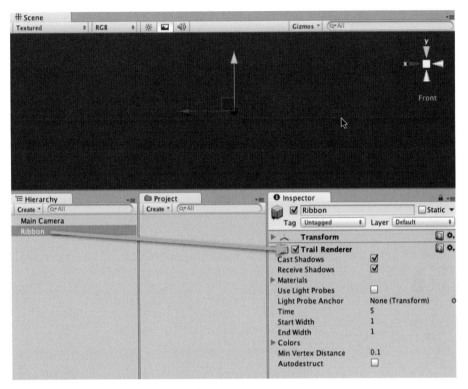

FIG 3.40 Adding a new game object with a Trail Renderer.

```
    // Use this for initialization
    void Start () {

}

// Update is called once per frame
void Update () {
    if(((Input.touchCount > 0 &&
        Input.GetTouch(0).phase ==
        TouchPhase.Moved) ||
        Input.GetMouseButton(0)))
    {
      Vector3 touchPos = Camera.main.ScreenToWorldPoint(
            new Vector3(Input.mousePosition.x,
                Input.mousePosition.y, 0));

      this.transform.position = new
            Vector3(touchPos.x,touchPos.y,0);
        }
    }
}
```

FIG 3.41 Drawing with a Trail Renderer.

Step 5: Save the script. Attach it to the Ribbon game object. Play. You will be able to draw on the screen as illustrated in Figure 3.41.

Step 6: The previous code implements a method that will allow you to run and test touch programs on a device and with a mouse as it employs the `GetMouseButton()` function as well as a `GetTouch()`. As you will have gathered by now, writing a mobile game program and building it for testing is a laborious activity. The more you can test in the editor, the quicker development will be. Therefore, programming for mouse and touch input in the same code is important.

Step 7: To color the trail, create a new material in the Project, call it Ribbon. Change the shader to a Particle/Additive. This will default to white. Drag and drop this material onto the Ribbon game object in the Hierarchy. Select the Ribbon in the Hierarchy then in the Inspector locate the Trail Renderer component. Look for the Colors array. Select each of the five colors in turn and set them to a desired value. These colors will be applied over the top of the white material as the ribbon is drawn (see Figure 3.42).

Step 8: Save the project and build out to a mobile device for testing.

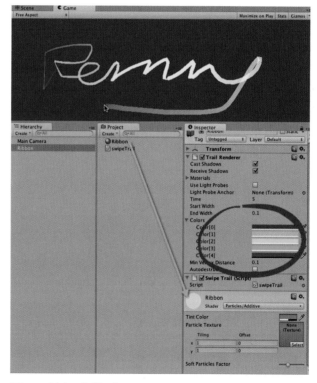

FIG 3.42 Coloring a Trail Renderer.

3.8.3 Tilt and Acceleration

Today's mobile devices have finger-nail sized microelectromechanical systems called *accelerometers* integrated to calculate tilt and acceleration by sensing motion and vibration. Accelerometers measure the downward force of gravity to determine how the device is angled and whether or not it is moving. The same types of accelerometers employed in the Nintendo Wii Remote and its Nunchuk and the PlayStation 3 Dual Shock 3 controller are used in mobile devices. These consist of a small cantilever beam attached to a seismic mass sealed in a gas pocket. When the device moves, the beam bends under accelerative forces and these are measured and reported.

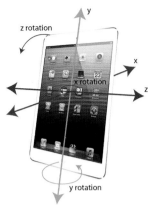

FIG 3.43 The rotational axes of the iPad mini.

Acceleration is measured around the axes of the mobile device as shown in Figure 3.43. This illustration shows the axes around which each rotational acceleration is measured on the iPad Mini. Depending on the actual orientation of the physical accelerometer in the device, these axes may be different. For example, from our own testing we know the accelerometer axes in Android Samsung and HTC phones are different to those in Apple devices. For these Android devices, the *x* and *z* axes are switched.

To test the accelerometers in your own device try the code in Listing 3.1 in Unity. Create a script called *tilt*, add the code and then attach it to the Main Camera.

Listing 3.1 A C# Script to Monitor Mobile Accelerometer Readings.

```csharp
using UnityEngine;
using System.Collections;

public class tilt : MonoBehaviour {

    Vector3 dir = Vector3.zero;

    void OnGUI()
    {
        GUI.Label( new Rect(10, 10, 100, 20), "x: " +
        dir.x);
        GUI.Label( new Rect(10, 30, 100, 20), "y: " +
        dir.y);
        GUI.Label( new Rect(10, 50, 100, 20), "z: " +
        dir.z);
    }

    // Update is called once per frame
    void Update () {

        if(Mathf.Abs (Input.acceleration.x) > 0.1)
            dir.x = Input.acceleration.x;

        if(Mathf.Abs (Input.acceleration.y) > 0.1)
            dir.y = Input.acceleration.y;
```

```
        if(Mathf.Abs (Input.acceleration.z) > 0.1)
            dir.z = Input.acceleration.z;

    }
}
```

◉ Unity Hands On

Tilt

Step 1: Create a new Unity Project for iOS or Android. In the Scene select the *y* axis on the gizmo to place it in Top view. Next, select the Main Camera and then choose GameObject > Align With View from the main menu. This will create a world in which the camera is looking straight down at the ground. It also means that, with a normal physics system, anything under the influence of gravity will fall away from you into the camera's view volume.

The idea is to create a small plane with a sphere on top. You will have to keep the mobile steady to keep the ball from rolling off. Therefore, create a sphere. Color it red. Add a plane just beneath it and make it smaller than the screen resolution. Add a Rigidbody to the sphere (Component > Physics > Rigidbody). Make sure the sphere sits above the plane as shown in Figure 3.44.

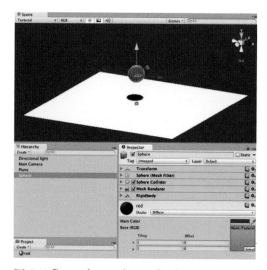

FIG 3.44 The setup for an accelerometer based game.

Step 2: Create a C# script called *rollBall*. Add the following code:

```
using UnityEngine;
using System.Collections;
public class rollBall : MonoBehaviour {
    float speed = 10.0f;
```

```
// Use this for initialization
void Start () {
}
// Update is called once per frame
void Update () {
    float newX;
    float newZ;

    newX = this.transform.position.x +
           Input.acceleration.x/speed;
    newZ = this.transform.position.z +
           Input.acceleration.y/speed;

    this.transform.position = new
           Vector3(newX,this.transform.position.y, newZ);
    }
}
```

Save the project and build out to a mobile device for testing.

3.8.4 Orientation

Data from the accelerometer can also determine the fixed orientation of a device as it is assumed the mechanical component of the accelerometer is fixed with respect to the body of the device. There are six orientations that may be registered. These are landscape right, landscape left, portrait upright, portrait upside-down, face-up, and face-down. The orientations as recorded on a HTC Google Nexus One with Android are shown in Figure 3.45.

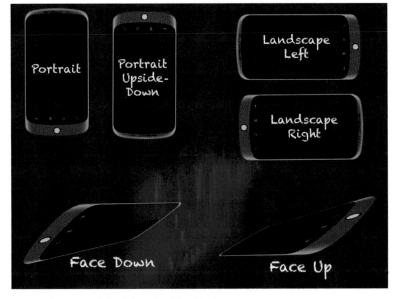

FIG 3.45 Orientations of a Google Nexus One HTC mobile phone.

Unity reports the device orientation via the Input class. The same one we have used for getting touches, mouse-clicks and acceleration. The code in Listing 3.2 can be used in a C# script attached to the camera to report back on the device orientation.

Listing 3.2 Unity C# to Report Device Orientation

```csharp
using UnityEngine;
using System.Collections;

public class getOrientation : MonoBehaviour
{
    string orientString = "Unknown";
    Vector2 pivotPoint = new Vector2 (200, 200);
    float rotAngle = 0;

    void OnGUI ()
    {
        if (Input.deviceOrientation == DeviceOrientation.
        FaceDown) {
            orientString = "Face Down";
            rotAngle = 0;
        }
        if (Input.deviceOrientation == DeviceOrientation.
        FaceUp) {
            orientString = "Face Up";
            rotAngle = 0;
        }

        if (Input.deviceOrientation == DeviceOrientation.
        Portrait) {
            orientString = "Portrait";
            rotAngle = 0;
        }

        if (Input.deviceOrientation == DeviceOrientation.
        PortraitUpsideDown) {
            orientString = "Portrait Upside Down";
            rotAngle = 180;
        }

        if (Input.deviceOrientation == DeviceOrientation.
        LandscapeLeft) {
            orientString = "Landscape Left";
            rotAngle = 90;
        }

        if (Input.deviceOrientation == DeviceOrientation.
        LandscapeRight) {
            orientString = "Landscape Right";
```

```
            rotAngle = -90;
        }

    GUI.BeginGroup (new Rect (Screen.width / 2-200,
            Screen.height / 2-200, 400, 400));
    GUIUtility.RotateAroundPivot (rotAngle, pivotPoint);
    GUI.Label (new Rect (0, 0, 400, 400), orientString);
    GUI.EndGroup ();

  }
}
```

3.8.5 Global Positioning Systems (GPS) and Compasses

Because mobile devices are . . . well . . . mobile, it makes sense to give them the ability to determine where exactly they are. Thanks to the Department of Defense who deployed the GPS in 1978 and later made it free for civilian use in 1993, mobile devices with the appropriate circuitry can determine where they are on the Earth. Today, the GPS consists of 30 solar-powered satellites orbiting the earth at 20,200 km. At any time, four satellites are visible from any one location on the Earth's surface. This allows for a GPS receiver, like the ones used in mobile phones, to *trilaterate* its position, to within ten meters, by determining its position from any four satellites. A number of mobile games that have evolved around GPS were discussed in Chapter 1.

GPS coordinates are recorded in longitude and latitude based on the spherical coordinate system used for mapping the Earth. Lines of longitude (also called meridians) run vertically on the globe beginning with 0° which runs through the Royal Observatory, Greenwich, London, UK. At right-angles to these fall the lines of latitude circling the Earth, parallel to (and including) the equator. Whereas the lines of latitude are equidistant, the lines of longitude come together at the North and South Poles. Near the equator, the distance between each line of latitude and each line of longitude is approximately 111 km.

Longitude and latitude are traditionally measured in degrees, minutes, and seconds where 60 seconds makes a minute, 60 minutes makes a degree, and one revolution around the earth is 360 degrees. Coordinates are given in values either north and south of the equator for latitude or east and west of the prime meridian for longitude. More recently, and especially in the case of Google Maps, the minutes and seconds have been dispensed with in favor of a single degree value with decimal points. For example, Bond University is at 28 degrees, 4 minutes, and 27.58 seconds south by 153 degrees, 25 minutes, and 5.18 seconds east—this equates to -28.074328, 153.418107 for latitude and longitude respectively.

☉ Unity Hands-On

GPS

Step 1: Create a new iOS or Android Unity project.

Step 2: Depending on your actual mobile device, you might only get an estimated location based on your mobile network service which *guestimates* your location depending on which towers your phone is connected to. However, if it works, you should be able to get some values from this anyway. Create a new C# script called GPS and add the code:

```
using UnityEngine;
using System.Collections;

public class GPS : MonoBehaviour {

    string message = "";

    IEnumerator Wait(int seconds) {
        yield return new WaitForSeconds(seconds);
    }

    void OnGUI() {
        GUI.Label (new Rect(10,10,400,50),"Message: " + message);
        GUI.Label (new Rect(10,30,200,50),"Longitude: " +
                    Input.location.lastData.longitude);

        GUI.Label (new Rect(10,50,200,50),"Latitude: " +
                    Input.location.lastData.latitude);
    }

    // Use this for initialization
    void Start () {

        // First, check if user has location service enabled
        if (!Input.location.isEnabledByUser)
            return;

        // Start service before querying location
        Input.location.Start (1,1);

        // Wait until service initializes
        int maxWait = 20;
        message = "Starting Location Services";

        while (Input.location.status ==
            LocationServiceStatus.Initializing && maxWait > 0)
            {
                StartCoroutine(Wait(1));
                maxWait-;
            }

            // Connection has failed
            if (Input.location.status ==
                LocationServiceStatus.Failed)
```

```
            {
                    message = "Unable to determine device location";
            }
            else
                    message = "Location Services Started!";

    }

    // Update is called once per frame
    void Update () {
    }
}
```

Step 3: Save the script and attach to the *Main Camera*. Build to the device to test and find your longitude and latitude.

In addition to knowing where they are, most smartphones can tell you which direction you are facing with respect to the Earth's magnetic field. They can do this via a small integrated circuit called a magnetometer. Magnetometers measure the strength and direction of magnetic fields. This allows them to detect the direction of the Earth's poles, however they are susceptible to magnetic fields produced by proximities to iron. In fact, there are metal detection apps in the marketplace that take advantage of this. Not surprisingly one of these, available for iOS and Android, is called *Metal Detector*.

◉ Unity Hands On

Compass

Step 1: Create a new Unity Android (this does not work for iOS builds) project. Set the camera to be looking down the *y* axis.

Step 2: Add a plane into the Scene. By default it will be in the XZ plane and thus the camera should be looking straight at it. Onto the plane place an image of an arrow. You can create this image in a paint package but it must be created pointing *downwards*. Other arrow icons may be found at http://iconarchive.com. Place this image onto the plane. Because of the way in which images are placed onto the default Unity plane, they will be upside down. In this case, because we created the arrow upside-down, it will not be facing upwards. It is imperative that the direction of the arrow image and the *z* axis of the plane line up as shown in Figure 3.46 An arrow placed on the default Unity plane to line up with the *z* axis. The reason being that the compass needle direction will be based on the plane's *z* axis.

The idea is to rotate this arrow around the *y* axis based on the heading of the mobile device so the arrow always faces north like a real compass. The Unity compass function that returns the magnetic heading determines the angle between the top of the device and magnetic north. For example, if you had the top of the device pointing at magnetic north,

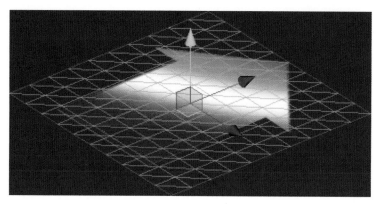

FIG 3.46 An arrow placed on the default Unity plane to line up with the z axis.

then you would have a magnetic heading value of 0 degrees. If you were facing south, you'd want the compass needle to be pointing down at the bottom of the device. Therefore, you want to rotate the arrow in the negative direction to the magnetic heading of the device.

Step 3: Create a C# script called *compassControl* and add the following:

```
using UnityEngine;
using System.Collections;

public class compassControl : MonoBehaviour {

    // Update is called once per frame
    void Update () {

        this.transform.localEulerAngles = new Vector3(
                this.transform.localEulerAngles.x,
                -Input.compass.magneticHeading,
            this.transform.localEulerAngles.z);
            }
    }
```

Step 4: Save this script and attach it to the plane. Play. Hold the device like a compass in front of your body. Turn on the spot and watch how the compass needle continues pointing to north. Depending on your device and any other electromagnetic interference nearby you'll get differing levels of accuracy.

3.9 Joysticks

The first known use of a joystick was for the control of an aircraft in 1908. However, it wasn't until Ralph Baer introduced the first television video game in 1967 complete with a joystick controller that they became a household name. Nowadays, the traditional form of the *stick* joystick has been replaced with more fancy and streamlined console controllers but the idea of it and the intuitive navigational interface it provides lives on.

◉ Unity Hands-On
The Joystick

Step 1: Create a new Unity iOS or Android Project. When the Create Dialog box comes up ensure you tick to include Standard Assets (Mobile). unityPackage.

Step 2: In the Project, locate the Single Joystick prefab in the Standard Assets | Prefabs folder and drag it into the Hierarchy as shown in Figure 3.48. You will see the joystick image appear in the bottom left corner of the Scene and Game.

FIG 3.47 Creating a new Unity project with mobile assets.

FIG 3.48 Adding a Single Joystick to the Scene.

Step 3: In order to use the joystick we need to apply its movements to something. Therefore create a cube and position it in front of the camera. Now create a new C# file *drive* and add the code:

```
using UnityEngine;
using System.Collections;

public class drive : MonoBehaviour {
    public Joystick moveJoystick;
    float speed = 1.0f;
    float turnSpeed = 1.0f;

    void Update () {
        this.transform.Translate(Vector3.forward *
            moveJoystick.position.y * speed);
        this.transform.Rotate(Vector3.up *
            moveJoystick.position.x * turnSpeed);
    }
}
```

Save. Back in Unity you will get an error saying the Joystick can't be found. This is because the C# script is referencing something called Joystick, but the compiler can't find it. This can happen because of the order in which classes get compiled. To fix this issue, in the Project create a folder called Plugins. Things placed in the Plugins folder get priority compilation. Because the drive script requires the Joystick script, we need to force Joystick to compile first. Take the Joystick out of the Standard Assets | Scripts folder and drag it into Plugins as shown in Figure 3.49. The error coming from the drive script will be removed.

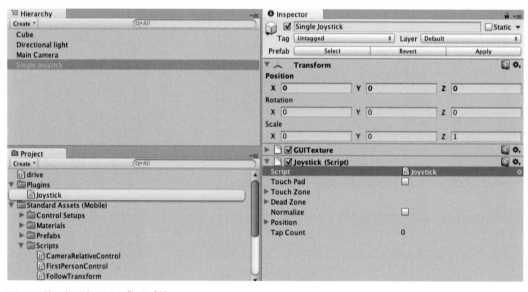

FIG 3.49 Move Joystick script into Plugins folder.

Step 4: Attach the *drive* script to the cube. Select the cube in the Hierarchy. Locate the drive script in the Inspector and drag and drop the Single Joystick from the Hierarchy onto the exposed Move Joystick variable as shown in Figure 3.50.

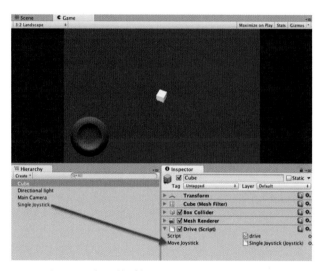

FIG 3.50 Assign Joystick variable of drive script.

Save and build to your device for testing. The Joystick on the screen can be used to drive the cube around on the XZ plane.

While a single joystick is useful for driving a simple player character model around on a flat surface, other interfaces require two joysticks; one for movement and one for looking around or orientation. In the next hands-on session the use of double joysticks will be examined.

◎ Unity Hands-On
Double Joystick First-Person Controller

Step 1: Create a new iOS or Android Unity Project and include the Standard Assets (Mobile) and Skyboxes Unity packages. After importing the extra assets there1 will be a Standard Assets and Standard Assets (Mobile) folder in the Project.

Step 2: From the main menu select Edit > Render Settings. A RenderSettings panel will appear in the Inspector. Locate a Skybox material in the Standard Assets Folder in the Project and drag it onto the RenderSettings Skybox Material as shown in Figure 3.51.

Step 3: To see the skybox in action switch over to the Game view.

Step 4: Next, add a plane to the Scene. Resize it to stretch over a larger area. A scale of 5 for the *x* and *z* scale values in the plane's transform will suffice.

183

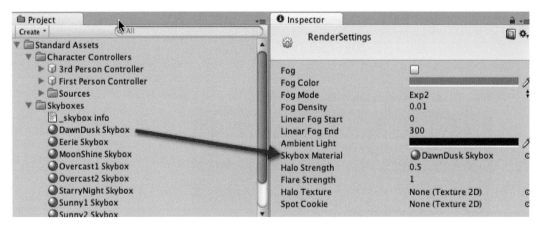

FIG 3.51 Adding a Skybox to the Scene.

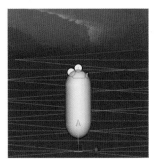

FIG 3.52 Adding First Person Controls to a Scene.

FIG 3.53 The left and right touch pad game objects.

Step 5: In the Standard Assets (Mobile) | Prefabs folder in the Project locate the First Person Controls Prefab. Drag it into the Scene and position it just above the plane as shown in Figure 3.52. Once you do this a warning will appear in the Unity console saying "There are 2 audio listeners in the scene . . ." An audio listener picks up sounds in the environment for interpolating the 3D sound experience of the player. Each camera you create has an audio listener. It is essentially the ears of the camera. Because the First-Person Controls has a camera, it also has an audio listener as does the existing Main Camera. To fix this issue, delete the pre-existing Main Camera.

Step 6: At this point you will have dashed line boxes in each lower corner of the Scene. This is the same setup for the player in the *Minecraft* exercise from the previous chapter. However, now we want to replace these touchpads with joysticks.

Step 7: Locate the Dual Joysticks prefab in the Standard Assets (Mobile) > Prefabs folder and drag into the Hierarchy. In the Hierarchy expand the First Person Controls to reveal the LeftTouchPad and RightTouchPad as shown in Figure 3.53. Delete both. A message will pop up warning about breaking a prefab. This is OK.

Step 8: Select the Player child object of the First-Person Controls to reveal its settings in the Inspector. Expand the Dual Joysticks object in the Hierarchy. Drag the LeftJoystick component onto the Move Touch Pad exposed variable in the Hierarchy and the RightJoystick onto the Rotate Touch Pad as shown in Figure 3.54.

Step 9: The script controlling the First Person Controls will now be linked to the dual joysticks. Save and build to a device for testing.

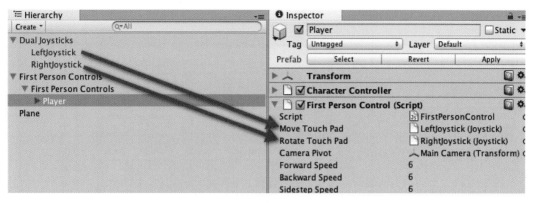

FIG 3.54 Add joystick to the First Person Controller.

3.10 Handling Multiple Resolutions

When it was just the iPhone original, life was simple for game developers. There was but one screen size to deal with if you were publishing in the Apple App Store. Then came the iPads, retina displays, and iPhone 5. Each provides a new challenge in designing the game environment to best display on the resulting resolutions. If you add Android devices to the list you'd be forgiven to thinking there are an unmanageable amount of differing screen sizes to deal with. However, the majority of devices fall into four groups of aspect ratio; 4:3, 3:2, 16:10, 16:9.

3.10.1 Aspect Ratios

The aspect ratio of a screen is the ratio of the longest side to the shortest side and can be determined by the pixel width and height. For example, the original iPhone on the longest side was 480 pixels and 320 on the shortest. This equates to an aspect ratio of 3:2, which is 480 divided by 320 or 1.5. Ratios are written in the format 3:2 as it helps visualize the screen space. In this case *3 is to 2*, as it is said, tells us that the screen is three units long and two units wide. If the screen were divided into equal sized squares such that exactly three of these squares could fit side-by-side within the length, then two of these same squares would fit along the width. To calculate a ratio from the pixel dimensions you need to make a fraction of the longest side divided by the shortest side and then reduce the fraction to its lowest terms. To do this you first need to find the greatest common divisor for both values and then divide the values by it. For example, the greatest common divisor for 480 and 320 is 160; 480 divided by 160 is 3 and 320 divided by 160 is 2. Hence the aspect ratio is 3:2.

If you are not targeting a single device then you need to create a game environment design that fits best with all aspect ratios. This might sound like an impossible task, however by analyzing the situation and what this might mean to your game it's actually easy to cater for a variety of resolutions. This is of course assuming you can live with the fact that your game is just going to look slightly different on different mobile phones.

FIG 3.55 Aligning three popular screen resolutions to see the overlapping space.

If you lay the different resolutions over the top of each other as shown in Figure 3.55 then you can easily see the common screen area. The ratio 4:3 shares screen space with both 3:2 and 16:9. In this case you need to put the playable area of your game into the space of 4:3.

However, this does not mean that you design only for 4:3 as on wider ratios the background color will show through. This is because Unity is a 3D engine and we are faking 2D using an orthographic camera as shown in Figure 3.56 (a). When the ratio changes, it's just the camera's near plane size that widens or shortens. As can be seen in Figure 3.56 (b), when the camera is widened from a 4:3 design to a 16:9 ratio the camera can see the side of the background image plane and the camera's color setting can be seen. If you wanted your game to function like this it would be desirable to have the camera's background set to black instead of Unity blue. This is always the case in Unity whether or not you're working in landscape or portrait mode.

Because Unity's environment is 3D and it's only the camera's opening that is being widened, the actual environment does not get stretched or squashed with ratio changes. If it did, the result from a 16:9 design to a 4:3 design would be that shown in Figure 3.56 (c). This may not happen in 3D, but if you built an entire game using the Unity GUI and based the sizes of the elements on proportions of screen height and width, you would get a disastrous result.

As the shorter aspect is always stretched to fill the camera view in landscape mode, you can be assured that the game environment will not get cut off at the top and bottom. Only the sides will be affected. In Figure 3.56 (d), (e), and (f) you can see how more of the background is revealed as the ratio increases. This extra space can be used for more background detail, but never for game play elements.

Because the positioning of objects in the 3D world do not move or resize with ratio changes a GUI made using the method of the drawcall button menu

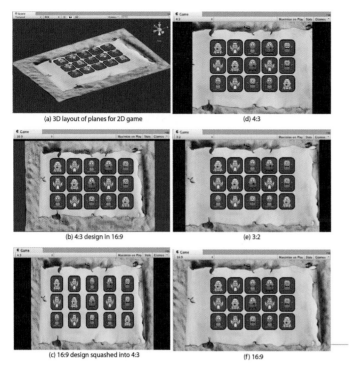

(a) 3D layout of planes for 2D game

(d) 4:3

(b) 4:3 design in 16:9

(e) 3:2

(c) 16:9 design squashed into 4:3

(f) 16:9

FIG 3.56 The result of changing aspect ratios on game display.

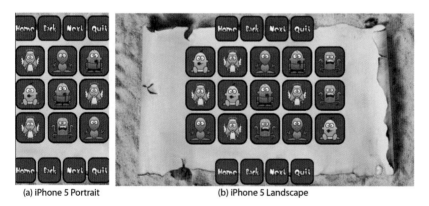

(a) iPhone 5 Portrait

(b) iPhone 5 Landscape

FIG 3.57 Menus created with 2D planes in the 3D environment placed at the top and bottom of the view stay fixed.

used in the previous hands-on session in Section 3.9 is ideal. However, as it's the sides of the camera view that are cut with resolution changes, you should restrict GUI elements on the left or right. This side cutting also occurs when orientation changes as shown in Figure 3.57. In order to keep any left or right menus clamped to the side of the camera, view code is required to dynamically move them with the changing orientations. This is the topic of the next hands-on session.

⊙ Unity Hands-On
Right- and Left-Side Menu Clamping

Step 1: Download and unzip the Unity project *MenuClamp.zip* and open the *mainscene*. In the Scene there is a background image and a plane with a dummy menu image on it. Open the *mainscene* in the project. When you press play, the GUI elements discussed in a previous hands-on will display on the screen. The project is in iOS mode. If you don't have iOS, then switch it to Android. You can also play with the menu clamping just in the normal PC/desktop version inside the editor.

Step 2: Change the Game view's aspect to something that is taller than it is wide. You'll notice the menu plane disappears and you are left with part of the background image. Remember it won't resize but you'll always be able to see the full height of it if it is originally a perfect fit with the camera's field of view.

Step 3: Create a new C# script called *clampMenu* and add the following:

```
using UnityEngine;
using System.Collections;

public class clampMenu : MonoBehaviour
{
    public enum clampmode {left , right }
    public clampmode clampSide;

    Vector3 p;

    void Start ()
    {
        Rect r = Camera.main.pixelRect;

        if(clampSide == clampmode.left)
            p = Camera.main.ScreenToWorldPoint( new Vector3(r.
            xMin, 0, this.transform.position.y));
        else if(clampSide == clampmode.right)
            p = Camera.main.ScreenToWorldPoint(new Vector3
            (r.xMax, 0, this.transform.position.y));

            this.transform.position = new Vector3 (p.x,
            this.transform.position.y, this.transform.
            position.z);
    }
}
```

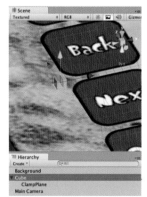

FIG 3.58 Adding a Cube to Anchor the Menu Plane onto.

188

Save the script.

In the Scene create a Cube. Position it to the left of the menu plane and child the ClampPlane object to the Cube in the Hierarchy by dragging ClampPlane and dropping it onto the Cube as shown in Figure 3.58. The Cube will act as the anchor for aligning the menu to the left side of the camera view. If you want to anchor to the right, place the Cube on the right side of the menu plane. Remove all of the Cube's components except the transform from the Inspector.

Step 4: Attach the clampMenu script to the Cube. With the Cube selected in the Hierarchy locate the script in the Inspector. Notice you can set the clamp side to left or right. The preceding code creates this dropdown box with *left* and *right* in it using the enumerators from the line of code with `enum clampMode`.

More Information: Enumerators

Enumerators are a data type consisting of integer values that are referred to by name. You can create an enumerated list for all sorts of uses. For more information about enumerators in C# see http://msdn. microsoft.com/en-us/library/sbbt4032(v=vs.80).aspx.

Step 5: To turn this into a right clamped menu you would need to position the little cube on the other side of the plane and change the *clampMode* to `right`.

The value `Camera.main.pixelRect` holds the size of the near plane in screen pixel coordinates. By using the `xMin` and `xMax` values of this, we are determining the edges of the camera's left and right extents. This point in screen space is then converted to a location in world space as the same distance from the camera as the menu plane. The menu plane is then repositioned to that point thus putting it at the edge of the field of view as shown in Figure 3.59.

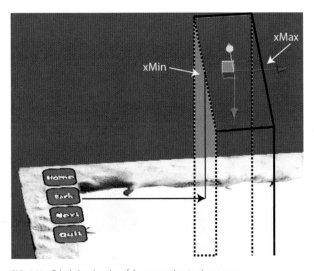

FIG 3.59 Calculating the edge of the camera view to place a menu.

3.10.2 Resolution and the Graphical User Interface

Unlike the 3D environment, the GUI resides is a different coordinate system and is dramatically affected by screen resolution. Figure 3.60 shows the GUI created in the previous hands-on exercise as it would appear (a) on the original iPhone and (b) on the iPhone 5. Although the screens of both devices are physically similar in size, the higher resolution means that the 50×50 buttons in the corners are half the size on the iPhone 5, making the same GUI interface under different resolutions impractical.

One solution is to draw different sized buttons scaled in proportion with the resolutions. This can make for quite messy code as you will have a lot of if statements in the OnGUI function in the form:

```
if( the resolution is iPhone original)
        draw this button
else if (the resolution is iPhone 4)
        draw this button
else if (the resolution is the iPhone 5)
        draw this button
else if (the resolution is the iPad retina)
        draw this button
else if (the resolution is the Samsung Galaxy 3)
        draw this button
else if ...
```

As you can imagine, this is quite impractical but can work if you are targeting limited devices. A more dynamic approach, however, is to scale the entire GUI relative to the screen size for which it was designed. It's possible to do this in Unity by rescaling the GUI matrix. This matrix is the transform component of the screen holding information on the scale, rotation, and position of the screen space. It can't be accessed in the Inspector but can be manipulated by code as shown in Listing 3.3.

(a) iPhone Original (3:2, 480 x 320)   (b) iPhone 5 (16:9, 1136 x 640)

FIG 3.60 GUI button size differences between the original iPhone and iPhone 5.

Listing 3.3 Manipulating the GUI.matrix to resize GUI objects[2]

```
void OnGUI()
{
    //work out scale for screen matrix based
    //on original design resolution
    Vector3 guiScale;
    guiScale.x = Screen.width/(float) designWidth;
    guiScale.y = Screen.height/(float) designHeight;
    guiScale.z = 1.0f;

    //save the current gui matrix
    Matrix4x4 saveCurrentMatrix = GUI.matrix;

    //create new scaled one
    GUI.matrix = Matrix4x4.TRS(Vector3.zero,
    Quaternion.identity, guiScale);

    //draw items to be affected by scale
    GUI.Label( new Rect(10,10,100,30),
    "Hello World", myGUIStyle);

    //reset to original for drawing other things
    GUI.matrix = saveCurrentMatrix;
}
```

The only unfortunate side-effect to scaling the GUI matrix in this way is that if the aspect ratio changes then the items will be stretched and squashed accordingly. For example, a button designed for 4:3 will become long and stretched in 16:9.

Therefore, while these types of solutions will work, there is no perfect answer for dealing with screen resolution changes. However, working with 3D buttons and planes in the world environment will cause far less headaches in the future. The added bonus of creating your own GUI in the 3D world is that you also reduce the number of drawcalls.

As a final word on changing resolutions, if you are working with 3D objects and want to take advantage of the extra screen space provided in longer aspect ratios, a solution is to move the camera closer to the objects in the scene to fill the view volume. Inspiration for the code in Listing 3.4 was taken from original code provided by the author's former student Jackson Hall. The code determines the screen resolution and then sets the *y* position of

---

[2] Code modified from the original in the Unity forums at http://answers.unity3d.com/ques tions/150736/script-gui-units.html.

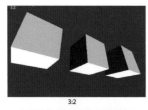

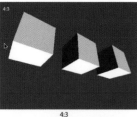

3:2

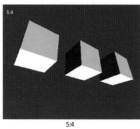

4:3

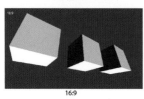

16:9

5:4

FIG 3.61 Camera position changing to fit in 3D objects based on aspect ratio.

the camera thus zooming in or out to fit the scene in the view as shown in Figure 3.61. In this example, it is assumed the camera is in perspective mode and positioned to look straight down the *y* axis. To determine the *y* heights for each ratio initially the camera is manipulated manually and the height recorded. If you want to do this with an orthogonal camera, change the camera's size value rather than its position.

Listing 3.4 Using screen resolution to control camera.

```
using UnityEngine;
using System.Collections;

public class testScreenRes : MonoBehaviour
{
    string currentScreenRes = "";
    string lastScreenRes = "";

    //print screen resolution
    void OnGUI()
    {
        ScreenRatio(Screen.width, Screen.height);
        GUI.Label( new Rect(10,10,100,30),
        currentScreenRes);
    }

    //calculate the scree ratio
    void ScreenRatio (int n1, int n2)
    {
        currentScreenRes = (((float) n1/gcd((float) n1,
        (float) n2)) + ":" +
        (n2/gcd((float) n1,
        (float) n2)));
    }

    //calculate the greatest common denominator
    float gcd(float a, float b)
    {
        float tmp;
        //Swap the numbers so a > = b
        if(a < b)
        {
            tmp = a;
            a = b;
            b = tmp;
        }
        //Find the gcd
        while(b ! = 0)
        {
```

```
            tmp = a % b;
            a = b;
            b = tmp;
        }
        return a;
}

void Update()
{
        //if the screen resolution changes reposition the
        //camera in the y position to fit scene in
        if(  currentScreenRes ! = lastScreenRes )
        {
            Vector3 pos = Camera.main.transform.position;
            if(currentScreenRes == "16:9")
                pos.Set(pos.x, 30.2f, pos.z);
            if(currentScreenRes == "4:3")
                pos.Set(pos.x, 31.2f, pos.z);
            if(currentScreenRes == "5:4")
                pos.Set(pos.x, 31.5f, pos.z);
            if(currentScreenRes == "3:2")
                pos.Set(pos.x, 30.7f, pos.z);

            Camera.main.transform.position = pos;
            lastScreenRes = currentScreenRes;
        }
    }
}
```

3.11 Summary

Interface design is a critical factor in the success of your mobile game. It determines how attractive the game appears as well as making it usable. Often interface design is left to the final stages of the project, but it really should be integrated as an essential design element from the outset. The theme of the GUI must emulate the theme of the game. The controls in the GUI must effectively assist the player in their quest to enter and conquer the world you have created for them. The type of experience you want for your player will impact on your design. If it's a rich immersive 3D world such as *The Room*, you'll want a more diegetic design that draws the player in and supports their suspension of disbelief. If it's a game environment in which the player is obviously looking into another world in a god-like way to control proceedings, such as with *Mini Motor Racer*, then a non-diegetic interface may be more appropriate.

However it appears, the interface is the games communication channel with the player. It must be able to convey to the player what they are currently doing and what they must do next. Without the interface your game becomes a window into a non-interactive fantasy world.

CHAPTER 4

Aesthetics and Visual Literacy

One might argue that the essence of much of art is in forcing us to see things as they really are rather than as we assume them to be.

Raph Koster

4.1 Introduction

In a study conducted by the University of Wales,[1] researchers found that the most important features of computer games for players were, in descending order, playability, graphics, online gaming, the interface, and sound. While a great deal of effort is spent on the programming, in a mobile game this is all for nothing if the game doesn't engage with the player. The majority of very successful mobile games have vibrant graphics, brilliant sounds, and awesome animations that grab the player's attention.

---

[1] Source: www.glyndwr.ac.uk/cunninghams/research/game_audio.pdf.

In this chapter we will look at a variety of visual aesthetics and how they can be used in mobile games as well as the optimization techniques you can employ to get as much visual impact out of the device hardware as possible.

4.2 Third-Party Assets

If you are more inclined towards the programming of games rather than the art creation you'll be pleased to know there is a plethora of third-party resources available to you. Some of these have been discussed in previous chapters.

Using game assets created by others can be a very cost-effective solution. Before buying, however, consider how much of your own time it would take to create the asset and what your time is worth. Then you can make a rational judgment as to the suitability of the resource.

One of the downfalls to purchasing assets from others is that each artist has their own style. In the same way as you can judge a Monet from a Picasso, the same is true of any creative medium. Trying to create a game with visual assets from multiple artists may leave you with a mish-mash of incompatible styles, making your game appear incoherent and aesthetically displeasing. Therefore, try to get as many of the visual assets as possible from the same artist. To assist the process, make a list of the assets you require in groups. For example, graphical user interface, environment, characters, etc. Then try and source these groups from the same artist.

There are numerous online websites from which you can obtain free and inexpensive models for use in your own games. Do make sure you check the licensing on the models before you put them into commercial games.

● Note

Unity's native 3D model format is FBX. These can be created with Autodesk's Maya or 3D Studio Max. The open source modeling software Blender will also create FBX files. To add a model to your Project simply drag and drop it into the Project along with any associated textures. If you place the model and its texture into a folder and drop the entire folder into Unity, the textures are *usually* automatically assigned to the model.

Unity also provides its own Asset Store. It contains purpose-built models and code resources especially created for Unity. The Asset Store is accessed within Unity by selecting Window > Asset Store from the main menu.

⊕ Unity Hands-On

Adding External Models into Unity

Step 1: Create an account on TurboSquid by visiting http://turbosquid. com and follow the prompts.

Step 2: Search on TurboSquid for "frog." When the results appear, arrange the order by price to find the free ones. Unity can import 3D models in the format OBJ, 3DS, or FBX.

Step 3: Create a new Unity project. Drag and drop the models into the Project. Once they have been imported you can drag them from the Project into the Hierarchy. They will then appear in the Scene. Issues you will encounter when using free models from multiple artists are that they won't be scaled to the same size, may not be textured, and might not work at all. Some models may also come with a ground plane.

For the purpose of this exercise, four free models that appeared when "frog" was searched for were imported into Unity. Two of the models didn't work. Sometimes if you can see a model it could be very, very small or very, very large. So before dismissing it, try rescaling. Another model came with textures and a ground plane. The last model didn't have any textures. These are shown in Figure 4.1.

FIG 4.1 Models imported into Unity.

In the case of the frog model shown in Figure 4.1, it has a ground plane attached. If you do not want this plane, simply delete it from the Hierarchy and this will remove it from the scene.

4.3 The Anatomy of a 3D Polygon

In a 3D game environment, all objects are made from polygons. We've already used several models composed of many polygons. A polygon (or *poly* as it is affectionately known in games) is a flat surface in 3D space. It is usually represented by three or four vertices as shown in Figure 4.2.

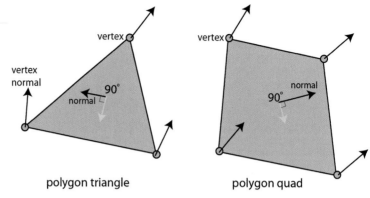

vertex

vertex

vertex
normal

normal

90°

90°

normal

polygon triangle

normal

polygon quad

FIG 4.2 Polygons.

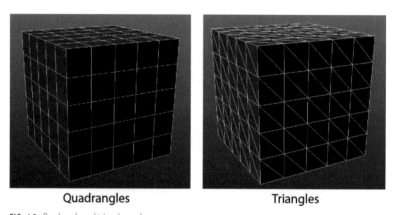

Quadrangles

Triangles

FIG 4.3 Quadrangle and triangle meshes.

A 3D model is more efficiently stored as a set of triangular polygons than quads as each face has one less vertex. However quadrangle poly models tend to keep their shape better when dynamically modified. As most models tend to keep their original shape in a game environment, triangles are most popular. Cubes made from (a) quadrangles and (b) triangles are shown in Figure 4.3.

Every polygon has a face normal and a set of vertex normals. The face normal is projected at 90 degrees to the surface of the plane. Vertex normals project out at 90 degrees to each of the edges that meet at the vertex to which it belongs. In 3D space, a polygon has one visible side. Because the polygon is flat, it's not possible to see it from both sides at the same time. The face normal represents the side on which textures are placed. As only one side of the polygon is visible, it makes no sense processing-wise to have a texture on a side that is never seen. In addition, the side with the normal is the side that lighting effects are calculated on. In fact, when viewed from the side without the normal, the polygon appears as if it is not there. Figure 4.4 (a) shows a

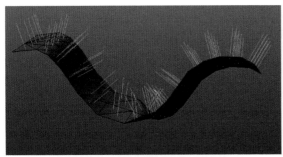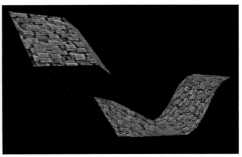

(a) Polygon Strip in Maya displaying
Face Normals in green

(b) Same Polygon Strip displayed
in Unity with a Texture

FIG 4.4 Normal and textured faces.

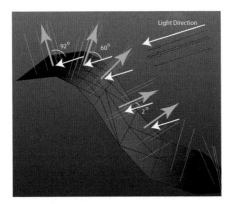

FIG 4.5 The angle between a light source and face normals
affects poly illumination.

twisted strip created in Maya with the face normals displayed in green. The same model when placed in Unity only has texture applied to the side with normals, as in Figure 4.4 (b). Where the back face of the polygon is facing the camera, the polygon appears as though it's not there.

Besides indicating the visible side of a poly, the normals also determine how the polygon is shaded. The angle of the incoming light source is compared against the surface normal. When the angle between the normal and the light source is 0 degrees then the poly is fully lit. When the angle is greater than 90 degrees, the light is on the other side of the poly and therefore not illuminating it. This principle is illustrated in Figure 4.5.

Using just one face normal is the cheapest way to store the direction of a poly, however it does not necessarily produce the best illumination and shading. Figure 4.6 (a) demonstrates a sphere shaded by using just the face normal. This makes each face a constant color across its surface and is hence called

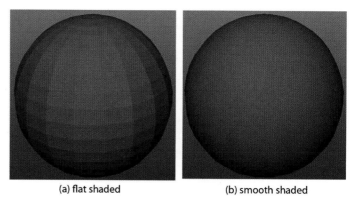

<table>
<tr><td>(a) flat shaded</td><td>(b) smooth shaded</td></tr>
</table>

FIG 4.6 Flat and smooth shading applied to the same sphere.

flat shading as the actual nature of the poly is revealed. However, by using an average of the vertex normals and face normal across the poly at multiple points a smoother result can be achieved as shown in Figure 4.6 (b). Note each sphere in the illustration is exactly the same with the respect to the number of polygons.

Having an understanding of the difference polygon faces and normals makes is essential for understanding how textures and shaders affect the surface rendering. By dynamically manipulating the normals across the surface a large variety of effects can be achieved from rough bumpy surfaces to water.

4.4 Textures and Shaders

The word texture refers to the tactile surface characteristic and appearance of an object. Of course in games we don't (yet) have the ability to touch objects, but the textures used give the virtual objects visual substance, believability, and distinction. As with the metaphors used with graphical interfaces, the textures applied to virtual objects communicate non-verbal messages about themselves to the player. Besides the way a surface might feel to touch, the texture can relay information about weight, composition, temperature, age, and purpose. For example, a sword would be textured with a grey image indicating steel or a similar material as shown in Figure 4.7 (a). If this image were to have red, orange and yellow applied it would make the sword appear as though it was hot (see Figure 4.7 (b)).

On top of the use of a texture for applying color and tactility to a virtual object, a *shader* is applied. A shader dictates how the texture will be treated before it is rendered. You could imagine the paint you put on timber furniture as the texture and then the varnish placed over the top as the shader. This is a very simple analogy of course. Unlike a texture, which is an image, a shader is a computer program. It is run on the pixels of the texture in association

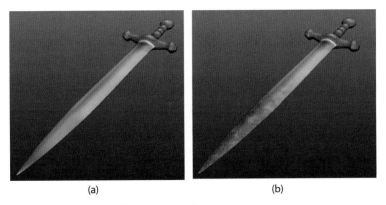

(a)   (b)

FIG 4.7 A sword treated with different textures for different states.

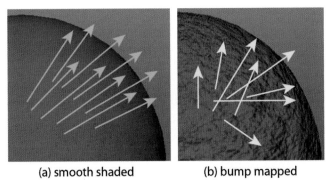

(a) smooth shaded   (b) bump mapped

FIG 4.8 (a) Normals averaged for smooth shading, (b) averages manipulated for bump mapping.

with information about the shape of the object that it is on and the lighting conditions. It can use multiple textures to create stunning visual effects and give virtual objects details that make them seem much more tangible.

As the number of polygons in a 3D scene places an ever-increasing strain on the CPU and GPU, textures and shaders can be used in the place of actual modeled detail to fake depth and extra surface detail that's not really there. The most common form of this is the bump map.

Jim Blinn introduced the technique of bump mapping in 1978. It is a technique by which the perceived height of a surface is modified by manipulating the normals and affecting the light calculations for a poly. Instead of showing the true shading for a flat surface as defined by the angle between the normals and the light source, the normals are manipulated to give the flat surface light and dark areas thus making it appear bumpy. It's not unlike the averaging of normals across the surface to create smooth shading; however, instead of averaging, the normals take on more erratic positions as shown in Figure 4.8.

Since its introduction, the term "bump mapping" has been replaced in the games domain with the term "normal mapping." Bump mapping itself has taken on the more literal meaning for defining surface tactility with normal maps manipulating the surface not only for surface quality but also for lighting purposes. The normal map can make a flat surface look curved by manipulating the way light is rendered on the surface. It also defines bumps and ridges on the surface, but nowadays the real texture in height displacement is integrated into bump maps and another type of map called a *displacement map*. Whereas the bump map just makes a model look bumpy, a displacement map actually changes the position of vertices to physically make the model bumpy.

There are a plethora of map types that can be applied to the surface of a polygon for differing effects. Some of the more popular ones used in games are shown in Figure 4.9. The diffuse map is the actual texture or color that you want to apply to the surface. Bump maps and normal maps we have already discussed.

In Figure 4.10 you will notice how the normal map takes on a light blue color. This is because each pixel of the normal map maps to a pixel on

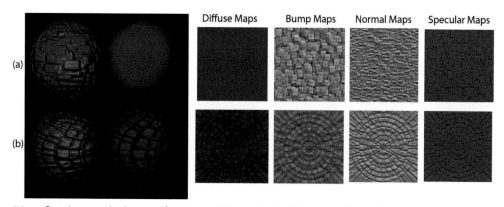

FIG 4.9 Two spheres treated with a variety of texture maps; (a) has a color as the diffuse map and (b) uses an image.

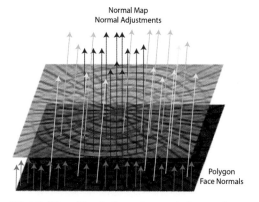

FIG 4.10 Values of the color blue used as normal adjustments for polygon face normals.

the diffuse map and the pixel value represents a normal at that pixel location. If we consider the diffuse map to exist in the XY plane, any normal would be perpendicular (or close) to this and thus take the form of the vector (0,0,1). As red, green, and blue (RGB) is represented in a vector by values (R,G,B) where (0,0,1) indicates no red, no green and all blue, any RGB value with a larger *z* value than red and green will appear bluish.

4.4.1 Shaders and Textures in Unity

As previously discussed, shaders are programs that work on textures to produce rendered effects. Unity provides numerous shaders. These shaders are applied to textures on materials. Shaders can be set on a material in Unity by selecting the material in the Project and viewing its properties in the Inspector, as shown in Figure 4.11.

FIG 4.11 Accessing and setting the shaders in Unity.

Depending on the chosen shader, you'll get the opportunity to add different textures. For example, the plain *Diffuse* shader requires just one texture. This texture is then placed onto the model to which the material belongs. The *Bumped Diffuse* texture introduces a normal map and the *Bumped Specular* allows for a normal map and the ability to add shininess. You can play around with these at will to get the effect you would like.

More Information: Shaders

For a comprehensive list of the built-in Unity shaders visit http://docs. unity3d.com/Documentation/Components/Built-inShaderGuide.html.

The shaders of most interest to 2D mobile game developers in Unity are the *Unlit/Transparent* and the *Unlit/Texture*. These are required in making 2D elements in Unity appear clear, bright, and—when required—transparent. If you are using a PNG file with transparent areas then you must set the shader to Unlit/Transparent if you want to take advantage of the transparent areas of the image. The "unlit" part ensures any surface you add the material to is not affected by the scene lighting.

4.4.2 Texels

Often beginners are disappointed by the lack of clarity in their images when viewed on the mobile device or even in the Unity Editor. Their instinct is to

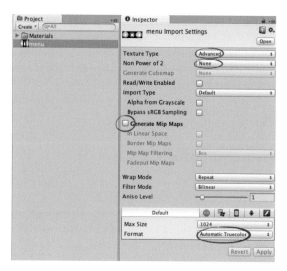

FIG 4.12 Setting an image for highest clarity.

make the original image bigger. However, this is not necessarily the solution, as there are a number of factors influencing texture quality.

In Chapter 3 we discussed how to make an image on a plane crisp and clear for use as a menu button through the texture settings in Unity (again shown in Figure 4.12). These settings touch on several issues relating to images that will now be further elucidated. Setting the texture type to Advanced allows access to a number of crucial settings. The first is the *Non Power of 2*.

Computer processors work with binary code at their core. Values are represented by 1s and 0s. A single 1 or 0 is the smallest amount of computer memory and it is referred to as a *bit*. Putting two bits together gives you four value possibilities; 00, 01, 10, 11. Three bits can store eight values: 000, 001, 011, 010, 100, 101, 111, 110. To calculate the number of values that can be stored based on the number of bits the formulae is a power of 2; $2^{number\ of\ bits}$. In eight bits, which is also called a byte, 2^8 256 values can be stored. Each processing cycle the CPU and GPU push through data in groups of bytes. Making sure your data is in full groups of bytes optimizes it for the processor. The following analogy is taken from *Holistic Game Development with Unity*.

> Imagine it as though you have a dishwasher that can hold four plates. You need to wash nine plates. You would do two full cycles and then have only one plate in the third cycle. For the same amount of dishwashing you could have invited another three guests to dinner.

And it's the same for texture processing. You want a texture to be the size of a power of 2 to make it more efficient. This means images whose height and width are power of 2 in pixel resolution. For example, 256 × 256, 64 × 1,024, 16 × 16 or 32 × 256. Note, the image does not need to be square. If your image is not a power of 2, Unity will attempt to compress it automatically for you. This can make the image blurry. If you must have an image that is not a power of 2 you need to set the non-power of 2 value for the texture to *None*.

The next setting of importance for image clarity is the *Generate Mipmaps* tick box. *Mipmaps* are a set of lower resolutions images generated by a game engine to accompany the original image. They are smaller in size and clarity and used on the surface of models when the player is further away from the object. Thus they give objects a blurrier surface the further away the camera is from them. This simulates human visual acuity in real-world perspective. If your image is being used in a 2D game or for a menu you do not need *mipmaps* generated and may as well turn this setting off.

While we are discussing the texture settings another to take note of is the Wrap Mode. This can be set to repeat or clamp. By default it is set to repeat. This allows you to seamlessly tile textures across the surface of a polygon. The unfortunate side-effect, if you have a partially transparent image on a plane that is not tiled, is a strip of extra pixels from the bottom of the image, this is the image starting to repeat again. To remove this line of pixels if they appear in your transparent textures, set the Wrap Mode to clamp. That will force them to the entire extent of the plane they are on.

Now we've come this far and haven't even addressed the subsection title; *texels*. A *texel* is a rendered pixel. It represents the pixel of an image after it has been projected from the 3D environment onto the screen as shown in Figure 4.14. The amount of texels taken up by an image is the maximum size you need to consider when making a texture. In the given example, the

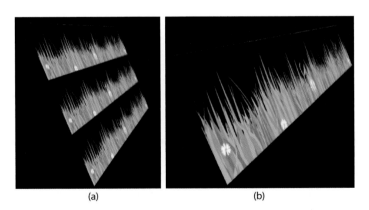

(a) (b)

FIG 4.13 Tiling and not tiling the same image on a single plane: (a) between the images the extra line of pixels is not evident until the very top, (b) the same extra line of pixels at the top of a single use of the texture.

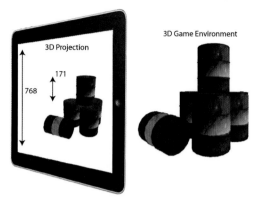

FIG 4.14 A pile of barrels in a 3D environment rendered on a mobile screen.

barrels, when rendered, are only 171 texels in height. This means that if you use a texture on the barrels that is any larger than 171 pixels, it is an inefficient image size. If you were to use a barrel texture that was only 50 pixels in height, then by the time it was rendered it would have been stretched over three times. This will create a blurry rendered image.

This goes for all images in your game environment. Do not make them any bigger than they will be on the screen as they will become distorted. If you are creating a button menu from a 2D plane and image where the buttons are to display at 64 × 64 then you want to create the image of them at 64 × 64. It's not possible to know in all circumstance how textures will be viewed by the player in a 3D space especially if the player is free to move around at leisure, but you can know that if your game is only going to run on screens with a resolution of 1,024 × 768 then no texture in your game environment needs to be any bigger.

4.5 Investigating Graphics Processing

When it comes to creating a mobile game it is essential to consider the amount of processing the device will have to do to get your game onto the screen. Each polygon and texture in the environment adds extra strain on the processor as it needs to be processed by the CPU and/or GPU. With each game loop, the visual element of the game needs to be calculated and pushed to the screen. This act is called a *drawcall*.

In the case of Unity, every material used in a scene equals one drawcall. If you have 100 materials to render it will cost 100 drawcalls. But why should you care? Drawcalls affect frame rates. The frame rate of a game refers to the number of times the screen is updated in a second. This relates back to the motion picture and animation industries that rely on the number of frames they can project onto a screen in a second to fool the human brain

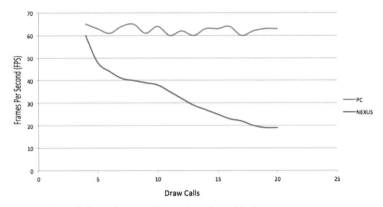

FIG 4.15 Drawcall effect on frame rate: PC versus Nexus One mobile phone.

into seeing smooth motion. When the frame rate falls below 15 frames a second, an animation begins to look jittery. The target frame rate for your games should therefore be around 20 if you don't want to affect the player's performance.

The way in which the drawcalls affect processing depends on the hardware running the game. As you would expect, a desktop machine will be able to handle more drawcalls than a mobile phone. To illustrate the effects, the graph in Figure 4.15 shows how frame rate is affected as the drawcalls increase on a PC versus a Google Nexus One.

The biggest pitfall when developing mobile games is to build and test them in the IDE and emulator on the desktop machine without pushing out to the mobile on a regular basis. A developer who does not test the current build on a mobile will quickly be led into a false sense of security about how fast their game will run and then be bitterly disappointed when it runs at a snail's pace on the actual device.

◉ Unity Hands-On

Drawcalls

Step 1: Create a new Project in Unity.

Step 2: Add two planes to the Scene.

Step 3: Position the camera so the planes are visible in the Game.

Step 4: Click the Stats button in the top right of the Game tab. Notice the number of drawcalls is currently one.

Step 5: Create two new materials in the Project called Material 1 and Material 2. You don't need to give them any particular settings.

Step 6: Add Material 1 to one plane and Material 2 to the other. Now look at the number of drawcalls. It will be two, the same as the number of materials.

Step 7: Right-click on one of the planes in the Hierarchy and select Duplicate. The number of drawcalls will remain at two as there are still only two materials being used.

Step 8: Create another material and add it to the latest plane. The number of drawcalls will increase to three.

As the number of drawcalls increases, the slower your game will run. It would require a great number of drawcalls to make any noticeable difference on a high performance gaming machine. However, if you port your application to a mobile device, a dramatic effect on performance is seen after around 15 drawcalls.

Materials aren't the only things that will increase the number of drawcalls. As the polycounts of the meshes in the game environment increase, so too will the drawcalls. However, polycounts don't have a one-to-one relationship with performance. Therefore, it is essential to consider the way in which materials are handled.

4.6 Sprites

Sprites would have to be the very first form of moving graphics used in games. The concepts are as old as games and computer graphics. A sprite is simply a moveable 2D image. While it is a given that 2D images be used in 2D game environments, they can also be used in 3D environments for special effects and faking high-quality background objects. In fact, because of the processing limitations on mobile devices, knowing how to implement sprites will greatly enhance the look and feel of your game.

4.6.1 Billboards

A billboard is another name for a 2D plane with an image on it. In games they are used to fake 3D objects that are in the distance or never move—such that you cannot tell they are just a flat image with no depth—or in close-up situations where a lot of a single object is required to give a certain illusion such as grass. In Figure 4.16 a student mobile tower game is shown in which the original central character, Bob, was a 3D model. Bob had so many polygons that the model was affecting the game's performance. In the end the students replaced Bob with a billboard containing a 2D image of Bob. As Bob didn't need to move with respect to the player's view, they would be none the wiser that Bob was, in fact, flat!

Billboards when used en masse can create the illusion of millions of single objects, such as blades of grass and clouds as shown in Figure 4.17. If each billboard is made from the same image and material, you can place hundreds of them in a scene without affecting the number of drawcalls.

The only issue when using 2D objects to fake 3D in a 3D environment occurs when the player wants to move around them. As shown in Figure 4.17 (b)

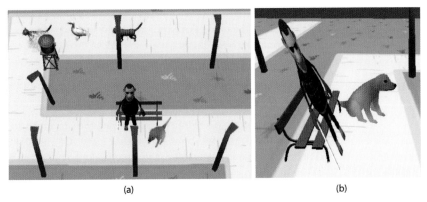

(a) (b)

FIG **4.16** A billboard being used to fake a 3D object: (a) the player's view of the game, (b) the plane with the 2D image on it.

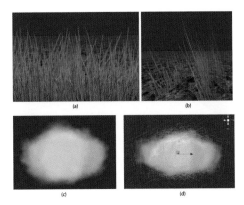

FIG **4.17** Grass and clouds created from billboards: (a) grass billboards viewed from the front, (b) side view of grass billboards, (c) a cloud, (d) the individual billboards of a cloud.

billboard grass loses its effect when viewed from the side. But there is a way to fix this problem; have the grass always face the player's camera. That way the side of the billboard with the image on it is always parallel to the screen. This method is often used with grass, distant trees, and other scenery. In fact, in Unity, when grass is painted onto a terrain (using the terrain editor) as you walk around the terrain you will notice the grass is programmed to always face the camera, giving the illusion of 3D grass.

⊙ Unity Hands-On
Camera-Orientated Billboards
Step 1: Create a new Unity Project and import the packages for Character Controller and Terrain Assets.
Step 2: Add a plane and directional light to the scene. Resize the plane to be quite large. This will act as the ground. From the Standard Assets >

Character Controller folder in the Project, drag and drop a First-Person Controller into the scene. Position it above the ground plane. As the First-Person Controller has a camera, you can remove the existing one from the root of the Hierarchy.

At this stage you can press play and walk the character around on the plane using the mouse and WASD keys.

Step 3: Add another plane into the scene. Find the Grass texture in the Project in Standard Assets > Terrain Assets > Terrain Grass and drag it onto this new plane in the scene. The material on the plane will default to *diffuse* as shown in Figure 4.18 (a). Set the shader to Unlit/Transparent to make the grass look as it does in Figure 4.18 (b).

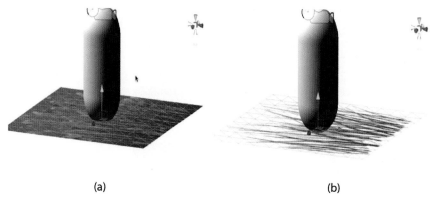

(a)   (b)

FIG 4.18 A grass texture placed on a plane with (a) a diffuse shader and (b) an unlit transparent shader

Step 4: Next we want to add a script onto the plane to make it always face the player's camera. If you remember back to the LookAt function used previously you will remember that it orientates the z axis of an object to point at something else. Examine the grass plane. Notice it's the y axis that points perpendicular from the plane and not the z. If we performed a LookAt on this plane, it would not sit upright and face the player. It would remain lying down.

There are two ways to fix this. First you could program a LookAt and then multiply this with another axis rotation to get the plane to sit correctly or you could simply add a parent object for the plane that does have its z axis aligned correctly. We will perform the latter here, as you'll find it extremely useful for moving other objects around when their z axis isn't pointing forward.

FIG 4.19 Adding a parent cube to another object to fake its z axis.

Add a cube to the scene. Rotate the grass plane by 90 degrees around the x axis so the grass is sitting upright. This is illustrated in Figure 4.19. In the Hierarchy drag and drop the grass plane onto the cube. This will make the grass a child object of the cube. Whatever transformation happens to the cube will now happen to the grass. Notice when the cube is selected, its z axis faces forward and is perpendicular with the grass plane.

Step 5: Create a C# script called *lookAtPlayer* and add the following code:

```
using UnityEngine;
using System.Collections;

public class lookAtPlayer : MonoBehaviour {

    // Use this for initialization
    void Start () {

    }

    // Update is called once per frame
    void Update ()
    {
        this.transform.LookAt
        (Camera.main.gameObject.transform.position);
    }
}
```

Attach this script to the cube. Play. Move the character controller about and watch how the grass realigns to always face the player. This is how you want it to react.

Step 6: Because you don't want a big grey cube with the grass, at this stage select the cube and in the Inspector remove its Cube (Mesh Filter), Box Collider, and Mesh Renderer. This will make it into an empty game object. You could have started with an empty game object rather than the cube; however, having the cube mesh visible while you are aligning the grass plane is rather useful.

Also remove the Mesh Collider from the grass plane. You won't want the character controller colliding with the grass as it moves through it.

Step 7: Select the cube in the Hierarchy and make duplicates of it by right-clicking and selecting Duplicate. Spread these objects around on the plane to make a field of grass.

Play and walk the first-person controller around to see the effect.

4.7 UV Mapping

Thus far we have been working with whole textures displayed on polygons. But what if you wanted to use just part of a texture on a polygon? You would need a method of cutting out parts of the image and stretching them across the surface of the poly. This in fact is already happening when you apply a texture to an object. Each vertex of the poly is mapped to part of an image using a *UV Map*. The UV Map defines which coordinates of the 2D image are allocated to the 3D vertices of a polygon and the pixels contained within the 2D coordinates are painted onto the poly's surface between the vertices. This process is shown in Figure 4.20.

Each face of the cube has four vertices. These are mapped to four coordinates in the image. The locations 1, 2, 3, and 4 in the image in Figure 4.20 are mapped

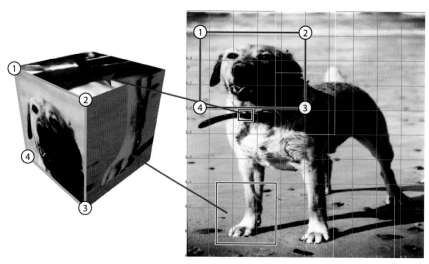

FIG 4.20 UV Mapping.

to the vertices 1, 2, 3, and 4 on the cube's face. The mapping can be scaled such that only a small portion of the image is spread across a surface or even rotated.

In the Unity Editor you have a limited amount of control over the UV points of a texture on an object. In the material settings, you can change the values for Tiling and Offset. Tiling sets the number of times an image repeats across the surface of an object. It can be set to tile vertically up the surface by modifying the *x* value or horizontally with the *y* value. The offset is a value between 0 and 1 that moves the image by a proportion of its own size across the surface. For example, as shown in Figure 4.20 an offset of 0.8 for the Y will move the image down by 80% thus beginning it near the bottom of the surface and having it wrap around again from the top.

Being able to manipulate UVs on a polygon is useful for creating animation and reducing drawcalls. To create an animation, the UVs can be programmed to change with code. Listing 4.1 provides a C# script that, when attached to a plane with an image will scroll the image across the surface. It is set to scroll in the *y* direction, but you can change this with the uvSpeed variable. This effect is useful for faking movement in the 3D world, such as flowing water or conveyor belts.

Listing 4.1 UVScroller.cs

```
using UnityEngine;
using System.Collections;

public class UVScroller : MonoBehaviour {

        public Vector2 uvSpeed = new Vector2(0.0f,
        1.0f);
```

```
Vector2 uvOffset = Vector2.zero;

void LateUpdate()
{
        uvOffset + = ( uvSpeed * Time.deltaTime );
        renderer.materials[0].SetTextureOffset
        ("_MainTex", uvOffset);
        }
        }
```

To use UVs to reduce the drawcalls in a game, the use of a special composite image called a texture atlas is employed.

4.8 Texture Atlases

One way to reduce drawcalls dramatically is to cut the number of materials being used. You can do this by combining the images you want to use into one bigger image. This bigger image is called a texture atlas. An example texture atlas is shown in Figure 4.21 for the iPhone game *Just 4*. In this game, players slide tiles around the screen to make words containing four letters before the screen becomes congested with so many tiles that they are no longer moveable.

Each tile in *Just 4* is a single four vertex plane. *But each tile shares the same material.* This allows the game to run on one drawcall. Assigning UVs to planes can be achieved in Unity using code to readjust the position of the image.

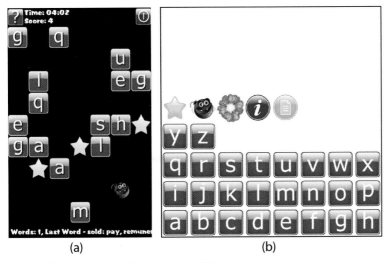

(a)   (b)

FIG 4.21 (a) Screen shot from the iOS game *Just 4* and (b) its texture atlas.

⚙ Unity Hands-On

Texture Atlas

Step 1: Create a new Unity Project. Download and add sprite.fbx and textureAtlas.png from the website. Sprite.fbx is a plane with four vertices. If you are using the latest version of Unity, you'll find a game object called Quad. This is essentially the same thing. Adjust the settings of textureAtlas to improve the image quality.

Step 2: Add the sprite object into the scene. It is a simple plane. Orient the camera to look straight at it. Drag and drop the textureAtlas from the Project onto the sprite. Select the sprite and change the material shader to Unlit/Transparent. As the scene stands you should see a plane with the entire texture atlas spread over the surface as shown in Figure 4.22.

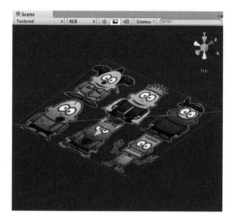

FIG 4.22 A plane with a whole texture atlas displayed.

Step 3: Create a new C# file called *setSprite* and add the following code. It sets the UV values to position the texture on the plane with the values uvs[0], uvs[1], etc. Unity 3 and 4 treat the order of these UVs differently and therefore depending on the version of Unity you are using you'll require the appropriate set of code given here.

Unity 3 code:

```
using UnityEngine;
using System.Collections;

public class setSprite : MonoBehaviour {

public Vector2 startPixel;
public Vector2 endPixel;

void Start () {

    //get object mesh
    Mesh mesh = GetComponent<MeshFilter>().sharedMesh;
```

```
    //get existing uvs
    Vector2[] uvs = new Vector2[4];

    //get existing material
    Texture2D texture =
        (Texture2D) renderer.sharedMaterial.mainTexture;

    //create new uvs from the start and end pixel values
    uvs[0] = new Vector2(startPixel.x/texture.width,
        (texture.height – endPixel.y)/texture.height);

    uvs[1] = new Vector2(startPixel.x/texture.width,
        (texture.height – startPixel.y)/texture.height);

    uvs[2] = new Vector2(endPixel.x/texture.width,
        (texture.height – startPixel.y)/texture.height);

    uvs[3] = new Vector2(endPixel.x/texture.width,
        (texture.height – endPixel.y)/texture.height);

    //reset the mesh uvs
    mesh.uv = uvs;
    }
}
```

Unity 4 code:

```
using UnityEngine;
using System.Collections;

public class setSprite : MonoBehaviour {

public Vector2 startPixel;
public Vector2 endPixel;

void Start () {

    //get object mesh
    Mesh mesh = GetComponent<MeshFilter>().sharedMesh;

    //get existing uvs
    Vector2[] uvs = new Vector2[4];

    //get existing material
    Texture2D texture =
        (Texture2D) renderer.sharedMaterial.mainTexture;

    //create new uvs from the start and end pixel values
    uvs[2] = new Vector2(startPixel.x/texture.width,
        (texture.height – endPixel.y)/texture.height);

    uvs[1] = new Vector2(startPixel.x/texture.width,
        (texture.height – startPixel.y)/texture.height);

    uvs[3] = new Vector2(endPixel.x/texture.width,
        (texture.height – startPixel.y)/texture.height);

    uvs[0] = new Vector2(endPixel.x/texture.width,
        (texture.height – endPixel.y)/texture.height);
```

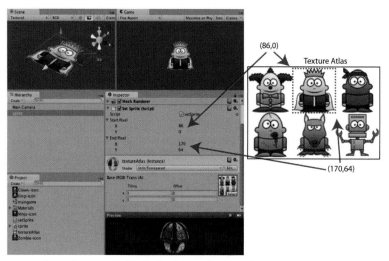

FIG 4.23 Setting the Start and End Pixels of a subsection of a texture atlas.

```
//reset the mesh uvs
mesh.uv = uvs;
    }
}
```

Note: If you are using Unity 4 you'll find a Quad game object available in the Create Object menu. This is a plane with four vertices and works with the above code.

Save and add the script to the sprite.

Step 4: Select the sprite in the Hierarchy and locate the attached code in the Inspector. The script has two exposed variables; Start Pixel and End Pixel. Both are 2D vectors and represent the uppermost-left and bottommost-right pixels of the subsection of the texture atlas that you want to put on the plane. It's just like specifying the part of the larger image that you'd like to cut out and paste onto the sprite surface. This process is illustrated in Figure 4.23.

To make the king appear on the plane, the Start Pixel should be set to (86,0) and the End Pixel set to (170,64). Press play in the editor to see the result. Note that whenever you create sprites using a texture atlas in this manner, until you press play you won't be able to see the final UV mapping result. All planes will just look like they have the entire texture atlas applied.

Step 5: Make a prefab from the sprite game object. Add multiple copies into the scene. Modify each of the Start and End Pixels to have different characters from the texture atlas shown on each plane.

The UV mapping that occurs in the previous hands-on exercise is not the only way to use texture atlases. A much easier way, if you know how, is to do the UV mapping in a 3D modeling package such as Maya.

Video Tutorial

Easy UV Mapping with Maya for Unity,
www.holistic3d.com/?page_id=122.

4.9 Particles

Billboards are also used for creating particle systems. A particle system is the mass creation of animated sprites, each representing single particles whether it is for snow, dust, or water. Although they can look spectacular, particle systems are a processor killer on any platform. Each particle is its own game object and is processed as though it is in the physics system with gravity, velocity, acceleration, and life.

A particle system is much like a water hose. The nozzle represents the particle emitter; this is the location the particles spawn from. As they are created, the particles are given a starting velocity and a life. The velocity dictates the direction and speed the particle starts moving in and life is how long the particle exists for. A particle cannot exist forever or the system would become congested with game objects. Forces such as wind and gravity can be applied for all types of effects from water fountains to tornados.

Particle systems in their purest form are not recommended for use on mobile platforms. The particle generators that come with Unity, while creating spectacular effects, are very processor-heavy and their use should be kept at a minimum. There are ways, of course, to fake a particle system for equally impressive effects. But first we will have a look at the ones that do come with Unity.

☉ Unity Hands-On
Starting a Fire
Both the games *Little Inferno* and *Year Walk* include a touch mechanic whereby a flame appears on the screen beneath the player's finger. We will replicate this here.

Step 1: Create a new Unity Project for iOS or Android and include the Particles package as shown in Figure 4.24.
Step 2: In the Project, locate the small flames particle prefab as shown in Figure 4.25. Drag and drop it into the Hierarchy.

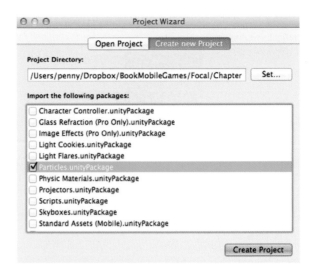

FIG 4.24 Including the particles package at the same time as creating a new project in Unity.

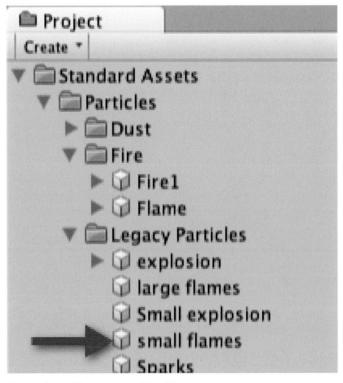

FIG 4.25 The small flames legacy particle prefab.

Step 3: With the small flames object selected in the Hierarchy, locate its Particle Emitter component in the Inspector and change its settings as shown in Figure 4.26.

The majority of the default settings will remain the same. The values for energy specify the minimum and maximum life any particle can have. Energy is set randomly within this range for each new particle. The minimum and maximum emissions relate to the number of particles the emitter is in control of at any one time. The more particles, the smoother the effect, but the more labor-intensive for the processor.

Step 4: Immediately below the Particle Emitter component in the Inspector you will find the Particle Animator component. Untick the Autodestruct tickbox at the bottom. We are going to be turning the emitter on and off with script. If at any point, the emitter runs out of particles, if the autodestruct box is ticked, the whole emitter will be destroyed. We don't want this.

Step 5: Create a new C# script called *createFlame* and add the following code:

```
using UnityEngine;
using System.Collections;

public class createFlame : MonoBehaviour {

    void Start () {
        particleEmitter.emit = false;
```

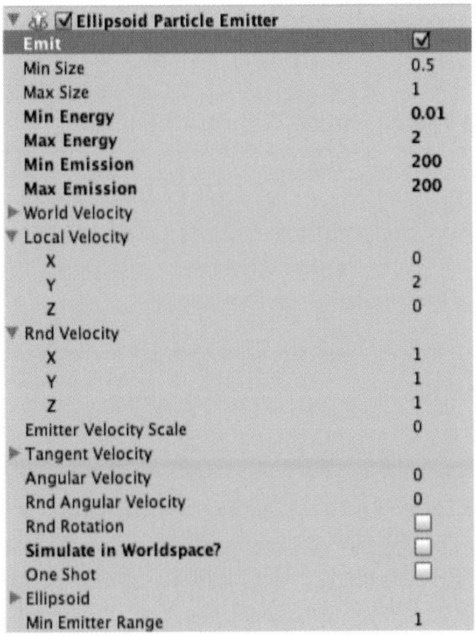

▼ ☑ Ellipsoid Particle Emitter	
Emit	☑
Min Size	0.5
Max Size	1
Min Energy	0.01
Max Energy	2
Min Emission	200
Max Emission	200
▶ World Velocity	
▼ Local Velocity	
X	0
Y	2
Z	0
▼ Rnd Velocity	
X	1
Y	1
Z	1
Emitter Velocity Scale	0
▶ Tangent Velocity	
Angular Velocity	0
Rnd Angular Velocity	0
Rnd Rotation	☐
Simulate in Worldspace?	☐
One Shot	☐
▶ Ellipsoid	
Min Emitter Range	1

FIG 4.26 The Particle Emitter Settings.

219

```
    }
    void Update ()
    {
        if(Input.GetMouseButtonDown(0))
        {
            particleEmitter.emit = true;
        }
        else if(Input.GetMouseButtonUp(0))
        {
            particleEmitter.emit = false;
        }

        if(Input.GetMouseButton(0))
        {
            Vector3 pos = Camera.main.ScreenToWorldPoint(
                new Vector3(Input.mousePosition.x,
                Input.mousePosition.y,
                Camera.main.nearClipPlane + 10.0f));
            this.transform.position = pos;
        }
    }
}
```

Save and attach to the small flame object in the Hierarchy. Run in the editor. A flame should appear under the mouse when the button is down and go out when the button is up. Build to your mobile device. The flame will go on and off with your finger touch.

The code in this exercise is very similar to ones we've seen before with respect to controlling objects in 3D space with touches on the screen. The familiar `ScreenToWorldPoint` function is employed once again and this time it sets the position of the particle emitter.

Although Unity's built in particle effects are visually stunning, they aren't optimized for use on mobile devices and often you can get away with something much simpler. In the next hands-on you will learn how to use an animated sprite to fake a particle system.

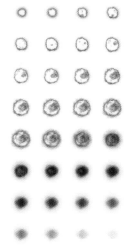

FIG 4.27 The texture map for an animated sprite.

⊙ Unity Hands-On
Sprite Particles

Step 1: Download *explode.png* and *sprite.fbx*[2] from the website. The explode.png image is shown in Figure 4.27. It is a texture map consisting of all the frames for an explode animation. The even column and row structure is required by the code in this exercise to ensure the animation is cycled correctly to give the correct effect.

---

[2] Or use the Unity 4 Quad game object.

● **Note**

Explode.png was created with the particle effect animation TP Editor available from www.rigzsoft.co.uk.

Step 2: Create a new Unity Project and add *explode.png* and *sprite.fbx* to the Project. Change the texture settings for *explode.png* to best suite a transparent image as per Figure 4.12.

Step 3: Add the plane (called sprite) to the Hierarchy. Select and set the Shader component to *Mobile/Particles/Alpha Blended*. You could use the default Unity plane for this, but it has far more vertices, making this four vertex model more efficient. The following code is also designed to work specifically with this four vertex plane. The plane will be in the XZ. Reposition the camera to be looking down the *y* axis at it.

● **Note**

When importing static FBX files, sometimes they get an Animation Component attached to them. Select the object after you've added it to the Hierarchy for the first time. In the Inspector, look for an Animation Component. If your model doesn't have any animations *remove this component*. It will inadvertently cause unnecessary drawcalls.

Step 4: Create a C# file called *animateParticle* and add the following code:

```
using UnityEngine;
using System.Collections;

public class animateParticle : MonoBehaviour {

    public int frameWidth;
    public int frameHeight;
    public int columns;
    public int fCount;

    public Texture2D spriteAtlas;
    public float framesPerSecond;
    public bool oneShot = true;

    private Mesh mesh;
    private Texture2D texture;
    private float nextFrame = 0;
    private float timeBetweenFrames;
    private int currentFrame = 0;

    void Start () {
        this.renderer.material = new
            Material(Shader.Find(
                "Mobile/Particles/Alpha Blended"));
```

```
                    this.renderer.material.mainTexture = spriteAtlas;
                    mesh = this.GetComponent<MeshFilter>().mesh;
                    texture = (Texture2D) renderer.material.mainTexture;
                    timeBetweenFrames = (float) 1.0/framesPerSecond;
                    UpdateSprite();
                }

                void UpdateSprite()
                {
                    Vector2[] uvs = new Vector2[4];
                    Vector2 startPixel;
                    Vector2 endPixel;
                    int col;
                    int row;

                    if(this.audio)
                    {
                        if(currentFrame == 0 && this.audio.clip)
                        {
                            audio.Play();
                        }
                    }

                    col = currentFrame % columns;
                    row = currentFrame / columns;

                    startPixel.x = frameWidth * col;
                    startPixel.y = frameHeight * row;

                    endPixel.x = frameWidth * (col+1);
                    endPixel.y = frameHeight * (row+1);

//USE THIS FOR UNITY 3
                    uvs[0] = new Vector2(startPixel.x/texture.width,
                    (renderer.material.mainTexture.height -
                    endPixel.y)/texture.height);

                    uvs[1] = new Vector2(startPixel.x/texture.width,
                    (renderer.material.mainTexture.height -
                    startPixel.y)/texture.height);

                    uvs[2] = new Vector2(endPixel.x/texture.width,
                    (renderer.material.mainTexture.height -
                    startPixel.y)/texture.height);

                    uvs[3] = new Vector2(endPixel.x/texture.width,
                    (renderer.material.mainTexture.height -
                    endPixel.y)/texture.height);
//END UNITY 3 CODE

//USE THIS FOR UNITY 4
                    uvs[2] = new Vector2(startPixel.x/texture.width,
                    (renderer.material.mainTexture.height -
                    startPixel.y)/texture.height);
```

```
        uvs[1] = new Vector2(endPixel.x/texture.width,
        (renderer.material.mainTexture.height -
        startPixel.y)/texture.height);

        uvs[3] = new Vector2(endPixel.x/texture.width,
        (renderer.material.mainTexture.height -
        endPixel.y)/texture.height);

        uvs[0] = new Vector2(startPixel.x/texture.width,
        (renderer.material.mainTexture.height -
        endPixel.y)/texture.height);
    //END UNITY 4 CODE

        mesh.uv = uvs;
        currentFrame++;

        if(currentFrame > = fCount)
        {
        if(oneShot)
        {
            Destroy(this.gameObject);
            return;
        }
        currentFrame = 0;
        }
        Invoke("UpdateSprite", timeBetweenFrames);
    }

    void Update ()
    {
        transform.LookAt(Camera.main.transform);
    }
}
```

Attach this code to the plane. Select the plane in the Hierarchy and then in the Inspector, locate the code and set the values for each property as shown in Figure 4.28. The frame width and height will be 128 each. This is the size of the individual images that make up the whole image. Set the number of columns to four—as the image we are using has four columns—and set frame count to 32. Drag and drop the texture atlas with the particle effect onto the Sprite Atlas property. Set the frames per second to 15. Finally, the One Shot value, if ticked, will cause the particle to display once and then be destroyed. If you untick One Shot, the particle will loop over and over.

Save and play. The code works by displaying each frame at a time using the UVs to adjust the part of the image that is on the plane in any frame. It sequentially works its way from frame to frame using the frame width and height as a guide as to the pixels to map next. For example if the width starts at 0 and the frame is 128 wide, then the last width wise pixel for that frame will be at 127. The next frame will start at 128 and go until 255, and so on.

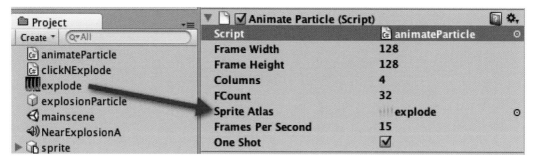

FIG 4.28 Setting particle sprite details in the Inspector.

⦿ **Note**

The code for this exercise only works on planes that have four vertices. It will not work on the default Unity plane. Reuse the plane given here for your own effects or create one in Maya.

Step 5: Download *NearExplosionA.ogg* from the website and drop it into the Project. Select the plane from the Hierarchy and then Component > Audio > Source from the main menu to attach a sound source to it. Drag and drop NearExplosionA from the Project onto plane's Audio Source in the Inspector. Untick *Play On Awake*.

Step 6: Next, select NearExplosionA in the Project and look at its properties in the Inspector. By default, sounds are set to 3D: this will affect how they play in your game. In a 2D game you won't be concerned where a sound is coming from and therefore want to hear it playing all the time. As such, untick the 3D sound box in the Inspector and click on Apply.

Play. The sound will play as the explosion particle occurs.

Step 7: The particle plane is now ready to become a prefab to be used over and over. In Project create a new prefab and call it *explosionParticle*. Drag and drop the particle plane from the Hierarchy onto the new prefab in the Project.

Step 8: Create a new C# script called *clickNExplode*. Add the following code.

```
using UnityEngine;
using System.Collections;

public class clickNExplode : MonoBehaviour {

public GameObject explosionPrefab;

    void Update ()
    {
```

```
if(Input.GetMouseButtonDown(0))
{
        Vector3 pos = Camera.main.ScreenToWorldPoint(
            new Vector3(Input.mousePosition.x,
            Input.mousePosition.y, Camera.main.nearClipPlane +
            0.05f));

        Instantiate(explosionPrefab, pos,
            Quaternion.identity);
}
    }
}
```

Save and attach the code to the Main Camera. Select the Main Camera in the Hierarchy and locate the *clickNExplode* code in the Inspector. Drag and drop the *explosionParticle* prefab from the Project onto the Explosion Prefab exposed variable as shown in Figure 4.29. Delete the sprite plane from the scene as it's no longer needed.

Play. Wherever you click an explosion will occur. The One Shot setting for the explosion means it will destroy itself after each animation. Therefore the scene won't get overloaded with objects. This will also work if you build out to a mobile device.

The above code takes the mouse-click or touch location and turns it into a world position 0.05 units in front of the camera. At this location the prefab is used to instantiate an explosion. You could use the exact same method to instantiate the explosion at the location of any object in your scene to add particle effects to it.

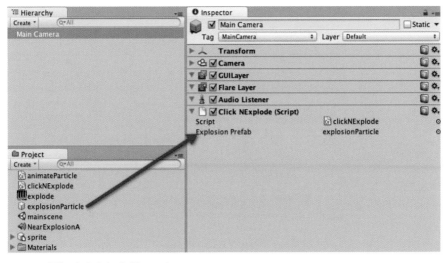

FIG 4.29 Adding the Explosion Prefab to a script.

Video Tutorial

Making texture atlases for particle effects with TP Editor,
www.holistic3d.com/?page_id=122.

4.10 Animations

Constructing animations for any media is a simple yet highly effective technique for adding realism and life into the game world. Whether it is through simple sprite-based characters or complex, lifelike 3D models. Animations really are yet another feature in the artist's aesthetic toolbox for creativity. Animations, when well-constructed and used appropriately, add to the overall experience of the game. However, when either overused or poorly executed, the result can detract from the overall quality of the game. Fortunately, simple animations are sometimes the best.

When learning the fundamentals of animation, look to some of the great works produced by Disney, Pixar, and DreamWorks to name a few. These fictitious characters (whether they be human or not), all follow a consistent framework of principles for producing real and often hyper-real character movements and motions. As outlined in what is regarded as one of the most crucial guides to animation, *The Illusion of Life* by Ollie Johnston and Frank Thomas, 12 fundamental animation principles are presented. Although traditionally applied to film, many of these same principles also apply to games of every shape and size. Several of the principals such as *straight-ahead action* and *pose-to-pose*, *solid drawing* and *appeal* are more relevant to drawing and animation and will not be discussed here.

4.11 Squash and Stretch

This relates to the deformation of objects in reaction to the laws of physics. For example, a tennis ball hitting a wall squashes on collision. As shown in Figure 4.30, a ball when bouncing becomes elongated as it is falling or moving away from a surface. When it hits something, depending on the material it is made from it deforms and squashes into surface.

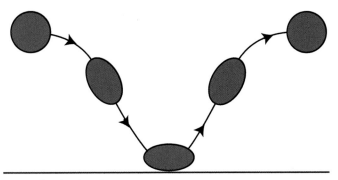

FIG 4.30 Squash and stretch.

Use of squash and stretch on rigid bodies in game environments is not a popular effect, as it would require considerable calculations to deform the object. It is possible to achieve such an effect by scaling the object in question in response to a collision, but 2D games that use sprite-based characters don't tend to bother unless they purposely create an animation for the effect. For example, in *Angry Birds*, you'd expect the bird to squash and stretch on being flung through the air and then hitting a building. But the developers didn't go to such lengths because the extra effort would have had little payoff. Instead, they more easily hide any potential squash from a bird with a puff of feathers—a simple particle-type animation as discussed in the previous section.

Where you do see squash and stretch in games it is usually animated. It could be something as simple as a bouncing icon trying to get the player's attention or the natural rise and fall in a character's gait as they walk along.

⊙ **Unity Hands-On**

Bouncy Clown

In this hands-on session we are going to use the same code from the sprite based particle explosion to create an animated character.

Step 1: Create a new Unity Project. Add the *sprite.fbx* and the *animateParticle.cs* files used in the previous exercise. Download and include *bouncyClown.png*. Set the texture properties of this PNG file for best clarity.

Step 2: Add the sprite plane to the Scene. Reposition the camera to look at it. Set the *Shader* component to *Unlit/Transparent*.

Step 3: Attach the *animateParticle* code to the sprite.

Step 4: Set the *animateParticle* variables for the sprite in the Inspector to those shown in Figure 4.31. The frames are 128 × 128. The image contains four columns of frames in two rows. Assign the *bouncyClown* image to the script at the Sprite Atlas. Set the frames per second to 15 and untick the One Shot box.

Step 5: Save and play. The animation of a bouncing clown will play looped on the surface of the plane.

FIG 4.31 Sprite Atlas.

● **Note**

If the clown is on its side, make the following changes to *animateParticle* script.

```
void UpdateSprite()
{
...

    uvs[2] = new Vector2(startPixel.x/texture.width,
            (renderer.material.mainTexture.height -
            endPixel.y)/texture.height);

    uvs[1] = new Vector2(startPixel.x/texture.width,
            (renderer.material.mainTexture.height -
            startPixel.y)/texture.height);

    uvs[3] = new Vector2(endPixel.x/texture.width,
            (renderer.material.mainTexture.height -
            startPixel.y)/texture.height);

    uvs[0] = new Vector2(endPixel.x/texture.width,
            (renderer.material.mainTexture.height -
            endPixel.y)/texture.height);
}
```

The animation was created in Photoshop by taking the clown icon, which is 128 × 128, and repeating it in the image in exact size side-by-side 128 × 128 spaces as shown in Figure 4.32. To get the squashing effect with each frame the clown is scaled slightly smaller until the lowest point in the first frame of the second row, then it is scaled up again. This sequence makes a seamless loop so it can be played over and over again.

Remember, if you only want the animation to play once then tick the One Shot box.

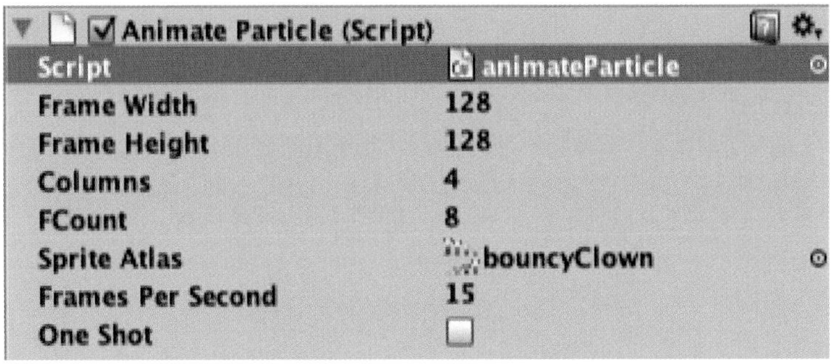

FIG 4.32 Settings for an animated sprite.

4.12 Anticipation

Anticipation occurs when the viewer is presented with short actions or hints of what is about to happen. For example, a person about to jump in the air will bend their knees first. If the player is presented with a timer in a game they will anticipate something will happen when the time runs out. Or maybe, as is the case in many first-person shooter games, the music takes on a sinister tone, and the player can almost feel an enemy approaching from behind.

As well as inciting anticipation from animated movements and sounds, a game can also use lighting to increase tension and play on the gamer's expectations as to what is about to happen. In the next hands-on session we are going to take some inspiration from the free horror indie game *Slender* (http://slendergame.com), for ways to instantiate lighting-based anticipation.

⦿ Unity Hands-On
Anticipation

Step 1: Download *anticipation.zip* from the website, unzip and open the *maingame* scene in Unity. There's a Unity terrain, some trees, and thumbstick controllers. In the Hierarchy you will notice two First-Person Controllers. *Editor Controller* is the character controller that will work in the Unity Editor. *Mobile Controller* is the character controller that will work on your mobile device. To test in the Editor, enable the Editor Controller by activating it in the Inspector as shown in Figure 4.33. When you tick the box it may ask you if you want to Activate Children as well. Do this. If not you will need to activate each child separately. If you turn on the Editor Controller you will need to deactivate the Mobile Controller. To do this, select it in the Hierarchy and then untick the box at the very top in the Inspector. Deactivate all the children.

There are two controllers in the game to allow for testing in the editor. This reduces the number of times you will need to build out to your device. At this point, press play and take a walk around.

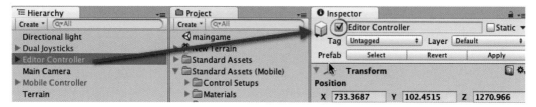

FIG 4.33 Activating a game object.

FIG 4.34 Setting a skybox material in Unity.

More Information: Unity Terrains

This exercise uses a Unity terrain. To learn more about creating your own terrain see http://docs.unity3d.com/Documentation/Components/script-Terrain.html.

Step 2: We want to make the terrain a scary place: dark and horror-type environments always invoke anticipation. At the moment the scene is more like a walk in the park, so let's turn the lights off. In the Hierarchy, select the Directional Light and delete it. This will make the environment go dark. The sky will remain the same.

The sky in 3D games is treated differently as it's not actually in the game. Rather it represents the infinite extent of the environment that you can never get to. The default Unity blue doesn't make for a very scary scene so let's add a skybox. From the main menu select Assets > Import Package > Skyboxes. Import all selected. *Slender* has a starry night sky that we will now replicate.

Select Edit > Render Settings and then go to the Inspector. You will find the Skybox Material property here as shown in Figure 4.34.

If you click on the little round icon next to the Skybox Material box it will allow you to make a selection. The window that pops up will show you all the materials in the system. You can restrict the choice by typing "sky" in the search box. In this example, *StarryNight* skybox has been selected.

Play. The game will be too dark to move around in effectively, but you will be able to make out individual trees.

Step 3: What better to help light your way in a dark spooky forest than a flashlight? Select GameObject > Create Other > Spotlight from the main menu. A spotlight will appear in the Scene. Take this spotlight and

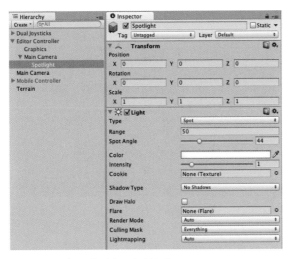

FIG 4.35 Attaching a Spotlight to the Main Camera.

drag and drop it onto the Main Camera of the Editor Controller. This will attach it to the camera. Set its position and rotation to (0,0,0) as shown in Figure 4.35.

Set the Range to 50. You can modify this as you see fit later. This value determines how far into the environment the spotlight reaches. Duplicate the spotlight by right-clicking on it and selecting Duplicate. Take the duplicate and child to the Main Camera under the Mobile Controller, ensure its position and rotation are still set to (0,0,0).

Play. Just by making the environment dark you're invoking emotions of fear, uncertainty, and anticipation.

Step 4: If you have an old mobile device then chances are, as it stands, the current version of the game will struggle to run as there are about 194 drawcalls. This needs to be optimized as the spotlight feature itself requires a lot of GPU power. The first thing you can do is reduce the camera's far plane. The more objects inside the frustum, the more drawcalls. In this case, trees that are far away from the player don't need to be visible and we can use the camera to cull them as shown in Figure 4.36.

To limit the far plane, select the Mobile Controller's Main Camera and set the far plane to 20. This will bring the drawcalls down to around 50. With this number, older devices will still struggle.

Step 5: As we are using a Unity Terrain and trees painted onto the mesh, you can control the detail and distance of the trees and their details. Select the Terrain and in the Inspector reduce the values for the terrain trees as shown in Figure 4.37. As you change the values watch in the Scene how the trees change. You'll notice that you can determine

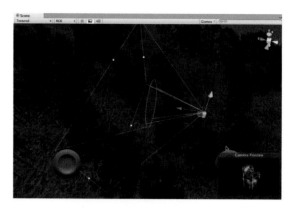

FIG 4.36 A reduced camera frustum.

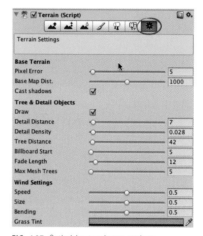

FIG 4.37 Optimizing terrain tree settings.

the distance at which the trees become billboards. This means the trees in the distance will be represented as flat billboards, further reducing strain on the processor.

Be sure to play around with these settings until you get something you are happy with. If you have the billboard distance too close, trees will pop from billboard to 3D too obviously. Start with the settings as low as possible and slowly increase them until you get the effect you want.

Step 6: A clever way to *hide* some of the optimizations is to add fog into the environment. Although the original *Slender* doesn't use fog, this effect does add an extra level of suspense into a scene. The cost of having fog is that you have to remove the skybox.

To turn on the fog, select Edit > Render Settings from the main menu. In the Inspector you will find a checkbox to turn on fog. Also set the density to 0.05 as shown in Figure 4.38.

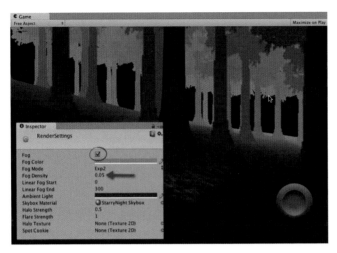

FIG 4.38 Turning on fog and setting the density.

As previously stated, the skybox is an object that isn't in the game environment and therefore is not affected by fog. As you can see in Figure 4.38, the landscape and trees have fog, but the sky does not. It still shows through with its original starry night material. To fix this you need to turn the skybox off and set the camera's background color to the same color as the fog.

While still in the Render Settings, select a dark, almost black color for the fog. Take note of the color settings. Select the Main Camera for the Editor Controller and set the Main Camera's Clear Flags to Solid Color and the Background to the fog color. Do this also for the Mobile Controller's Main Camera.

Play. If while walking through the environment you still see objects popping into view, make the fog thicker to hide the effect.

Step 7: We will now add some background nighttime sounds. Visit http://freesound.org and find an appropriate nighttime sound. Search for something like "crickets loop." I chose an mp3 called *Summer Night*. Add the sound to your Project and make it a 2D sound.

Select the Editor Controller (I assume you are still working and testing in the Editor) and then select Component > Audio > Audio Source from the main menu. An Audio Source for the Editor Controller will now appear in the Inspector. Drag and drop the background sound onto this. Tick the Play On Awake and Loop check boxes to ensure the sound starts playing straight away and continuously loops as shown in Figure 4.39.

Repeat the process for the Mobile Controller.

Step 8: On the http://freesounds.org website search for a footsteps sound track. We will use this as the sound effect of walking through the game.

233

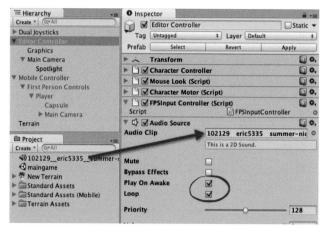

FIG 4.39 Setting the background sound to start immediately and loop.

You may need to speed up or slow down the sound to match the speed of the player in the game. To do this you can use Audacity, a free downloadable sound editing tool. In it you can change the speed of a sound clip. There is also one available for download from the website.

Create an empty game object in the Hierarchy and call it *SoundController*. To it add an Audio Source component. Make your walking sound 2D and assign to the Audio Source.

Step 9: Create a C# script called *walkingSound* and add the following code:

```csharp
using UnityEngine;
using System.Collections;

public class walkingSound : MonoBehaviour {

    public AudioSource walking;
    public Joystick joystick;
    bool joystickMove = false;

    void Start () {
    }

    void Update ()
    {
        if(joystick)
        {
            if(Mathf.RoundToInt(joystick.position.x) != 0
            || Mathf.RoundToInt(joystick.position.y) != 0)
            {
                joystickMove = true;
            }
```

```
            else
                joystickMove = false;
        }

        if (Input.GetAxis( "Horizontal" ) ! = 0 ||
            Input.GetAxis( "Vertical" ) ! = 0 ||
            joystickMove)
            {
            if(!walking.isPlaying)
                walking.Play();
            }
        else
            {
            if(walking.isPlaying)
                walking.Stop();
            }
        }
    }
}
```

Save and attach to the Sound Controller. The code has been created to determine if the player is moving with either the Editor Controller or the Mobile Controller. It uses the `Input.GetAxis()` function to determine if the Editor Controller is moving and requires access to the LeftJoystick of the Mobile Controller. Because Joystick is a JavaScript file, you may currently be receiving an error from the above code informing you that it has never heard of anything called Joystick. This is because the JavaScript file is invisible to the C#. To force it to become visible, in the Project, create a new folder called Plugins. Drag and drop the Joystick script that is in Standard Assets (Mobile) and place it into Plugins as shown in Figure 4.40.

With the *SoundController* selected in the Hierarchy, drag and drop the attached Audio Source onto the Walking variable of the script as shown in Figure 4.41.

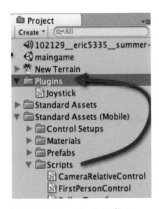

FIG 4.40 Moving a JavaScript file into Plugins for priority compilation.

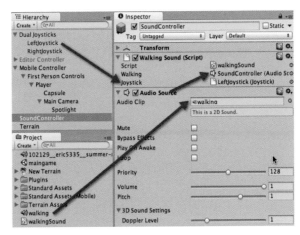

FIG 4.41 Setting up the walking sound.

Test everything is working in the Editor, then swap over controllers and build to your device. Note: before building, take the LeftJoystick of the Dual Joystick control and drop it onto the Joystick variable of the walkingSound script. When you switch back to the Editor controller you will need to remove it otherwise you will hear a constant walking sound.

Step 10: We will now create more anticipation by adding a scary sound that occurs randomly in the scene. Find a sound file of a wolf howling or something similar and put it into the project. Set it to 2D and turn off Play On Awake. Add another Audio Source onto the Sound Controller game object and link it with the new sound.

Create a new C# file called *playRandom* and add the following:

```
using UnityEngine;
using System.Collections;

public class playRandom : MonoBehaviour {

    public AudioSource sound;

    void Start ()
    {
        //play for the first time in 30 seconds
        Invoke("PlaySoundRandomly",30);
    }

    void PlaySoundRandomly()
    {
        if(!sound.isPlaying)
        {
            sound.Play();
        }

        //play again randomly between 30 and 60 seconds
        Invoke("PlaySoundRandomly", Random.Range(30,60));
    }
}
```

Attach this code to the Sound Controller and assign the input for the sound variable to the recently added Audio Source as shown in Figure 4.42.

FIG 4.42 Playing a Random Sound.

Play. After 30 seconds the sound will play for the first time. Then it will repeatedly replay at random intervals between 30 and 60 seconds. You may want to shorten these values the first time you test and then extend them when the game is deployed.

Step 11: In *Slender*, the screen plays a quick burst of static with a louder than normal sound when the "Slenderman" is nearby. To replicate this, download static.png from the website and bring into your Project with the *animatedParticle* script and *sprite.fbx* that we've used before.

Place the sprite plane into the Scene and child to the Main Camera of the controller you are using. Position it as close to the camera as possible and rotate and scale to fit the screen as shown in Figure 4.43. Attach the *animateParticle* to the sprite. Set its sprite atlas to be the static image you downloaded. Set the frame width and height to 64, columns to 4 and frame count to 16. Set the frames per second to 10.

As the plane is a child of the Main Camera it will stay fixed in its location with respect to the camera as the camera moves. Therefore we can remove the `transform.LookAt()` line from the Update function of the animateParticle script. In addition change the code:

```
new Material(Shader.Find("Unlit/Transparent"))
```

to

```
new Material(Shader.Find("Transparent/Diffuse"));
```

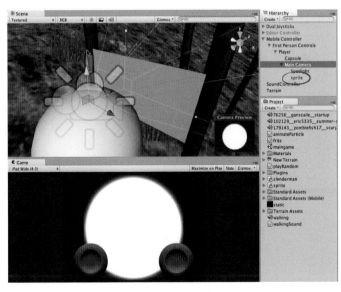

FIG 4.43 Adding the sprite with static animation in front of the Main Camera.

and remove the audio control code:

```
if(this.audio)
{
    if(currentFrame == 0 && this.audio.clip)
    {
        audio.Play();
    }
}
```

The shader needs to be changed so we can later control the transparency of the static plane and the audio code is not needed as we will control it via the Inspector shortly.

Save and play. The game should only show the plane with animated static and the two thumbstick controllers. The static was made in Photoshop as a 512 × 512 image and the application of noise filters.

Step 12: Now we can't leave the static plane as it is because it obscures the rest of the view. It needs to jump in and out of view quickly to give a frightening, panicked affect. To do this we will create some script that changes the opacity of the material of the plane. Create a C# script called *fritz* and add the following code:

```
using UnityEngine;
using System.Collections;

public class fritz : MonoBehaviour {

    Color c;

    IEnumerator fizzle()
    {
        c.a = 0.1f;
        renderer.material.color = c;
        yield return new WaitForSeconds(0.1f);

        c.a = 0.9f;
        renderer.material.color = c;
        yield return new WaitForSeconds(0.2f);

        c.a = 0.4f;
        renderer.material.color = c;
        yield return new WaitForSeconds(0.1f);

        c.a = 0.0f;
        renderer.material.color = c;
        yield return new WaitForSeconds(0.8f);

        c.a = 0.7f;
        renderer.material.color = c;
        yield return new WaitForSeconds(0.1f);

        c.a = 0.3f;
        renderer.material.color = c;
        yield return new WaitForSeconds(0.1f);
```

```
    }
    void Start () {
        c = renderer.material.color;
    }
    void Update () {
        StartCoroutine(fizzle());
    }
}
```

Attach the code to the sprite with the static image. Play. The image will display static that fades in and out erratically by changing the alpha value of the plane's material color. Alpha represents how transparent a color is; 0 means totally clear and 1 is fully opaque. The shader of the material needed to be changed to Transparent/Diffuse beforehand to deal with the alpha changes. You cannot change the alpha on all shader types.

To modify the static effect, you can change the number of seconds between each alpha change or the alpha values themselves.

Step 13: Locate a scary static sound to accompany the static animation. There is one on the website called scarynoise.mp3 you can use. Set to a 2D sound. To the sprite plane with the static add an Audio Source. Set the source for this to the scary sound you just added. Set the Audio Source to Play On Awake and Loop.

Play. The static animation will have become that much scarier. Remember to make a duplicate of this sprite and child it to the other controller's Main Camera so the effect is repeated in whichever mode you decide to play.

Step 14: We don't want the static to play all the time only when the Slenderman is near. First we need a model for Slenderman. You can get one from http://thefree3dmodels.com or download the one on the website. Drop the model into the Project. After it has been imported, drag and drop it into the Scene in front of the camera and scale it as shown in Figure 4.44.

● **Note**

If the model has an Animation component that is not being used, delete it in the Inspector, otherwise any scaling or rotation you do on it could be reverted when you press play.

Later we will make Slenderman move randomly around the map. When he gets near the player, the static will start up. Therefore, we will add code onto the Slenderman model that monitors the distance to the player. If the player is within that distance, the static will play. Create a C# file called *monitorPlayer* and add the following code:

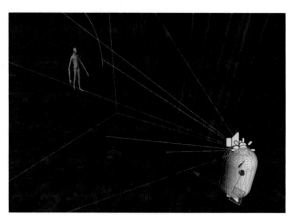

FIG 4.44 Adding the Slenderman model into the Scene.

```
using UnityEngine;
using System.Collections;

public class monitorPlayer : MonoBehaviour {

    public GameObject thePlayer;
    public GameObject staticPlane;

    void Start () {
        //initially turn off the staticPlane
        staticPlane.active = false;
    }

    void Update () {
        if(Vector3.Distance(thePlayer.transform.position,
            this.transform.position) < 10)
        {
            if(!staticPlane.active)
                staticPlane.active = true;
        }
        else
        {
            staticPlane.active = false;
        }
    }
}
```

Save the code and attach it to the Slenderman game object. Select Slenderman in the Hierarchy and locate the code in the Inspector. Set the Player variable to the Mobile Controller (or Editor Controller if you are working with that) and the Static Plane variable to the sprite with the static effect as shown in Figure 4.45.

The code works by calculating the distance from Slenderman to the player's controller. If the player is within ten units of Slenderman then the static animation and sound will play. You can test this in the Editor by playing and

FIG 4.45 Setting up the code to monitor the player's distance from Slenderman.

going to the Scene view. Select *Slenderman* in the Hierarchy and move him toward and away from the player's controller. The static will cut in and out.

Step 15: We now want Slenderman to move around the environment and pop back and forth at random near the player. If Slenderman stays near the player for a set amount of time we shall deem the game over. First download a screaming sound. Add it to the Project, set it to 2D, turn off Play On Awake and add it as an Audio Source on the Slenderman game object. To control Slenderman's movements create a new script called *slenderController* and add the following code:

```
using UnityEngine;
using System.Collections;

public class slenderController : MonoBehaviour {

    public GameObject player;
    int timesNearPlayer;

    void Start ()
    {
        //start model at zero
        transform.position = Vector3.zero;

        //start travelling toward player in 10 seconds
        //and then every second thereafter
        InvokeRepeating("TravelToPlayer",10,1);
    }

    void TravelToPlayer()
    {
        Vector3 directionToPlayer =
            (player.transform.position -
            transform.position).normalized;

        float distanceToPlayer =
            Vector3.Distance(player.transform.position,
            transform.position);

        //stop Slenderman from getting too close
```

241

```
                    if(distanceToPlayer > 10)
                    {
                        transform.position = transform.position +
                            directionToPlayer * Random.Range(1,
                            distanceToPlayer-1);

                        timesNearPlayer = 0;
                    }
                    else
                    {
                        //right near the player
                        timesNearPlayer ++;

                        //if near the player for a set amount of time
                        if(timesNearPlayer >= 5)
                        {
                            //game over

                            //turn player to face Slenderman
                            player.transform.LookAt(
                            this.transform.position);

                            //play scream audio
                            this.audio.Play();

                            //turn off travelling
                            CancelInvoke("TravelToPlayer");
                        }
                    }

                    //on the odd occasion go back to the start
                    if(Random.Range(0,100) < 20)
                    {
                        transform.position = Vector3.zero;
                    }
                }

                void LateUpdate()
                {
                    //get terrain height for positioning model
                    Vector3 pos = new Vector3(transform.position.x,
                        Terrain.activeTerrain.SampleHeight(
                        transform.position), transform.position.z);

                    transform.position = pos;
                    //turn model to look at the player
                    transform.LookAt(player.transform.position);
                }
            }
```

Save and attach to Slenderman. With Slenderman selected in the Hierarchy, locate the script in the Inspector and set the Player variable to the current controller. As shown in Figure 4.46 the character controller you are currently using and its associated static sprite plane will need to be set in both Slenderman scripts.

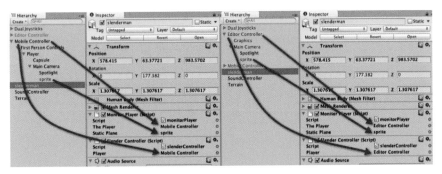

FIG 4.46 Ensure the controller you are using for the player is set correctly with the Slenderman scripts.

In the code, the Slenderman begins as (0,0,0), it then calculates the direction and distance to the player. Using this information, it begins moving toward the player in random-sized jumps. When it is close enough to the player, the static will start to play. To provide a bit of variety, the Slenderman randomly goes back to (0,0,0). If the Slenderman is near the player for five seconds, the game is over. Note: this is not the same algorithm used in the real game, but works for our purposes of creating anticipation and suspense.

Step 16: Last but not least, we are going to black out the screen when Slenderman has *got* the player. To do this first create a GUI Texture with GameObject > Create Other > GUI Texture from the main menu. A Unity logo will appear in the center of the screen and a game object called *UnityWatermark-small* in the Hierarchy. Rename this as *BlackOut*.

Make a small black image with Photoshop—it only need be 16 × 16—and bring it into the Project. Set this image as the texture for the *BlackOut* game object. A GUI Texture resides in screen space. Resize it in the Inspector to fill the screen with black as shown in Figure 4.47.

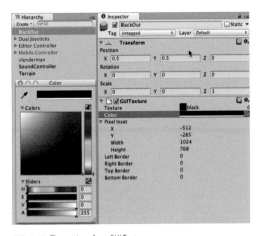

FIG 4.47 The settings for a GUI Texture.

Create a script called *fadeIn* and add the following code:

```
using UnityEngine;
using System.Collections;

public class fadeIn : MonoBehaviour {

    Color c;
    float fadeSpeed = 0.005f;

    void Start ()
    {
        c = guiTexture.color;
        c.a = 0f;
        guiTexture.color = c;
    }

    void Update ()
    {
        if(c.a < 1)
        {
            c.a + = fadeSpeed;
            guiTexture.color = c;
        }
    }
}
```

Save and attach to the *BlackOut*. You can now test the fading in of the script in the Editor. However, as we want the fade out to black to occur at the end of the game, create a new prefab in the Project called blackout. Drag and drop the BlackOut GUI Texture from the Hierarchy onto the new prefab. Delete the original BlackOut game object from the Hierarchy.

Modify the *slenderController* script to instantiate the *BlackOut* prefab at the end of the game thus:

```
using UnityEngine;
using System.Collections;

public class slenderController : MonoBehaviour {

    public GameObject fadeToBlack;
    public GameObject player;
    int timesNearPlayer;

    ...

    void TravelToPlayer()
    {
        ...

        //stop Slenderman from getting too close
        if(distanceToPlayer > 2)
        {
            ...
```

```
        }
    else
    {
        //right near the player
        timesNearPlayer ++;

        //if near the player for a set amount of
        time
        if(timesNearPlayer >= 5)
        {

            ...

            //play scream audio
            this.audio.Play();

            Instantiate(fadeToBlack,
                fadeToBlack.transform.position,
                Quaternion.identity);

            //turn off travelling
            CancelInvoke("TravelToPlayer");
        }
    }
    ...
```

Save the script. Find the newly exposed variable *fadeToBlack* in the Inspector for the Slenderman and drag and drop the *BlackOut* prefab from the Project onto it as shown in Figure 4.48.

This is not a complete game, unless you consider trying to stay away from Slenderman for as long as possible the aim of the game. There are many other elements in the actual game that we will not be exploring here. You, however, are encouraged to explore the possibilities within this skeleton.

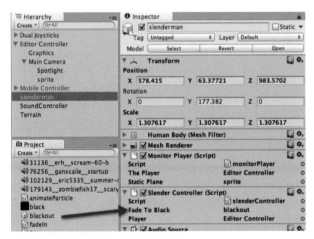

FIG 4.48 Adding the *BlackOut* prefab to the *slenderController* script for instantiation at the end of the game.

4.13 Staging

Staging refers to presenting an idea in such a way that no mistake can be made regarding is happening. For example, viewing an angry person's face gives a better impression of their mood than the back of their head. *Angry Birds* is viewed from the side. Imagine looking at it from the location of the sling shot. You probably wouldn't be able to see much or determine exactly what you were shooting at. However, *Catapult King* stages the exact same mechanics, quite successfully, taking the player for a ride with the projectile as it hurtles toward the castle.

4.14 Follow-Through and Overlapping Action

This is the way in which momentum acts on a moving object to cause extra motion even after the initial force has stopped. For example, a baseball pitcher's arm does not stop moving the moment the ball leaves their hand. In addition, their legs and body also move in response to the action. The physics system in a game naturally handles follow-through by applying the laws of physics to objects under its control. For example, if a force is applied to an object then it will move. If two objects collide then there is a reaction that results in the objects moving according to the forces involved.

Overlapping action occurs when secondary objects move with the main object. In animation it can refer to a character doing more than one activity at a time, for example reading the paper and taking a drink. No single action tends to occur by itself. In games, your character should be able to walk and shoot or run and swing a sword at the same time. These realistic touches in today's games mean you can't get away with a character that must stop moving in order to take a shot at an enemy because the animation system doesn't support it.

4.15 Arcs

Motion in animals and humans occurs along curved paths. This includes the rotation of limbs and the rise and fall of a body when walking. The same curved movement is also found in the trajectory of thrown objects.

4.16 Secondary Actions

These are animations that support the principal animation. They give a scene more realism. For example, a person walking along the street won't just be moving their legs. Their arms might swing, they may be talking, and their hair could be flowing with the breeze.

Secondary actions and animations can bring extra life to the game's characters. Something as simple as a blinking eye animation can make a world of difference to how a character appears.

☉ Unity Hands-On

Blinking Clown

In this hands-on session we will make the clown sprite from the previous bouncy clown example blink.

Step 1: Create a new Unity Project. Download and include *sprite.fbx* and *blinkClown.png* in the Project. Also add the *animateParticle* script we've used previously in the *Bouncy Clown* Hands on. Add the sprite to the Hierarchy and reposition the camera to look at it. Remember to delete the Animation component that automatically comes with fbx files, from the sprite game object in the Inspector. Set the *blinkClown* image as shown in Figure 4.49 for best clarity.

Step 2: Attach the *animateParticle* script to the sprite. Set the frame width and height to 128, the columns to 2, the frame count to 2, the Sprite Atlas to the *blinkClown* image, frames per second to 15, and turn off One Shot.

Play. The clown sprite will blink constantly.

☉ Note

If the clown is on its side, make the following changes to *animateParticle* script.

```
void UpdateSprite()
{
...

        uvs[2] = new Vector2(startPixel.x/texture.width,
            (renderer.material.mainTexture.height -
            endPixel.y)/texture.height);

        uvs[1] = new Vector2(startPixel.x/texture.width,
            (renderer.material.mainTexture.height -
            startPixel.y)/texture.height);

        uvs[3] = new Vector2(endPixel.x/texture.width,
            (renderer.material.mainTexture.height -
            startPixel.y)/texture.height);

        uvs[0] = new Vector2(endPixel.x/texture.width,
            (renderer.material.mainTexture.height -
            endPixel.y)/texture.height);
}
```

Step 3: The current animation plays far too quickly. We want the clown to blink but not constantly. If we set frames per second to 1 then the clown would have its eyes open for one second and then closed for one second. We'd rather the eyes were open for most of the time and the animation for the blinking happen at longer intervals. To achieve this modify the *animateParticles* script thus:

FIG 4.49 The blinking clown animation with two frames. One for eyes open and one for eyes closed.

```
public class animateParticle : MonoBehaviour {

    ...
    public Texture2D spriteAtlas;
    public float framesPerSecond;
    public bool oneShot = true;
    public float playInterval = -1.0f;

    ...

    void Start () {
        ...
        texture =
        (Texture2D)renderer.material.mainTexture;
        timeBetweenFrames = (float) 1.0/framesPerSecond;

        if(playInterval == -1)
        {
            playInterval = timeBetweenFrames;
        }

        UpdateSprite();
    }

    void UpdateSprite()
    {
        ...
        mesh.uv = uvs;
        currentFrame++;

        if(currentFrame == 1)
        {
            Invoke("UpdateSprite", playInterval);
            return;
        }

        if(currentFrame >= fCount)
        {
            ...
```

```
        }
        Invoke("UpdateSprite", timeBetweenFrames);
    }
    ...
```

Save. Locate where the script is attached to the sprite game object in the Inspector. Set the new exposed *playInterval* variable to 2. Play. The blinking animation will run every two seconds at 15 frames per second. The code also caters for use in the way we've applied it before. If the playInterval is set to -1 we are indicating that no special treatment is requires and the animation should run as per usual. If the playInterval is anything other than -1 it will provide a pause between runnings of the animation.

4.17 Slow In and Out

Slow in and out refers to natural movement in which there is a change in direction, decelerating into the change and accelerating out. For example, a car turning a corner slows into the corner and accelerates out. A person jumping will slow into the impact with the ground and speed up as they push off the ground with their legs.

In the hands-on in the next section we will illustrate slow in and out with a camera that follows an object as though it were on a spring.

4.18 Timing

This refers to the speed of actions and is essential for establishing mood and realism. For example, a fast-moving character will appear to be in a hurry whereas a slow-moving character portrays lethargy or disinterest. For realism, the correct timing of actions with motion and sound is critical. A slow animated walking character can look like they are slipping across the ground if their forward movement and leg cycles are not matched. In the previous Slenderman exercise, the speed at which the player appeared to be walking needs to be matched closely with the walking sound to have it feel realistic to the player.

Time is also used in games as an actual mechanic. Racing games for example work with time. The speed of the car is based on time, time is used to record how fast the player went around a track and it may also be used as a countdown. In the next hands-on we will explore some of these concepts.

⊙ Unity Hands-On
Timing
Step 1: Download and open the Timers.zip project from the website. It is set for iOS, so if you are using Android then change the build settings. Open the *maingame* scene. In it you will find a blue car and thumbstick controller. The car is perched on top of a long plane. It has a rigidbody that is constrained from movement

in the *x* and rotation in the *y*. This will ensure it stays on the narrow strip of the plane that represents a road and does not rotate around its up axis, keeping it pointing forward.

Step 2: We will now connect the thumbstick to drive the car. First, create a C# file called *drive* and add the following:

```
using UnityEngine;
using System.Collections;

public class drive : MonoBehaviour {

    public Joystick moveJoystick;
    float speed = 15.0f;

    void Update ()
    {
        #if UNITY_EDITOR
        //running in the editor
        this.transform.Translate(Vector3.forward *
            Input.GetAxis("Horizontal") *
                speed * Time.deltaTime);
        #else
        //running externally
        this.transform.Translate(Vector3.forward *
            moveJoystick.position.x * speed *
                Time.deltaTime);

            #endif

    }
}
```

Save. Attach the code to the *minicar* game object in the Hierarchy. Select this object in the Hierarchy and locate the attached code in the Inspector. Drag and drop the Single Joystick object from the Hierarchy onto the exposed joystick variable in the script.

Play in the editor and use the arrow keys to move the car back and forth.

In the code `Time.deltaTime` has been introduced as a multiplier for the car's movement. The reason being that if you simply move the car by a set amount with each `Update()` you can't be assured of moving it by the same amount each second. Time between calls to the `Update()` function is not constant and fluctuates with the amount of processing occurring each game loop. `Time.deltaTime` stores the time since the last `Update()` and therefore by using it as a multiplier for the car's speed you can be assured of the same speed per second. `Time.deltaTime` should be used when moving objects in your environment to ensure reliable speeds based on real-world time.

Step 3: To keep the car within sight of the camera you could attach the camera to the car game object. However this will create a rather rigid moving camera. Instead we'll create a simple smooth camera following algorithm. Make a new C# file called *smoothFollow* and add the following code:

```
using UnityEngine;
using System.Collections;

public class smoothFollow : MonoBehaviour {

    public GameObject target;
    Vector3 cameraTargetPos;
    Vector2 distanceFromTarget;

    void Start()
    {
        //determine initial distance of camera from car
        //in the x and y
        distanceFromTarget = new
            Vector2(this.transform.position.x
            - target.transform.position.x,
            this.transform.position.y
            - target.transform.position.y);
    }

    void Update ()
    {

        cameraTargetPos = new Vector3(
            this.target.transform.position.x +
            distanceFromTarget.x,
            this.target.transform.position.y +
            distanceFromTarget.y,
            target.transform.position.z);

        transform.position =
            Vector3.Lerp(this.transform.position,
            cameraTargetPos, Time.deltaTime * 2.0f);
    }
}
```

Save and attach to the Main Camera. Select the camera in the Hierarchy and locate the attached code. It will have an exposed variable called "target." Drag and drop the car game object from the Hierarchy onto this variable to make the car the camera's target. Play. Notice how the camera smoothly follows the car like it's on a spring? This is an excellent example of "slow in and out" animation.

The above code first determines how far the camera is away from the car in the *x* and *y* direction. It then uses this information to ensure the camera stays at that same distance and only follows the car along in the *z* direction. The *z* axis in this case, because of the camera orientation runs across the screen. During the Update() the camera is lerped along with the car. The Lerp function in this case moves the camera smoothly by 2.0 * Time.deltaTime along the distance between where the car is and where the camera should be. If you want to make the camera move tighter with the car, you can increase the 2.0 value.

Step 4: Move some distance along the road and add a cube to the Scene, rename it *FinishLine* and make it red with a new material as shown in Figure 4.50.

At this point, if you drive the car up to the finish line it will collide with it, as primitive objects automatically come with a collider. We want to use this cube to record the player's time in driving from one end of the track to the other. If we remove the collider, there will be no way to test if the car and the cube have interacted. Instead, the collider should be turned into a *trigger*. A trigger will register collisions of rigid bodies but will not act upon them in a physical sense. To make the cube's collider a trigger, select the *FinishLine* game object and locate its box collider. Tick the box next to Is Trigger as shown in Figure 4.51.

Create a C# script called *detectCar*. Add the following code:

```
using UnityEngine;
using System.Collections;
```

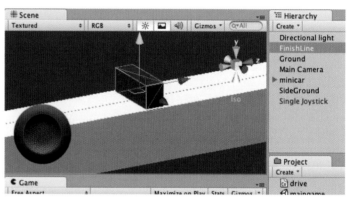

FIG 4.50 Using a cube for a finish line.

FIG 4.51 Turning a collider into a trigger.

252

```
public class detectCar : MonoBehaviour {

    void OnTriggerEnter(Collider other)
    {
        Debug.Log("hit");
    }
}
```

Save and attach this code to the finish line. The `OnTriggerEnter()` function detects when a rigidbody has collided with the trigger of the game object. Play. Drive the car up to the finish line and, as you drive through it, the message "hit" will appear in the console. You can use this to test your code is working.

Step 5: The *detectCar* script is going to present the time on the screen and stop it when the car goes over the finish line. To do this, modify the code thus:

```
using UnityEngine;
using System.Collections;

public class detectCar : MonoBehaviour {

    float theTime = 0.0f;
    bool finished = false;

    void OnTriggerEnter(Collider other)
    {
        finished = true;
    }

    void OnGUI()
    {
        if(!finished) //keep recording time
        {
            theTime = Time.realtimeSinceStartup;
        }
        GUI.Label(new Rect(10,10,100,50),
            theTime.ToString());
    }
}
```

Save and run. The `Time.realtimeSinceStartup` is the time since the game began. It is being used to set the value in the `theTime` variable, which is then printed on the screen. When the car goes through the finish line, the finished variable is set to true which stops `theTime` being updated.

Step 6: To display the time in a more familiar format you can use the `string.Format()` function in the *detectCar* script thus:

```
    . . .

public class detectCar : MonoBehaviour {

    float theTime = 0.0f;
```

```
    bool finished = false;
    string timeString = "";

    ...

    void OnGUI()
    {
        if(!finished) //keep recording time
        {
            theTime = Time.realtimeSinceStartup;

            int milliseconds = (int)
                ((theTime - (int) theTime) * 10);

            int secs = (int) theTime % 60;
            int mins = (int) theTime / 60;
            timeString = string.Format(
                "{0:00}:{1:00}:{2:00}",
                mins, secs, milliseconds);
        }

        GUI.Label(new Rect(10,10,100,50), timeString);

    }
}
```

Step 7: To make this a bit more challenging, we'll add a previous time display and reset the car to the beginning of the track after it hits the finish line. Modify *detectCar* thus:

```
    ...
public class detectCar : MonoBehaviour {

    ...

    void OnTriggerEnter(Collider other)
    {
        finished = true;
        PlayerPrefs.SetString("score", timeString);
    }

    void OnGUI()
    {
        if(!finished) //keep recording time
        {
            theTime = Time.timeSinceLevelLoad;

            int milliseconds =
                (int)((theTime - (int) theTime) * 10);
            ...
        }
        else
        {
            //start the level again
            Application.LoadLevel("maingame");
        }
```

```
GUI.Label(new Rect(10,10,100,30), timeString);
GUI.Label(new Rect(10,30,100,30),
    PlayerPrefs.GetString("score"));
    }
}
```

Save and play. On the first run you will just see the time as before. After you hit the finish line, a value for the time is stored in the Player Preferences. This is an internal value that you can set and retrieve at any time. In this case, the player preference is a string called score, but it can be any number of datatypes and you can call it what you like. This value is retrieved in the `OnGUI()` function and printed on the screen.

More Information: Unity Player Preferences

For more information on Unity player preferences see http://docs. unity3d.com/Documentation/ScriptReference/PlayerPrefs.html.

You may also have noticed that the time value has changed to `Time. timeSinceLevelLoad`. Unlike the previous value, this one resets to zero when a level restarts. `Application.LoadLevel` is called when finished becomes true. This occurs when the car hits the trigger. It reloads the level and resets all values. The only values that remain are those set by *PlayerPrefs*. Because everything is reset, the car is also repositioned back to the start.

To make the game a little more challenging, consider adding some cubes into the scene, rotate them to create peaks and add them to the track as shown in Figure 4.52.

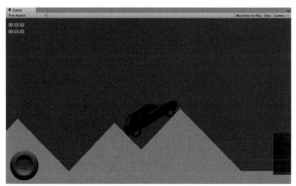

FIG 4.52 Turning a plain racing track into an obstacle course.

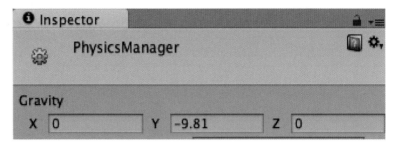

FIG 4.53 Setting the value for gravity in Unity.

4.19 Exaggeration

Perfect imitations of the real world in animation can appear dull and static. Often it is necessary to make things bigger, faster, brighter, etc., to present them in an acceptable manner to a viewer. Overexaggeration is also used in physical features of characters for the effects of physics. For example, in Warner Bros.' Coyote and Roadrunner cartoons, when the Coyote is about to fall from a great height, the time he spends in the air realizing his predicament is exaggerated far beyond what normal gravity would allow. This effect is fondly referred to as *coyotus interruptus*.

Although the default physic system works according to the laws of physics as we know it, it is possible to tweak the values for a variety of effects. For example, gravity in Unity is set with a Vector3 which means "down" can be in any direction. To change the gravity vector select Edit > Project Settings > Physics from the main menu and in the Inspector you will find gravity as shown in Figure 4.53. It is set by default to 9.81 meters per second[2] straight down as it is on Earth.

4.20 The Little Things

As they say, the devil is in the detail, and with respect to games the little finishing touches of detail you add can make all the difference to the player experience. In this section we will examine some of the simple things you can do to make your game that much better with little effort.

4.20.1 Blob Shadows

Probably the simplest thing you can do to add a little bit of polish to your game environment is to put in shadows. It might sound like a minor thing to add but it makes a world of difference to the scene by grounding the game objects in the environment. We encounter shadows everywhere in the real world and when they are missing in a game—although you may not quite be able to put your finger on what is wrong—the environment will just look that much more artificial.

There are two types of shadows that you can deploy; baked and dynamic. Baked shadows are actually colored into the object textures pixel by pixel as can be seen in Figure 4.54. Where shadows fall in a virtual environment with lighting are pre-calculated in the modeling package and then colored into the texture. In Figure 4.54 you can see the texture map has very dark areas representing the shadows. This all occurs before the game is run, even before the model makes its way into the game engine. It means they cannot change and stay fixed. This works well in a mobile environment as it does not add any processing load.

Dynamic shadows are created in real time and have only just become supported in Unity 4 Pro as beforehand the available technology could not handle the processing required. You may have noticed in the Slenderman exercise that the environment was dynamically lit and shaded, but the trees did not cast shadows. Unless you have high-end mobile hardware dynamic shadows are not an option.

So while you can freely use baked shadows in your mobile game, you also need a method of adding shadows to moving objects. The most optimized technique that doesn't impact a great deal on drawcalls is the blob shadow. This is exactly as its name suggests a small round dark blob situated beneath an object to simulate a shadow.

Unity provides a method for creating blob shadows called a projector. There is a package built into Unity under Assets > Import Package > Projectors. This package comes with a shadow and light projector prefab. In short, the projector is attached to an object and projects an image onto a surface, much like a movie projector. In can however, ignore certain surfaces and therefore one placed above a character can ignore the character and just cast a black blob onto the ground.

Sewer Room Mesh with Texture

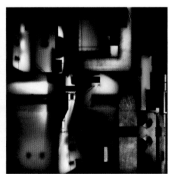
Sewer Room Texture

FIG 4.54 The Unity sewer room model and its texture map with baked shadows.

> **More Information: Unity Pojectors**
>
> For more information on Unity projectors see http://docs.unity3d.com/Documentation/Components/class-Projector.html.
>
>

Unfortunately projectors become drawcall-heavy the more you have. In a simple environment, the cheapest and easiest type of blob shadow is a plane with a black fuzzy ball texture on it.

● Unity Hands-On
Blob Shadows

Step 1: Download and open the *SheepController* project from the website. Open the *maingame* scene. In the scene you will find a large green plane, a sheep and a thumbstick controller. If you play the scene you'll be able to move the sheep around with the arrow keys, or thumbstick on a mobile device.

Step 2: To the scene add a new plane. Resize the plane and position under the sheep as shown in Figure 4.55 (a). This will hold the shadow image. Next, set the texture of the plane to the shadow material provided in the Materials folder in the Project. The plane will change to represent that in Figure 4.55 (b). This material has an Unlit/Transparent shader.

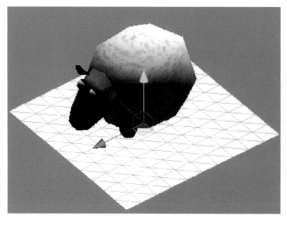
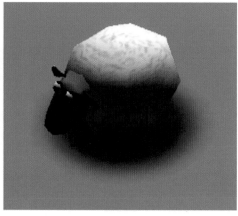

(a)   (b)

FIG 4.55 Creating a simple blob shadow.

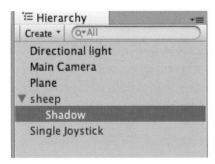

FIG 4.56 The shadow plane is a child of the sheep game object.

Step 3: Drag and drop the plane that is the shadow in the Hierarchy onto the sheep to child it as shown in Figure 4.56. Now when the sheep moves, the shadow will move with it.

4.20.2 Audio and Visual Feedback on Actions

Animations, floating text messages, and sounds are played in numerous mobile games as points and coins are accumulated. This provides the player with visual and audio feedback and makes the game more fun to play. Without these cues, a player could become confused as to whether they are doing the right or wrong thing.

FIG 4.57 An example of text floating up to represent points gained in *Flock 'Em!*

🔘 **Unity Hands-On**
Pickup Scores, Sounds and Animation

Step 1: For this exercise, open the project from the previous hands-on session.

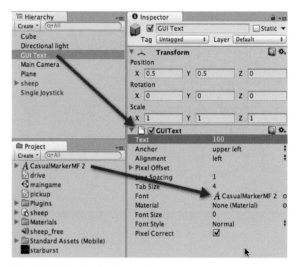

FIG 4.58 Setting values for a GUI text item.

Step 2: Create a cube and add it to the scene in front of the sheep. Scale it to the size of the sheep. Make the collider a trigger.

Step 3: Add a GUI text into the Scene with GameObject > CreateOther > GUI Text. You will see the text "GUI text" appear in the center of the scene. Set the text for this to 100. Set the font for the GUI text to the one provided in the Project. This process is illustrated in Figure 4.58. To resize the font, select the font in the Project, then in the Inspector set the size, then hit Apply. You will see the font size change on the screen.

Step 4: Create a new C# file called *floatUp* and add the following code:

```
using UnityEngine;
using System.Collections;

public class floatUp : MonoBehaviour {

    float fadeDuration = 2.0f;
    void Start ()
    {
        StartCoroutine(Fade(1.0f, 0.0f, fadeDuration));
    }
    public IEnumerator Fade (float startLevel,
        float endLevel, float time)
    {
        float speed = (float) 1.0/time;
        Color c = guiText.material.color;
        for (float t = 0.0f; t < 1.0f; t + =
        Time.deltaTime*speed)
```

```
            {
                    c.a = Mathf.Lerp(startLevel, endLevel, t);
                    guiText.material.color = c;
                    yield return true;
            }
                    Destroy(this.gameObject);
    }
    void Update ()
    {
            this.transform.Translate(Vector3.up * 0.005f);
    }
}
```

Save and attach to the GUI text in the Hierarchy. Play. The 100 should rise up the screen and fade away. When it has completed fading out, the game object will be destroyed.

Make a prefab from this GUI text called *score*. Remove the original GUI text from the Hierarchy when you are done.

Step 5: Bring into the Project the *sprite.fbx* and *animateParticle.cs* files used in previous examples. Add the sprite to the Hierarchy. Attach the animateParticle.cs script to it. Set the sprite atlas for the script to the starburst image provided in the Project. Set the frame width and height to 128, the columns to 4, frame count to 20 and frames per second to 15. Leave it set as a One Shot.

Inside the *animateParticle* script ensure the LookAt() function is active in the Update() as we previously commented it out. This will ensure the particle effect always faces the camera. Position the sprite in the scene where it can be seen by the camera, for example over the sheep or cube.

Play. You will see a star burst particle system play. If it is too small, increase the scaling of the sprite in its transform component in the Inspector. If the sprite is culled because it intersects with the cube or sheep when you play it, move it closer to the camera.

Step 6: Add an Audio Source to the sprite. Set the sound to the sheep_ free one provided in the Project. Ensure the sound file is in 2D format. Play to see the particle and hear the sound play.

Step 7: Create a prefab from the sprite. Call it *stars*. Delete the original sprite in the Hierarchy. Check the Shader component is set to *Mobile/ Particles/Alpha Blended*.

Step 8: We want the sheep to cause a trigger when it hits the cube. To do this, the sheep needs to have a collider and rigidbody. With the sheep selected in the Hierarchy, select Component > Physics > Rigidbody and Component > Physics > Sphere Collider from the main menu. Both items will be added to the model. In the Inspector, turn off gravity for the sheep's rigidbody.

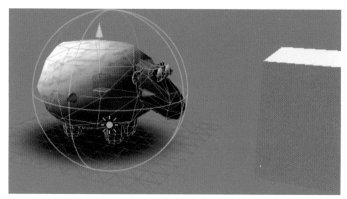

FIG 4.59 Adding a collider to the sheep mesh.

Step 9: Create a new C# script called *pickup* and add the following code:

```
using UnityEngine;
using System.Collections;

public class pickup : MonoBehaviour

{
    public GameObject particles;
    public GameObject score;

    void OnTriggerEnter(Collider collider)
    {
        Instantiate(particles,this.transform.position,
            Quaternion.identity);
        Vector3 viewPos = Camera.main.WorldToViewportPoint
            (this.transform.position);
        Instantiate(score, new Vector3(viewPos.x,viewPos.y,0),
            Quaternion.identity);
        Destroy(this.gameObject);
    }
}
```

Save and attach to the cube. Select the cube in the Hierarchy and locate the attached script. Set the particles value to the stars prefab and the score to the scores prefab as shown in Figure 4.60.

Play. On hitting the cube, the sheep will cause the particle animation to play and a floating score to go up the screen.

The GUI text of the score lives in screen space and therefore, before instantiating it, we need to convert the position of the cube in world coordinates to screen coordinates. This is the reason for the use of the WorldToViewportPoint() function.

Step 10: Create a new C# script called *ginterface* and add:

```
using UnityEngine;
using System.Collections;
```

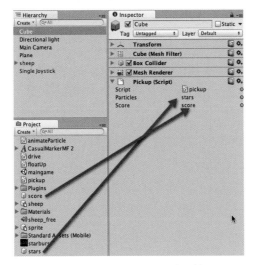

FIG 4.60 Setting values in the pickup script with prefabs.

```
public class ginterface : MonoBehaviour
{
    public static int totalScore = 0;

    void OnGUI()
    {
        GUI.Label(new Rect(10,10,100,30), "Score: " +
            totalScore.ToString());
    }
}
```

Save and attach to the Main Camera. This code will display a score on the screen. Notice the use of the word `static` with the declaration of `totalScore`. This will allow us to access this variable and modify it from other code.

Now modify the pickup script thus:

```
...
public class pickup : MonoBehaviour
{
    ...
    void OnTriggerEnter(Collider collider)
    {
        ...
        Instantiate(score,
            new Vector3(viewPos.x,viewPos.y,0),
            Quaternion.identity);

        ginterface.totalScore += 100;
        Destroy(this.gameObject);
    }
}
```

Save. Notice how the variable of `totalScore` that is in the *ginterface* script is accessed? Because it has been declared as a static value, all we need to do to reference it is put its script name in front of it.

Play. When the sheep hits the cube, the score will increase by 100.

Step 11: The cube object is now complete. You can make a prefab from it and place multiple copies around the scene. For each one the sheep walks into, 100 will be added to the score.

4.20.3 Music Control

Although audio wasn't rated highly by the participants in the aforementioned University of Wales study, game players would notice its absence. Giving the player the ability to control the music as well as have it sound seamless are two things you can provide to make the experience that much better.

Continuous Music
Unity allows for a game to be divided up into numerous scenes. This is convenient for dividing up the functionality of the game and managing which resources are loaded at any one time. As you begin jumping from scene to scene with `Application.LoadLevel()`, you'll soon realize any background music and sounds you have playing stop as the scene unloads and start from the beginning on the new scene load. Of course they will only start playing again if they are also in the new scene. Unity provides a way to keep objects from being destroyed on scene loads. For example, music created in the main menu scene can be kept enabled and playing into the next scene. The only issue occurs when the player switches back to the main scene, as the object that created the first instance of the music will be loaded again. The trick is to test on the loading of a scene if the music already exists and, if it does, not to let another instance exist.

⊚ **Unity Hands-On**
Seamless Music Between Scenes
Step 1: For this exercise, open the project from the previous hands-on session.
Step 2: From the main menu select File > New Scene. A blank scene will open. It will only contain a camera. Create a new C# file called *mainmenu* and add the following code:

```
using UnityEngine;
using System.Collections;

public class mainmenu : MonoBehaviour {

    void OnGUI()
    {
        if(GUI.Button(new Rect(10,10,100,30), "Play"))
        {
```

```
            Application.LoadLevel("maingame");
        }
    }
}
```

Save and attach to the Main Camera. Select File > Save Scene from the main menu and name the current scene *firstscene*.

Step 3: From the main menu select File > Build Settings. Drag both scenes from the Project into the Scenes In Build area as shown in Figure 4.61. If a scene isn't in this area it won't get included in the game build and you'll get errors when trying to access it. You can also drag and drop the scenes around in this window to get them in the correct order. The scene listed first will be the one that loads first. The order of the others doesn't matter so much as you control where the player goes with a GUI.

Play. A button will appear in the top left corner that when clicked will load the *maingame* scene.

Step 4: To get back to *firstscene* from the *maingame*, you will need to add a button similar to the one in Step 2 into the *ginterface* file except make it load first scene. To do this modify the existing OnGUI() in *ginterface* with:

```
void OnGUI()
{
    GUI.Label(new Rect(10,10,100,30), "Score: " +
        totalScore.ToString());

    if(GUI.Button(new Rect(Screen.width-100,10,100,30),
        "Back"))
    {
        Application.LoadLevel("firstscene");
    }
}
```

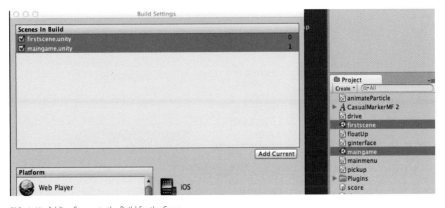

FIG 4.61 Adding Scenes to the Build for the Game.

Play. You'll be able to switch between scenes.

Step 5: In *firstscene* create a new empty game object called *Music*.Attach an audio source component to it. You'll need a sound loop to play as the background music. Select one and download from www.flashkit.com/loops. Add it to the Project and set it to 2D. Set it as the Audio Source on the Music game object. Ensure you tick the Loop box to make it play continuously. Test it works by playing *firstscene*. While doing this, notice how the sound is destroyed when you go to the next scene. But it will start again when you return to the main menu.

Step 6: As well as a game object's name, it can also be identified by a tag. This tag can be searched on to find all the game objects with the same one that exist in the Hierarchy. To create a tag, select the Music game object. In the Inspector just below its name you will see the title Tag and a dropdown box. Click on this and select Add Tag. In the Inspector you will have the opportunity to create a new tag. Make one called "music" as shown in Figure 4.62.

Now select the Music game object in the Hierarchy again and dropdown the Tag box and you'll find music as one of the tags to select. Set this for the Music game object.

Step 7: Create a new C# file called *musicController*. Add the following:

```
using UnityEngine;
using System.Collections;

public class musicController : MonoBehaviour
{
    void Awake()
    {
        if(GameObject.FindGameObjectsWithTag("music").Length
        > 1)
            Destroy(this.gameObject);
            DontDestroyOnLoad(this.gameObject);
    }
}
```

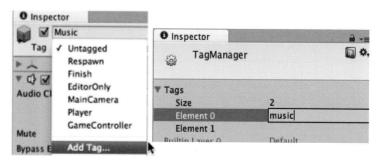

FIG 4.62 Creating a tag for a game object.

Save. Attach this code to the Music game object. When the scene starts the `Awake()` function will run. It will look for all objects in the scene with a tag of music. If there is already an object with tag in the scene, the one running the code will be destroyed. This stops multiple instances of the Music game object being created.

The `DontDestroyOnLoad` ensures the object exists across multiple scenes. Play the game now to see how it handles the music.

4.20.3.2 Volume and Muting

Adding a volume slider and a button for muting sounds is always a good idea. If it's a mobile game, sometimes the player may want to listen to their own music.

◎ Unity Hands-On
Music Controls
Step 1: For this exercise, open the project from the previous hands-on session.
Step 2: Open the *mainmenu* script and make the following modifications to add music controls for the volume and muting.

```
using UnityEngine;
using System.Collections;

public class mainmenu : MonoBehaviour {

    GameObject music;
    float hSliderValue = 0.5f;

    void Start()
    {
        music = GameObject.Find("Music");
        hSliderValue = PlayerPrefs.GetFloat("Volume");
    }

    void OnGUI()
    {
        if(GUI.Button(new Rect(10,10,100,30), "Play"))
        {
            Application.LoadLevel("maingame");
        }
        hSliderValue = GUI.HorizontalSlider (
        new Rect (120, 10, 100, 40),
        hSliderValue, 0.0f, 1.0f);

        music.audio.volume = hSliderValue;
        PlayerPrefs.SetFloat("Volume", hSliderValue);
```

```
if(GUI.Button( new Rect(250,10,50,50), "Mute" ))
{
    if(music.audio.isPlaying)
        music.audio.Stop();
    else
        music.audio.Play();
}
}
}
```

Play. The code adds a slider that controls the volume of the music. The value is also saved with PlayerPrefs and loaded the next time so the volume level is remembered. A simple button is used to mute and unmute the music.

4.20.4 Fade in and out of scene loads

When scenes load there can be an obvious pause in the game while one lot of objects unloads and another one loads. This pause can be covered up with a loading screen that fades in and out.

◉ Unity Hands-On
Fading Loader

Step 1: For this exercise, open the project from the previous hands-on session.

Step 2: Create a new script called *loading* and add the following code:

```
using UnityEngine;
using System.Collections;

public class loading : MonoBehaviour {

    public static string levelToLoad;
    public Texture2D theTexture;

    bool fadeOut = false;
    bool fadeIn = false;

    float fade = 1f;
    float fadeInTime = 1f;

    void Awake()
    {
        DontDestroyOnLoad(this.gameObject);
    }
    void Start()
    {
        StopCoroutine("FadeInCoroutine");
        StartCoroutine("FadeInCoroutine");
    }
```

```
IEnumerator FadeInCoroutine()
{
    while(true)
    {
        fade = 0;
        float time = 0f;
        while (time < fadeInTime)
        {
            yield return true;
            fade += Time.deltaTime / fadeInTime;
            time += Time.deltaTime;
        }
        fade = 1;
        time = 20;
        AsyncOperation async =
            Application.LoadLevelAsync (levelToLoad);
        yield return async;
        while (time < (20 + fadeInTime))
        {
            yield return true;
            fade -= Time.deltaTime / fadeInTime;
            time += Time.deltaTime;
        }
        fade = 0;
            Destroy(this.gameObject);
    }
}

void OnGUI()
{
    GUI.depth = 0;
    if (fade > 0)
    {
        Color c = Color.white;
        c.a = fade;
        GUI.color = c;
        GUI.DrawTexture(new Rect(0,0,
            Screen.width, Screen.height),
            theTexture);
    }
}
}
```

Step 3: In Photoshop or equivalent create a PNG file with "Loading …" in large letters in the center. It's best to make it the same resolution as the device you are aiming your game at. Add the image to the Project.

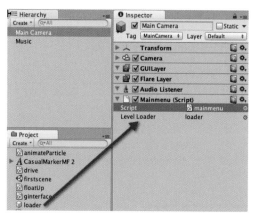

FIG 4.63 Assigning the fading loading screen to the main menu.

Step 4: Create an empty game object in the Hierarchy and call it *Loader*. Attach the above script. Set *The Texture* variable of the script to the image created in the previous step. Make the loader game object into a prefab and destroy the original.

Step 5: Modify the *mainmenu* script to now load the scene via the loading prefab thus:

```
...
GameObject music;
public GameObject levelLoader;
float hSliderValue = 0.5f;
...
void OnGUI()
    {
        if(GUI.Button(new Rect(10,10,100,30), "Play"))
        {
            Instantiate(levelLoader,
                levelLoader.transform.position,
                levelLoader.transform.rotation);
            loading.levelToLoad = "maingame";
        }

        hSliderValue = GUI.HorizontalSlider (
            new Rect (120, 10, 100, 40),
            hSliderValue, 0.0f, 1.0f);
    ...
```

Save. Select the Main Camera in the Hierarchy and in the Inspector locate the *mainmenu* script. Drag and drop the loader prefab from the Project onto the exposed Level Loader variable as shown in Figure 4.63.

Play. When you click on the play button the loader prefab will be instantiated and its texture slowly faded in. After the next level has loaded behind the loader texture it will fade out. Once the loader has completely faded out it is destroyed. Repeat the process for the Main Camera in the *maingame* scene if you want to use the loader to transition back to the main menu.

4.21 Summary

Before you can consider the visual elements of your game environment, you need to understand how a virtual world is constructed and what is possible. You are somewhat limited on today's mobile devices because of their hardware; however, what was impossible just two years ago is now a reality. For example, the latest Android and iOS architectures can process more polygons and even handle real-time shadows. Therefore, we can only imagine what will be possible in another two years. Yet living in the now, designers and developers have to push the envelope and come up with little tricks to get the best visuals and game experience with limited CPU and GPU capabilities.

In this chapter we've examine the nature of 2D and 3D games with respect to creating the visuals for both types in a 3D game engine. While moving virtual objects are key components in a game, several techniques have been considered that are linked to the principles of animation. In addition, optimization techniques have been discussed to assist the reader in assessing the suitability of their designs for the mobile platform.

CHAPTER 5

Learning from the Masters: Part One

No man is so foolish but he may sometimes give another good counsel, and no man so wise that he may not easily err if he takes no other counsel than his own. He that is taught only by himself has a fool for a master.

Hunter S. Thompson

5.1 Introduction

Today there are so many different games available on the mobile platform and while many of them reuse the same simple mechanics over and over again, a few unique and novel experiences have arisen that make us sit up and take notice of the opportunities these devices, with their touchscreens and peripherals, provide with respect to delivering a truly unique player experience. The great majority of games still implement simple touch-and-drag interfaces reminiscent of point-and-click adventures, as these are easiest to program and not a lot of innovation is required to port such games from desktop computers to devices.

On the rare occasion an idiomatic game comes to market that not only provides a strong narrative but also takes a different approach to the interface through exploration of the affordances of the physical capabilities of mobile devices. One of these games was *Year Walk*, released in 2012. It implemented clever game mechanics that had to be explored in order for puzzles to be completed. In one scene, after the player has spent quite a bit of time playing the game in landscape mode, they are required to collect a series of game objects. One of these objects is located slightly off the screen with the only clue that it is there being blood dripping upward from the bottom. Turning the device upside-down causes the object to fall down (or up relative to the game environment), allowing the player to retrieve it.

Inventing new and clever ways to interact with such tangible and haptic devices is not an easy assignment. However, knowing what is possible and how to implement it goes some way to assisting designers to push these boundaries. To this end, this chapter presents a series of hands-on sessions of some well-known games that primarily implement touch- and orientation-based interfaces in the hope that a new generation of game developers will understand what is possible and come up with their own exceptional gameplay experiences.

5.2 Touch

The primary mechanic on any mobile device is touch due to the inherent nature of the technology. As discussed in previous chapters, the surfaces of these devices are sensitive to fingertips and some styluses derived from the technology contained within. Touch replaces all basic mouse functionality with one exception. Unlike a mouse that has a cursor that can move around the screen without activating anything, a mobile device cannot sense a fingertip unless it's actually performing a touch. This does affect the interactions with the game world. For example, on a desktop machine, it is possible to highlight buttons when the mouse is over them. This is not possible on a mobile device. However the absence of this hardly affects the gameplay experience.

In this section we will examine two touch-based games. The first, *Bejeweled*, is created with simple touches and the second, *Year Walk*, uses dragging.

5.2.1 *Bejeweled*

PopCap's *Bejeweled* implements a match-three mechanic within a tiled grid of images in which the player must get three matching tiles in a row. When three or more tiles match they vanish, the player gets points, and all tiles above the matched tiles file down into the new space. This makes room for new tiles to enter the game board at the top.

◉ Unity Hands-On
Lesser Bejeweled

Step 1: Start a new 2D Unity iOS or Android Project. As of Unity 4.3, the option to setup the environment for pure 2D functionality is given in the New Project dialog as shown in Figure 5.1. The camera will be facing down the *z* axis.

Step 2: Check that the camera is set to orthographic as shown in Figure 5.2.

Step 3: Add a quad with GameObject > Create Other > Quad. A plane will appear in the Scene with a scale of (1,1,1) and position at (0,0,0). Don't change the settings for the quad. Instead, adjust the camera's size so the plane becomes about as big as a single tile in *Bejeweled*. In this example, the Game view is set to Android portrait 10:16 and the camera has a size of 5.

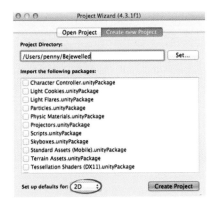

FIG 5.1 Creating a new 2D project in Unity.

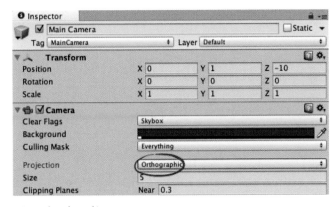

FIG 5.2 An orthographic camera.

275

FIG 5.3 Positioning the camera with respect to the tiles and determining tile distances.

We are going to procedurally generate the tiles with a two dimensional array. The tile at (0,0,0) will belong to array position [0,0], the tile diagonally a distance of one from this tile will be in position [1,1]. Its world location will depend on how far away this new tile will be from the initial tile when placed in the world. To experiment we can just add in another tile of the same dimensions and work out the distance. As shown in Figure 5.3, the diagonal tile should have coordinates of (1,1,0). We are not working with the *z* axis and therefore it will not change for any tiles, but we know from this information that all the tiles are 1 × 1 in the world.

As also shown in Figure 5.3, the camera has been moved so tile [0,0] is in the bottom-left corner of the view. As each tile is added, the height and width of the grid will grow up and to the right. Therefore we want to make room on the screen to fit the grid as it is generated.

Step 4: Create a prefab in the Project and call it *tile*. Drag and drop the original quad from the Hierarchy onto the tile prefab. Delete the quad from the Hierarchy.

Step 5: Create a new C# script called *CreateGame* and add the following code:

```
using UnityEngine;
using System.Collections;

public class Tile
{
    public GameObject tileObj;
    public string type;

    public Tile(GameObject obj, string t)
    {
        tileObj = obj;
        type = t;
    }
}

public class CreateGame : MonoBehaviour {
    public GameObject tile;
    static int rows = 8;
    static int cols = 5;

    Tile[,] tiles = new Tile[cols,rows];

    // Use this for initialization
    void Start ()
    {
        //initialise tile grid
        for(int r = 0; r < rows; r++)
        {
            for(int c = 0; c < cols; c++)
            {
                Vector3 tilePos = new Vector3(c,r,0);
```

```
                    GameObject o = (GameObject)
                    Instantiate(tile, tilePos,
                        tile.transform.rotation);

                    tiles[c,r] = new Tile(o,o.name);
                }
            }

        }
        // Update is called once per frame
        void Update () {
        }
}
```

Save and attach the script to the Main Camera.

In this file you will have noticed two classes being defined. The first up the very top is a small class called Tile. Because each tile in the game must have a number of attributes assigned to it—including its physical form and the image it will have on it (identified by type)—it's easier to manage all the tiles if their attributes remain separated. It's quite legitimate to have more than one class definition in a file. In this case we are merely creating a new container for tile information.

Step 6: Download from the website the six FBX files whose names start with *smiley* and the `smileyAtlas.png` shown in Figure 5.4. Select all of the files at once and drag and drop these into the Project. Adjust the settings for the *smileyAtlas* image for the best clarity and check the material created automatically for it has an Unlit/Transparent shader. Each of these planes was texture-mapped with the `smileyAtlas.png` such that each one has a different image on it. The planes were created in Maya with a width and height of 100. This makes them the same size in Unity as the default Unity quad.

Drag each of them in turn into the Hierarchy. They will be orientated the wrong way, so rotate each 90 on the *x* axis and 180 on the *y* axis. Remove any animation component they may have (inherently added because they are an FBX file). Add a box collider to each (Component > Physics 2D > Box

FIG 5.4 A texture atlas of smiley face icons courtesy of www.codicode.com.

277

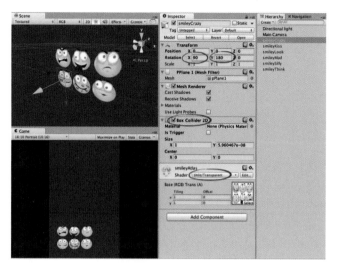

FIG 5.5 Making tiles for the *Bejeweled* game.

Collider 2D). Make prefabs from each of them. Check that the Box Collider size is set to 1 for *x* and *y*. The key settings are shown in Figure 5.5.

Remove the originals from the Hierarchy.

⬤ **Note**

The quick way to make a prefab is to drag the object from the Hierarchy and drop it onto the Project.

Step 7: To accommodate the six different tiles we need to modify the *CreateGame* script thus:

```
using UnityEngine;
using System.Collections;
using System.Collections.Generic;

public class Tile
{
    ...
}

public class CreateGame : MonoBehaviour {

    public GameObject[] tile;
    List<GameObject> tileBank = new List<GameObject>();
    static int rows = 8;
    static int cols = 5;

    public Tile[,] tiles = new Tile[cols,rows];
```

```
    void ShuffleList()
    {
        System.Random rand = new System.Random();
        int r = tileBank.Count;
        while (r > 1) {
            r--;
            int n = rand.Next(r + 1);
            GameObject val = tileBank[n];
            tileBank[n] = tileBank[r];
            tileBank[r] = val;
        }
    }
}

void Start ()
{
    //instantiate a bunch of tile
    //gameobjects from the prefabs
    int numCopies = (rows*cols)/3;
    for(int i = 0; i < numCopies; i++)
    {
        for(int j = 0; j < tile.Length; j++)
        {
            GameObject o = (GameObject)
                Instantiate(tile[j],
                new Vector3(-10,-10, 0),
                tile[j].transform.rotation);
            o.SetActive(false);
            tileBank.Add(o);
        }
    }

    ShuffleList();
    //initialise tile grid
    for(int r = 0; r < rows; r++)
    {
        for(int c = 0; c < cols; c++)
        {
            Vector3 tilePos = new Vector3(c ,r , 0);

            for(int n = 0; n < tileBank.Count; n++)
            {
                GameObject o = tileBank[n];
                if(!o.activeSelf)
                {
                    o.transform.position =
                        new Vector3(tilePos.x,
                        tilePos.y,
                        tilePos.z);
                    o.SetActive(true);
                    tiles[c,r] = new Tile(o,o.name);
```

```
                                         n = tileBank.Count + 1;
                            }
                    }
                }
            }
        }
    . . .
```

In the above, each of the tile prefabs are loaded into a public array. Next a large list is created into which multiple copies of each clone are added. This is the pool of game objects that will be used throughout the game. It removes the need to instantiate and destroy objects inside the `Update()` loop, thus making the game much more memory-friendly. The list is shuffled into a random order. Initially all tiles in the list are set to inactive. This list is then searched one-by-one to use the tile in the game. If a tile is inactive, it is set to active and placed into the screen grid. All inactive tiles are still in the pool. When an active tile is finished in the grid it will be made inactive, hence placing it back in the pool.

Save the script. Select the Main Camera in the Hierarchy and locate the exposed tile array in the Inspector. Assign each of the tile prefabs to it as shown in Figure 5.6.

Save and run to see the grid of smileys established on the screen.

Step 8: Now for the interactive component. We want to select a tile on a finger or mouse-down event and swap it with the tile that is under a finger or mouse-up event. To do this, modify *CreateGame* thus:

```
    . . .
    public class CreateGame : MonoBehaviour {

        public GameObject[] tile;
        List<GameObject> tileBank = new List<GameObject>();
        static int rows = 8;
        static int cols = 5;
```

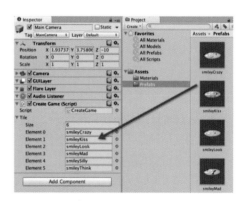

FIG 5.6 Adding tiles to the array in the script.

```
public Tile[,] tiles = new Tile[cols,rows];

GameObject tile1 = null;
GameObject tile2 = null;
...

// Update is called once per frame
void Update ()
{
    if(Input.GetMouseButtonDown(0))
    {
        Ray ray = Camera.main.ScreenPointToRay
            (Input.mousePosition);
        RaycastHit2D hit =
            Physics2D.GetRayIntersection(ray,1000);
        if (hit)
        {
            tile1 = hit.collider.gameObject;
        }
    }
    // if finger up is detected after
    // an initial tile has been chosen
    else if(Input.GetMouseButtonUp(0) && tile1)
    {
        Ray ray = Camera.main.ScreenPointToRay
            (Input.mousePosition);
        RaycastHit2D hit =
            Physics2D.GetRayIntersection(ray,1000);

        if (hit)
        {
            tile2 = hit.collider.gameObject;
        }
        if(tile1 && tile2)
        {
            Vector3 tempPos = tile1.transform.position;
            tile1.transform.position =
                tile2.transform.position;

            tile2.transform.position = tempPos;

            //reset the touched tiles
            tile1 = null;
            tile2 = null;
        }
    }
}
```

Save and play. You will be able to swap tiles by selecting one, dragging to another and then releasing your finger or mouse. This works in the editor and on a mobile device. The code works by including two placeholders, tile1 and tile2. The object hit with the finger-down raycast becomes `tile1` and the object underneath the finger when the touch finishes is set to `tile2`. The code then tests that both placeholders have a tile before swapping their position.

Thus far we have swapped the physical tiles, but not the ones held in the grid matrix. Remember, this grid matrix constructed in the `Start()` function stores the items of type Tile (the class defined at the top). Therefore, besides moving the tile model in the game environment, we also need to update its position in the grid matrix. The reason for this will become clear shortly. Add the following code to the `Update()` function in the *CreateGame* script:

```
else if(Input.GetMouseButtonUp(0) && tile1)
{
...

        if(tile1 && tile2)
        {
    Tile temp = tiles[(int)tile1.transform.position.x,
        (int)tile1.transform.position.y];

    tiles[(int)tile1.transform.position.x,
        (int)tile1.transform.position.y] =
        tiles[(int)tile2.transform.position.x,
        (int)tile2.transform.position.y];

    tiles[(int)tile2.transform.position.x,
        (int)tile2.transform.position.y] = temp;

    Vector3 tempPos = tile1.transform.position;
            tile1.transform.position =
            tile2.transform.position;
```

Save. The above code uses the x and z world positions of the tiles as their indexes into the grid.

Step 9: A rule of the game is that only tiles vertically and horizontally next to each other than be switched. Currently any two tiles will be swapped. Therefore a test needs to be performed before we let the swap occur. Two tiles will be next to each other if either their *x* or *z* coordinates differ by only one. First we need to add some feedback for the player, so they know if they've made a wrong move rather than the tiles just not swapping.

Download a buzzer incorrect sound file. If you can't find a suitable one there is buzzer.wav on the website. Add an Audio Source onto the Main Camera and set it to play the buzzer sound. Ensure Play On Awake is turned off and the audio file is set for 2D sound.

Modify the `Update()` function thus:

```
void Update ()
{
  if(Input.GetMouseButtonDown(0))
  {
...
```

```
        if(tile1 && tile2)
        {
        int horzDist = (int)
        Mathf.Abs(tile1.transform.position.x –
        tile2.transform.position.x);

        int vertDist = (int)
        Mathf.Abs(tile1.transform.position.y–
        tile2.transform.position.y);

        if(horzDist == 1 ^ vertDist == 1)
        {
    Tile temp =
    tiles[(int)tile1.transform.position.x,
        (int)tile1.transform.position.y];

    tiles[(int)tile1.transform.position.x,
        (int)tile1.transform.position.y] =
    tiles[(int)tile2.transform.position.x,
        (int)tile2.transform.position.y];

    tiles[(int)tile2.transform.position.x,
        (int)tile2.transform.position.y] = temp;

Vector3 tempPos = tile1.transform.position;
    tile1.transform.position =
    tile2.transform.position;

    tile2.transform.position = tempPos;
    }
    else
    {
        audio.Play();
    }
    //reset the touched tiles
    tile1 = null;
    tile2 = null;
    ...
```

Save. The above code calculates the horizontal and vertical distance between the tiles and converts the value to an integer. By converting it to an integer we can be sure we are working with exact position values, for example 1 instead of 1.00001. It makes the values easier to compare. The if statement then tests if the tiles are next to each other. The ^ symbol performs a logical XOR. This requires that the first or the second value is true, but not both at the same time. If both were indeed true, the tiles we would be comparing would be diagonally next to each other and this is not allowed.

If the XOR fails, the tiles are not swapped and the audio file is played.

Play to test this out.

Step 10: Now to test if there are three tiles in any row or column that are the same and make them vanish. This is where the grid matrix comes in.

Because each position in the grid links to an actual tile in the world, we can loop through the matrix to process the tiles. This is much easier than trying to determine where all the tiles are in relation to each other in the actual game world. Add a new function into the *CreateGame* called CheckGrid() thus:

```
void CheckGrid()
{
    int counter = 1;

    //check in columns
    for(int r = 0; r < rows; r++)
    {
        counter = 1;
        for(int c = 1; c < cols; c++)
        {
        if(tiles[c,r] != null && tiles[c-1,r] != null)
        //if the tiles exist
        {
            if(tiles[c,r].type == tiles[c-1,r].type)
            {
                counter++;
            }
            else
                counter = 1;    //reset counter

            //if three are found remove them
            if(counter == 3)
            {
                if(tiles[c,r] != null)
                    tiles[c,r].tileObj.SetActive(false);
                if(tiles[c-1,r] != null)
                    tiles[c - 1,r].tileObj.SetActive
                    (false);
                if(tiles[c-2,r] ! = null)
                    tiles[c - 2,r].tileObj.SetActive
                    (false);

                tiles[c,r]   = null;
                tiles[c-1,r] = null;
                tiles[c-2,r] = null;

                renewBoard = true;
            }
        }
        }
    }
    //check in rows
    for(int c = 0; c < cols; c++)
```

```
    {
        counter = 1;
        for(int r = 1; r < rows; r++)
        {
            if(tiles[c,r] ! = null && tiles[c,r-1]
            ! = null)
            //if tiles exist
            {
                if(tiles[c,r].type == tiles[c,r-1].type)
                {
                    counter++;
                }
                else
                    counter = 1;     //reset counter

                //if three are found remove them
                if(counter == 3)
                {
                    if(tiles[c,r] ! = null)
                        tiles[c,r].tileObj.SetActive
                        (false);
                    if(tiles[c,r-1] ! = null)
                        tiles[c,r-1].tileObj.SetActive
                        (false);
                    if(tiles[c,r-2] ! = null)
                        tiles[c,r-2].tileObj.SetActive
                        (false);

                    tiles[c,r]   = null;
                    tiles[c,r-1]   = null;
                    tiles[c,r-2]   = null;;

                    renewBoard = true;
                }
            }
        }
    }
    if(renewBoard)
    {
        RenewGrid();
        renewBoard = false;
    }
}
```

At the top of the class, add a new variable to be set when the board needs renewing thus:

```
...
public class CreateGame : MonoBehaviour {

    public GameObject[] tile;
    List<GameObject> tileBank = new
    List<GameObject>();
    static int rows = 8;
```

```
static int cols = 5;
bool renewBoard = false;

Tile[,] tiles = new Tile[rows,cols];

GameObject tile1 = null;
GameObject tile2 = null;
...
```

Then call the CheckGrid() function as the first line in the Update() thus:

```
...
void Update ()
{
    CheckGrid();
    if(Input.GetMouseButtonDown(0))
    {
...
```

Save and play. Groups of three tiles that match either vertically or horizontally will vanish. You will notice two embedded for loops in the CheckGrid() function. The first loops through and examines each row for horizontal matches. The second reverses the search and looks through columns for vertical matches. When three tiles are counted as matching, their game objects are destroyed. Note, that just after the actual tile objects are destroyed, the corresponding grid matrix position is set to null. Null is the term that says a variable is absolutely empty. We will now need to check for these empty grid positions and replace them with new tile.

Step 11: When tiles vanish in *Bejeweled*, the whole game board shuffles down the tiles from the top to fill in the gaps and then new tiles are added at the top. We now need to write a function to do this. Add the following function to the CreateGame class just below CheckGrid().

```
...
void RenewGrid()
{
    bool anyMoved = false;
    ShuffleList();
    for(int r = 1; r < rows; r++)
    {
        for(int c = 0; c < cols; c++)
        {
            if(r == rows-1 && tiles[c,r] == null)
            //if in the top row and no tile
            {
                Vector3 tilePos = new Vector3(c, r, 0);
                for(int n = 0; n < tileBank.Count; n++)
                {
                    GameObject o = tileBank[n];
                    if(!o.activeSelf)
                    {
```

```
                        o.transform.position = new
                        Vector3(tilePos.x, tilePos.y,
                        tilePos.z);
                        o.SetActive(true);
                        tiles[c,r] = new Tile(o,o.name);
                        n = tileBank.Count + 1;
                    }
                }
            }

            if(tiles[c,r] != null)
            {
                //drop down if space below is empty
                if(tiles[c,r-1] == null)
                {
                    tiles[c,r-1] = tiles[c,r];
                    tiles[c,r-1].tileObj.transform.
                    position = new Vector3(c, r-1, 0);
                    tiles[c,r] = null;
                    anyMoved = true;
                }
            }
        }
    }
    if(anyMoved)
    {
        Invoke("RenewGrid",0.5f);
    }
} ...
```

This function gets called as the last thing inside the CheckGrid() function thus:

```
...
                if(counter == 3)
                {
                    ...

                    renewBoard = true;
                }
            }
        }
    }

    if(renewBoard)
    {
        RenewGrid();
        renewBoard = false;
    }
}
```

Save and play. After you make a match, any empty positions are filled by tiles above. When positions in the top of the grid become empty, new tiles are generated.

Step 12: Last but not least, *Bejeweled* restricts the swapping of tiles if a match will not be made following the change. To replicate this we need to perform a test on matches before the tiles are swapped and then allow the swap if the test returns true. Add a new function to the *CreateGame* class thus:

```
...
bool PreCheckGrid(int c, int r)
{
    int counter;

    counter = 1;
    for(int i = 1; i < cols; i++)
    {
        if(tiles[i, r].type == tiles[i-1, r].type)
            counter++;
        else
            counter = 1;
        if(counter == 3) return true;
    }

    counter = 1;
    for(int i = 1; i < rows; i++)
    {
        if(tiles[c, i].type == tiles[c, i-1].type)
            counter++;
        else
            counter = 1;
        if(counter == 3) return true;
    }

    return false;
}
```

This code is very similar to the `CheckGrid()` function except it looks in just the row and column of the swapped tile. If there is a match it returns true otherwise false. This function is then used in a test inside the `Update()` function thus:

```
void Update ()
{
    ...
    if(tile1 && tile2) //swap
    {
        ...
        if(horzDist == 1 ^ vertDist == 1)
        {
            ...
            tile2.transform.position = tempPos;

            if(!PreCheckGrid((int)tile1.transform.position.x,
                (int)tile1.transform.position.y))
```

```
        {
            //swap back
            temp =
            tiles[(int)tile1.transform.position.x,
                (int)tile1.transform.position.y];

            tiles[(int)tile1.transform.position.x,
                (int)tile1.transform.position.y] =
                tiles[(int)tile2.transform.position.x,
                (int)tile2.transform.position.y];

            tiles[(int)tile2.transform.position.x,
                (int)tile2.transform.position.y] = temp;

            tempPos = tile1.transform.position;
            tile1.transform.position =
                tile2.transform.position;
                tile2.transform.position = tempPos;
        }
    }
    else
    {
        audio.Play();
    }
    ...
```

Save and play. The above code checks if there will be a match after a swap. If there is not a match, the tiles that were swapped are swapped back. You will not see this as an animation as the entire logic occurs inside one `Update()` loop and therefore there is not enough time to draw out a frame of the tiles before they are swapped back.

● Note
If no tiles can be swapped you will need to hit stop and play again. Obviously you would have to add code to deal with this if it is developed any further.

From this point, you should be able to finish off the game with techniques taught in the previous chapters. You could add sounds and particle effects to the tiles being matched and a scoring system with appropriate GUI.

This hands-on has given you an insight into the way in which tile and grid type games work. It is essential to have a memory-based grid matrix to keep track of the game objects that live on or in the grid. However, you must ensure that, as game objects move around, the grid matrix is updated so the right game objects are in the correct place.

5.2.2 *Year Walk*

The iOS game *Year Walk* by Simogo took home the "Best 2D Artistic Experience" award at the 2013 Unity Awards. It is indeed worthy of this accolade and so much more. Its interactive experience is unlike any mobile game that has come before it. The use of touch mechanics and phone orientation is innovative and very clever.

It is a 2D-come-3D game that implements parallax scrolling to give the illusion of depth within a series of 2D images. Parallax scrolling can best be described as the moving scene you witness from a train. Things in the background tend to move slowly across your view while close up objects fly past quickly. Parallax scrolling imitates this effect using numerous layers of 2D images that move slower across the field of view the further they are away from the camera.

In *Year Walk*, the scene moves across the screen by means of the player's finger dragging across the device surface from left to right and vice versa. The player can also move forward and backward to move into and out of the scene but only when special paths that they can take to do this become available.

In the following hands-on session we will explore the touch mechanics and parallax scrolling in *Year Walk*.

◉ Unity Hands-On
***Partial recreation of* Year Walk**
Step 1: Download the *YearWalk* project files. Unzip and open in Unity. The project will have been created for iOS, if you are using Android then switch the platform in the build settings. Open the maingame scene. In it you will find five planes and an orthographic camera looking down the *y* axis.

The first thing we are going to do is scroll the background sideways with *x* movements of the player's finger. The code will also include mouse drags so you can test it in the Unity Editor. Create a new C# file called *dragScreen* and add the following:

```
using UnityEngine;
using System.Collections;

public class dragScreen : MonoBehaviour {

    public GameObject layer;

    float dragSpeed = 0.01f;
    float mousePosXStart = 0f;

    // Update is called once per frame
    void Update ()
```

```
{
    if(Input.GetMouseButtonDown(0))
    //calculate change in mouse position
        //from the moment it is put down
    {
        mousePosXStart = Input.mousePosition.x;
    }

    if(Input.touchCount == 1 &&
        Input.GetTouch(0).phase == TouchPhase.Moved
        || Input.GetMouseButton(0))
    {
        Vector3 newPosition;
        float deltaX = 0f;

        if(Input.touchCount == 1)
            //otherwise on the device
        {
            deltaX = Input.GetTouch(0).deltaPosition.x;
        }
        else
        {
            deltaX = Input.mousePosition.x -
                mousePosXStart;
        }

            newPosition = new Vector3(
            layer.transform.position.x + deltaX
            * dragSpeed,
                layer.transform.position.y,
                layer.transform.position.z);

        layer.transform.position = newPosition;
    }
}
}
```

Save and attach this script to the Main Camera, as shown in Figure 5.7. The script has an exposed variable called *Layer*, as it was declared public in the script. With the Main Camera selected in the Hierarchy and this exposed variable visible in the Inspector, drag and drop the background game object onto *Layer* in the Inspector.

Step 2: Any operation performed on *Layer* in the script will actually be happening to the background game object. In this case, the background's *x* position will be updated with the amount of finger- or mouse-drag in the *x* direction.

Run in the Editor and test with the mouse or build out to your mobile device to try it. If the movement is too fast, decrease the value of the dragSpeed at the top of the code. The background will also continue scrolling off the screen. We will deal with this later.

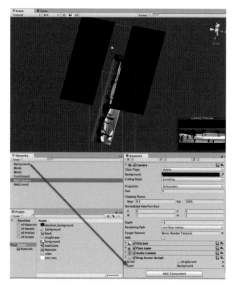

FIG 5.7 Attaching the *dragScreen* script to the Main Camera and assigning a game object to the layer variable.

Step 3: Let's add the next layer—the middle layer. Because it is closer to the camera than the background, its movement adjustment will need a multiplier to make it move faster than the background. Modify your code with:

```
...
public class dragScreen : MonoBehaviour {

    public GameObject layer;
    public GameObject layer2;

    float dragSpeed = 0.005f;
    float mousePosXStart = 0f;

    // Update is called once per frame
    void Update ()
    {
        if(Input.GetMouseButtonDown(0))
        {
            mousePosXStart = Input.mousePosition.x;
        }

        if(Input.touchCount == 1 &&
            Input.GetTouch(0).phase ==
            TouchPhase.Moved
            || Input.GetMouseButton(0))
        {
            ...
```

```
        newPosition = new Vector3(
        layer.transform.position.x +
        deltaX * dragSpeed,
        layer.transform.position.y,
        layer.transform.position.z);

        layer.transform.position = newPosition;

        //note below is layer2 <- don't forget the 2
        //and * 1.5f added to the dragSpeed
    newPosition = new Vector3(
        layer2.transform.position.x +
        deltaX * dragSpeed * 1.5f,
        layer2.transform.position.y,
        layer2.transform.position.z);

        layer2.transform.position = newPosition;

        }
    }
}
```

Save the code. With the Main Camera selected and the code visible in the Inspector, drag and drop the MidGround game object onto the exposed `Layer2` variable. Run. Note how the MidGround moves at 1.5 times the speed of the Background.

Step 4: To add yet another layer you could repeat the process and add code for a Layer3 variable. However we will leave that to you as an exercise. Imagine you had to cater for 10 or 100 layers, think how many lines of code this would take. Instead we can make the program much more expansive by using an array and dealing with any number of layers. Modify your code thus:

```
...
public class dragScreen : MonoBehaviour {

    public GameObject[] layers;

    float dragSpeed = 0.005f;
    float mousePosXStart = 0f;

    // Update is called once per frame
    void Update ()
    {
        ...

        if(Input.touchCount == 1 &&
            Input.GetTouch(0).phase ==
            TouchPhase.Moved
            || Input.GetMouseButton(0))
        {
        ...

            else
```

```
        {
                deltaX = Input.mousePosition.x -
                        mousePosXStart;
        }
        for(int i = 0; i < layers.Length; i++)
        {
                newPosition = new Vector3(
                        layers[i].transform.position.x +
                        deltaX * dragSpeed * i/10.0f,
                        layers[i].transform.position.y,
                        layers[i].transform.position.z);

                layers[i].transform.position = newPosition;
        }
    }
  }
}
```

This small change will make a world of difference to your program as you can now have as many layers as you like. The *GameObject* array at the very top holds all the layers and the for loop goes through each, moving it by drag amount and a multiple of its position in the array. This allows us to make closer layers move faster with some simple mathematics.

Save this code and locate it in the *Inspector* attached to the *Main Camera*. The exposed variables will change to those shown in Figure 5.8. There is now an array called Layers. Initially the size will be 0, set it to 3. This will reveal three elements. Drag and drop Background, MidGround, and Foreground from the Hierarchy into these positions as shown.

Run and test. Each layer will move at a different speed based on its position in the array.

Step 5: Now we need to clamp the layer movement so the layers don't scroll off the screen. Given that the layer closest to the camera, the one last in the array, will move the fastest, all movement should cease when it reaches its limits on either side.

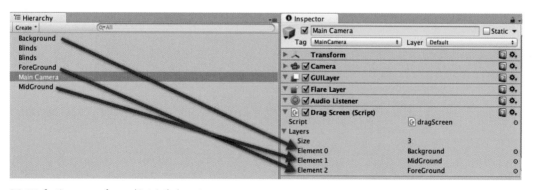

FIG 5.8 Creating an array of game objects in the Inspector.

```
...
public class dragScreen : MonoBehaviour {

    public GameObject[] layers;

    float dragSpeed = 0.01f;
    float mousePosXStart = 0f;
    float minDragX = -8.0f;
    float maxDragX = 8.0f;

    // Update is called once per frame
    void Update ()
    {

        ...

        if(Input.touchCount == 1 &&
            Input.GetTouch(0).phase ==
            TouchPhase.Moved
            || Input.GetMouseButton(0))
            {

                ...

                for(int i = 0; i < layers.Length; i++)
                {
                    float newX = Mathf.Clamp(
                        layers[i].transform.position.x +
                        deltaX * dragSpeed *
                        (i+1)/10.0f, minDragX, maxDragX);

                    if(i == layers.Length - 1)
                    {
                        newPosition = new Vector3(newX,
                            layers[i].transform.position.y,
                            layers[i].transform.position.z);

                        layers[i].transform.position =
                            newPosition;
                    }
                    else if( layers[layers.Length -
                        1].transform.position.x <
                        maxDragX && layers[layers.Length -
                        1].transform.position.x > minDragX)
                    {

                        newPosition = new Vector3(newX,
                            layers[i].transform.position.y,
                            layers[i].transform.position.z);

                            layers[i].transform.position =
                            newPosition;
                    }
                }
            }
    }
}
```

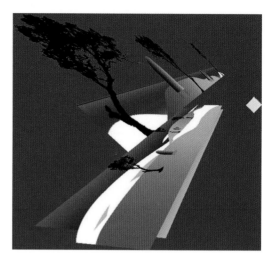

FIG 5.9 A layer attached to a pivot point for rotation.

Save and run. The layers will stop scrolling when the extremes of the topmost layer are reached. To achieve this, the code deals with the top layer separately. It is last in the array and therefore in the array at position (`layers.Length -1`). The `Mathf.Clamp` function is used to set the value of the *x* position while ensuring it doesn't stray between a minimum and maximum distance. In this case, these values are −8.0 and 8.0 respectively. To determine these limits, in the Scene, grab the topmost layer's *x* axis and drag it until it reaches its visible limits in the Game window. Record the layer's *x* value as shown in its transform component in the Inspector. You can do this for both sides of the layer. If you haven't moved any of the layers out of the original file, the extremes of −8.0 and 8.0 should suffice.

Step 6: Besides scrolling from side to side, the layers in *Year Walk* also fold forward and backward as you drag your finger up and down the screen. To achieve this, we need to rotate each layer towards the camera in turn around a pivot point object as shown in Figure 5.9. The cube in this illustration acts as a parent object, grabbing hold of the layer and rotating it between 0 and 90 degrees towards and away from the camera.

The pivot object, which in this case is a cube, requires code to control its rotation as well as the layer currently being rotated. A single layer pivots at a time. When it reaches 90 degrees to the camera it is made inactive and the next layer in order starts to rotate.

Create a new C# script called *roller* and add the following code to achieve this effect.

```
using UnityEngine;
using System.Collections;
public class roller : MonoBehaviour {
    public GameObject[] layers;
```

```
float dragSpeed = 1.0f;
float mousePosYStart = 0f;
int currentLayer = 0;

void Start()
{
    layers[currentLayer].transform.parent = this.transform;
}

void Update ()
{
    if (Input.GetMouseButtonDown (0))
    {
        mousePosYStart = Input.mousePosition.y;
    }

    if (Input.touchCount == 1 &&
        Input.GetTouch (0).phase == TouchPhase.Moved ||
        Input.GetMouseButton (0))
    {
        float deltaX = 0f;

        if (Input.touchCount == 1)
        {
            //otherwise on the device
            deltaX = Input.GetTouch (0).deltaPosition.y;
        }
        else
        {
            deltaX = Input.mousePosition.y -mousePosYStart;
        }
        if(this.transform.rotation.eulerAngles.x < = 90 &&
            this.transform.rotation.eulerAngles.x > = 0)
        {
            this.transform.Rotate(Vector3.right,
                - Time.deltaTime * deltaX * dragSpeed);

            if(this.transform.rotation.eulerAngles.x > 300)
            {
                this.transform.rotation =
                    Quaternion.Euler(0,0,0);

                if(currentLayer > 0)
                {
                    //detach current child
                    layers[currentLayer].transform.parent =
                    null;
                    currentLayer-;

                    layers[currentLayer].transform.parent =
                        this.transform;
```

```
                                        layers[currentLayer].SetActive(true);
                                        this.transform.rotation =
                                            Quaternion.Euler(90,0,0);
                                }
                        }
                        else if(this.transform.rotation.eulerAngles.y
                        > = 180)
                        {
                                this.transform.rotation =
                                    Quaternion.Euler(0,0,0);
                                //if there is another layer
                                if(currentLayer < layers.Length - 1)
                                {
                                        //detach current child
                                        layers[currentLayer].transform.parent =
                                        null;
                                        layers[currentLayer].SetActive(false);

                                        //get next layer
                                        currentLayer++;

                                        layers[currentLayer].transform.parent =
                                            this.transform;
                                }
                                else
                                {
                                        this.transform.rotation =
                                            Quaternion.Euler(90,0,0);
                                }
                        }
                }
        }
    }
}
```

Create a cube to act as the pivot point and position it at the bottom of the layers but outside the camera's view. Rename it *PivotPoint*. Also move the black blinds closer to the camera so that, as the layers rotate forward, they do not intersect with them.

Save. Attach the preceding code to the cube. With the cube selected in the Hierarchy, locate the attached code in the Inspector. Add each of the layers of your Scene into the layers array with the exception of the background as shown in Figure 5.10. Ensure you add the layers in order, starting with the topmost.

Save and play. As you swipe down the screen, the layers will start to fold upwards.

Step 7: The code works by assigning each layer in turn as a child to the cube. As the cube rotates according to finger-swipes, the attached layer goes with it. At the start, the topmost layer is attached to the cube. When it is rotated through 90 degrees, it is detached and made inactive. At

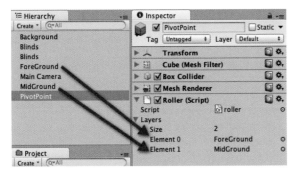

FIG 5.10 Assigning the layers for pivoting to the pivot object.

the same time, the next layer is attached to the cube. The same process happens in reverse as each layer is returned to a flat position.

Attaching and detaching of layers occurs when the cube is at 0 or 90 degrees rotation. Testing for this is somewhat difficult when working with Euler angles as when the cube reaches 90 degrees around the *x* axis (the axis we are rotating around) its values don't continue to increase as you would expect, they start to go down again and it is the *y* and *z* axis that become 180 degrees initially. Remember Unity works with Quaternions and visualizing these as Euler angles is mind-bending and impractical. Suffice it to say, the code requires a little magic to occur. Therefore we test for the cube being rotated by 90, not with the *x* rotation but with the *y* rotation.

Yes, this is confusing, however if you rotate the cube by hand in the Scene and watch how the rotation values in its transform component change it will become clear why the code is written as it is. Using a clamp function in this instance will not work as the values for *x* throughout a full 360 degree rotation are not linear in nature.

In one part of *Year Walk*, the player is trying to locate objects that are slightly off the screen. The first few objects are above the top of the screen and when found, fall under gravity to the ground. One of these particular objects is difficult to find and the clue to its location comes by way of a pool of blood dripping upward. At this point, if the player rotates the mobile device upside down, thus to make the blood drip downwards, the object that was hidden below the screen, now positioned at the top, falls down into the scene. This mechanic, the topic of the following hands-on session, can be achieved by harnessing the mobile device's orientation.

Unity Hands-On
Blood Defying Gravity
Step 1: Create a new Unity Project. Turn the *Build Settings* on for your mobile device type and in the Game set the view to Landscape as shown in Figure 5.11.

In the player settings set the Default Orientation to Landscape Right to prevent the screen being rotated by the player as shown in Figure 5.12.

FIG 5.11 Game view.

Step 2: Set up the camera as orthographic with size 10 and add a plane. Orientate the camera to look down the *z* axis such that *y* is up and down. Position the camera and the plane as shown in Figure 5.13. Place a background image onto the plane to represent the scene we are recreating, alternatively you can download *yearwalkbloodscene.png* from the website. In this case there will be a pool of blood that drips upward. Note the shader on the plane is set to Mobile/Unlit.

Step 3: Create a PNG of a blood drop. This only need be 32 × 32 pixels with a white background. Bring the image into Unity and create a new material with it. Set the shader to Mobile/Particles/Multiply.

Step 4: Add a particle system into the scene with GameObject > Create Other > Particle System. Rename it *Blood*. With the *Blood* object selected in the Hierarchy, scroll down to the bottom of the Inspector and select Renderer in the Particle System Component. In it you will find a material property. Drag and drop your new *Blood* material onto this property as shown in Figure 5.14.

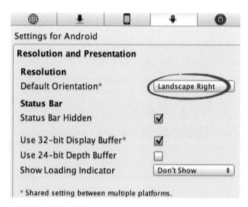

FIG 5.12 Default Orientation.

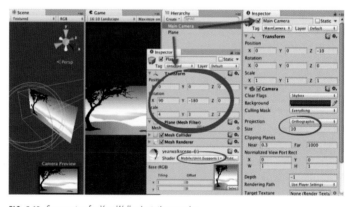

FIG 5.13 Scene setup for *Year Walk* orientation exercise

Reposition the particle system so that it appears to be coming from the pool of blood on your background plane.

Normally you should stay away from particle systems when creating mobile games as they create a mass of drawcalls and can significantly slow down the running of your game. However in this case, it's only one particle system and is only going to have a few particles, therefore it's easier to implement than writing your own code.

Step 5: To make the blood drip straight up and slow down the rate, select the *Blood* object and modify the emission and shape attributes of its Particle System as shown in Figure 5.15. The default particle shape is a cone. That will have the particles beginning at a single point and spreading out as they move up. Instead a box will keep the particles

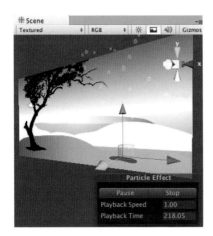

FIG 5.14 Assigning the *Blood* material to a particle system.

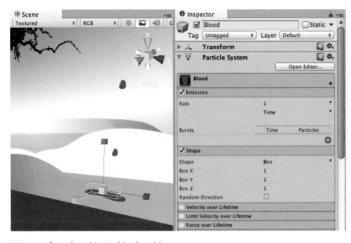

FIG 5.15 Setup for a dripping blood particle system.

moving directly upward but allow us to resize it such that the emission location is the size of our blood puddle.

Step 6: Create a Sphere with GameObject > Create Other > Sphere. Put a red material on it. Position it below the blood puddle but off the screen so it is out of the camera's view. Also add a ground in the Scene. Make it out of a cube and stretch it across the bottom of the scene, as shown in Figure 5.16. Remove the cube's Mesh Render so that it becomes a collision object that is not seen.

Add a rigidbody to the Sphere and tick *isKinematic* of the rigidbody component in the Inspector as shown in Figure 5.17. This will keep the Sphere from reacting to physics until we want it to.

For the ground plane, tick *isTrigger* of its collider component. This will allow the Sphere to pass through it as it drops into the upside-down scene, after which we will use code to turn the trigger off and allow normal physics reactions between the ground and the ball.

Step 7: Create a new C# script called *dropBall* and add the following code:

```
using UnityEngine;
using System.Collections;
public class dropBall : MonoBehaviour {

    public GameObject theSphere;
    bool ballReleased = false;

    void OnTriggerExit(Collider other)
    {
        this.collider.isTrigger = false;
    }
    void Update ()
    {
```

FIG 5.16 Adding a sphere just outside the camera view.

FIG 5.17 Setting a game object to be excluded from the physics system.

302

```
if(Input.deviceOrientation == DeviceOrientation.
LandscapeLeft && !ballReleased)
    {
    theSphere.rigidbody.isKinematic = false;
    theSphere.rigidbody.AddForce(Vector3.up * 1000);
    ballReleased = true;
    }
}
}
```

Attach this script to the ground plane object. In the Inspector set the *theSphere* property of the script to the red ball already in the scene.

This script works by detecting the orientation of the device with `Input.deviceOrientation`. This is independent to screen orientation, which is a good thing as it means we can stop the scene from flipping about but yet determine how the device is being held.

When the device is turned to the `LandscapeLeft` position, the `isKinematic` setting for the sphere is turned off. This will put the sphere back under the influence of the physics system, including gravity. However, before we let gravity take a hold, we push the sphere up into the scene. As it passes through the ground plane it will turn its `isTrigger` off, which makes it solid again (as far as the physics system is concerned). When the red sphere starts to fall, after it reaches the peak of its initial upward thrust it will have the ground to land on and thus remain in the scene.

Save all, build to your device and run.

After a lot of gameplay with single-finger touches and drags in *Year Walk*, the game throws up a puzzle that requires the player to place two fingers on an artifact to unlock the next phase in the game. This is a very elegant and simple mechanic to implement. The method presented can be extended to more than two multiple touches with iPhones and iPods capable of detecting up to five touch points and the iPad up to ten touches running iOS 7. Other devices will have different capabilities according to their hardware specifications.

The next hands-on session investigates the detection of multiple simultaneous touches.

◉ Unity Hands-On
Year Walk *Two-Touch Activation*
Step 1: Setup a new Unity project in the same way as the dripping blood hands-on exercise. For the image on the background plane you can download *yearwalkfingerprints.png* from the website.
Step 2: To make this work, not only do we need to ensure that the player has two fingers on the screen, but the finger touches must be located over the fingerprints on the background illustration. We can't rely on screen coordinates only, as the 3D world coordinates with respect to

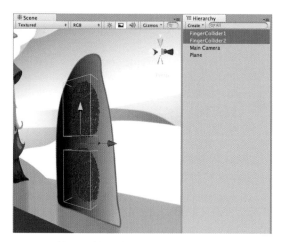

FIG 5.18 Adding invisible colliders to a Scene.

the screen coordinates could change depending on the mobile device resolution.

Therefore, we place colliders over the areas where the fingerprint images are on the plane. The easiest way to do this is to add two cubes to the scene, position them over the fingerprint images and resize them to cover the area of the prints. Once you're done remove the Mesh Filter and Mesh Render of each cube as shown in Figure 5.18.

Rename the colliders FingerCollider1 and FingerCollider2.

Step 3: Create a C# script called *detectTouch* and add the following code:

```
using UnityEngine;
using System.Collections;

public class detectTouch : MonoBehaviour {

    void Update ()
    {
        if(Input.touchCount == 2)
        {
            GameObject focusObj1 = null;
            GameObject focusObj2 = null;

            RaycastHit hit1;
            Ray ray = Camera.main.ScreenPointToRay(
                Input.GetTouch(0).position);

            if (!Physics.Raycast (ray, out hit1, 10000))
                return;

            //determine if first finger has touched
            //anything of interest
            if(hit1.transform.gameObject.name ==
            "FingerCollider1" ||
                hit1.transform.gameObject.name ==
                "FingerCollider2")
```

```
{
     focusObj1 = hit1.transform.gameObject;
}
RaycastHit hit2;
ray = Camera.main.ScreenPointToRay(
     Input.GetTouch(1).position);

if (!Physics.Raycast (ray, out hit2, 10000))
     return;

//determine if second finger has touched
//anything of interest
if(hit2.transform.gameObject.name ==
"FingerCollider1" ||
     hit2.transform.gameObject.name ==
     "FingerCollider2")
{
     focusObj2 = hit2.transform.gameObject;
}

     //if we've touched two objects
     //and they aren't the same objects
     if (focusObj1 != focusObj2)
     {
          Handheld.Vibrate();
     }
}
     }
}
```

Save and attach this code to the Main Camera.

Build to your mobile device and try it out. When you place two fingers over the fingerprint images, the phone will vibrate. It's within this same `if statement` that you would put code to do whatever it is the two-finger touch unlocks.

Another interactive mechanic implemented in *Year Walk* is the dragging of the environment to move sideways through a scene. In one particular part of the game, objects the player needs to locate are hidden off to the side of the screen; a place it seems unlikely the player can get to by scrolling. After the player drags their finger across the screen to scroll the scene, on lifting their finger, the scene springs back to the start. The secret in maintaining a continual scroll of the environment is to scroll the scene as far as possible with one finger and then while keeping the first finger on the screen, using a second finger to keep the screen scrolling across. The mechanic is akin to using your index and middle finger as a pair of legs and walking them across the screen.

One way to implement this mechanic is shown in the next hands-on session.

☉ Unity Hands-On

Year Walk: Drag Scene

Step 1: Create a Unity project with the same scene setup as the previous two *Year Walk* hands-on sessions. This time, however, make the background plane three times the width of the screen. You'll need a longer background image to achieve this. Download the file *yearwalklong. png* from the website and use it for the image. Position the plane such that the extreme left of it is visible by the camera leaving the other two thirds outside the view volume to the right as shown in Figure 5.19.

Step 2: Next we implement a script to drag the plane across the camera view similar to that used in the first *Year Walk* hands-on session. Create a new C# script called *dragScreen* and add the following code:

```csharp
using UnityEngine;
using System.Collections;

public class dragScreen : MonoBehaviour {

    public GameObject layer;

    float dragSpeed = 0.01f;
    float mousePosXStart = 0f;
    float initialXPos;
    float finalXPos;
    bool springback = false;

    void Start()
    {
        //remember where the layer starts
        //so we can't scroll back past it.
        initialXPos = layer.transform.position.x;

        finalXPos = -40;
        Debug.Log(finalXPos);
```

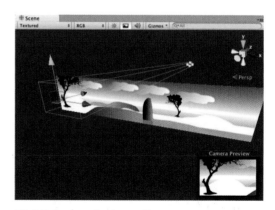

FIG 5.19 Scene setup for a long scrolling scene.

```
    }

    bool TouchesMoved()
    {
        for(int i = 0; i < Input.touchCount; i++)
        {
            if(Input.GetTouch(i).phase == TouchPhase.Moved)
            {
                return (true);
            }
        }
        return false;
    }

    int TouchesDeltaX()
    {
        float delta = 0;
        for(int i = 0; i < Input.touchCount; i++)
        {
            delta += Input.GetTouch(i).deltaPosition.x;
        }
        return ((int) delta);
    }

    // Update is called once per frame
    void Update ()
    {
        if(Input.GetMouseButtonDown(0))
        {
            mousePosXStart = Input.mousePosition.x;
        }

        if(TouchesMoved() || Input.GetMouseButton(0))
        {
            Vector3 newPosition;
            float deltaX = 0f;

            if(Input.touchCount > 0)
            {
                deltaX = TouchesDeltaX();
            }
            else
            {
                deltaX = Input.mousePosition.x -
                        mousePosXStart;
            }
            float newX = layer.transform.position.x
                + deltaX * dragSpeed;

    //swap greater than and less than signs if your x
    //axis gets larger moving to the right
    if(newX > initialXPos) newX = initialXPos;
    if(newX < finalXPos) newX = finalXPos;

    newPosition = new Vector3(
```

```
                    newX, layer.transform.position.y,
                    layer.transform.position.z);

            layer.transform.position = newPosition;
        }
        else if(Input.touchCount > 0 &&
            Input.GetTouch(0).phase == TouchPhase.Ended ||
            Input.GetMouseButtonUp(0))
        {
            springback = true;
        }

        if(springback)
        {
            Vector3 newPosition;
            float newX = layer.transform.position.x + 1;

            if(newX > initialXPos)
            {
                newX = initialXPos;
                springback = false;
            }
            newPosition = new Vector3 (
                newX,layer.transform.position.y,
                layer.transform.position.z);

            layer.transform.position = newPosition;
        }
    }
}
```

In the `Start()` function you'll find a setting for the `finalXPos`. This is the *x* coordinate of the plane that determines how far the plane can be scrolled to the right. In this example it is assumed the positive *x* axis points to the right and therefore as the plane moves to the left, the *x* values will be getting smaller. If your camera is facing in the other direction, your *x* values will be increasing as the plane is scrolled. This will affect the value you place in the `Start()` function for `finalXPos` and also the greater-than and less-than signs in the code where indicated in the `Update()` function.

To determine the `finalXPos` for your plane, drag it with its *x* axis as far across the screen as you will allow it to be scrolled by the player. Record its *x* position and include in the code. Remember to move it back to its starting position before playing.

Because the mechanic allows multiple fingers moving on the screen, two functions have been written to determine if any finger has been moved and to calculate the total finger *x* drag amounts. This removes the need to include numerous tests inside the `Update()` function testing for the phase and movement of individual fingers.

Save this script, attach to the camera, assign the plane to the exposed variable *Layer* and try it out. It will work in a limited capacity in the Unity Editor with the mouse. The effect is far better experienced on a mobile device.

In a hidden cave, in the *Year Walk* forest, is a creepy wooden doll hanging from a rope. The player can tap on the doll to move it. Swiping its head causes the head to rotate around. After the correct number of rotations, more of the game clues are revealed to the player. This doll is a 3D model. To recreate this scene we will begin by creating a ragdoll in the next hands-on session.

☺ Unity Hands-On
Creepy Head-Turning Doll
Step 1: Create a new Unity project and set for a mobile build. The camera can remain in the default perspective setting for this exercise. For a spooky look, add a single directional light and set the camera's background color to black. Download the *doll.fbx* and *hessian.png* from the website. Drag and drop these into the Asset window together. Unity will automatically assign the *hessian.png* texture to the doll model.

Drop the doll into the scene and position and orientate it such that it sits nicely in the view volume as shown in Figure 5.20. Ensure the doll's forward vector is facing toward the camera. With the doll selected in the Hierarchy, remove the Animator component in the Inspector.

Step 2: Select the doll in the hierarchy. Rename and reorganize all the parts of the doll such that they reflect the names shown in Figure 5.21. You will need to select each part to identify it on the model in the scene before renaming.

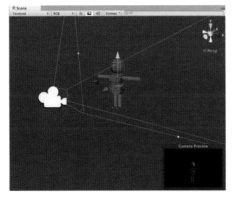

FIG 5.20 Adding doll model to Scene and positioning in the camera view.

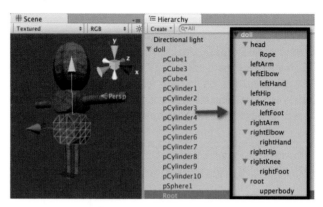

FIG 5.21 Renaming doll parts.

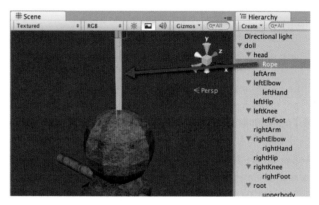

FIG 5.22 Adding a rope object to the doll game object.

Note that the bottom half of the body is named the root.

Also note how some parts are parented to others. For example, the *leftFoot* is childed to the *leftKnee*. This is because we want the *leftFoot* to be physically attached to the *leftKnee* so that when the knee joint moves so does the foot. The *leftKnee* is not childed to the *leftHip* at this time as the *ragdoll* game object will take care of this later.

Create a cylinder with GameObject > Create Other > Cylinder and resize it to become a rope protruding from the top of the model's head as shown in Figure 5.22. Attach this cylinder to the head part of the doll model.

Step 3: GameObject > Create Other > Ragdoll. A dialog box will open requiring you to assign all the model parts for constructing a ragdoll as shown in Figure 5.23. Take each associated part that you have just renamed from the doll model and drag and drop into the associated positions.

When you are finished, select the Create button at the bottom of the popup and a ragdoll will be constructed from the model. Selecting the doll in the Hierarchy will reveal the joints and colliders added by the ragdoll constructor as shown in Figure 5.24.

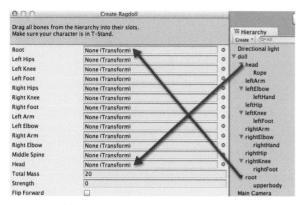

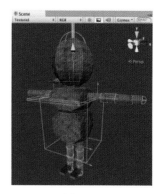

FIG 5.23 Ragdoll dialog box.

FIG 5.24 Ragdoll joints and colliders.

At this stage you can test the ragdoll by placing a plane beneath it to act as the ground and then pressing play. The ragdoll will fall under gravity and the physics system will control its movements.

Step 4: We will now suspend the ragdoll by the rope. Select the head in the Hierarchy and then Component > Physics > Hinge Joint.

Select the head in the Hierarchy and locate the attached Hinge Joint in the Inspector. The head will have a Character Joint (added by the Ragdoll creator) and a Hinge Joint. Make sure you locate the correct one.

The Hinge Joint will act as a suspender for the entire doll as the head is connected to the rest of the body by the ragdoll elements. The rope cylinder is just for show. You could remove it and the doll would react in the same way.

Note at the top of the head where the Hinge Joint has been added, there is a small orange arrow as shown in Figure 5.25. This arrow is defined in the Inspector of the Hinge Joint component and specifies the axis around

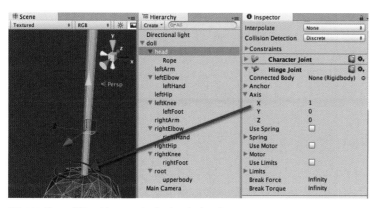

FIG 5.25 The small hinge joint arrow showing the axis of rotation.

which the joint will swing. In this case it is along the *x* axis. It will allow the doll to swing back and forth.

Press play and see how the doll reacts. The ragdoll components will be affected by gravity and collisions, but the whole model will still be suspended by the Hinge Joint.

You may notice that one of the ragdoll arms hangs a little funny. The reason being that the ragdoll creator doesn't always make a perfect ragdoll. However it has given you access to all the tools so you can make a few tweaks. The ragdoll works through a system of capsule colliders connected by anchor points. The anchor point is used to connect one collider to another. The issue with the doll's arm is that the hinge is located in the middle of the lower arm rather than up where the elbow should be as shown in Figure 5.26.

To fix this you can move the capsule collider further up into the arm using the Capsule Collider component's Y center value and relocate the joint's anchor up near the elbow. This is shown in the after image in Figure 5.26.

More Information: Physics Joints

For more information on the variety of physics joints in Unity see http://unity3d.com/learn/tutorials/modules/beginner/physics/joints.

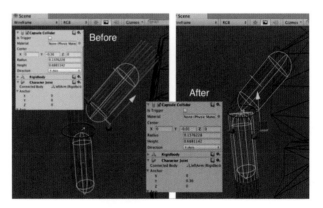

FIG 5.26 Adjusting ragdoll colliders and joints.

Step 5: To allow tap interaction with the doll, create a new C# script called *interact* and add the following code:

```
using UnityEngine;
using System.Collections;

public class interact : MonoBehaviour {

    void Update ()
    {
        if(Input.GetMouseButtonDown(0) || (Input.touchCount
        > 0 &&
            Input.GetTouch(0).phase == TouchPhase.Began))
        {
            RaycastHit hit;
            Ray ray = Camera.main.ScreenPointToRay(
                Input.mousePosition);

            if (!Physics.Raycast (ray, out hit, 10000))
                return;

            hit.rigidbody.AddForce(ray.direction * 1000);
        }
    }
}
```

Save and attach to the main camera. Try it out. This code will allow you to click or tap on the doll and add a force to it in the same direction as the physics raycast from the touch-point. Because the doll contains numerous colliders, it is the collider that gets hit by the ray that has the force applied to it. The ragdoll setup of the model allows the physics from one part to affect the whole.

At this point you can get quite a swing up on the doll if you keep tapping on it. If you want to reduce the amount of movement you can limit the angle of the joints. Limits can be applied on all joints. To limit the Hinge Joint on the head to only allow it to swing backward to a maximum of 10 degrees apply the settings shown in Figure 5.27. Notice the Use Limits tick box needs to be ticked.

Try this out. You'll see a dramatic effect on the swing of the head. Remember the rest of the body doesn't have this restriction throughout so you'll still get a lot of movement.

Step 6: We are now going to add a head to the doll that can be spun around when a finger is dragged over it.

Create a basic sphere and add to the Scene. Locate it over the top of the existing head. The existing head is required by the ragdoll system and therefore instead of deleting it we are leaving it. You can, however, turn off or remove the existing head's Mesh Renderer so it doesn't interfere with the drawing of the new head. Name this sphere *SpinHead* and child it to the existing head as shown in Figure 5.28.

FIG 5.27 Limiting the swing of a Hinge Joint.

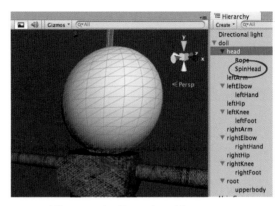

FIG 5.28 Adding an extra head layer to the ragdoll.

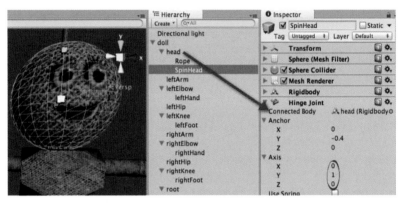

FIG 5.29 Setup for the spinning head.

Step 7: To the *SpinHead* add a Rigidbody and a Hinge Joint. Set the angular drag of the *SpinHead* to 20. Locate the Hinge Joint component of the *SpinHead* and set the Connected Body property to be the original head. Also set the Hinge Joint axis to (0,1,0) as shown in Figure 5.29. There is also a texture file called *goodDolly.png* you can download from the website to put onto the head.

Setting the Hinge Joint axis to the *y* axis will allow it to spin around its up direction.

Step 8: To make the head spin around modify the Update() function of the *interact* script thus:

```
void Update ()
{
    if(Input.GetMouseButtonDown(0) ||
        (Input.touchCount > 0 &&
        Input.GetTouch(0).phase == TouchPhase.Began))
```

```
        {
            . . .
        }
        else if((Input.touchCount > 0 &&
            Input.GetTouch(0).phase == TouchPhase.Moved))
        {
            RaycastHit hit;
            Ray ray =
                Camera.main.ScreenPointToRay(Input.mousePosition);
            if (!Physics.Raycast (ray, out hit, 10000))
                return;
            if(hit.rigidbody.gameObject.name == "SpinHead")
            {
                hit.rigidbody.AddTorque(Vector3.up *
                Input.GetTouch(0).deltaPosition.x * -10);
            }
        }
    }
}
```

This provides the ability to add a torque (circular) force to the *SpinHead* game object when a finger is dragged over the top of it. If the head spin is too fast or too slow for you, adjust the angular drag and/or the added torque.

Step 9: Last but not least, we are going to count the number of times the player spins the head and then, just because we can, after five spins, blow-up the doll. Begin by importing the detonator package used in Chapter 3. Now add four generic cubes to the scene. Reshape three of these cubes and position them coming out of the *SpinHead* as shown in Figure 5.30. Name them 1, 2, and 3 and make them children of the *SpinHead* object. Create a new tag called *spinner* and set it as the tag for these three blade objects.

Imagine each of these cubes as blades on a fan. As the *SpinHead* rotates, they rotate with it.

Now resize the fourth cube and position in just to the front right of the first blade. Make it big enough that it will be able to register each blade

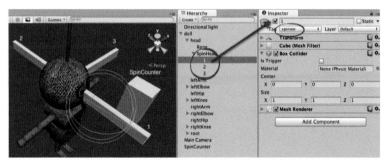

FIG 5.30 Adding collider blades to a spinning object.

moving through it. Call it *SpinCounter*. Make its Box Collider a trigger by ticking its *isTrigger* tick box. Don't attach it to anything.

Step 10: As the head spins around—and thus the blades—we will be able to tell how the head is rotating by the sequence in which the blades hit the *SpinCounter*. For one full revolution to the right, the sequence would be blade 1 followed by 2, then 3, and then 1 again. Two revolutions to the right would give the sequence 1231231. We will now write some code to place onto the *SpinCounter* to keep track of the blade hit sequence. Create a new C# script called *countSpins* and add the following:

```
using UnityEngine;
using System.Collections;

public class countSpins : MonoBehaviour
{
    public GameObject explosion;
    public GameObject explodingObject;

    private string recordHits = "";
    private string matchString = "1231231231231231";

    void OnTriggerEnter(Collider other)
    {
        if(other.gameObject.tag == "spinner")
        {
            recordHits + = other.gameObject.name;
            if(recordHits.Contains(matchString))
            {
                Instantiate(explosion,
                explodingObject.transform.position,
                Quaternion.identity);

                Destroy(explodingObject);
            }
            //clean out recordHits string to
            //stop it getting too big
            if(recordHits.Length >
            (matchString.Length * 2))
            {
                //remove first set of characters
                //that are the same length but
                //don't match the string
                recordHits = recordHits.Substring(
                    matchString.Length);

                    Debug.Log(recordHits);
            }
        }
    }
}
```

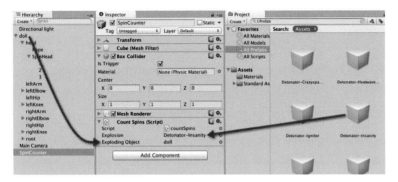

FIG 5.31 Setup for an explosion to be triggered.

More Information: Strings

This code introduces the functionality of the C# .net string class with the Substring and Contains methods. For more detail on this see http://msdn.microsoft.com/en-us/library/system.string.aspx.

Save and attach the script to the *SpinCounter*. In the exposed public variables for Explosion and Exploding Object add the explosion prefab and the doll as shown in Figure 5.31.

Finally, you will want to turn off the Mesh Renderers for all four cubes so they are not visible in the final scene. Once you've done this, build to your mobile device and try it out.

The beauty of this script is that it will allow you to extend it to other puzzle-solving problems where the user must move or rotate objects in a certain order to achieve some goal. This could be attached to a locked safe in which the player has to rotate a dial back and forward in the right sequence to unlock. The `matchString` does all the work for you.

5.3 Drawing on the Screen

Drawing on the screen is an extension of finger-dragging, which uses the same sensing of finger-down, finger-moving, and finger-up but leaves behind actual evidence of the drag on the screen by way of a drawn line. The two games examined in this section implement this mechanic. First, *Fruit Ninja* deals with short, sharp swipe actions and second, *Master Harbor* allows the user to draw paths on the screen to guide boats to safety.

5.3.1 *Fruit Ninja*

Fruit Ninja is a swipe-and-slice game in which the player swipes their finger across pieces of fruit in order to slice them into smaller pieces. In this hands-on session we will recreate this main game mechanic and also revisit trail rendering.

◎ Unity Hands-On
Fruit Frenzy

Step 1: Create a new Unity Project with an orthographic camera set to look down the *z* axis with a size of 5. To easily set the camera to look in this direction, click on the axis gizmo in the top corner of the Scene until it says Front as shown in Figure 5.32. Then with the camera selected in the Hierarchy, select GameObject > Align With View from the main menu. The camera will now be viewing the environment in the same way you are viewing the Scene.

Step 2: Add an empty game object to the Scene and name it *Swipe*. This object will be the same as the ribbon effect created in Chapter 3. With Swipe selected in the Hierarchy add a Trail Renderer with Component > Effect > Trail Renderer from the main menu. Set its Time, Start Width, and End Width values to 0.5, 0.5 and 0.1 respectively.

We want the ribbon to follow our finger as it swipes across the screen. To do this create a new C# file called *swipeTrail* and add the following code:

```
using UnityEngine;
using System.Collections;

public class swipeTrail : MonoBehaviour {

    // Use this for initialization
    void Start () {

    }

    // Update is called once per frame
    void Update ()
    {
        if(((Input.touchCount > 0 && Input.GetTouch(0).phase ==
            TouchPhase.Moved) || Input.GetMouseButton(0)))
        {
            var mPos = Camera.main.ScreenToWorldPoint(
                new Vector3(Input.mousePosition.x,
                    Input.mousePosition.y, 0));
```

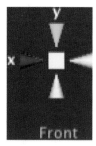

FIG 5.32 The Scene view set to look along the *z* axis.

```
        this.transform.position = new
            Vector3(mPos.x,mPos.y,0);
    }
  }
}
```

Attach the *swipeTrail* script to the *Swipe* object.

Save and play. You will be able to draw a ribbon on the screen.

Step 3: To color the ribbon, create a new material and set the Shader to *Mobile/Particles/Additive*. By default it will be white. Add this material to the Trail Renderer. In the Trail Renderer settings in the Inspector, change the colors to give the ribbon a rainbow effect. Set the Trail Renderer time to 0.1 or smaller. This will give you a little trail behind the mouse position.

Step 4: We are now going to add some apples for swiping and cutting. Download the file *Apples.zip* from the website. Unzip the file and drag and drop the contents into the Project. Unity will automatically create a material for the models. Set this material's shader to Mobile/Bumped Diffuse and assign the two image files to this material as shown in Figure 5.33. Ensure the same material is applied to each of the imported models.

Drag the *SingleApple* model into the Hierarchy or Scene so it is visible by the camera. It may appear quite large. Remembering the camera is in orthogonal view, moving the apple backwards will not make it smaller. You will need to resize the object itself. With the *SingleApple* selected in the Hierarchy press the R key and then drag the mouse over the center white cube of the axes that appear to change the apple's size.

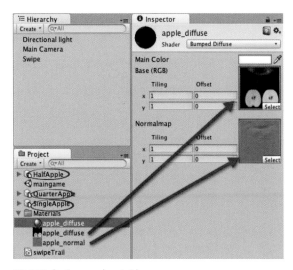

FIG 5.33 Creating an apple material.

FIG 5.34 The Apple's mesh intersects with the camera's near plane, thus obscuring part of it.

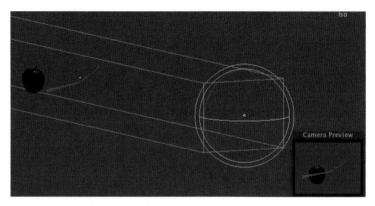

FIG 5.35 Positioning the apple behind the swipe trail with respect to the camera.

It may also be intersecting with the camera's near plane and appear as though it has a hole in it as shown in Figure 5.34. In this case, move it backwards along the *z* axis.

Step 5: In order for the swipe trail to be drawn in front of the apple, the apple will have to be further back in the *z* than the swipe trail. The code for the swipe trail always draws it on the XY plane at $z = 0$, therefore positioning your apple with $z = -10$ will ensure it is drawn behind, as shown in Figure 5.35.

Once you have the apple sized and positioned appropriately, select the apple object in the Hierarchy. In the Inspector, locate the attached animation component. Remember, these get imported as part of the FBX file import. As the apple isn't an animated model and we want to ensure as few drawcalls as possible, delete the animation component.

Next, with the apple selected in the Hierarchy, add a sphere collider and a rigidbody component via the main menu Component > Physics > Rigidbody and Component > Physics > Sphere Collider. Change the collider's radius so that it's approximately the same size as the apple. The apple will now become part of the physics system and collisions and gravity will automatically affect its behavior.

Step 6: Draw and drop the *SingleApple* object in the Hierarchy onto the Project window. This will create a new prefab of this apple as shown in Figure 5.36.

After the prefab has been created, delete the original object from the Hierarchy.

FIG 5.36 Drag and drop an object from the Hierarchy into the Project to create an instant prefab.

Drag and drop the *HalfApple* model into the Hierarchy. Scale it to the same size you used for the *SingleApple*. To find the scale used for the *SingleApple*, select its prefab in the Project and look in the Inspector for its Scale in the Transform component. Turn the apple 90 degrees around its *y* axis so you can see that it is half an apple. Remove the Animation component and add a rigidbody and a box collider. The sphere collider will not work in this instance as it won't fit the half apple well.

Step 7: With the *HalfApple* selected in the Hierarchy use CTRL+D (Windows) or CMD+D (Mac) to duplicate it. Rotate the second half −90 degrees around the *y* and position it next to the other half such that they line up to make a whole as shown in Figure 5.37.

Create an empty game object called *TwoHalves*. Drag and drop both *HalfApple* objects onto this new object to child them to it as shown in Figure 5.38.

Step 8: Next, move one of the halves towards the other so their colliders overlap as shown in Figure 5.39. The reason for doing this is so the halves will push away from each other when the object is instantiated, providing some initial movement. To see the effect, press play. The halves will push apart from each other while dropping under the force of gravity.

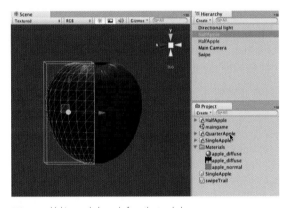

FIG 5.37 Making a whole apple from the two halves.

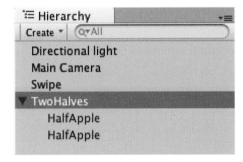

FIG 5.38 An empty game object acting as a parent for the two apple halves.

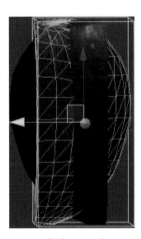

FIG 5.39 Overlapping apple colliders.

321

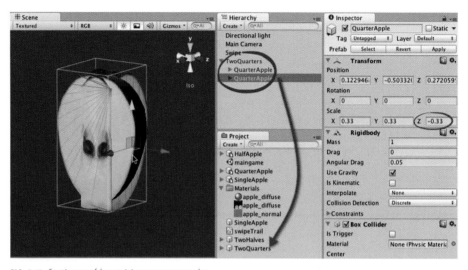

FIG 5.40 Creating a prefab containing two quarter apples.

FIG 5.41 Creating unique tags for each type of apple prefab.

Make a prefab out of the *TwoHalves* object and then delete the original.

Step 9: Repeat Steps 7 and 8 with the *QuarterApples*. You'll need two quarters lined up to make a half, contained in an empty game object with overlapping colliders. Note, when you duplicate the first quarter, in order to mirror it, set its *z* scale value to negative as shown in Figure 5.40.

Remember to remove the original object from the Hierarchy when you are done.

Step 10: Select each of the apple prefabs in turn and create and set a new tag for them as shown in Figure 5.41. Tag the whole apple *SingleApple*, the halved apple *TwoHalves* and the other *TwoQuarters*. Also create a tag *HalfApple* and set it for the child halves of the *TwoHalves* prefab and a tag *QuarterApple* and set it for the child quarters of the *TwoQuarters* prefab.

Create a cube and position it in the bottom-right corner of the camera's view. Position it at the same distance from the camera you decided to have the apples. In this case it is -10. Rotate the cube so the *z* axis points to the upper left as shown in Figure 5.42. Remove its collider.

Step 11: Create a new C# script called *spawnApples* and add the following code:

```
using UnityEngine;
using System.Collections;

public class spawnApples : MonoBehaviour {

    public GameObject apple;
```

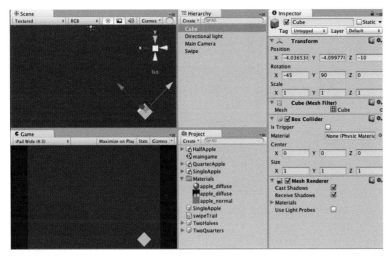

FIG 5.42 Creating a cube and positioning it in the lower right corner.

```
void Start ()
{
    InvokeRepeating("SpawnBall",1,1);
}

void SpawnBall()
{
    GameObject appObj = (GameObject) Instantiate(
        apple, this.transform.position,
        this.transform.rotation);

    appObj.rigidbody.AddForce(this.transform.forward * 800);
}
}
```

Attach this code to the Cube and set the exposed apple variable to the *SingleApple* prefab as shown in Figure 5.43.

Play. The apples should spawn and shoot across the screen as shown in Figure 5.44. Note that in this particular illustration, the time between apples is 0.3 seconds instead of the one second set in the previous code. You can modify this value as you see fit for more or less apples per second. At this stage if you want to resize the spawned apples you can do so by changing the scale within the transform component of the *SingleApple* prefab.

Step 12: To cause the apple to split into halves and then quarters when swiped, modify the Update() function of the *swipeTrail* code thus:

```
void Update ()
{
```

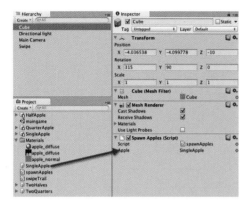

FIG 5.43 Setting the spawn code to create *SingleApple* objects.

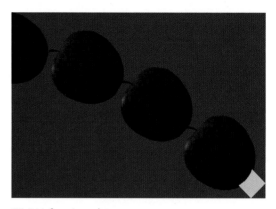

FIG 5.44 Spawning apples.

```
if((((Input.touchCount > 0 &&
    Input.GetTouch(0).phase == TouchPhase.Moved)
    || Input.GetMouseButton(0)))
{
    var mPos = Camera.main.ScreenToWorldPoint(
        new Vector3(Input.mousePosition.x,
        Input.mousePosition.y, 0));

    this.transform.position = new Vector3
    (mPos.x,mPos.y,0);

    RaycastHit hit;
    Ray ray = Camera.main.ScreenPointToRay
        (Input.mousePosition);

    if (!Physics.Raycast (ray, out hit, 10000))
        return;

    //we've hit an apple
    if(hit.transform.gameObject.tag == "SingleApple")
    {
        GameObject halfObj = (GameObject)
            Instantiate(appleHalves,
            this.transform.position,
            this.transform.rotation);

        halfObj.transform.position =
            hit.transform.gameObject.transform.position;

        Destroy(hit.transform.gameObject);
    }
    else if(hit.transform.gameObject.tag == "HalfApple")
    {
        GameObject quartObj = (GameObject)
            Instantiate(appleQuarters,
            this.transform.position,
            this.transform.rotation);
```

```
        quartObj.transform.position =
            hit.transform.gameObject.transform.position;

        Destroy(hit.transform.gameObject);
        }
    }
}
```

Also add these two public variables to the top of the script:

```
    public class swipeTrail : MonoBehaviour {

        public GameObject appleHalves;
        public GameObject appleQuarters;

        void Start () {
        ...
```

Save the code. Select the Swipe object in the Hierarchy and locate the *swipeTrail* script in the Inspector. Assign the *appleHalves* and *appleQuarters* variables the appropriate prefabs as shown in Figure 5.45.

Play. You will be able to swipe the whole apple into halves and the half into quarters. The code works by detecting a raycast hit from the mouse or finger movement, takes the hit game object and replaces it with either a two halves or two quarters depending on the tag on the object. The hit object is then destroyed to remove it from the game environment.

Step 13: Unfortunately after the apple is split it loses momentum, as the original object's movement does not translate to the newly created object that replaces it. We can fix this using the hit object's velocity as an added force on the new object. However, remember

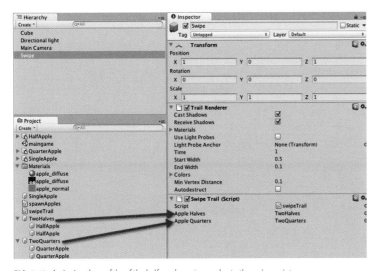

FIG 5.45 Assigning the prefabs of the half- and quarter-apples to the swipe script.

each new instantiated object is just a holder object with two children representing the half apple pieces. The parent object itself does not have a rigidbody and therefore cannot have a force applied to it. We need to apply the initial force to the children. To do this we use the `GetComponentsInChildren` function. This returns an array of the children of a certain type that belong to the parent. In this case we want to get all rigidbodies that are attached to the parents and apply a force to them. To do this, modify the *swipeTrail* code in its `Update()` function thus:

```
...
RaycastHit hit;
Ray ray = Camera.main.ScreenPointToRay (Input.mouse
Position);
if (!Physics.Raycast (ray, out hit, 10000))
    return;

    //we've hit an apple
    if(hit.transform.gameObject.tag == "SingleApple")
    {
        GameObject halfObj = (GameObject) Instantiate
        (appleHalves,
            this.transform.position,
            this.transform.rotation);

        Rigidbody[] halves;
        halves = halfObj.GetComponentsInChildren<Rigidbody>();

        foreach(Rigidbody r in halves)
            r.AddForce(hit.rigidbody.velocity * 50);

        halfObj.transform.position =
        hit.transform.gameObject.transform.position;

        Destroy(hit.transform.gameObject);
    }
    else if(hit.transform.gameObject.tag == "HalfApple")
    {
        GameObject quartObj = (GameObject) Instantiate
        (appleQuarters,
            this.transform.position, this.transform.
            rotation);

            Rigidbody[] quarters;
            quarters = quartObj.
            GetComponentsInChildren<Rigidbody>();

            foreach(Rigidbody r in quarters)
                r.AddForce(hit.rigidbody.velocity * 50);
    ...
```

Save and play. The apples are now sliced and given an extra push. You will notice that sometimes the halves just seem to fall down. This will be due to the colliders on each half hitting in a way that they negate any sideways velocity. You can play around with the velocity multiplier in the preceding code if you want to change how this is affected.

● Note

Ensure you add code onto the apple prefabs that ensure they are destroyed when they become invisible to the camera. This will stop the CPU becoming cluttered with unused game objects. The method for achieving this was covered in the Chapter 3 hands-on exercise Touch 3D Objects.

This completes the main mechanic in *Fruit Ninja* of the swipe-and-slice. You can finish off the game by adding an image in the background, moving the apple spawn cube slightly off the screen and devising a point-scoring system complete with floating text. Other fruit can be added by duplicating the apple-spawn-cube and giving it a different set of fruit model prefabs.

5.3.2 *Harbor Master*

Harbor Master is now becoming one of the "original" mobile games. It implements a drawing mechanic in which players draw a path for little boats to follow. The player must guide the boats into the harbor and back out without boats colliding with one another or the land.

◎ Unity Hands-On
Harbor Master

Step 1: Download and open the HarbourMaster.zip project. Open the *maingame* scene to reveal a large plane with an image of the Sydney Harbor on it. This will be background for the game. You can change it to your liking later. In the Project you will find a *BoatPrefab*. This will be the basis for the little boats that come into the harbor. Note, the camera is set to orthographic and looking down the z axis.

The project is also setup for iOS. Change this if you are building for Android.

Step 2: Drag and drop the *BoatPrefab* into the Scene. Ensure its z position places it closer to the camera so it is not obscured by the background plane. To make the boat move forward create a new C# script called *driveBoat* and add the following code:

```
using UnityEngine;
using System.Collections;

public class driveBoat : MonoBehaviour {

    float speed = 1.0f;
    void Start () {
    }
    void Update ()
    {
        this.transform.position - =
            (this.transform.forward *
            Time.deltaTime * speed);
    }

}
```

Save and attach to the boat in the Hierarchy. Play. This will drive the boat object along its forward axis.

Step 3: With the boat selected in the Hierarchy, add a Trail Renderer with Component > Effects > Trail Renderer. Set the material of the renderer to Default-Particle and the Time, Start Width, and End Width respectively to 2, 1, and 0.5 as shown in Figure 5.47. Now, when you play, the boat will have a nice water wake following it.

Step 4: To update the changes made to the boat prefab, with the boat object selected in the Hierarchy, click on the Apply button as shown in Figure 5.48.

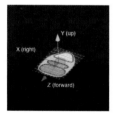

FIG 5.46 The boat prefab and its axis system.

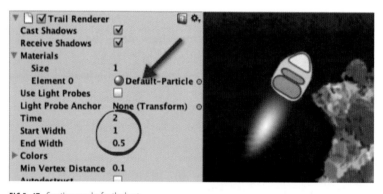

FIG 5 47 Creating a wake for the boat.

FIG 5.48 Applying the changes made to a prefab onto the master object.

Step 5: Remove the boat from the Hierarchy.

Step 6: Create a cube and place it outside the camera's view in the bottom-left corner of the environment. This will act as the spawn point for boats. Create a new C# script called *spawnBoats* and add the following:

```
using UnityEngine;
using System.Collections;

public class spawnBoats : MonoBehaviour {

    public GameObject boatPrefab;

    void CreateBoat()
    {
        GameObject boatObj = (GameObject)
            Instantiate(boatPrefab,
            this.transform.position,
            boatPrefab.transform.rotation);
        Invoke("CreateBoat",2);
    }
    void Start ()
    {
        //create the first boat in 2 seconds
        Invoke("CreateBoat", 2);
    }
}
```

Save. Attach this code to the cube. With the cube selected in the Hierarchy, locate the attached code and set the *boatPrefab* variable to the actual boat prefab by dragging it across from the Project.

Play. The code spawns a new boat every two seconds. It uses the boat prefab's set rotation as the starting rotation and therefore all the boats created will move off in the same direction as shown in Figure 5.49.

Step 7: At this point, you could make a prefab from the cube and place them multiple times around the game environment. They would spawn boats every two seconds and they would all move off in the same direction. However, we need more control over the direction the boat is initially moving in. Therefore we need to rotate each boat slightly around its up axis.

To determine the values of rotation we are dealing with, drag and drop a *boatPrefab* into the Scene and examine its rotation values in the Inspector as shown in Figure 5.50. In this case the boat has been rotated 45 degrees around the *x*. The *y* and *z* axis are rotated by 90 as the boat has been set to face the camera.

Leaving the *y* and *z* axes as 90, if you set *x* to 90, the boat will point to the top of the screen. If you set it to 0, the boat will face to the right. If you set

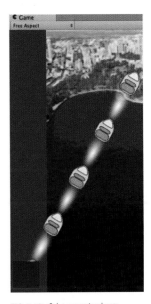

FIG 5.49 Cube spawning boats.

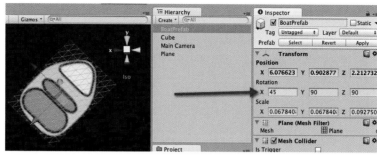

FIG 5.50 Investigating the angle a boat is facing.

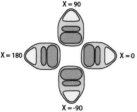

FIG 5.51 The *x* rotation values to turn the boat in different directions.

it to 180 it will point to the left. These values are illustrated in Figure 5.51. You will notice the values increase counter-clockwise to 180 at which point they become negative and count back up to 0. Note 180 and –180 in this case are the same! This is due to the way quaternions work.

Step 8: Working with these axis rotations can be quite confusing so rather than considering values ranging between 0 and 180 and 0 and -180, we could set the initial boat prefab to face 0 degrees and then use the Rotate function to turn it around. This way we aren't setting a particular rotation, we are turning the object by a certain angle. Unity's mathematics then does all the work for us. We can use a random function to generate rotation values by modifying *spawnBoats.cs*, thus:

```
. . .
public GameObject boatPrefab;
public float minBoatTurnAngle = 0;
public float maxBoatTurnAngle = 90;

void CreateBoat()
{
    GameObject boatObj = (GameObject) Instantiate
    (boatPrefab,
        this.transform.position,
        boatPrefab.transform.rotation);

        boatObj.transform.Rotate(0, -
            Random.Range(minBoatTurnAngle,
            maxBoatTurnAngle), 0);

    Invoke("CreateBoat",2);
}
. . .
```

Save and run. Boats will be spawned and rotated by random amounts between 0 and 90 degrees thanks to the Random.Range() function. To ensure this works, set the *x* rotation of the boat prefab to 0. The angle randomly generated then turns the boat through that amount around its *y* axis. The result will be boats produced as shown in Figure 5.52.

Step 9: We are now going to create the line-drawing functionality to allow the player to draw paths on the screen for the boats to follow. Begin by adding an empty game object to the Hierarchy called *Line*. To this, select the *Line* object, then Add Component > Effects > Line Renderer. Create an Unlit/Texture material that is white and set this as the line renderer's material as shown in Figure 5.53. Tag the object with the word "Line" and make a prefab from it.

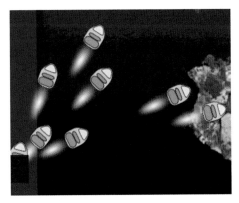

FIG 5.52 Boats being spawned then turned between 0 and 90 degrees.

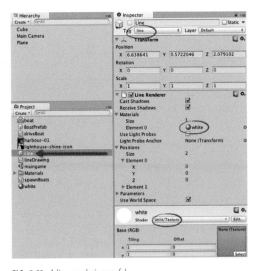

FIG 5.53 A line-rendering prefab.

Create a new C# script called *lineDrawing* and add the code:

```
using System.Collections.Generic;
using UnityEngine;

public class lineDrawing : MonoBehaviour
{
    public GameObject line;

    List<Vector3> linePoints;
    LineRenderer lineRenderer;
    public float startWidth = 0.01f;
    public float endWidth = 0.01f;
    public float threshold = 0.001f;

    Vector3 lastPos;

    void Update()
    {
        if((Input.touchCount > 0 && Input.GetTouch(0).phase ==
            TouchPhase.Began) || Input.GetMouseButtonDown(0))
        {
            Vector3 mousePos = Input.mousePosition;
            mousePos.z = 1;

            GameObject newLine = (GameObject) Instantiate
            (line,
                this.transform.position,
                Quaternion.identity);

            linePoints = null;
            lastPos = Vector3.one * float.MaxValue;
            lineRenderer = newLine.
            GetComponent<LineRenderer>();
            linePoints = new List<Vector3>();
        }
        else if((Input.touchCount > 0 && Input.GetTouch(0).
        phase ==
            TouchPhase.Moved) || Input.GetMouseButton(0))
        {
            Vector3 mousePos = Input.mousePosition;
            mousePos.z = 1;

            Vector3 mouseWorld =
                Camera.main.ScreenToWorldPoint(mousePos);

            float dist = Vector3.Distance(lastPos, mouseWorld);

            if(dist < = threshold)
                return;

            lastPos = mouseWorld;
            linePoints.Add(mouseWorld);
```

```
            UpdateLine();
        }
    }

    void UpdateLine()
    {
        lineRenderer.SetWidth(startWidth, endWidth);
        lineRenderer.SetVertexCount(linePoints.Count);

        for(int i = 0; i < linePoints.Count; i++)
        {
            lineRenderer.SetPosition(i, linePoints[i]);
        }

        lineRenderer.materials[0].mainTextureScale =
        new Vector2 (linePoints.Count-1,1);
    }
}
```

Save and attach to the ground plane object. Set the exposed Line variable in the script to the Line prefab as shown in Figure 5.54. Play. You will be able to draw white lines on the screen.

Step 10: On close inspection you'll be able to see that the line being drawn is a dynamically created mesh using the mouse location to determine the vertices as shown in Figure 5.55. The code works by creating a new line renderer on each touch. As the player drags their finger across the screen, the new mouse position becomes another vertex in the line. To ensure the line doesn't have vertices at each and every pixel location, a threshold value is used to determine when a new vertex is recorded. This makes the line a construction of small straight segments. The bigger the threshold, the less smooth the line will appear.

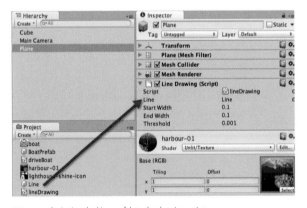

FIG 5.54 Assigning the Line prefab to the drawing script.

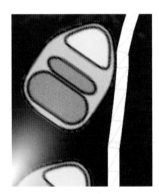

FIG 5.55 Close up of a line showing the polygon construction.

The paths drawn in *Harbor Master* must start on a boat. Therefore before a new line is drawn we must ensure a boat is under the player's finger (or mouse). To do this, first ensure the boat prefab has a tag of "boat." The boat already has a Mesh Collider on it so we will take advantage of the fact. To determine if a boat has been pressed on before drawing a line we will add a Boolean value to the code and set it to true if a physics raycast of the touch location hits something tagged with "boat." Modify *lineDrawing* thus:

```
...
public float startWidth = 0.01f;
public float endWidth = 0.01f;
public float threshold = 0.001f;

bool started = false;

Vector3 lastPos;
    void Update()
    {
        if((Input.touchCount > 0 && Input.GetTouch(0).
        phase ==
            TouchPhase.Began) || Input.
            GetMouseButtonDown(0))
        {
            Vector3 mousePos = Input.mousePosition;
            started = false;

            RaycastHit hit;
            Ray ray = Camera.main.ScreenPointToRay
                (Input.mousePosition);

            if (!Physics.Raycast (ray, out hit, 10000))
                return;

            //we've hit a boat
            if(hit.transform.gameObject.tag ! = "boat")
                return;

            started = true;

            mousePos.z = 1;

            ...
        }
        else if(((Input.touchCount > 0 &&
            Input.GetTouch(0).phase ==
            TouchPhase.Moved) || Input.GetMouseButton(0))
            && started)
        {
    ...
```

Save and play. You will only be able to draw a line if the line starts on top of a boat.

Step 11: Before we go any further we need to modify the boat prefab. Previously we discovered the image on the plane faces in the opposite

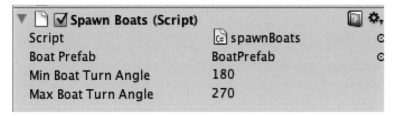

FIG 5.56 Modifying the starting spawn angle range.

direction to the forward-facing z axis. When we start moving objects around relative to other objects, like we are about to do with the boat following the path, the code and mathematics is a lot neater if the graphics of the object face in the right direction according to the z axis. Therefore, to fix this, open the boat.png image in Photoshop or equivalent and turn the image upside down. Then reassign to the boat prefab. You can also download this boat image from the website as *boatupsidedown.png*.

In addition, the Cube's *spawnBoat* script will need its minimum and maximum boat turn angles modified as shown in Figure 5.56. To ensure the boat rotates right around before starting its journey from the bottom-left of the screen.

To make a boat follow a line modify the *driveBoat* script thus:

```
using System.Collections.Generic;
using UnityEngine;
using System.Collections;

public class driveBoat : MonoBehaviour {

    public LineRenderer path;
    public List<Vector3> pathPoints;

    float speed = 1.0f;
    int pathIndex = 0;

    void Update ()
    {
        if(path && pathPoints.Count > 0)
            //if there is a path, follow it
        {
            Vector3 targetPos = new Vector3(pathPoints[0].x,
                pathPoints[0].y,
                this.transform.position.z);

            this.transform.LookAt(targetPos, Vector3.forward);

            //if boat is close enough to the point
            if(Vector3.Distance(targetPos,
            this.transform.position) < 1)
            {
                //remove point from lineRenderer
```

```
                                        //and array to make boat move to next point
                                        pathPoints.RemoveAt(0);
                                        UpdatePath();
                                    }
                                }
                                this.transform.Translate(Vector3.forward *
                                    Time.deltaTime * speed);
                            }
                            //after vertex is removed from the path
                            //update the line renderer to remove it too
                            void UpdatePath()
                            {
                                if(pathPoints.Count > 0)
                                {
                                    path.SetVertexCount(pathPoints.Count);
                                    for(int i = 0; i < pathPoints.Count; i++)
                                    {
                                        path.SetPosition(i, pathPoints[i]);
                                    }
                                    path.materials[0].mainTextureScale =
                                        new Vector2 (pathPoints.Count-1,1);
                                }
                            }
                        }
```

Next make the following changes to *lineDrawing*:

```
        ...
        public class lineDrawing : MonoBehaviour
        {
            public GameObject line;
            public GameObject boat = null;

            List<Vector3> linePoints;
            ...
```

and inside the first if statement in the Update() function add a line to assign the boat object:

```
        ...
        RaycastHit hit;
        Ray ray = Camera.main.ScreenPointToRay (Input.mouse
        Position);
        if (!Physics.Raycast (ray, out hit, 10000))
            return;

        //we've hit a boat
        if(hit.transform.gameObject.tag ! = "boat")
            return;

        started = true;
        boat = hit.transform.gameObject;
```

```
mousePos.z = 1;
...
```

then add another `else if` clause to the bottom of the `if` statement in the `Update()` function thus:

```
...
else if(((Input.touchCount > 0 &&
Input.GetTouch(0).phase == TouchPhase.Ended) ||
Input.GetMouseButtonUp(0)) && started)
{
    if(boat)
    {
        boat.GetComponent<driveBoat>().path = lineRenderer;
        boat.GetComponent<driveBoat>().pathPoints = linePoints;
        boat = null;
    }
}
...
```

Step 12: The new code in *lineDrawing* will assign a line and the line's points to the boat that was touched. This is then used by the new code in *driveBoat* loops through each of the vertices in the line and has the boat turn to look at each in turn as it gets close to them. The forward driving code keeps the boat moving forward as before and the turning code allows it to change directions. Remember we turned the boat image upside-down so now we don't need to make allowances for the *z* axis being reversed.

Save and play. You will be able to click and drag a line out from a boat and when you release the mouse the boat will follow that line. When it reaches the end of the line it will continue moving forward from that point.

Step 13: We now want to have a boat destroyed if it collides with another boat or land. The first thing that needs to be done is to place colliders over the areas of land. The easiest way to do this is to use primitive objects such as cubes and spheres. Place them over your ground plane to block the areas of land. Then remove their Mesh Filters and Mesh Renderers so that all is left are the colliders as shown in Figure 5.57.

Ensure the colliders intersect with the ground and are also high enough that a boat will collide with them and not pass over the top. Tag all the land colliders with "land."

Once again, place the *BoatPrefab* back into this Scene. This time we want to adjust its collider. Currently it is a flat mesh collider. This type of collider is processor-heavy for the physics system to process and should only be used when absolutely required. Also, because it is flat with no real depth, you could run into issues when two boats collide. The collision

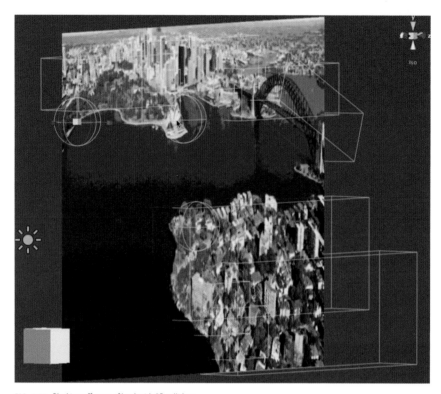

FIG 5.57 Blocking off areas of land with 3D colliders.

may be ignored. To ensure a better collision, with the boat selected in the Hierarchy, add a Box Collider with Component > Physics > Box Collider. This will replace the mesh collider but still be wafer thin. Therefore, in the Inspector adjust the box collider's *y* size to make it more cube-shaped as shown in Figure 5.58. Tick the Is Trigger box on the collider. Also add a rigidbody to the boat and tick its *Is Kinematic* box.

Apply the changes to the boat prefab and then delete the one in the Scene.

Step 14: Making a collider a trigger places it in the physics system but it is not affected by physics events. It does however register any collision that occurs. In addition, for the physics system to register a collision has occurred, an object needs to have a rigidbody. In this case, we've set the rigidbody to be kinematic. This means the object will not be affected by any physics. For example, the boat will be able to register a collision with another collider, but it will not be repelled by any resulting forces.

To destroy each boat when it hits the land or another boat, add this new function to the *driveBoat* script:

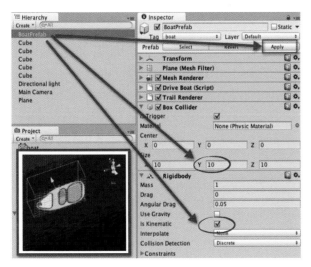

FIG 5.58 Adding a box collider onto the boat prefab.

```
void OnTriggerEnter(Collider other)
{
    if(other.gameObject.tag == "land" ||
        other.gameObject.tag == "boat")
    {
        Destroy(this.gameObject);
    }
}
```

This function runs when a trigger object experiences a collision. In this case we are destroying the object itself if it runs into something tagged with "land" or "boat."

Step 15: In the Project there is a small lighthouse image (courtesy of www.fatcow.com/free-icons). Place this image onto a new plane in the Scene. The lighthouse will represent the harbor location that the boat must get to. Add a Box Collider to it. Ensure the collider is cube shaped and not too flat—just like you did for the boat. Make the collider a Trigger.

Create a new C# script called *processBoat* and add the following:

```
using UnityEngine;
using System.Collections;

public class processBoat : MonoBehaviour {

    GameObject boat;

    void OnTriggerEnter(Collider other)
    {
```

```
if(other.gameObject.tag == "boat")
{
    boat = other.gameObject;

    //rotate the boat around
    boat.transform.Rotate(0,180,0);
    //stop boat moving
    boat.GetComponent<driveBoat>().speed = 0;

    //align boat with lighthouse
    boat.transform.position =
        this.transform.position;

    //start boat moving again in 2 seconds
    Invoke("StartBoat",2);
}
}
void StartBoat()
{
    if(boat)
        boat.GetComponent<driveBoat>().speed = 1.0f;
}
}
```

Make the speed variable in *driveBoat* public so the script can access it.

Attach this code to the lighthouse. Save and play. When a boat hits the lighthouse, its speed will be reduced to zero for two seconds. It will also be turned around by 180 degrees, ready to leave.

Step 16: Finally for this tutorial, you may have noticed that a boat's path stays on the screen even after the boat has been destroyed. To make sure it gets deleted, you need to include an OnDestroy() function in the *driveBoat* script. This function runs just before an object is removed from the game environment. In this case you will want to add it thus:

```
void OnDestroy()
{
    if(path)
        path.SetVertexCount(0);
}
```

To complete your *Harbor Master* game you can now add a scoring system, user interface, floating up scores, explosions on impact and all other manner of special effects and features. You may also want to add destroys for the boats in OnBecameInvisible() functions. The lighthouse could also be made into a prefab and multiple copies added around your game scene.

5.4 Using Motion

In this section we examine the use of the mobile device's accelerometer in creating engaging gameplay. Using acceleration and orientation on a mobile device is unique from other motion sensing devices such as the Nintendo Wii and Sony PlayStation EyeToy (apart from Virtual Reality headsets) as the player is rotating the screen itself. Because the screen can rotate away from the player's vision, the game designer must keep in mind how visible the game graphics will be when the screen is rotated in certain ways. The majority of games that use the accelerometers in gameplay rotate the screen while keeping it perpendicular to the player's view, having it rotate like a car's steering wheel. It's not a surprise that many games using this type of motion are racing games that require the player to turn a vehicle, such as *Real Racing 3* and *Riptide GP 2*.

Other games use motion to orientate the game environment. A popular example is explored in the following section.

5.4.1 *Super Monkey Ball*

Super Monkey Ball by Amusement Vision started out life in 2001 as an upright arcade cabinet game and later as a launch title for the Nintendo GameCube. The game mechanics see the player attempting to control a transparent sphere containing a running monkey. The objective is to pick up bananas while keeping the ball balanced on and moving along a game track that sits in midair without any safety rails. The challenge comes from orienting the game track by tilting it to control the movement of the ball.

Joysticks and game controllers originally controlled the tilting of the game track; however, with the proliferation of mobile phones, the accelerometer lent itself perfectly to the same tilting mechanic. This saw *Super Monkey Ball* and *Super Monkey Ball: Tip 'n Tilt* released for mobiles in 2007.

⬤ **Unity Hands-On**
Super Rubber Ball
Step 1: Download and open the *SuperRubberBall* project from the website. Open the main scene. In it you will find a game track and a sphere as shown in Figure 5.59. The sphere has a *Rigidbody* added to it and the track has a mesh collider. Play. The sphere will fall onto the surface of the track.
Step 2: Before we use the accelerometers of a device, we will use the arrow keys to tilt the track so we can debug the gameplay in the editor. Create a new C# script called *tiltTrack* and add the following code:

```
using UnityEngine;
using System.Collections;

public class tiltTrack : MonoBehaviour {

    // Use this for initialization
    void Start () {

    }

    // Update is called once per frame
```

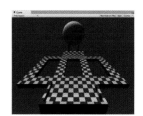

FIG 5.59 The starting scene for the Super Rubber Ball game.

```
void Update ()
{
    if(Input.GetKey(KeyCode.RightArrow))
    {
        this.transform.Rotate(Vector3.forward * 1);
    }
    else if(Input.GetKey(KeyCode.LeftArrow))
    {
        this.transform.Rotate(Vector3.forward * -1);
    }
    else if(Input.GetKey(KeyCode.UpArrow))
    {
        this.transform.Rotate(Vector3.right * -1);
    }
    else if(Input.GetKey(KeyCode.DownArrow))
    {
        this.transform.Rotate(Vector3.right * 1);
    }
}
}
```

Save and attach the script to the *superballtrack* game object in the Hierarchy. Play. The arrow keys will tilt the track and the sphere will react appropriately.

Something you may notice is that if the sphere is allowed to fall and hit the track and then you start tilting it, the physics system will appear to not be working. It is not a glitch but rather that the physics system is ignoring your manual movements of the track model. To ensure the track is a physics object, select it in the Hierarchy and add a rigidbody to it. In the track's new rigidbody component, ensure the *isKinematic* tickbox is checked. This will allow the track to cause physics events without being affected by them.

● **Note**

If you find the sphere too hard to keep on the track, try changing the sphere's rigidbody drag value to 5.

Step 3: To make the camera follow the sphere as it moves along the track we will create a 3D version of the smooth camera following algorithm used in Chapter 4. Create a new C# script called *cameraFollow* and add the following code:

```
using UnityEngine;
using System.Collections;

public class cameraFollow : MonoBehaviour {

    public GameObject target;
```

```
Vector3 cameraTargetPos;
Vector3 distanceFromTarget;

void Start()
{
    distanceFromTarget = new Vector3(
        this.transform.position.x-target.
        transform.position.x,
        this.transform.position.y-target.
        transform.position.y,
        this.transform.position.z-target.
        transform.position.z);
}
void Update ()
{
    cameraTargetPos = new Vector3(
        this.target.transform.position.x +
        distanceFromTarget.x,
        this.target.transform.position.y +
        distanceFromTarget.y,
        this.target.transform.position.z +
        distanceFromTarget.z);

    transform.position = Vector3.Lerp(
        this.transform.position, cameraTargetPos,
        Time.deltaTime * 2.0f);
}
}
```

Save and attach the script to the Main Camera. Set the Target value of the script, in the Inspector, to the sphere.

Play. The camera will now smoothly follow the sphere keeping its relative distance. You may like to adjust the camera's position such that it is slightly above the sphere and looking down at it as shown in Figure 5.60.

Step 4: Now that we have the basic movement mechanics in place, it's time to add the accelerometer. This requires two lines of code to access the accelerometer values examined in Chapter 3. Modify the *tileTrack* script thus:

```
...
public class tiltTrack : MonoBehaviour {

    public float sensitivity = 5.0f;
    // Use this for initialization
    void Start () {

    }

    // Update is called once per frame
    void Update ()
```

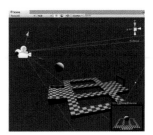

FIG 5.60 Positioning the camera relative to the sphere.

343

```
{
    this.transform.Rotate(Vector3.forward *
        Input.acceleration.x/sensitivity);
    this.transform.Rotate(Vector3.right *
        Input.acceleration.z/sensitivity);
    if(Input.GetKey(KeyCode.RightArrow))
    {
        this.transform.Rotate(Vector3.
        forward * 1);
    }
    ...
```

Save and build the game out to a mobile device for testing. Note that the code has a sensitivity adjustment for the accelerometer readings. The larger you make this value, the slower the rotations will be applied.

Step 5: Next we will add some pickup items to the game. Create a cube and place it in the scene in front of the sphere. Add a material to it. In this example it will be shown as green. Give the cube a tag of *GreenCube*, attach it to the *superballtrack* game object and set its Box Collider to be a trigger as shown in Figure 5.61.

Step 6: Create a C# script called *gInterface* and add the following code:

```
using UnityEngine;
using System.Collections;

public class gInterface : MonoBehaviour
{
    static public int score = 0;
```

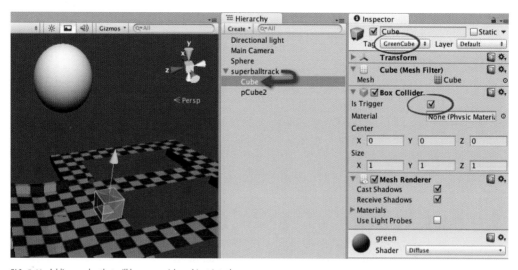

FIG 5.61 Adding a cube, that will become a pickup object, into the scene.

```
    void OnGUI()
    {
        GUI.Label(new Rect(10,10,100,20), "" + score);
    }
}
```

Save and attach to the Main Camera. When the game is run a *GUI Label* will display the score in the top left corner of the screen.

Step 7: Create a C# script called *pickup*. Add the following code:

```
using UnityEngine;
using System.Collections;

public class pickup : MonoBehaviour
{
    void OnTriggerEnter(Collider other)
    {
        if(other.gameObject.tag == "GreenCube")
        {
            gInterface.score++;
            Destroy(other.gameObject);
        }
    }
}
```

Save and attach to the sphere. Now when the sphere rolls over any objects that are triggers, the pickup code will run and add one to the score before deleting the trigger object (in this case the green cube). Try it out.

● A note about static variables

In the preceding code for *gInterface* the variable of score is declared as a static variable. The keyword *static* creates a variable that exists in the same location in computer memory for the entire run of a program. As such it allows us to access it using the name of the script that contains it and its name, e.g., `gInterface.score`. You can only refer to static variables in this way. You should also ensure you have but one static variable of any name to avoid confusion.

Because static variables are in the computer's memory for the entire execution of your game you should ensure you only use them for items that need to exist for that long. Using them to store player statistics is perfect.

Step 8: Create a prefab from the cube and remove it from the scene. Use the prefab to create multiple copies of the cube and scatter them throughout the scene. Remember to attach them to the track otherwise

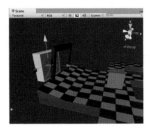

FIG 5.62 Adding a cube that will trigger the end of the level.

they will not move with the track as it tilts. Play. Roll the sphere over the cubes and watch your score increase.

Step 9: To end the level, the sphere must pass between the goalposts at the opposite end of the track. The pickup script that detects trigger objects can be added to detect the end of a level. First create a cube and place it just behind the goal posts as shown in Figure 5.62.

Step 10: Make the cube a trigger and remove its Mesh Renderer. This will make it invisible. Attach it to the track. Give the cube a tag of *LevelOver*.

Step 11: Modify the *gInterface* script like this:

```
. . .
static public bool levelOver = false;
void OnGUI()
    {
        GUI.Label(new Rect(10,10,100,20), "" + score);
        if(levelOver)
        {
            GUI.BeginGroup (new Rect (Screen.width / 2 – 50,
                Screen.height / 2 – 50, 100, 100));
                GUI.Box (new Rect (0,0,100,100),"Level Over");
            GUI.EndGroup ();
        }
    }
. . .
```

Save. This new code will display a GUI Box in the middle of the screen when the level is over. The `levelOver` value is initially set to false in this script. In the next step, it is set to true by the sphere colliding with the end of level cube.

Step 12: Modify the pickup script thus:

```
public class pickup : MonoBehaviour
{
    void OnTriggerEnter(Collider other)
    {
        if(other.gameObject.tag == "GreenCube")
        {
            gInterface.score++;
        }
        else if(other.gameObject.tag == "LevelOver")
        {
            gInterface.levelOver = true;
        }
    }
}
```

Save and play. When the sphere passes through the goalposts at the end of the track, the "level over" GUI will display. Within this code you could add extra commands to take the player to the next level in the game or to restart the level.

To add further enhancements to this type of game you might consider putting in particle effects and floating up scores as each cube is triggered by the sphere. The code to achieve this was presented in Section 4.8.

5.5 Summary

In this chapter we have primarily examined touch and orientation mechanics, as they provide the primary methods of user interaction in mobile games. Without a mouse, players are required to use a series of single and multiple touches as well as swipes and drags to interact with the game environment. Touch alone provides a plethora of differing gameplay experiences.

In addition, with onboard accelerometers, it makes sense to include orientation and movement data into mobile games. While not providing the range of functionality of touch, device orientation and movement can allow for natural motion input such as tilting the game world as in *Super Monkey Ball* or delivering quirky gameplay like the dripping blood in *Year Walk*.

In the next chapter, we will continue learning from existing successful games, and extend our exploration into physics, procedurally generated content, and artificial intelligence.

Learning from the Masters: Part Two

You can teach a student a lesson for a day; but if you can teach him to learn by creating curiosity, he will continue the learning process as long as he lives.

Clay P. Bedford

6.1 Introduction

Creating great games is time-consuming. In the distant past, game developers had to write all the code for a game from the ground up. If they wanted physics, they'd have to write a module; if they wanted sound, they'd have to develop the code for that too. Eventually many people noticed the same code was being used over and over again in games and this code evolved into plugin modules that other developers could use in place of writing their own systems. Today there are a plethora of external modules—otherwise known as engines—that game developers can use that take the hard work out of reinventing graphics systems, physics systems, artificial intelligences, mathematical systems, audio systems, and more.

Unity implements numerous external engines. For graphics rendering it employs Direct X (for Windows), OpenGL (for Mac, Windows, Linux, and PS3), and OpenGL ES (for mobile development). The C# scripts you write are processed by the Mono engine, an open source implementation of Microsoft's .NET Framework. This is the reason you'll see the term `MonoBehaviour` in the top of the scripts you write.

For physics, Unity implements the NVIDIA PhysX engine. This allows Unity to support real-time cloth simulation, thick raycasts, and collisions.

● Note

Unity uses spheres to perform a thick raycast. Imagine it like shooting out a pipe instead of a piece of string to perform a collision hit. For more information see http://docs.unity3d.com/Documentation/ScriptReference/Physics.SphereCast.html

---

Of all the plugins in game development engines it is the physics system that provides the most value in terms of dynamic object movement and interactions. Many games play on this strength, allowing the game engine to create game object behavior rather than scripting for it specifically.

Another system that requires in-depth knowledge of mathematics is artificial intelligence (AI). In games, AI is used primarily to give computer-controlled characters the ability to traverse game environments, find the player, and converse with them. Unity has an inbuilt system, available in Unity Pro, for movement called Navigation Meshes and NavMeshes. These grid-like systems sit over the top of existing terrain and game maps that determine safe routes along which characters can travel to get to a goal position without colliding with objects in the environment. Such a Unity plugin, that you don't need Unity Pro for, that will do this for you is investigated at the end of the chapter.

Both the physics and AI systems procedurally generate content as it is the mathematics and algorithms contained within that dynamically affect the game environment and character behavior. By extending these ideas to the manipulation of the physical game environment at runtime we can also make a game build and extend on itself. Numerous games implement algorithms that build game environments automatically and generate infinite game maps. One example, *Temple Run*, infinitely generates paths for the player to run along as long as the player's character remains alive. This type of game world generation is advantageous as it extends gameplay and the size of a game level without placing extra onus on modelers to model gigantic game maps. With just a few simple building blocks, an endlessly interesting game environment can be produced, just like the terrains in *Minecraft*.

In the following sections we will explore how many popular mobile games have implemented physics, procedural generation, and AI to create extended game and character dynamics on the fly.

6.2 Exploiting the Physics System

In the distant past of game development, physics systems were programmed from scratch for all games. Thankfully, now we have physics engines that take care of all the mathematics and physics principles embedded in games that determine object behavior when placed under force. What this means is that we can simply create an object, allocate its size and mass, and then push it around. How the object reacts with the environment and other game objects is all calculated. This dramatically reduces development time.

The two elementary components in any physics system are colliders and rigidbodies. These will be examined before we dive into their use with recreations of the professional games *Angry Birds* and *Catapult King*. While these games implement the same mechanic of projectile-throwing, they implement the physics system in different spaces; 2D for *Angry Birds* and 3D for *Catapult King*.

6.2.1 Colliders and Rigidbodies

A collider is a bounding area around an object that specifies its physical limits. It is used by the physics system to calculate the size of an object to determine when one object comes into contact (collides) with another. Without a collider, a game object has no substance. A wall without a collider would allow a player's avatar to pass straight through.

In Unity there are several collider types that can be added to a game object via the Inspector as a component. The most common of these is shown in Figure 6.1. The only collider that can be a perfect match to your game object's mesh is the mesh collider as it uses the same mesh as the renderer to define the object's boundary. However, the mesh collider is the most expensive collider type to add to an object due to its complexity.

In order for the physics system to determine if one object has collided with another, it needs to calculate if the boundaries have overlapped. This is an elementary calculation for two sphere colliders, as only the position and radius are needed to determine if there is any overlap. If the sum of the radii (r1 + r2) of the spheres is less than the distance between the center positions (determined using Pythagoras' theorem) the spheres will not be over lapping. A 2D example of this is shown in Figure 6.2. The more complex the collider's shape, the more complex the calculations involved to determine if there has been a collision. The simpler collider shapes are a better choice for mobile games.

To add a collider to a game object in Unity is a matter of selecting it in the Hierarchy and then adding a physics component. There are both 2D and 3D collider types. The more common 3D colliders are shown in Figure 6.3. When

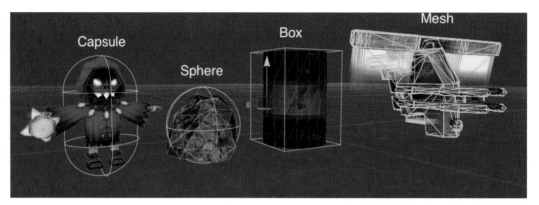

FIG 6.1 The capsule, sphere, box, and mesh collider types shown around models.

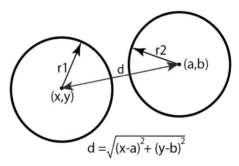

$$d = \sqrt{(x-a)^2 + (y-b)^2}$$

FIG 6.2 Calculating a sphere collision.

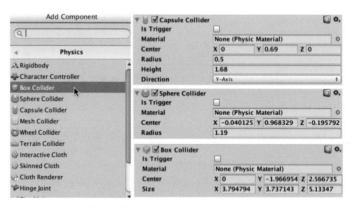

FIG 6.3 The Unity collider available in the physics components.

adding a collider to an object with an existing mesh, Unity does its best to resize and fit the collider around the object. If however this doesn't work, you can manually tweak the position of the collider in its settings in the Inspector. All colliders have a center position that moves the entire boundary and other values that change its size.

Colliders can also be set as triggers in the Inspector. This allows you to capture when one object has entered the boundary of another, but the trigger is not in the physics system as a hard entity and therefore objects can pass straight through it.

A rigidbody assigns physical properties to objects with colliders. While the collider determines the physical boundary of an object, a rigidbody gives that object solidity. Within a rigidbody component, you are able to set the object's mass, drag, angular drag, and whether or not the object is affected by gravity. A rigidbody is a physics component and added to an object in the Inspector.

The mass of an object determines the amount of force required to move the object as well as the energy it exerts on collision with another object. This obeys Newton's first law of motion; force = mass × acceleration. The greater the mass, the more destruction it causes. The biggest mistake programmers make in Unity when starting out with a rigidbody component is to use the object's mass to make it move faster. For example, if a ball is falling from the sky and they want it to fall faster, they increase the mass. This will not work as mass does not affect an object's velocity. You might remember the story about the bowling ball and feather dropped from the same height on the moon. Which one hits the ground first? They do in fact hit the ground at exactly the same time. The reason this experiment takes place on the moon is to eliminate the effect of drag caused by air friction. On Earth, the bowling ball would indeed hit the ground first as the feather has far more drag affecting it. Drag and angular drag (friction when rotating) can also be set in an object's rigidbody component. These values can be used to simulate the effect of friction on an object. If you want to make an object fall faster, reduce its drag, add a force to it, or change the gravitational force in the game. Under Edit > Project Settings > Physics, in the Inspector you will find the gravity vector. It will be set, as default, to that of Earth's gravity; 9.81 meters per second^2 downwards. You'll notice you are free to set gravity in your game environment to be in any direction and any magnitude.

Further, physical properties for an object can be manipulated through the addition of a physics material. The collider component has an exposed variable to which you can add a physics material. These can be created in the Project as shown in Figure 6.4.

The properties of a physics material provide you with control over bounce and friction. When playing around with these settings, remember it takes two objects to cause a collision and the physics material on both will come into play.

FIG 6.4 Creating a new physics material.

> ● **Note**
>
> For more detailed information on colliders, rigidbodies, and physics materials in Unity check out the Unity reference manual at http://docs. unity3d.com/Documentation/Manual/Physics.html.
>
>

6.2.2 Dice Rolling

We begin our practical examination of the physics system in Unity with a simple dice-rolling mechanic.

● **Unity Hands On**

Die Rolling

A number of board games that have made their way to mobile devices include die rolling graphics, such as the digital version of *Trivial Pursuit*. By exploiting Unity's physics system this mechanic is easily implemented.

Step 1: Create a new Unity Project. Set the camera to orthographic with a size of 5. Orient the camera to look down the *y* axis. Add a plane to the scene and put a green material on it. Download from the website *dice. fbx* and add to your assets. Drag a copy of it into the Scene. Resize the die as required and make sure it is sitting above the plane. Change the build settings for a mobile device and then change the view in the Game to landscape. Resize the plane to fill the Game view as required. The scene setup should look like that in Figure 6.5.

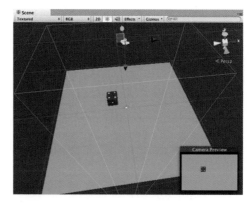

FIG 6.5 The Scene setup for die rolling exercise.

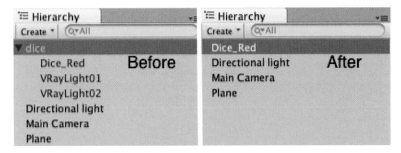

FIG 6.6 Changing the structure of the dice game object.

Step 2: The die (sourced from http://turbosquid.com) has some undesirable components that we don't need. Locate the dice game object and expand the contents as shown in Figure 6.6 (Before). The *Dice_Red* object is the actual model and that is all we need in for this exercise. Drag it out of the dice structure and drop it at the bottom of the Hierarchy. This will make it an object by itself. The remaining dice game object with the two *VRay* components can be deleted.

Step 3: Create a C# script called *rolldice* and add the following code:

```
using UnityEngine;
using System.Collections;

public class rollDice : MonoBehaviour {

    GameObject focusObj;
    Vector3 lastPos;
    Vector3 lastVelocity;

    void Update ()
    {
        if(Input.GetMouseButtonDown(0) ||
            (Input.touchCount > 0 &&
            Input.GetTouch(0).phase == TouchPhase.Began))
        {
            RaycastHit hit;
            Ray ray = Camera.main.ScreenPointToRay
            (Input.mousePosition);
            if (!Physics.Raycast (ray, out hit, 10000))
                return;
            if(hit.transform.gameObject.tag == "dice")
            {
                focusObj = hit.transform.gameObject;
            }
        }
        else if(focusObj && (Input.GetMouseButtonUp(0) ||
            (Input.touchCount > 0 &&
            Input.GetTouch(0).phase == TouchPhase.Ended)))
```

```
    {
        focusObj.rigidbody.AddForce( lastVelocity * 1000);
        focusObj = null;
    }
    else if(focusObj && ((Input.touchCount > 0 &&
        Input.GetTouch(0).phase == TouchPhase.Moved)||
        Input.GetMouseButton(0)))
    {
        Vector3 mPos = Camera.main.ScreenToWorldPoint(
            new Vector3(Input.mousePosition.x,
            Input.mousePosition.y, 0));

        focusObj.transform.position = new Vector3(mPos.x,
            focusObj.transform.position.y, mPos.z);

        lastVelocity = (focusObj.transform.position -
            lastPos);

        lastPos = focusObj.transform.position;
    }
}
}
```

Attach this code to the Main Camera. It is implementing the code we've used before for dragging and dropping objects. It works with the mouse as well as touch.

On a touch (or mouse-down) the code performs a raycast to determine if an object tagged with "dice" has been hit. If so, it remembers this object by setting focusObj to point to it. When the finger is then dragged around on the screen, the object moves with it. With each move, the last position of the object is remembered so we can compare the last position with the current position and calculate the object's velocity (the magnitude and direction in which it is moving). When the touch ends, this velocity is added as a force to the die.

Step 4: To make this code work, tag the die with "dice" and add a box collider and rigidbody to it.

Run. You'll be able to flick the dice with the mouse or a finger swipe. The die will slip, rather than roll across the screen at this stage. Hold tight! We'll deal with that shortly.

Step 5: As the program currently works, the die is flicked off the screen. To make it more interactive and exciting we should add some barriers around the game area to stop the die rolling off the plane. Add four cubes to the Scene and resize them into long sections to create a fence around the outside of the camera view volume as shown in Figure 6.7.

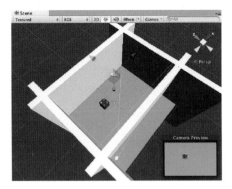

FIG 6.7 Creating physics reactive barriers to the Scene to keep the die contained.

Play, the die should be contained on the game board when rolled.

Step 6: On the off-chance the die gets through the barriers, you won't want the game to be devoid of a die, therefore you can add some code to the die to bring it back onto the board when it goes outside the camera's view. Create a C# script called *makeVisible* and add this:

```
using UnityEngine;
using System.Collections;

public class makeVisible : MonoBehaviour {

    Vector3 defaultPos;

    void Start()

    {
        defaultPos = this.transform.position;
    }

    void OnBecameInvisible()
    {
        this.transform.position = defaultPos;
    }
}
```

Attach this script to the die. Now, when it goes outside of the screen, it will simply pop back to its starting position.

Step 7: To stop the die from sliding across the plane we should increase the friction on the plane's material. This will cause the die to grab onto the plane and flip itself over. In the Project, create a new Physics Material and call it *felt* as shown in Figure 6.8.

Step 8: Select *felt* in the Project and locate its properties in the Inspector. Set the dynamic and static friction values to 1 as shown in Figure 6.9.

FIG 6.8 Creating a new Physics Material.

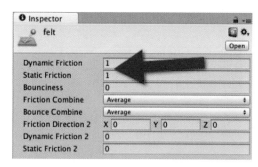

FIG 6.9 Changing the friction of a physics material.

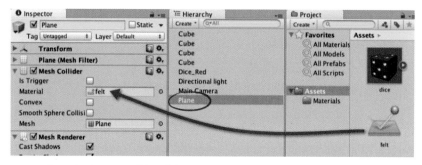

FIG 6.10 Setting the physics material for a collider.

Step 9: Now select the Plane in the Hierarchy and locate its Mesh Collider in the Inspector. Drag and drop the *felt* physics material onto its Physics Material property as shown in Figure 6.10.

Play. Try rolling the die to see the difference.

Step 10: Next we will create a script to record and display the value on the die. Create a new C# script called *scores* and add the following:

```
using UnityEngine;
using System.Collections;

public class scores : MonoBehaviour {

    static int totalScore = 0;
    static int diceValue = 0;

    public static void UpdateScore(int value)
    {
        diceValue = value;
        totalScore + = diceValue;
    }

    void OnGUI()
    {
```

```
GUI.Label(new Rect(20,10,100,30),"Score:" +
    totalScore);

GUI.Label(new Rect(20,30,1000,30),"Last Roll:" +
    diceValue);
    }
}
```

Save and attach to the Main Camera. Play. A value for Score and Last Roll
will appear on the screen.

We will now create code to pass the value on the rolled dice to the
UpdateScore() function in the *scores* script. Create a C# script called
getRoll and add:

```csharp
using UnityEngine;
using System.Collections;

public class getRoll : MonoBehaviour {

void Update ()
{
    if(this.rigidbody.velocity.magnitude == 0)
    {
        if(Vector3.Angle(this.transform.right,-Vector3.up)<1)
            scores.UpdateScore(4);
        else if(Vector3.Angle(this.transform.right,
        Vector3.up)<1)
            scores.UpdateScore(3);
        else if(Vector3.Angle(this.transform.up,Vector3.up)< 1)
            scores.UpdateScore(6);
        else if(Vector3.Angle(this.transform.up,-Vector3.up)< 1)
            scores.UpdateScore(1);
        else if(Vector3.Angle(this.transform.forward,Vector3.
        up)<1)
            scores.UpdateScore(2);
        else if(Vector3.Angle(this.transform.forward,-Vector3.
        up)< 1)
            scores.UpdateScore(5);
    }
  }
}
```

Save and attach to the die.

In the preceding code, the value of the die roll (the number on the top
side of the die) is reported to the UpdateScore function. The value of
the die is determined by its orientation. If you examine the die closely
you'll notice how its axes align with its sides and how those in turn align
with the world axis. This can be seen in Figure 6.11.

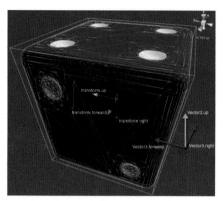

FIG 6.11 The axes of the die with respect to the world axes.

When the value of the die is a four, the *x* axis (`transform.right`) is pointing down. If we were to compare the transform.right axis of the die with the world's down (`-Vector3.up`) we'd find the axes to be almost parallel. To determine just how parallel, we can find the angle between these two axes and, if it is very small, we could be certain the value on the die was a four. Similarly when the die is right way up, that is its transform. up is pointing up and parallel with the world's `Vector3.up`, the die will have a value of six. By comparing all the axes of the die against those of the world's up axis we can determine the die's value.

Furthermore, we only want to get the value on the die when it is not rolling around. Therefore we check the magnitude of the die's velocity to determine if it has stopped moving. When it's not moving the value can be passed through to the `UpdateScore()` function that displays it on the screen.

Step 11: The issue we now face is a repetitive updating of the score when the die is not moving. To ensure a roll is recorded only once we should use a Boolean value to turn score recording on and off.

In the *scores* script add the following declaration at the top of the class:

```
public static bool gameStarted = false;
```

Next in the `Update()` function of *getRoll* add:

```
void Update ()
{
    if(this.rigidbody.velocity.magnitude == 0
        && scores.gameStarted)
    {
        . . .
        scores.gameStarted = false;
    }
}
```

And finally we need to set `gameStarted` to true after a touch has ended to signify that when it stops moving the score should be recorded. In the `Update()` function of *rollDice* inside the touch ended clause add:

```
...
else if(focusObj && (Input.GetMouseButtonUp(0) ||
    (Input.touchCount > 0 &&
    Input.GetTouch(0).phase == TouchPhase.Ended)))
{
    focusObj.rigidbody.AddForce( lastVelocity * 1000);
    focusObj = null;
    scores.gameStarted = true;
}
...
```

Save all scripts and play. The score will only be updated after each roll.

6.2.3 *Angry Birds*

Angry Birds is a projectile-throwing game in which wingless birds are flung via slingshot into a structure containing green pigs. The aim is to knock the structure down and destroy the pigs. The game is simple to recreate with Unity as the physics system does most of the work for you. With just a few tricks used to manipulate the physics, the slingshot system can be quickly recreated.

⬤ Unity Hands-On
Angry Birds

Step 1: Create a new Unity project with the 2D default setting. Set the camera to orthographic. It will have a size of 5 and be looking down the *z* axis. The *x* axis will extend in the positive direction to the right. Change the Build Settings for either iOS or Android.

Step 2: Create a Quad and add a grass texture to it to represent the ground. Stretch it out so it is twice the length of the screen as shown in Figure 6.12. The grass needs to be at least twice as long as the camera so you have one area where the sling is and another where the building will go. After a bird is shot in *Angry Birds*, the camera pans across to where the buildings and pigs are. The grass needs to extend this far to give a seamless ground plane. Also add another quad to represent a catapult. You can download appropriate images from the website called grass.png and stickthing.png. After importing into your project you should set the texture quality appropriately and ensure the wrap mode is clamp.

Remove the colliders from the grass and slingshot planes.

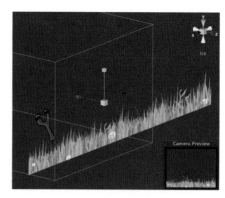

FIG 6.12 The setup for the game environment with the grass extending twice the width of the camera's view

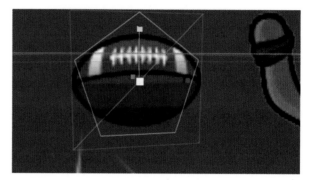

FIG 6.13 Adding a polygon collider to the football quad.

Step 3: Create a quad near the sling and put a ball image on it. This one being used here was found at http://icons.iconarchive.com. Tag the ball game object with "ball." Remove the Mesh Collider and then add a polygon collider around the ball (Add Component > Physics 2D > Polygon Collider) as shown in Figure 6.13. Position the ball near but slightly behind the slingshot.

Add a *rigidbody2D* to the ball and tick the *IsKinematic* box of the component in the Inspector. Doing this will take the ball out of the physics system. When the ball is at the end of the slingshot at the beginning of each game, we don't want it falling to the ground. The *rigidbody2D* will be turned on when the ball is released.

Step 4: Create a C# file called *shootBall* and add the following code:

```
using UnityEngine;
using System.Collections;

public class shootBall : MonoBehaviour {

    GameObject focusObj = null;
```

```csharp
// Use this for initialization
void Start () {

}

// Update is called once per frame
void Update ()
{
    //if we've started a mouse or finger press
    if(Input.GetMouseButtonDown(0) ||(Input.touchCount > 0
    &&
        Input.GetTouch(0).phase == TouchPhase.Began))
    {
        Ray ray = Camera.main.ScreenPointToRay
            (Input.mousePosition);

        RaycastHit2D hit =
            Physics2D.GetRayIntersection(ray,10000);

        if(!hit)
            return;

        //if the object the mouse or finger is on is the ball
        //remember it
        if(hit.transform.gameObject.tag == "ball")
        {
            focusObj = hit.transform.gameObject;
        }
    }
    //if we've released the mouse or finger
    else if(Input.GetMouseButtonUp(0) || (Input.touchCount > 0 &&
        Input.GetTouch(0).phase == TouchPhase.Ended))
    {
        focusObj = null;
    }

    //if we are moving the mouse or finger
    //and the ball is selected
    else if(focusObj && ((Input.touchCount > 0 &&
        Input.GetTouch(0).phase == TouchPhase.Moved)
        || Input.GetMouseButton(0)))
        {
            Vector3 mPos = Camera.main.ScreenToWorldPoint(
                new Vector3(Input.mousePosition.x,
                Input.mousePosition.y, 0));

            focusObj.transform.position = new Vector3( mPos.x,
                mPos.y, focusObj.transform.position.z);
        }

    }
}
```

Save and attach to the Main Camera in the Hierarchy. Play. You will be able to select the ball with the mouse (or finger-touch) and move it around the screen.

Step 5: To create the elastic on the sling we will use a line renderer. To represent the elastic at a minimum we need three locations: the position where the elastic attaches to the first fork of the sling; the position behind the ball where the elastic wraps around; and the position where the elastic attaches to the other fork. Rather than mess around and try and find these values by hand, we will simply get the script to work them out for us.

First, add three cubes to the scene. Name them *SlingTie1*, *SlingTie2*, and *SlingJoin*. Make *SlignJoin* a child of the *Ball*. This will ensure it moves when the ball moves. Place them in the locations shown in Figure 6.14. SlingTie1 goes on the slingshot's left fork in the same *z* location as the slingshot plane. SlingTie2 is placed in line with the slingshot's right fork when viewed from the front, but placed further back in the *z* direction than the ball. SlingJoin is placed on the back tip of the ball in the same *z* location.

Remove the colliders, mesh filters, and mesh renders from each of these cubes so they don't interfere with rendering or the physics. They will become empty game objects with just a transform.

Modify the *shootBall* code to draw the elastic around the slingshot thus:

```
using UnityEngine;
using System.Collections;

public class shootBall : MonoBehaviour {

    GameObject focusObj = null;
    public GameObject slingtie1;
    public GameObject slingtie2;
    public GameObject slingjoin;
```

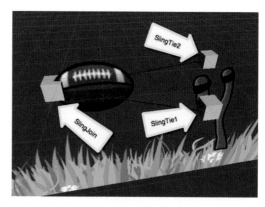

FIG 6.14 Adding marker locations for the sling elastic.

```csharp
public Texture2D elasticTexture;

LineRenderer lineRenderer;

// Use this for initialization
void Start ()
{

    lineRenderer =
        this.gameObject.AddComponent<LineRenderer>();

    lineRenderer.material = new Material
        (Shader.Find("Unlit/Texture"));

    lineRenderer.material.mainTexture = elasticTexture;
    lineRenderer.SetWidth(1,1);
    lineRenderer.SetVertexCount(3);

    lineRenderer.SetPosition(0,
        slingtie1.transform.position);

    lineRenderer.SetPosition(1,
        slingjoin.transform.position);

    lineRenderer.SetPosition(2,
        slingtie2.transform.position);

}
// Update is called once per frame
void Update ()
{
    ...
    else if(focusObj &&((Input.touchCount > 0 &&
        Input.GetTouch(0).phase == TouchPhase.
        Moved)
        || Input.GetMouseButton(0)))
    {
            Vector3 mPos = Camera.main.
            ScreenToWorldPoint(
                new Vector3(Input.mousePosition.x,
                Input.mousePosition.y, 0));

            focusObj.transform.position = new
            Vector3(mPos.x,
                mPos.y, focusObj.transform.position.z);

            lineRenderer.SetPosition(0,
                slingtie1.transform.position);

            lineRenderer.SetPosition(1,
                slingjoin.transform.position);

            lineRenderer.SetPosition(2,
                slingtie2.transform.position);
            }
    ...
```

Save.

Create a small texture in Photoshop or similar to represent the color of the elastic. In this example it will be a 16 × 16 red PNG. Add this image to the project.

Now select the Main Camera and locate the attached *shootBall* script. Set all the exposed variables by dragging across the sling cubes and texture as shown in Figure 6.15.

Play. Drag the ball around on the screen and notice how the elastic moves with it.

Step 6: To make the ball move according to the amount of stretch and direction of the elastic, a force needs to be added. This force will be proportional to the distance between the *SlingJoin* and *SlingTie1* and the angle vector between these same two locations.

To add this to your code, modify the mouse up part of the `Update()` function of *shootBall* thus:

```
...
//if we've released the mouse or finger
else if(Input.GetMouseButtonUp(0) ||
(Input.touchCount > 0 &&
    Input.GetTouch(0).phase == TouchPhase.Ended))
{

    //apply force to ball proportional to length of elastic
    //and in direction of sling base
```

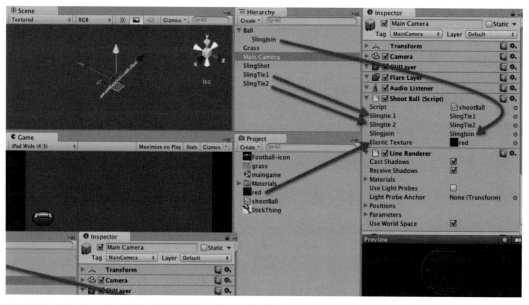

FIG 6.15 Assigning sling cubes as the elastic join locations and setting the color.

```
focusObj.gameObject.rigidbody2D.isKinematic = false;
focusObj.gameObject.rigidbody2D.mass = 5.0f;

float dist = Vector3.Distance(
        focusObj.transform.position,
        slingtie1.transform.position);

Vector3 dir3D = slingtie1.transform.position -
        focusObj.transform.position;

Vector3 dir = new Vector2(dir3D.x, dir3D.y);
focusObj.rigidbody2D.AddForce( dir * dist * 25);

//take the elastic off the ball
lineRenderer.SetPosition(1,slingtie1.transform.position);

focusObj = null;
    }
    ...
```

Save and play. You will be able to pull the ball back and release it. If the ball seems to move too slowly for your liking add a multiplying factor into the AddForce() function to ramp up the force applied to the ball, for example:

```
focusObj.rigidbody2D.AddForce( dir * dist * 50);
```

Step 7: In the preceding code you will notice the *rigidbody2D* being applied to the ball with code. This allows the AddForce() function and gravity in the physic system to affect the ball.

When the ball reaches the right-hand side of the screen, we want the camera to start sliding to the right to reveal the other part of the game—the building and pigs. To determine the right moment to do this, take the ball and slide it across in the *x* until it is near the right side of the screen and take note of its *x* position in the Inspector as shown in Figure 6.16. Also note

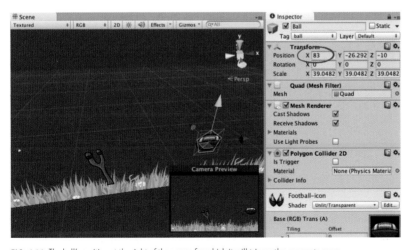

FIG 6.16 The ball's position at the right of the screen for which it will trigger the camera to move.

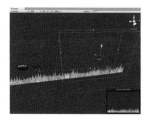

FIG 6.17 Moving the camera as far right as possible while keeping the grass in the shot.

the direction of the *x* axis as you move the ball. In the project used as the example here as the ball moves further to the right its *x* position changes in the positive. This will be the case if you have used the default Unity 2D project settings and not changed the camera's orientation. Move the ball back to its starting position. In this example the rightmost *x* value is 83.

Step 8: Now do the same with the camera. Drag it as far right as you can in the x direction to the very edge of the grass quad as shown in Figure 6.17. Take note of the camera's x value at this position then move it back to its starting position. In the example being used the rightmost *x* value is 178.

Step 9: Create a new C# file called *moveCamera* and add the following code:

```
using UnityEngine;
using System.Collections;

public class moveCamera : MonoBehaviour {

    void Update ()
    {
        if(this.transform.position.x > 83)
        {
            //final position of the camera, use your own
            Vector3 targetPos = new Vector3(178,
                Camera.main.transform.position.y,
                Camera.main.transform.position.z);

            float speed = 1.0f;

            Camera.main.transform.position = Vector3.Lerp
                (Camera.main.transform.position, targetPos,
                Time.deltaTime * speed);

        }
    }
}
```

If you found that your *x* values decrease to the right you will need to modify the `if` statement to take this into consideration. For example, if the ball starts at *x* = 5 and at the right of the screen *x* = −180 the test in the `if` statement will need to change to:

```
if(this.transform.position.x < -180)
```

Notice how the condition is now less-than rather than greater-than.

Save and attach to the ball. Now play. When the ball reaches the edge of the screen, the camera will slide over to the second part of the game environment. In the code, the `Lerp()` function is used. Lerp is an abbreviation for linear interpolation. The function is used to set the position of the camera taking consideration where the camera is, where you want the camera to be, and how fast you want the camera to move

FIG 6.18 A simple plank texture.

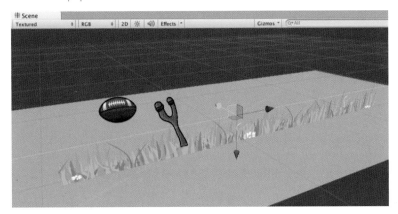

FIG 6.19 Adding a ground plane into the game environment.

towards its final location. It's a really useful function for moving game objects around without having to calculate vectors.

Step 10: This next part of the game development involves the creation of the buildings in the other half of the screen. The buildings are going to be constructed from plank images as shown in Figure 6.18. You can create your own or download and use plank.png from the website.

Before starting to build we need to add a ground quad. This will give the buildings something to rest on as well as stopping the ball from falling below the grass level. Select GameObject > Create Other > Quad from the main menu. Resize and move the quad as shown in Figure 6.19. You can leave the render on the quad if you wish. It won't show in orthographic view as it should be perpendicular to the camera. We don't want to be able to see it: it's for physics purposes only.

To make the quad a 2D physics object, remove its mesh collider and add a Physics2D > Edge Collider instead.

Create another quad facing the camera like the grass, ball, and slingshot. Put the plank texture on it. Remove the existing Mesh Collider. With it selected from the main menu choose Component > Physics 2D > Box Collider 2D. Attach a rigidbody 2D to it.

To test everything is working thus far, play. Fling the ball across. It should hit the plank, which in turn will topple over. You may want to modify the plank's physics properties to increase its mass if it goes flying off the screen when the ball hits it.

In Unity, when a rigidbody stops moving it is automatically put to sleep. This takes it out of the physics system and reduces load, allowing you to have a lot of rigidbodies in the scene. To force a rigidbody to sleep you can used rigidbody.Sleep in an `Awake()` or `Start()` function on each game object to reduce unnecessary processing when a level loads.

Step 11: Construct a building using the plank prefab in the other half of the game environment as shown in Figure 6.20.

To ensure the building doesn't fall over when you press play, the planks need to be positioned close to each but not with the colliders touching. Remember as soon as you press play, gravity and other physics will come into effect. If the colliders overlap, the planks will explode apart. If your structure is not balanced, it will tip over. After adding a few planks, press play to ensure your building settles nicely on the ground without falling over. Sling the ball across to test its interaction with the planks.

Step 12: Create a new C# script called *score*. Add the following code:

```
using UnityEngine;
using System.Collections;

public class score : MonoBehaviour {

    static public int points = 0;

    void OnGUI()
    {
        GUI.Label(new Rect(10,10,200,30),"Points: " + points);
    }
}
```

FIG 6.20 A building constructed from the plank prefab.

Save and attach to the Main Camera. The variable for points is declared as a static public integer so it is accessible by other code. We will use this benefit to update the score from the code attached to the pigs created in the next step.

Step 13: Create an object to represent the pig. It will be constructed in the same way as the planks with a quad, box collider 2D and rigidbody 2D. Use a pig image on the plane as shown in Figure 6.21. This image can be downloaded from the website and is called *pig-icon.png*.

Create a new C# script called *piggy* with the following code:

```
using UnityEngine;
using System.Collections;

public class piggy : MonoBehaviour {

    bool hit = false;
    public Texture2D pigHurt;
```

FIG 6.21 Adding a pig game object into the game environment.

```
void OnCollisionEnter(Collision collision)
{
    if(collision.relativeVelocity.magnitude > 20
        && !hit)
    {
        hit = true;
        this.renderer.material.mainTexture = pigHurt;
        score.points + = 100;
    }
}
}
```

Save and attach this code to the pig game object. The code works by detecting a collision and then, if the collision is large enough, the pig's image changes to a hurt pig texture and 100 is added to the score. The hit variable that is initially false is set to try once the pig has been hit hard enough, this then ensures the pig can only score once.

Step 14: Before you try the code, the hurtPig variable of the script needs to be assigned an image. This image will show after the pig is hit. For this you can download the blackeyedpig.png from the website or create your own. It is then assigned to the script attached to the pig as shown in Figure 6.22.

Add two more pigs to the scene with the script attached.

At this point, most of the functionality for an *Angry Birds*-type game will be in place and your scene should look somewhat like Figure 6.23.

Step 15: Last but not least we are going to add a few more dynamics that will help you on your way to completing the game. First let's modify

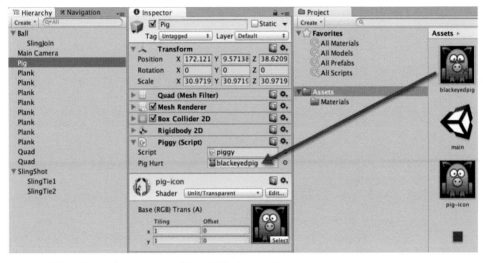

FIG 6.22 Adding code and an image to process collisions with the pig game object

FIG 6.23 A scene from our game.

piggy.cs to give a score relative to the force it has been hit with as well as register the pig as being hurt. The idea is that when all the pigs have been hurt, the game is over. Modify *piggy.cs* thus:

```
using UnityEngine;
using System.Collections;

public class piggy : MonoBehaviour {

bool hit = false;
public Texture2D pigHurt;

    void OnCollisionEnter(Collision collision)
    {
        if(collision.relativeVelocity.magnitude >
            20 && !hit)
        {
            hit = true;
            this.renderer.material.mainTexture =
            pigHurt;
            score.points + = (int) (100 *
                collision.relativeVelocity.magnitude);

            score.pigsHurt + = 1;

        }
    }
}
```

These changes will use the collision velocity as a multiplier on the amount of points received for disabling a pig. A new variable called pigsHurt to be placed in the score script will be incremented to keep track of the number of pigs that have been hit.

Next modify *score.cs* to record the number of hurt pigs with:

```
using UnityEngine;
using System.Collections;

public class score : MonoBehaviour {

    static public int points = 0;
    static public int pigsHurt = 0;

    void OnGUI()
    {
        GUI.Label(new Rect(10,10,200,30),
            "Points:" + points);
        if(pigsHurt > = 3)
        {
            GUI.BeginGroup (new Rect (Screen.width
                / 2 – 50, Screen.height / 2 – 50,
                100, 100));

            GUI.Box (new Rect (0,0,100,100),"Game Over");

            if( GUI.Button (new Rect (10,40,80,30),
                "Play Again"))
            {
                //reload this level
                points = 0;
                pigsHurt = 0;
                Application.LoadLevel(
                    Application.loadedLevel);
            }
            GUI.EndGroup ();
        }
    }
}
```

The new code here will track the number of pigs that have been hurt. When three or more pigs have been disabled, a GUI box will appear in the center of the screen displaying "Game Over" and a "Play Again" button. On pressing this button, the current scene will be reloaded. This will reset the entire environment except for any static variables that must be re-initialized by hand.

Step 16: Finally, the biggest change must be made to the *shootBall* script. The script is going to monitor the movement of objects in the environment after the ball has been released. When the objects stop moving, the ball and camera are repositioned at the start so the player can have another go at slinging the ball. The modifications you need to make are shown below:

```
using UnityEngine;
using System.Collections;

public class shootBall : MonoBehaviour
{
    ...
    LineRenderer lineRenderer;

    public GameObject ball;
    Vector3 startCamPos;
    Vector3 startBallPos;
    Quaternion startBallRotation;
    bool testForMovement = false;

    // Use this for initialization
    void Start ()
    {
        lineRenderer =
            this.gameObject.AddComponent<LineRenderer>();

        lineRenderer.material = new Material
            (Shader.Find("Unlit/Texture"));

        lineRenderer.material.mainTexture = elasticTexture;
        lineRenderer.SetWidth(1,1);
        lineRenderer.SetVertexCount(3);

        lineRenderer.SetPosition(0,
            slingtie1.transform.position);

        lineRenderer.SetPosition(1,
            slingjoin.transform.position);

        lineRenderer.SetPosition(2,
            slingtie2.transform.position);

        //remember starting position of camera and ball
        this.startCamPos = this.transform.position;
        this.startBallPos = ball.transform.position;
        this.startBallRotation = ball.transform.rotation;
    }

    void Reset()
    {
        this.transform.position = this.startCamPos;
        ball.transform.position = this.startBallPos;
        ball.transform.rotation = this.startBallRotation;
        ball.rigidbody2D.isKinematic = true;

        lineRenderer.SetPosition(0,
            slingtie1.transform.position);
```

```
            lineRenderer.SetPosition(1,
                slingjoin.transform.position);

            lineRenderer.SetPosition(2,
                slingtie2.transform.position);

            testForMovement = false;
    }
    //examine all rigidbodies in the scene
    //and count any that are still moving faster than 5
    void TestMovement()
    {
        int moveCount = 0;
        Rigidbody2D[] rbs =
            FindObjectsOfType(typeof(Rigidbody2D)) as
            Rigidbody2D[];

        foreach (Rigidbody2D body in rbs)
        {
            if(body.velocity.magnitude > 5)
            {
                moveCount++;
            }
        }
            if(moveCount == 0) //reset game
            {
                Reset();
        }
    }

    // Update is called once per frame
    void Update ()
    {
        if(testForMovement)
        {
            TestMovement();
        }
        //if we've started a mouse or finger press
        if(Input.GetMouseButtonDown(0) ||
        (Input.touchCount > 0 &&
        Input.GetTouch(0).phase == TouchPhase.Began))
        {
                ...
        }
        //if we've released the mouse or finger
        else if(focusObj && (Input.GetMouseButtonUp(0) ||
            (Input.touchCount > 0 &&
            Input.GetTouch(0).phase == TouchPhase.Ended)))
        {
                ...
```

```
//take the elastic off the ball
lineRenderer.SetPosition(1,
    slingtie1.transform.position);

testForMovement = true;

focusObj = null;
}
. . .
```

The new code needs access to the ball game object to record its starting position. To set this up, select the camera in the Hierarchy, locate the Shoot Ball script in the Inspector and drag and drop the ball from the Hierarchy onto the exposed `Ball` variable in the script as shown in Figure 6.24.

Step 17: One more thing. Before playing, extend the size of the ground plane and make it really large. This will allow game objects that fly off the screen to come to rest somewhere. If they are pushed over the edge of the existing ground plane, because the will fall forever, the code will count them as a moving object and the ball and camera will never be reset.

Save and play. The camera and ball will now reset after all objects stop moving after a collision to give the player another chance at hitting the pigs. If all three pigs are hit, the "Game Over" box comes up and the player can restart the level.

You will now have the base for an awesome version of *Angry Birds* as shown in Figure 6.25.

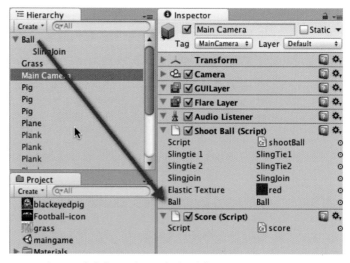

FIG 6.24 Assigning the ball game object to the shoot ball script.

FIG 6.25 The *Angry Birds* remake in action!

To complete the *Angry Birds* game from this section, you could add sounds, floating up text scores, make the pigs blink, add different building materials with different physics properties, and add different projectiles.

6.2.4 *Catapult King*

Catapult King is basically the 3D version of *Angry Birds* with a different backstory and characters. However, the basic premise remains to knock down a tower with a projectile and eliminate all enemies.

◉ Unity Hands-On
Catapult King
Step 1: Download then unzip the *Catapult* project from the website and open the project in Unity. Open the *maingame* scene, in it you will find a simple terrain and a cannon.
Step 2: To aim the cannon we will implement a simple finger-drag system to change the altitude and heading of the model. Add a cylinder to the Scene resize it and drag it around to align with the barrel of the cannon as shown in Figure 6.26. Tag the cylinder with "cannon." Child the

FIG 6.26 Creating a primitive object to use as a collider.

cylinder to the cannon and then remove the cylinder's mesh filter and renderer. This collider will be used to detect the player's finger touching the cannon, allowing it to be rotated.

To orient the cannon on finger-drags, create a new C# script called *alignCannon* and add the following code:

```
using UnityEngine;
using System.Collections;

public class alignCannon : MonoBehaviour {

    float horizontalSpeed = 30.0F;
    float verticalSpeed = 30.0F;

    void Update()
    {
        if((Input.touchCount > 0 && Input.GetTouch(0).phase ==
            TouchPhase.Moved) || Input.GetMouseButton(0))
        {
            RaycastHit hit;
            Ray ray = Camera.main.ScreenPointToRay
                (Input.mousePosition);

        if (!Physics.Raycast (ray, out hit, 10000))
            return;
        {
            if(hit.transform.gameObject.tag == "cannon")
            {
                Vector3 angles = transform.eulerAngles;

                angles.y += horizontalSpeed *
                    Time.deltaTime *
                    Input.GetAxisRaw("Mouse X");

                angles.y = Mathf.Clamp(angles.y, 163, 220);

                angles.z -= verticalSpeed * Time.deltaTime *
```

```
                Input.GetAxisRaw("Mouse Y");

            angles.z = Mathf.Clamp(angles.z, 0, 25);

            transform.eulerAngles = angles;

            }
        }
    }
}
}
```

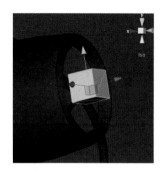

Save. Attach to the cannon parent object. Play. When the mouse (or finger)
touches the barrel of the cannon, the player will be able to drag on the
screen to reorient the object. The code uses the `Input.GetAxisRaw()`
functions to change the orientation of the cannon *using x* movement to
rotate the cannon around *its y* axis (up) and *y* movement to rotate the
cannon around its *z* axis. The way you rotate an object will depend on
its orientation in the game world. In this case, the cannon's *z* axis is not
forward but points to the side. The reason being that the cannon was
originally modelled facing in this direction in the software that created it.

Step 3: To shoot cannonballs from the cannon, we first need a spawn
point. Create a cube and place it in the mouth of the barrel. Rename
it *CannonSpawn*. Rotate it so its *z* axis is facing out from the barrel as
shown in Figure 6.27. This will be used as the initial trajectory for the
cannonballs.

Once the cube is in place, make it a child of the cannon so that when the
cannon moves, the cube will move with it. Remove the cube's mesh filter
and renderer. Also remove the cube's box collider as we don't want it to
interfere with the cannonballs.

Create a sphere to act as the cannonball. Place it near the mouth of the
cannon barrel and resize it to best represent a cannonball that would
come from this particular cannon. Add a rigidbody it. Make it into a
prefab called *cannonBallPrefab* and delete the original.

Create a new C# script called *spawnBalls* and add the following code:

```
using UnityEngine;
using System.Collections;

public class spawnBalls : MonoBehaviour {

    public GameObject cannonball;

    void Start ()
    {
        InvokeRepeating("Fire",2,2);
    }

    void Fire()
    {
        GameObject cball = (GameObject) Instantiate(
```

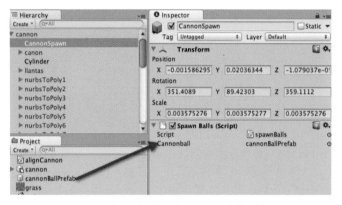

FIG 6.29 Adding a plane to the Scene to become the cannonball firing button.

FIG 6.28 Setting the exposed cannonball variable to the cannonball prefab.

```
            cannonball, this.transform.position,
            this.transform.rotation);

        cball.rigidbody.AddForce(this.transform.forward * 5000);
    }
}
```

Attach this code to the *CannonSpawn* object. With the *CannonSpawn* selected in the Hierarchy, locate the attached script and set the exposed cannonball variable to the cannonball prefab created in the last step.

Save and play. Every two seconds a cannonball will be fired from the cannon. Notice that if you change the cannon's orientation, the cannonball trajectories are affected appropriately.

Step 6: Add a plane to the Scene and rename it as *FireButton*. Put a red button type image on it and align it to the bottom right corner of the camera view as shown in Figure 6.29. Set the FireButton's tag to "fire".

To get the fire button to work, the *spawnBalls* script needs reworking. There are quite a few changes so all the code is given here:

```
using UnityEngine;
using System.Collections;

public class spawnBalls : MonoBehaviour {

    public GameObject cannonball;
    bool firing;

    private float vSliderValue = 0.0f;

    void OnGUI () {
        vSliderValue = GUI.VerticalSlider (
            new Rect (Screen.width - 30, 20, 100, 350),
```

```
                vSliderValue, 100.0f, 0.0f);
    }

    void Fire()
    {
        GameObject cball = (GameObject)
            Instantiate(cannonball,
            this.transform.position,
            this.transform.rotation);

        cball.rigidbody.AddForce(this.transform.forward *
                50 * vSliderValue);
    }

    void Update()
    {
        if((Input.touchCount > 0 && Input.GetTouch(0).phase
            == TouchPhase.Began) ||
            Input.GetMouseButtonDown(0))
        {

            RaycastHit hit;
            Ray ray = Camera.main.ScreenPointToRay
                (Input.mousePosition);

            if (!Physics.Raycast (ray, out hit, 10000))
                return;

            if(hit.transform.gameObject.tag == "fire")
            {
            firing = true;
            }
        }
        else if(((Input.touchCount > 0 &&
            Input.GetTouch(0).phase == TouchPhase.Moved) ||
            Input.GetMouseButton(0)) && firing)
        {
            vSliderValue + = 10.0f * Time.deltaTime;
        }
        else if(((Input.touchCount > 0 &&
            Input.GetTouch(0).phase == TouchPhase.Ended) ||
            Input.GetMouseButtonUp(0)))
        {
            if(firing)
            {
                firing = false;
                Fire();
                vSliderValue = 0.0f;
            }
        }
    }
}
```

Save and play. The code creates a vertical slider on the right of the screen. The value on the slider increases the longer you hold your finger on the fire button. When you release the fire button, the value on the slider is transferred to the power applied to the cannonball which then shoots out.

Step 5: Now it's time to build the castle that we are going to attempt to knock down with the cannonballs. In the Project is a model called *stone*. Drag it into the scene and resize it to your liking. Add a rigidbody and box collider to it. Make it into a prefab.

To build quickly, with the stone in the Scene selected, press CTRL+D or CMD+D to duplicate it. The duplicate will be in the same location as the original. Press the W key to get the translation axis. Drag the copy to where you want it on the ground. You can also select multiple stones at once, such as a row to duplicate, to make the building process quicker.

Build a tower like that shown in Figure 6.30. Ensure the stones are neatly lined up and that none of the colliders are overlapping. Press play occasionally during the building process to ensure the building doesn't fall over or explode apart. You want it to come to a nice rest as it settles under gravity.

When you are finished building you can try out the cannon on the structure. Because the cannonball and stone are prefabs you can also play with their physics settings such as mass to see how it affects the gameplay.

Step 6: In the Project you will find a *SpartanKing* folder. Inside there is a *SpartanKing* mesh. Drag this into the Scene. The model will be really small. Scale it up by 100 and place on top of your structure. Add to it a box collider and rigidbody. Modify the size and the position of the box collider to fit neatly around the mesh as shown in Figure 6.31.

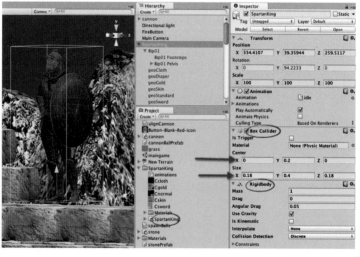

FIG 6.30 A simple tower built from the same stone prefab.

FIG 6.31 Adding the Spartan King to guard the tower.

Create a new C# script called *manageAnimations* and add the following:

```csharp
using UnityEngine;
using System.Collections;

public class manageAnimations : MonoBehaviour {

    bool alive = true;

    void OnCollisionEnter(Collision collision)
    {
        if(collision.gameObject.name == "Terrain" && alive)
        {
            alive = false;
            this.animation.CrossFade("diehard");
        }
    }

    void Update ()
    {
        if(this.rigidbody.velocity.magnitude > 3 && alive)
        {
            this.animation.CrossFade("resist");
        }
    }

}
```

Save and attach to the Spartan King object. Play. When the Spartan King's velocity goes over three the "resist" animation will run. If the object's collider hits the ground the "diehard" animation will play. The animations available to you can be seen in the Animation component attached to the object as shown in Figure 6.32. The name of the

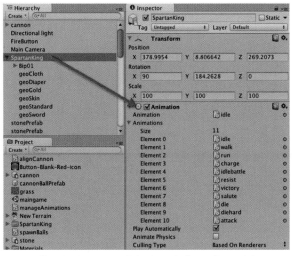

FIG 6.32 The animation sequences belonging to the Spartan King model.

animation is used in the `CrossFade()` function that blends the current animation with the named one.

Step 7: Unfortunately, however, when the object hits the ground and dies, the death animation physically moves the mesh, but does not move the actual object. Because the animation for the mesh was created in external software, Unity still considers the object's transformation to be static when playing animations. In this case, the Spartan King animation changes the meshes' location but not the objects. Now, this works fine if the object dies with the collider in an upright position as shown in Figure 6.33 on the left. However, as shown on the right in Figure 6.33, if the collider tips over, the death animation places the *Spartan King* mesh floating in mid-air. Of course this is undesirable and something you will encounter with externally animated models.

In this case we need to cater for such a situation. Ideally, when the death animation happens we want the object to be upright. That is, the *y* axis pointing up. The easiest way to do this is to restore the object's orientation to what it originally was at the start. We therefore record the starting rotation when the code starts to run and use this rotation when the object collides with the ground thus:

```
public class manageAnimations : MonoBehaviour {
...

    bool alive = true;

    Quaternion originalRotation;

    void Start()
```

FIG 6.33 Mesh animations do not affect the game object's transformation.

```
{
    originalRotation = this.transform.rotation;
}

void OnCollisionEnter(Collision collision)
{
    if(collision.gameObject.name == "Terrain" && alive)
    {
        alive = false;
        this.animation.CrossFade("diehard");
    }
}

void Update ()
{
    if(this.rigidbody.velocity.magnitude > 3 && alive)
    {
        this.animation.CrossFade("resist");
    }
    if(!alive)
    {
        this.transform.rotation = originalRotation;
    }
}
...
```

Save and play. Knock the Spartan King from the tower and watch the diehard animation run.

Step 8: One of nicest mechanics in *Catapult King* is the way in which the camera attaches itself to the last cannonball and takes the player on a ride with it. This mechanic is one of the critical things that really makes this game so special. When the player is aiming at and shooting a tower in a 3D environment in the distance, most of the action is lost because it can't be seen. However by travelling with the cannonball, none of the action is lost. To have the camera follow the cannonball make the following change to the Fire() function in *spawnBalls*:

```
void Fire()
{
    GameObject cball = (GameObject) Instantiate(cannonball,
        this.transform.position, this.transform.rotation);
    cball.rigidbody.AddForce(this.transform.forward *
        50 * vSliderValue);

    Camera.main.transform.parent = cball.transform;
}
```

This line makes the camera a child of the cannonball. The camera will then move relative to the cannonball. Save and play. What you will immediately notice is that the camera not only translates with the camera but rotates with it too. This is not desirable. We therefore want the cannonball to release the camera when it hits something. To achieve this, create a new C# script called *releaseCamera* and add the following code:

```
using UnityEngine;
using System.Collections;

public class releaseCamera : MonoBehaviour
{
    void OnCollisionEnter(Collision collision)
    {
        Camera.main.transform.parent = null;
    }
}
```

Save and attach to the *cannonballPrefab*. Now when the cannonball collides with something the camera will be released.

⬤ **Note**

If you find the camera does not follow the cannonball as it did before you attached the *releaseCamera* code, it could be because the cannonball on instantiation is colliding with the cylinder inside the cannon that is used for changing the cannon's orientation. Move the spawn point forward and the cylinder back a little so any cannonballs that are created do not collide with the cylinder.

After the Main Camera is released, you'll want the camera to be reset to its starting position. You could implement code similar to that in the *Angry Birds* hands-on that checks everything has stopped moving and then set the camera back to the start. But for now we will just add a simple button-press mechanism to do this.

Step 9: While we are at it, we will implement some simple code that will animate the camera after it has separated from the cannonball. The camera will slowly tilt down while rising up giving the player a bird's-eye view of the tower. At a certain height, the game will reset as though the reset button was pressed. The *releaseCamera* code now becomes:

```
using UnityEngine;
using System.Collections;

public class releaseCamera : MonoBehaviour {

    Vector3 CameraStartPos;
    Quaternion CameraStartRot;
```

```
bool camAttached = true;

void Start()
{
    CameraStartPos = Camera.main.transform.position;
    CameraStartRot = Camera.main.transform.rotation;
}

void OnGUI()
{
    if(GUI.Button(new Rect(Screen.width-70,
        Screen.height-70,50,50),"X"))
    {
        ResetCamera();
    }
}

void OnCollisionEnter(Collision collision)
{
    Camera.main.transform.parent = null;
    camAttached = false;
}

void ResetCamera()
{
    Camera.main.transform.parent = null;
    camAttached = false;
    Camera.main.transform.position = CameraStartPos;
    Camera.main.transform.rotation = CameraStartRot;
    Destroy(this.gameObject);
}

void Update()
{
    if(!camAttached)
    {
        Camera.main.transform.Translate(0,0.1f,
            -0.1f);
        Camera.main.transform.Rotate(0.05f,0,0);

        if(Camera.main.transform.position.y > 135)
        {
            ResetCamera();
        }
    }
}
}
```

Save and play. The code now animates the camera after it has been released and allows the player to reset to the starting position at any time after the cannonball is instantiated. Because this code belongs to the cannonball, it is only active when there is a live cannonball in the game environment. Therefore the GUI part is only visible after a cannonball is instantiated. There can never be more than one cannonball in the environment, as the button to release a cannonball is not accessible after the camera starts moving.

Step 10: The last thing we will do is to determine a game over state. Let's make this occur when all the Spartan Kings are dead. So far there is only one in the game. However, you could make the object into a prefab and add more into the environment. Whatever the case, the next piece of code will track all of these objects and determine if they are still alive or not.

First tag the Spartan King with "enemy". If you've made a prefab for it, ensure it is tagged there too. Create a new C# script called *monitorEnemies* and add the following:

```
using UnityEngine;
using System.Collections;

public class monitorEnemies : MonoBehaviour {

    GameObject[] enemies;
    bool gameOver = false;

    void OnGUI()
    {
        if(gameOver)
        {
            GUI.BeginGroup (new Rect (Screen.width / 2 - 50,
                Screen.height / 2 - 50, 100, 100));

            GUI.Box (new Rect (0,0,100,100), "Game Over");

            if( GUI.Button (new Rect (10,40,80,30),
                "Play Again") )
            {
                //reload this level
                Application.LoadLevel(
                    Application.loadedLevel);
            }

            GUI.EndGroup ();
        }
    }

    // Use this for initialization
    void Start ()
    {
        enemies = GameObject.FindGameObjectsWithTag("enemy");
    }

    // Update is called once per frame
    void Update ()
    {
        int countAlive = 0;
```

```
            foreach (GameObject e in enemies)
            {
                if(e.GetComponent<manageAnimations>().alive)
                    countAlive++;
            }
            if(countAlive == 0)
            {
                gameOver = true;
            }
        }
    }
```

Save and attach the code to the Main Camera. The function to point out here is `FindGameObjectsWithTag()`. It goes through the hierarchy and grabs all the game objects that are tagged with the string given to the function. In this case it will collect all the objects with "enemy" as the tag. These objects are placed in an array. Inside the `Update()` function, this array is looped through and each object examined.

Step 11: In addition, you will need to edit the *manageAnimations* script to make the alive variable accessible thus:

```
public class manageAnimations : MonoBehaviour {

    public bool alive = true;

    Quaternion originalRotation;

    void Start()
    {
        originalRotation = this.transform.rotation;
        alive = true;
    }
    ...
```

Save and play. A "Game Over" box will pop up when all enemies have been defeated.

This hands-on has given you the tools to recreate *Catapult King*. You can now have fun creating all sorts of towers and placing enemies throughout.

6.3 More Procedurally Generated Content

In the real version of *Super Monkey Ball*, the mechanic used on the monkey in the ball is to keep it continually moving forward without the assistance of the player. This same mechanic is implemented in *Temple Run*. This is a popular third-person game in which the player's character constantly runs forward and the objective is to keep the character out of harm's way by swiping to jump over hazards and turn corners when appropriate. As the character runs along its given path, it can be diverted slightly by tilting the device.

389

The same set of navigation mechanics is used in *Subway Surfer*. This toon-themed game features a character running along railway tracks into the paths of oncoming trains. The aim of the game is to keep the character alive as long as possible by swiping to change tracks and jump over obstacles and up on top of trains and other platforms. Just like in *Temple Run*, the character is forever running. The player has no control over the speed of the character just its left, right, up, and down position on the screen. *Subway Surfer* is another example of a procedurally generated game environment. If the player could keep their character alive indefinitely, the game will continuously create train track and oncoming trains.

As previously discussed, *Minecraft* landscapes are also procedurally generated. The difference between *Minecraft* and *Temple Run* is that the *Minecraft* landscape is created at the beginning of the game and the player then builds a world on top. With *Temple Run* and *Subway Surfer*, the only part of the environment that exists at any one time is what the player can see on the screen. Once the player moves over a platform or track, that part of the game environment is destroyed. It no longer exists and the player cannot ever go back where they came from.

All of these procedurally generated worlds required programmers to have a strong sense of the mathematics of 3D space and the positioning of game world elements. A game that was extremely successful in 2012, *Curiosity* by 22Cans, used probably the simplest procedurally 3D world that could be constructed; a cube of cubes.

6.3.1 *Temple Run*

Temple Run uses a procedural method to generate the path the character runs along. In theory, the game could continue to generate the game world forever, as long as the character were to stay alive. It works by detecting when the character is about to run out of game world and generates some more. In the next hands-on session you will find out how this can be done.

◉ Unity Hands-On
Temple Run

Step 1: Download the *Temple Run* starting project from the website. It will contain the character Astro Dude from a Unity Tech Demo project freely available in the Asset Store. In the main scene, Astro will be standing on a block with a rock texture. The character will also have a capsule collider and rigidbody. Before we begin, it is essential that the *x*, *y*, and *z* rotation of the character is frozen as shown in Figure 6.34.

Set the build settings according to the mobile device you are using and fix for portrait mode.

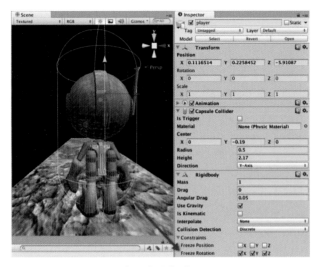

FIG 6.34 Freezing the rotation of a rigidbody for all axes.

Step 2: From the website, download *SmoothFollow.js*. This is a legacy Unity script used in previous tech demos that makes the camera follow the player's character. As we start moving the character, we will want the camera to follow along behind. Take this script and attach it to the Main Camera. Locate the script in the Inspector with the Main Camera selected in the Hierarchy. Drag and drop the player game object into the exposed Target variable and set the Distance to 4 and the Height to 0. You can adjust these values later if you think the camera is too low or close to the character.

Step 3: We will now create the first script that makes the character run forward. Start a new C# script called *playerNav* and add the following code:

```
using UnityEngine;
using System.Collections;

public class playerNav : MonoBehaviour {

    void Update () {

        this.transform.Translate(Vector3.forward * 0.1f);
    }
}
```

Attach this script to the *player* game object. Play. The character will run forward. The speed is controlled by the `0.1f`. Increase or decrease this value to modify the character's speed.

Step 4: To generate the track as the character moves along with program code we need to strictly control the size of the objects in the environment and their position. First we will consider the world as a very large (infinite) two-dimensional grid. Each grid in the world can support one platform object. For this project we will make the grid size 10 × 10 but you could make it anything you like. In order to place platforms accurately in each grid space so they line up, we need to make them the same length as a grid as well as centered.

Select the existing platform. Move it to (0,0,0) and scale it to (4,1,10). Make a prefab of this platform and call it *Platform1*. Add another copy of Platform1 to the scene and place it at (0,0,10). It will be end to end with the initial platform. This is shown in Figure 6.35.

Now that a platform is ten units long, we know if we space them ten units apart then they will touch end-to-end.

Make adjustments to the character and camera to reposition them on the platform.

Note

For the procedural world generation to work we will assume the world is flat and exists in the XZ plane at a height of 0 (e.g. $y = 0$). The x, y, and z axes of the game world are perfectly aligned with the x, y, and z of the Unity coordinate system. As the character initially moves off, it is running in a forward vector parallel to the z axis, that is (0,0,1). If your game world is rotated or slightly unaligned, you will get platforms appearing in strange places.

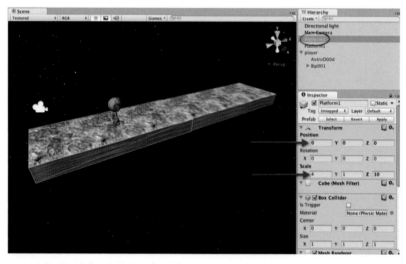

FIG 6.35 Ensuring platforms in the game fit into the environment grid size.

Step 5: Currently there are two platforms in the world. If you play now, the character will run the length of the two platforms and fall into the void of space. We want to create code that detects when the character is about to run off the edge of a platform and creates a new one right in front of it.

Because we are considering the world as one large two-dimensional grid with the character moving in the *x* and *z* directions, the world can be illustrated as that in Figure 6.36.

If we assume the current location of the character to be (x,z) and the character is facing in the forward *z* direction (0,1) then the grid position directly in front of it is (x, z+1). Similarly, if the character were facing in the positive *x* direction (1,0) the position directly in front of it would be (x+1,z). In *Temple Run*, when the character turns, it snap-turns 90 degrees each time. Therefore we know that it can only be moving in the *z* or the *x* direction, not both at the same time. We can then determine the next grid it is about to step into by adding its forward vector to its current grid position.

However, if you recall, we've made each grid in the world 10 units × 10 units. Therefore calculating the next grid using the character's exact location will not provide a platform location the neatly snaps to the grid. For example, the first platform is positioned at (0,0). If the player is moving in the positive *z* direction, a forward vector of (0,1), then the next location for a platform needs to be (0,10). If it is not, the new platform will overlap with the existing one. The character can be anywhere within a world grid space. If it is in the grid location containing (0,0) then it will still be in the same grid location when at (0,8). It won't be in the next grid position until its coordinates are greater than (0,10). If the character is at (0,8) and a platform is placed ten units in front of it, the new platform will be at (0,18). In this case, the platform will not be snapped to the grid.

The simplest way to deal with this issue is to round all coordinates to the closest value of ten. This way all platform positioning and trigger spawn points will be snapped to world positions that are multiples of ten.

Let's try this out. Create a new C# script called *generatePlatforms* and add the following code:

```
using UnityEngine;
using System.Collections;

public class generatePlatforms : MonoBehaviour {

    public GameObject[] platforms;
    float nextSpawnTriggerZ;

    void Start ()
    {
        nextSpawnTriggerZ = snap(this.transform.position.z
        + 10, 10);
```

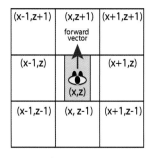

(x-1,z+1)	(x,z+1)	(x+1,z+1)
	forward vector	
(x-1,z)	↑ (x,z)	(x+1,z)
(x-1,z-1)	(x, z-1)	(x+1,z-1)

FIG 6.36 The coordinates in a grid layout 2D world.

```
}
void Update ()
{
    if(this.transform.position.z > nextSpawnTriggerZ)
    {
        Vector3 platformPosition = new
            Vector3(snap(this.transform.position.x,10),
            0, snap(this.transform.position.z + 10 *
            this.transform.forward.z,10));

        Instantiate(platforms[0], platformPosition,
            platforms[0].transform.rotation);

        nextSpawnTriggerZ = snap(this.transform.position.z + 10
            * this.transform.forward.z, 10);
    }
}
float snap(float value, float snapSize)
{
    return(Mathf.RoundToInt(value/snapSize)*snapSize);
}
}
```

Attach this code to the player. Locate the script in the Inspector for the player and drag and drop the *Platform1* prefab you created earlier onto the exposed platforms array as shown in Figure 6.33.

Save and play. Note the character runs right to the end of the platform and, just when you think it's going to fall over the edge, another platform snaps into place in front of it. The code works by generating a new spawn point ten units in front of the character. As the character passes it, a platform is generated and a new spawn point set. Note the code

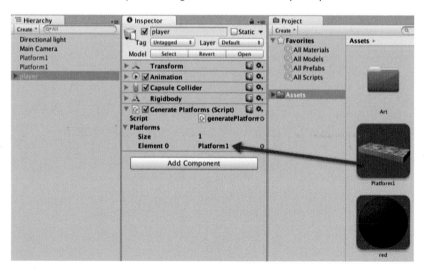

FIG 6.37 Attaching code to generate platforms in front of the player.

multiplies the platform position and the new spawn point location by the character's forward vector. This caters for the character pointing in the positive and negative *z* values. If the player is in grid (0,0) and facing (0,1) the platform is placed in (0,1). If the players is in grid (0,0) and facing (0,-1) the platform is placed in (0,-1).

Unfortunately the `if` statement testing the character against the next spawn trigger point only works if the player is facing in the positive *z* direction, as we will now see.

Step 6: To test platform spawning in all directions we need to be able to turn the character around. Modify the *playerNav* script thus:

```
using UnityEngine;
using System.Collections;

public class playerNav : MonoBehaviour {

    void Update () {

        this.transform.Translate(Vector3.forward * 0.1f);

        if(Input.GetKeyDown(KeyCode.RightArrow))
        {
            this.transform.Rotate(Vector3.up * 90);
        }
        else if(Input.GetKeyDown(KeyCode.LeftArrow))
        {
            this.transform.Rotate(-Vector3.up * 90);
        }
    }
}
```

Save and play. There is nowhere in the *x* direction to go at the moment, but if you double-tap an arrow key, you will be able to turn right around 180 degrees and retrace your steps. What happens when moving along the negative *z* direction when you get to the end of the platform track? That's right! You fall right off. The `if` statement in the *generatePlatforms* script has failed us.

It fails on two levels. First, the `if` statement only caters for movement in the positive *z* past a spawn point and, second, when the character turns right around, the next spawn trigger ends up behind the character. To fix this we need to generate a new spawn trigger when the character turns and make the `if` statement more robust.

Make these modifications to the *generatePlatforms* script:

```
...
void Start ()
{
    nextSpawnTriggerZ = snap(this.transform.
    position.z + 10, 10);
```

```
    }
    public void UpdateSpawnTrigger()
    {
        nextSpawnTriggerZ = snap(this.transform.position.z +
            10 * this.transform.forward.z, 10);
    }
    void Update ()
    {
        if( Mathf.Abs(this.transform.position.z -
            nextSpawnTriggerZ) < 1 )
        {
            Vector3 platformPosition = new
                Vector3(snap(this.transform.position.x,10),
                0, snap(this.transform.position.z + 10 *
                this.transform.forward.z,10));
    ...
```

The `if` statement now tests when the character is close to the spawn trigger point no matter what the direction. The `UpdateSpawnTrigger()` function creates a new spawn trigger point whenever it is called. We can now call this from the *playerNav* script thus:

```
void Update () {
    this.transform.Translate(Vector3.forward * 0.1f);
    if(Input.GetKeyDown(KeyCode.RightArrow))
    {
        this.transform.Rotate(Vector3.up * 90);
        this.GetComponent<generatePlatforms>().
            UpdateSpawnTrigger();
    }
    else if(Input.GetKeyDown(KeyCode.LeftArrow))
    {
        this.transform.Rotate(-Vector3.up * 90);
        this.GetComponent<generatePlatforms>().
            UpdateSpawnTrigger();
    }
}
```

Save and play. The character will cause platforms to be spawned in both *z* directions.

If you've turned left or right, at this point you'll notice *x* direction platforms are not spawned. This is because we haven't created any and haven't developed code to deal with movement in this direction. Let's add that now.

Step 7: Duplicate one of the platforms in the Scene. Change its transform values to: position (0,0,0) and scale (10,1,4). It will be longer in the *x* direction. Make this new platform into a new prefab and call it *Platform2*. For the copy of *Platform2* still in the scene set its position to (0,0,10). Create two more copies of *Platform2* and position them at (10,0,10) and (-10,0,10)

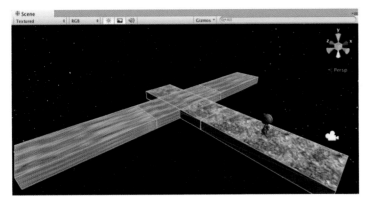

FIG 6.38 The starting platform configuration for our *Temple Run* game.

so your scene looks like that in Figure 6.38. You will now have an x direction path for the character to turn onto.

Save and play. The first thing you'll notice is that *x* direction platforms are not automatically spawned. To do this, modify the *generatePlatforms* script like this:

```
using UnityEngine;
using System.Collections;

public class generatePlatforms : MonoBehaviour {

    public GameObject[] platforms;

    Vector3 spawnTriggerPoint = new Vector3(0,0,0);

    void Start ()
    {
        UpdateSpawnTrigger();
    }
    public void UpdateSpawnTrigger()
    {
        spawnTriggerPoint = new Vector3(this.transform.position.x +
            10 * this.transform.forward.x,1,
            this.transform.position.z +
            10 * this.transform.forward.z);
    }
    void Update ()
    {
        if(Vector3.Distance(this.transform.position,
            spawnTriggerPoint) < 2 )
        {
            if(Mathf.Abs(Mathf.RoundToInt(this.transform.
            forward.z)) == 1)
            {
                Vector3 platformPosition = new Vector3(snap(
```

```
            this.transform.position.x,10),
            0, snap(this.transform.position.z + 10
            * this.transform.forward.z,10));

        Instantiate(platforms[0], platformPosition,
            platforms[0].transform.rotation);
    }
    else
    {
        Vector3 platformPosition = new Vector3(snap(
            this.transform.position.x + 10 *
            this.transform.forward.x,10),
            0, snap(this.transform.position.z,10));

        Instantiate(platforms[1], platformPosition,
            platforms[1].transform.rotation);
    }
    UpdateSpawnTrigger();
        }
    }
    float snap(float value, float snapSize)
    {
        return(Mathf.RoundToInt(value/
        snapSize)*snapSize);
    }
}
```

Examine all of the preceding code carefully as it has changed significantly. The spawn point trigger has changed to a vector that stores both the *x* and *z* trigger points. A new platform is spawned when the character gets within a distance of two from the trigger point. The location of the new platform is based on the character's forward vector.

Locate the *generatePlatforms* script in the *Inspector* for the player and drag and drop the *Platform2* prefab you created earlier onto the exposed platforms array.

Play.

As discussed in Chapter 1, instantiating game objects inside the Update() loop is a bad idea memory-wise. The longer this game is played the more and more platforms are added to the scene. Currently we aren't destroying them either so they will build up until the game crashes. We could use a Destroy() function that removes each platform as it goes outside the camera's view volume, however we'd still have the problem with many instantiations. Instead we should create all the platforms in the scene, place them in an array and move them around to create the game path as needed. When a platform is not part of the path it should be deactivated but not destroyed.

Step 8: Instead of using the default Unity cube to create these platforms we will use some models. Download *platformTSection.fbx*, *platformZThin. fbx*, and *platformZJump.fbx* from the website. Add these to your project. Add a single copy of each into the scene.

Step 9: For each of the new platforms delete any Animation Controller or Animator components that Unity may have added to the models when they were imported as shown in Figure 6.40. This is a common occurrence when bringing in FBX models. It can cause havoc with how your games behave if you have objects that don't have animations.

Notice in Figure 6.40 how *platformTSection* has a number of child objects. These are created by the modelling program that was used to construct the model file. They can usually cause a lot of headaches as most of them are empty. Later we will create code that controls the behavior of the platforms and cleans them up when they go outside the camera view. However, for this, the parent level game object will need to have the

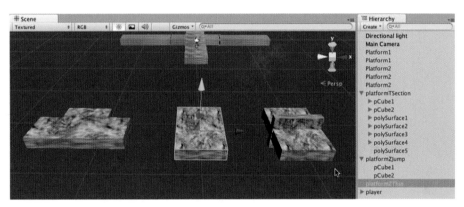

FIG 6.39 New pre-modeled platforms to use.

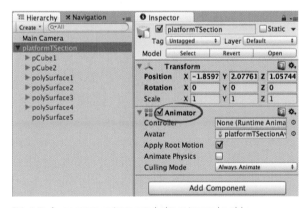

FIG 6.40 An unnecessary animator attached to an imported model.

object's mesh filter and mesh renderer. For *platformTSection*, the child called *polySurface5* is the actual object we want to work with. Therefore, drag *polySurface5* away from *platformTSection* to the bottom of the Hierarchy window. This will detach it and make it into a separate object. The remaining *platformTSection* can be deleted. Rename *polySurface5* to *platformTSection*.

You will need to repeat this for all the platforms to ensure they are just one object with no children and this object has the Mesh Renderer and Mesh Filter Components for the model.

You'll need to add Mesh Colliders to each of the platforms, remember to also check they have a Mesh Collider property assigned as they may not automatically have them like the default cube. Any models you bring from outside Unity will have to have colliders added in this manner if you want to use them in this way.

If the platforms are missing their texture, set the material on each new platform to that used for the initial platforms.

Make new prefabs from each of them.

Step 10: Duplicate the new platforms two more times so you end up with nine new platforms in total as shown in Figure 6.41. You can do this by shift-selecting the new three and then pressing CMD+D (Mac) or CTRL+D (PC).

Step 11: Select the player in the Hierarchy and locate the *generatePlatforms* script. Set the size of the `Platforms` array to 0. This will remove any old platforms you may have been using. Now add each of the nine new platforms into this array as shown in Figure 6.42.

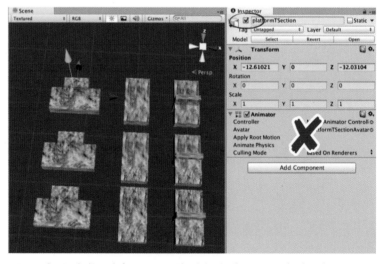

FIG 6.41 Creating duplicate platforms, removing their Animation Component, and making them inactive.

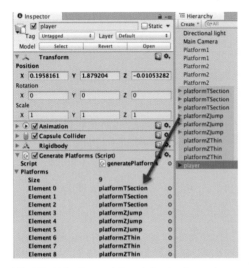

FIG 6.42 Adding the new platforms to the player's generate platforms array.

Step 12: With the new generate platforms array setup, select all the new platforms in the Hierarchy and untick the box at the very top left of the *Inspector* next to their name to make them inactive. The location of this tickbox is shown in Figure 6.41.

Step 13: Before modifying the platform generation code to deal with the new platforms, we need to change the player's navigation code to allow the character to jump over objects. This is a simple matter of adding a jump animation and throwing the character up into the air when the spacebar (or jump button on the screen) is pressed. We need to record when the player is in the process of jumping so we can disallow them from compounding the jump. Modify the *playerNav* code thus:

```
public class playerNav : MonoBehaviour {
    bool jumping = false;
    void OnGUI()
    {
        if(GUI.Button(new Rect(20,Screen.height - 70,
            50, 50),"Jump") && !jumping)
        {
            this.rigidbody.AddForce(0,300,0);
            this.animation.CrossFade("jump");
            jumping = true;
        }
    }

    void OnCollisionEnter(Collision collision)
    {
        if(!this.animation.IsPlaying("runforward"))
```

```
                    this.animation.CrossFade("runforward");

                    jumping = false;
            }
        void Update () {

            this.transform.Translate(Vector3.forward * 0.05f);

            if(Input.GetKeyDown(KeyCode.RightArrow))
            {
                ...
            }
            else if(Input.GetKeyDown(KeyCode.LeftArrow))
            {
                ...
            }
            else if(Input.GetKeyDown(KeyCode.Space) && !jumping)
            {
                this.rigidbody.AddForce(0,300,0);
                this.animation.CrossFade("jump");
                jumping = true;
            }
        }
    }
}
```

Save. Before playing, check the character has a jump animation. Select the player and examine the Animation component in the Inspector. Locate the Animations Size value and change it to 2. In the new space for an animation, select the small round icon to the right. A list of all available animations will pop up and you can select "jump" from them as shown in Figure 6.43.

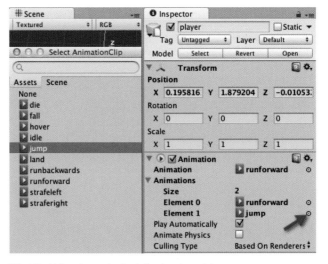

FIG 6.43 Adding a jump animation to the character model.

Play. The character will be able to jump when the spacebar or the new GUI jump button is pressed. To make the character jump higher or lower change the *y* value of the `AddForce` function in the preceding code.

Step 14: Now the character is capable of jumping over platforms with barriers on them we can start programming in the use of the new platforms. Modify the `Update()` function of *generatePlatforms* thus:

```
void Update ()
{
    if(Vector3.Distance(this.transform.position,
        spawnTriggerPoint) < 2 )
    {
        Vector3 platformPosition;

    if(Mathf.Abs(Mathf.RoundToInt(
        this.transform.forward.z)) == 1)
    {
        platformPosition = new
            Vector3(snap(this.transform.position.x,10), 0,
            snap(this.transform.position.z + 10 *
            this.transform.forward.z,10));
    }
    else
    {
        platformPosition = new
            Vector3(snap(this.transform.position.x + 10 *
            this.transform.forward.x,10), 0,
            snap(this.transform.position.z,10));
    }

    //random platform
    int pnum = Random.Range(0,platforms.Length);
    int tries = 0;

    //if this platform happens to be active
    while(platforms[pnum].activeSelf && tries < platforms.Length)
    {
        //get another one
        pnum = Random.Range(0,platforms.Length);
        tries++; //check if we run out of
            //inactive platforms
    }

    platforms[pnum].transform.position = platformPosition;
    platforms[pnum].SetActive(true);

    UpdateSpawnTrigger();
    }
}
```

Also note in the code the two `Instantiate` lines have been taken out. Instead, of creating new platforms all the time, we are reusing the ones that we have. The code searches for an inactive platform, places it into position and then activates it.

Save, but don't play at this point.

Step 15: A problem we now face is that eventually we will run out of inactive platforms, therefore when a platform pops out of view behind the character we need to make it inactive again.

Make a new C# script called *makeInactive* and add the following code:

```
using UnityEngine;
using System.Collections;

public class makeInactive : MonoBehaviour {

    void OnBecameInvisible()
    {
        if(this.gameObject.activeSelf)
            this.gameObject.SetActive(false);
    }
}
```

Save and attach to all the platforms in the Hierarchy (including the original T section ones). Now as the platforms are forever generated, the ones that become invisible to the camera are made available again for placement.

● Note

`OnBecameInvisible()` will only work on a `gameObject` that has a Mesh Renderer. If you put it on a parent object that has no Mesh Renderer, any children objects with Mesh Renderers will still be active.

Playing at this stage will reveal the new platform generation algorithm in action. You'll notice though that some of the platforms are facing the wrong way. If you are lucky, your character might be able to jump the gaps but that's not the type of game we are aiming for. We need to rotate the platforms as we snap them into place to ensure a smooth path.

Step 16: Examining the *platformTSection* reveals that the way it needs to be lined up will be to set its *z* axis to point in the opposite direction to the character's *z* axis. In other words, the platform should be rotated 180 degrees to that of the character. The other new platforms are constructed the same way and therefore we can treat them all in the same way. We just rotate the platform around its vertical axis toward the direction of the character. To do this, modify the *generatePlatform* code thus:

```
...
//random platform
int pnum = Random.Range(0,platforms.Length);
int tries = 0;
//if this platform happens to be active
while(platforms[pnum].activeSelf && tries
< platforms.Length)
{
    //get another one
    pnum = Random.Range(0,platforms.Length);
    tries++;
}
platforms[pnum].SetActive(true);
platforms[pnum].transform.position = platformPosition;
platforms[pnum].transform.rotation = this.transform.rotation;
platforms[pnum].transform.Rotate(new Vector3(0,180,0));

UpdateSpawnTrigger();
...
```

Save and run.

After running around the game environment for a while you'll notice a few glitches that need to be taken care of. First, sometimes two types of platform will be positioned in the same place. Second, when you run onto a T section in which you would expect you have to turn to avoid certain death, sometimes a platform appears directly ahead where it shouldn't.

Let's fix these.

Step 17: The position of the `spawnTrigger` is currently related to the character's position in the world. It doesn't get snapped to a position each time it is moved and therefore you can end up with inaccuracies that give you two spawn triggers on the same platform. This causes two platforms over the top of each other. To fix this we simply apply the snap function to the `spawnTriggerPoint` positioning. In addition, when the *spawnTriggerPoint* appears in the center of a T section, if the player is still facing forward and hasn't turned when they hit it, a platform will be created dead ahead with a gap between it and the player's current position. When the character is on a T section, we don't want it to be possible to spawn a platform straight ahead. Therefore we check if the `spawnTriggerPoint` is over a T section and, if it is, move it somewhere the player will not trigger it. When the player then turns a new `spawnTriggerPoint` will be created. Both these fixes occur in the `UpdateSpawnTrigger()` function of the *generatePlatforms* script thus:

```
public void UpdateSpawnTrigger()
{
    spawnTriggerPoint = new Vector3(
        snap(this.transform.position.x + 10 *
        this.transform.forward.x,10),1,
        snap(this.transform.position.z + 10 *
        this.transform.forward.z,10));

        //if the trigger is above a T Intersection then remove it
        RaycastHit hit;
        if(Physics.Raycast(spawnTriggerPoint,
            -Vector3.up, out hit, 1000))
        {
            if(hit.collider.gameObject.name ==
                "platformTSection" && Vector3.Distance(
                hit.collider.gameObject.transform.position,
                spawnTriggerPoint)<3)
            {
                spawnTriggerPoint = spawnTriggerPoint +
                new Vector3(0,-1000,0);
            }
        }
}
```

Step 18: Last but not least, we'll add swiping to code to allow for testing on a mobile device. Create two variables at the top of the `playerNav` class thus:

```
bool allowTurn = false;
Vector3 startTouch;
```

and modify the `Update()` function thus:

```
void Update ()
{
    this.transform.Translate(Vector3.forward * 0.05f);
    if(Input.touchCount > 0 &&
        Input.GetTouch(0).phase == TouchPhase.Began)
    {
        startTouch = Input.mousePosition;
        allowTurn = true;
    }

    if(Input.GetKeyDown(KeyCode.RightArrow) ||
        Input.touchCount > 0 &&
        Input.GetTouch(0).phase == TouchPhase.Moved &&
        Input.mousePosition.x > startTouch.x + 100 &&
        allowTurn && !jumping)
```

```
        {
            this.transform.Rotate(Vector3.up * 90);

            this.GetComponent<generatePlatforms>().
            UpdateSpawnTrigger();

            allowTurn = false;
        }
        else if(Input.GetKeyDown(KeyCode.LeftArrow) ||
            Input.touchCount > 0 &&
            Input.GetTouch(0).phase == TouchPhase.Moved &&
            Input.mousePosition.x < startTouch.x - 100 &&
            allowTurn && !jumping)
        {
            this.transform.Rotate(-Vector3.up * 90);

            this.GetComponent<generatePlatforms>().
            UpdateSpawnTrigger();

            allowTurn = false;
        }
        else if(Input.GetKeyDown(KeyCode.Space) ||
            Input.touchCount > 0 &&
            Input.GetTouch(0).phase == TouchPhase.Moved &&
            Input.mousePosition.y > startTouch.y + 100 &&
            !jumping)
        {
            this.rigidbody.AddForce(0,300,0);

            this.animation.CrossFade("jump");

            jumping = true;
        }
    }
}
```

Save and play.

By now you will have a decently running procedurally generated platform world.

6.3.2 Curiosity—What's Inside the Cube?

Curiosity was released in 2012. It was a massive multiplayer online game in which players tapped at the surface of a ridiculously large cube to destroy layers of the cube which in themselves were cubes. The winner was the player who tapped the very large cube to reveal what was inside.

The larger cube was initially constructed from 69 billion smaller cubes. That makes 552 billion vertices and 414 polygons. This is not a trivial number of cubes to hold in computer memory at any one time. Although players could see the entire cube, only the top layer was interactive until it was all tapped away, at which time the next layer down would be revealed. Therefore, it's only necessary to draw the outside layer of smaller cubes and make them interactive.

◉ Unity Hands-On
Curiosity Cube

In this hands-on session we will recreate the *Curiosity* cube with a simple generative algorithm and some 3D mathematics. The cubes are generated by an algorithm given the layer number where layer 1 is the cube in the middle, layer 2 is the layer of cubes encasing 1 and so on. As shown in Figure 6.44 there is a mathematical relationship between the layer number and the amount of cubes in that layer.

The relationship between the layer number and the cubes in that layer is:

$$(\text{layer number} + 2)^3 - \text{layer number}^3$$

Therefore in layer 3 there are $(3 + 2)^3 - 3^3 = 125 - 27 = 98$ cubes. Although in layer 3 the length of a side is five cubes, which would make the total 125 if the entire structure were composed of smaller cubes, the smaller cubes are only surface depth and therefore the number of cubes making up the interior must be subtracted.

If each small cube is made from a standard Unity cube of length 1, the math to determine the position of each is quite elementary. The center cube is placed at (0,0,0). With a size of 1 it extends from -0.5 to 5 along each *x*, *y*, and *z* axis. The position of the next layer begins at a distance of one from the previous layer. The distance from the center for the position of any layer is equal to the layer number. For example, layer 3 would begin at a distance of three from the center.

The number of cubes making up the side of a layer can be calculated by:

$$\text{layers} \times 2 - 1$$

For example on layer 3, the length of a side in cubes is equal to five and on layer 4, the length is seven. Once we know how many cubes will make up the length of the surface we need to draw, and considering the position of each cube in any axis will be a multiple of one based on the layer, it's only a matter of implementing a nested for loop that creates and places cubes according to their row, column, and depth position. In addition, we need to take care not to draw any interior cubes and not to repeatedly draw cubes on the edges and corners.

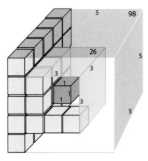

FIG 6.44 A cube made of layers of smaller cubes where each layer fully encases the next.

Step 1: Start a new Unity Project.
Step 2: Create a new C# script called *createCubeLayer* and add the following:

```
using UnityEngine;
using System.Collections;

public class createCubeLayer : MonoBehaviour {

    public GameObject cubePrefab;
    public int layers = 5;          //layers from centre
    float cubeSpacing = 0.05f;      //small gap between cubes
    GameObject largeC;              //the large middle cube

    Vector3 lastMousePos;
    float movementSensitivity = 0.1f;
    float pinchSensitivity = 0.01f;
    float previousDistance;

    Vector3 CameraZoomMax;
    Vector3 CameraZoomMin;

    void Start ()
    {
        int maxCubes = layers * 2 - 1;

        //generate a large inner cube
        Vector3 pos2 = new Vector3(
            (maxCubes -1)/2.0f + cubeSpacing*layers,
            (maxCubes -1)/2.0f + cubeSpacing*layers,
            (maxCubes -1)/2.0f + cubeSpacing*layers);

        largeC = Instantiate(cubePrefab, pos2,
            Quaternion.identity) as GameObject;

        largeC.transform.localScale = new Vector3(
            maxCubes-2 + cubeSpacing*layers,
            maxCubes-2 + cubeSpacing*layers,
            maxCubes-2 + cubeSpacing*layers);

        largeC.renderer.material.color = Color.red;
        largeC.transform.gameObject.tag = "Untagged";

        //generate outer cubes
        for(int row = 0; row < maxCubes; row++)
        {
            for(int col = 0; col < maxCubes; col++)
            {
                for(int dep = 0; dep < maxCubes; dep++)
                {
                    //if we are generating a cube on
                    //the outside
                    if(row == 0 || col == 0 || dep == 0 ||
                       row == maxCubes-1 || col == maxCubes-1 ||
                          dep == maxCubes-1)
                    {
                        Vector3 pos = new Vector3(
```

```
                                    row + row*cubeSpacing,
                                    col + col*cubeSpacing,
                                    dep + dep*cubeSpacing);

                        GameObject c = Instantiate(cubePrefab,
                                    pos, Quaternion.identity)
                                    as GameObject;

                        //give the cube a name relative
                        //to its position
                        c.name = "Cube_"+row+"_" + col + "_"
                        + dep;

                        //child to the centre cube
                        c.transform.parent = largeC.
                        transform;
                    }
                }
            }
        }
        largeC.transform.position = Vector3.zero;

        CameraZoomMax = new Vector3(0,0,
            (layers + layers*cubeSpacing)*5f);

        CameraZoomMin = new Vector3(0,0,
            (layers + layers*cubeSpacing)*2f);

        //set starting position of the camera
        this.transform.position = new Vector3(0,
            0,CameraZoomMax.z);

        this.transform.LookAt(largeC.transform.position);
    }
...
```

This code is quite long and its worthwhile pausing at this spot to consider what has already been added. As you will see, the nested for loops have been included to position smaller cubes as an enclosing skin around a single larger cube. The center cube is positioned at (0,0,0) and each small cube is a child of the center cube. This makes it much easier to rotate the entire structure as a whole in the game environment.

The second part of the code (following) takes care of cube rotation using finger-swipes or the mouse and camera zooming in and out.

```
// Update is called once per frame
void Update ()
{

    //drag and rotate
    if(Input.GetMouseButtonDown(0) || (Input.touchCount > 0 &&
        Input.GetTouch(0).phase == TouchPhase.Began))
    {
```

```
            lastMousePos = Input.mousePosition;
        }
        else if(Input.GetMouseButtonUp(0) ||
            (Input.touchCount > 0 &&
            Input.GetTouch(0).phase == TouchPhase.Ended))
        {
        }
        else if((Input.touchCount > 0 &&
            Input.GetTouch(0).phase == TouchPhase.Moved)||
            Input.GetMouseButton(0))
        {
        float mouseChangeX = (Input.mousePosition.x -
            lastMousePos.x) * movementSensitivity;

        float mouseChangeY = (Input.mousePosition.y -
            lastMousePos.y) * movementSensitivity;

        largeC.transform.RotateAround(largeC.transform.position,
            Vector3.up, -mouseChangeX * Time.deltaTime);

        largeC.transform.RotateAround(largeC.transform.position,
            Vector3.right, -mouseChangeY * Time.deltaTime);
        }

        //pinch and zoom
        if(Input.touchCount == 2 &&
            (Input.GetTouch(0).phase == TouchPhase.Began ||
            Input.GetTouch(1).phase == TouchPhase.Began) )
        {
            //calibrate previous distance
            previousDistance =
                Vector2.Distance(Input.GetTouch(0).position,
                Input.GetTouch(1).position);
        }
        else if (Input.touchCount == 2 &&
            (Input.GetTouch(0).phase == TouchPhase.Moved ||
            Input.GetTouch(1).phase == TouchPhase.Moved) )
        {
            float distance;
            Vector2 touch1 = Input.GetTouch(0).position;
            Vector2 touch2 = Input.GetTouch(1).position;
            distance = Vector2.Distance(touch1, touch2);

            float zChange = (distance - previousDistance);

            previousDistance = distance;
            this.transform.Translate(
                new Vector3(0f,0f,zChange*pinchSensitivity));

            if(this.transform.position.z > CameraZoomMax.z)
                this.transform.position = CameraZoomMax;

            else if(this.transform.position.z < CameraZoomMin.z)
```

```
            this.transform.position = CameraZoomMin;
    }
    //zoom with mouse wheel
    else if (Input.GetAxis("Mouse ScrollWheel") ! = 0)
    {
        this.transform.Translate(new
            Vector3(0f,0f,Input.GetAxis("Mouse ScrollWheel")));

        if(this.transform.position.z > CameraZoomMax.z)
            this.transform.position = CameraZoomMax;
        else if(this.transform.position.z < CameraZoomMin.z)
            this.transform.position = CameraZoomMin;
    }
}
}
```

Save the script. Attach to the Main Camera. Add a directional light to the scene to illuminate the cube.

Before playing add a default Unity cube to the scene and then make a prefab from it. Give the prefab a tag of "cube." Delete the original cube. With the *Main Camera* selected in the *Hierarchy*, locate the *createCubeLayer* script and the exposed *Cube* Prefab. Drag the newly created cube prefab from your assets into this exposed variable.

By default the layer number is set to 5 as you will see. You can increase this, however if you select a layer greater than 10 you'll begin to see a dramatic performance decrease. The distance the camera can zoom in and out is adjusted according to the layer.

When you run the code, either in the editor or on a mobile device, you will be able to rotate the cube and zoom in and out.

Step 3: As the objective of the game is to remove the outer layer of cubes by tapping on them, we will now add the appropriate code by which to do so. Because we are already touching the screen in order to rotate the cube, we don't want to destroy cubes at the same time as it might not be the player's intention. Rather, we will have a cube destroyed at the end of a touch on the provision that during the touch a move action did not occur. Modify the *createCubeLayer* script thus:

```
// Update is called once per frame
bool moving = true;
void Update ()
{
    //drag and rotate
    if(Input.GetMouseButtonDown(0) || (Input.touchCount > 0
    &&
        Input.GetTouch(0).phase == TouchPhase.Began))
```

```
        {
            lastMousePos = Input.mousePosition;
            moving = false;
        }
        else if((Input.GetMouseButtonUp(0) ||
            (Input.touchCount > 0 &&
            Input.GetTouch(0).phase == TouchPhase.Ended)) && !moving)
        {
            RaycastHit hit;
            Ray ray = Camera.main.ScreenPointToRay(Input.mousePosition);

            if (!Physics.Raycast (ray, out hit, 10000))
                return;

            if(hit.transform.gameObject.tag == "cube")
            {
                Destroy(hit.transform.gameObject);
            }
        }
        else if((Input.touchCount > 0 &&
            Input.GetTouch(0).phase == TouchPhase.Moved)||
            (Input.GetMouseButton(0) &&
            Vector3.Distance(Input.mousePosition,lastMousePos) > 0.5))
        {
            ...
            moving = true;
        }
    ...
```

Save and run. Cubes will be destroyed when you touch on them, but not while rotating the cube.

Step 4: After all the outer cubes have been removed from a layer, we want the next layer down to become covered in cubes. To achieve this we rerun the start script after decreasing the number of layers by 1 and resetting other key variables. Modify the *createCubeLayer* script thus:

```
...
int totalCubes;
int cubesDestroyed;

// Use this for initialization
void Start ()
{
    totalCubes = (int)(Mathf.Pow(layers+2, 3) −
        Mathf.Pow(layers, 3));

    cubesDestroyed = 0;
    int maxCubes = layers*2-1;
```

```
        //generate a large inner cube
    ...
    ...
void Update()
{
    //drag and rotate
    if(Input.GetMouseButtonDown(0) || (Input.touchCount >
    0 && Input.GetTouch(0).phase == TouchPhase.Began))
    {
        lastMousePos = Input.mousePosition;
        moving = false;
    }
    else if((Input.GetMouseButtonUp(0) ||
        (Input.touchCount > 0 &&
        Input.GetTouch(0).phase == TouchPhase.Ended))
        && !moving)
    {
        RaycastHit hit;
        Ray ray =
            Camera.main.ScreenPointToRay(Input.
            mousePosition);

        if (!Physics.Raycast (ray, out hit, 10000))
            return;

        if(hit.transform.gameObject.tag == "cube")
        {
            Destroy(hit.transform.gameObject);
            cubesDestroyed++;
        }
    }
    ...
    if(cubesDestroyed == totalCubes)
    {
        Destroy(largeC.gameObject);
        layers--;
        Start();
    }
}
```

Save and play. You might like to test by setting the layers to a small number such as three, otherwise it will take you quite a while to remove the outer layer to see the next layer created.

6.4 AI

AI has always proven to be one of the most complex elements in game development. AI as a field requires extensive knowledge of mathematics, computer science, and psychology. In games, AI implementation is less than perfect, while traditional AI researchers are interested in creating machines that do actually feel and think for themselves, in games we are more concerned about faking intelligence in a computer-controlled character. Such characters, in games, are referred to as non-player characters (NPCs).

It would be next to impossible to provide an entire elucidation of the inner workings of AI herein; Stuart Russell and Peter Norvig's 1995 popular text *Artificial Intelligence: A Modern Approach* is some 1,152 pages in length. Instead two of the most used AI concepts for implementing behavior in NPCs in mobile games will be given by way of examples in the context of a tower defense game. The AI package included in the pathfinding exercise below was used in the popular Unity-made mobile game *Cubemen*.

6.4.1 Line-of-Sight

The simplest form of AI that can be implemented in an NPC is line-of-sight. The method is, as the name suggests, determined if an NPC has a clear unobstructed view or route to a target location before initiating a behavior. For example, an NPC may remain idle until the player character comes into their line-of-sight.

⊙ Unity Hands-On
Look Before You Shoot

Step 1: Download the *AStar* project from the website. Open the *LineOfSight* scene. In it you will find a capsule with a simple turret on top. Place a cube in the scene near the bot but slightly higher than it.

Step 2: Create a new C# script called *Attack* and add the following:

```
using UnityEngine;
using System.Collections;

public class Attack : MonoBehaviour {

    public GameObject enemy;

    void Start () {

    }

    void Update () {
        this.transform.LookAt(enemy.transform.position);
    }
}
```

Save and attach this code to the *Turret Top* game object. It is a child of the bot. Set the exposed enemy value to be the cube as shown in Figure 6.45.

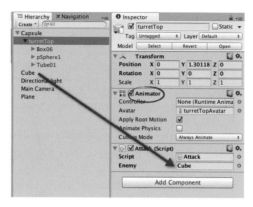

FIG 6.45 Setting up a simple enemy look at script.

While looking at the Turret Top components in the Inspector, remove the Animator component. As previously discussed, Unity will automatically add these to imported FBX models ready for animating. However, in this case we don't need it.

Play. The turret on the bot will turn to look at the enemy (cube). In order to use the above code, the object that you are rotating to look at something must have the *z* axis along what you would consider the front of the object. The `LookAt()` function turns the *z* axis of the model to point at the position it is given. In this case, *z* runs right along the barrel of the turret and therefore the `LookAt()` functions cause the barrel to aim right at the position of the enemy game object.

Step3: If you'd prefer the turret slowly turn towards the enemy rather than snap to position you can implement spherical interpolation. This basically splits a rotation up into a smaller set of rotations and adds them one at a time to give the appearance of a turn. To achieve this replace the `LookAt()` function line with:

```
transform.rotation = Quaternion.Slerp(
this.transform.rotation,
    Quaternion.LookRotation( enemy.transform.position -
    transform.position ), Time.deltaTime );
```

Save and play. The turret will turn slowly towards the cube. To speed this up you can add a multiplier to `Time.deltaTime`, e.g.,

```
Time.deltaTime * 10
```

Step 4: Because the turret is now turning toward the enemy, we want it to begin shooting when the enemy is within its sights, not from the moment it starts turning. To achieve this we need to examine the angle between the direction the turret is facing and the direction to the enemy. We are also going to add some ammunition to the turret for it to shoot when it is lined up.

To keep the number of instantiations to a minimum instead of creating bullets as needed we will load the turret with a set of pre-created bullets. Create a new cube in the scene and color it red. Resize it so it's small enough to come out of the end of the turret. Attach a rigidbody and create a prefab from it. Create four copies of the bullet so that there are five bullets in total in the scene. Position each bullet inside the sphere end of the turret and child them all to the *turretTop* game object.

Step 5: Modify the Attack script thus:

```
public GameObject enemy;
public GameObject[] bullets;
public float accuracy = 2.0f;
bool shooting = false;

void Start ()
{
    for(int i = 0; i < bullets.Length; i++)
    {
        bullets[i].transform.position = this.transform.position;
        bullets[i].SetActive(false);
    }
}
void Shoot()
{
    for(int i = 0; i < bullets.Length; i++)
    {
        if(!bullets[i].active)
        {
            bullets[i].SetActive(true);
            bullets[i].rigidbody.AddForce(
                this.transform.forward * 300);
            i = bullets.Length + 1;
        }
    }
}
void Update ()
{
    transform.rotation = Quaternion.Slerp( this.trans-
    form.rotation,
        Quaternion.LookRotation( enemy.transform.
        position—
        transform.position ), Time.deltaTime );

    if(Quaternion.Angle(transform.rotation,
        Quaternion.LookRotation(enemy.transform.position—
        transform.position )) < = accuracy && !shooting)
```

```
    {
        InvokeRepeating("Shoot",0f,1.0f);
        shooting = true;
    }
    else if(Quaternion.Angle(transform.rotation,
        Quaternion.LookRotation(enemy.transform.position -
        transform.position )) > accuracy)
    {
        shooting = false;
        CancelInvoke();
    }
}
```

Save. Select the *turretTop* game object and locate the script in the Inspector. You will now see an array to take the bullet game objects. Drag and drop each of the bullets into the array as shown in Figure 6.46.

Play. The code works by setting the bullets to inactive initially and then makes them active when needed. It will only select an inactive bullet to activate and fire. Any bullets already active are considered to have been fired. When the turret is aligned with the enemy to within 2 degrees as denoted by the accuracy property, shooting commences. The shoot function is called by an `InvokeRepeating` that will start it immediately and keep running it every two seconds. The shoot function invoke is cancelled when the alignment angle goes outside the accuracy setting.

The speed of the bullets can be adjusted by increasing or decreasing the force added to the bullets and adjusting the bullet's drag value on the rigidbody.

You may notice that the code causes all the bullets to be fired and then the turret stops firing. This is because it has run out of bullets. To reload the turret we should gather up the used bullets after they've hit something or gone outside the camera's view volume. Making them inactive will make them available again to the `Shoot()` function.

Step 6: Create a new C# script called *hitDeactivate* and add the following:

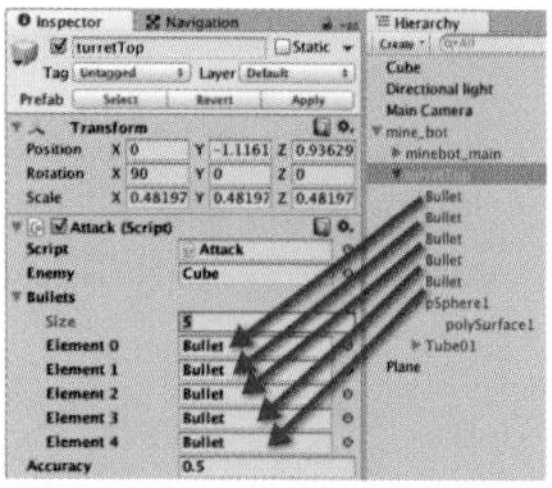

FIG 6.46 Creating an array of pre-created bullets to use in game.

```
using UnityEngine;
using System.Collections;

public class hitDeactivate : MonoBehaviour {

    Vector3 startPos;

    void OnBecameInvisible(){
        reset();
    }

    void Start()
    {
```

```
        startPos = this.transform.position;
    }

    void OnCollisionEnter(Collision collision){
        reset();
    }

    void reset()
    {
        this.gameObject.SetActive(false);
        this.gameObject.transform.position = startPos;
    }
}
```

Save and attach this code to the bullet prefab. It should automatically update all the bullets already in the scene (but you might like to check just in case). Play. The turret will continue firing bullets, constantly recycling the ones it has available to it. If you feel that more bullets are required, create more from the bullet prefab, attach them to the turret and place them in the bullets array of the *Attack* code.

Step 7: Currently the bullets leave the turret in the center of the sphere. When the force added is not enough they sometimes fall out the side rather than come from the center of the sphere. To fix this we can add a position holder to the turret that represents the bullets' starting positions. Create a cube and call it *Spawner*. Move it in the scene to the end of the turret's barrel and then child to the turretTop. Child all bullets to the spawner and set their positions to (0,0,0) as shown in Figure 6.47.

You won't want the cube to be visible in the game nor cause collisions so delete its Mesh Renderer, Mesh Filter and Box Collider. All you will be left with is the Transform component. At this time you will be able to see the red bullets at the end of the barrel, but these will become inactive when the game runs and therefore they will not be visible.

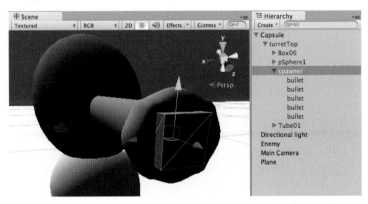

FIG 6.47 Using a game object to set the starting point for bullets.

419

The script *hitDeactivate* can be modified to use the bullet's new starting location thus:

```
public class hitDeactivate : MonoBehaviour {

    void OnBecameInvisible(){
        reset();
    }

    void OnCollisionEnter(Collision collision){
        reset();
    }

    void reset()
    {
        this.gameObject.SetActive(false);
        this.gameObject.transform.localPosition =
            Vector3.zero;
    }
}
```

Save and play. Notice the use of `localPosition` to reset the starting position of the bullet. Because it is a child of the spawner, it has to be locally reset to zero otherwise it will be placed globally at the world origin.

You now have a shooting bot that you can create a prefab from and spawn multiple copies of. They will all work in exactly the same way.

6.4.2 Waypoints and Pathfinding

Almost all AI techniques used in games rely on the programmers having an understanding of graphs. A graph in this context refers to a collection of nodes and edges. The nodes are represented graphically as circles and the edges are the lines that connect them. A graph can be visualized as the nodes representing locations and the edges as paths connecting them. A graph can be undirected, which means the paths between the nodes can be traversed in both directions or directed in which case the paths are one-way. Think of this as the difference between two-way streets and one-way streets. Graphs are drawn with the nodes represented as circles and the edges as lines as shown in Figure 6.48.

The nodes and edges can be drawn where the nodes represent coordinates such as those on a flight plan, or as symbolic states where the physical location in the graph is meaningless. For example, the state diagram in Figure 6.48 could be drawn with the nodes in any position and any distance from one another. Some directed graphs allow bi-directional traversal from one node to another in the same way as undirected graphs. However, if arrows are already being used in a directed graph to show some one-way-only paths, they should also appear on bi-directional edges for consistency. Both nodes and edges can have associated values. These values could be

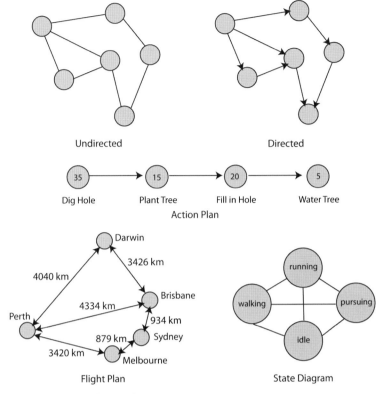

FIG 6.48 A variety of different graph types.

the distance between nodes like those representing the distances in a flight plan or the time it takes to complete an action such as the nodes in an action plan.

A waypoint is simply a remembered location on a map. Waypoints are placed in a circuit over the map's surface and are connected by straight-line paths. The paths and waypoints are connected in such a way that an AI controlled bot moving along the paths is assured not to collide with any fixed obstacles. The waypoints and their connecting paths create a graph. Moving from waypoint to waypoint along a path requires an algorithm to search through and find all the nodes and how they are connect to each other.

Usually you will want an NPC to move from one waypoint to another via the shortest path. Often the meaning of shortest refers to the Euclidian distance between points, but not always. In real-time strategy (RTS) games where maps are divided up into grids of differing terrain, the shortest path from one point to another may not be based on the actual distance, but on the time taken to traverse each location. The definition of shortest is therefore left up to a matter of *utility*. The term "utility" originates in classical game theory and refers to the preferences of game players. There are several methods to find the shortest path from one node to another in a graph. These include algorithms such as *Breadth-First Search*, *Depth-First Search*, and *A**.

The Breadth-First Search (BFS) takes the given starting node and examines all adjacent nodes. Nodes that are adjacent to a starting node are ones that are directly connected to the starting node by an edge. In turn, from each of the adjacent nodes, the nodes adjacent to these are examined. This process continues until the end node is found or the search for adjacent nodes has been exhausted. The algorithm can be written as Listing 6.1.

Listing 6.1 A Breadth-First Search Algorithm

```
1. Let i = 1;
2. Label starting node as i.
3. Find all unlabeled nodes adjacent to at least one node
   with label i. If there are no adjacent nodes, stop
   because we have run out of nodes. If the ending node is
   found, stop because we have found a path.
4. Label all nodes found in step 3 with i+1.
5. Let i = i+1, go to step 3.
```

This algorithm will always find the shortest path (Euclidean distance) from the start to the end vertices assuming that each vertex is the same distance apart. An example of the labeling process of a BFS is illustrated in Figure 6.49.

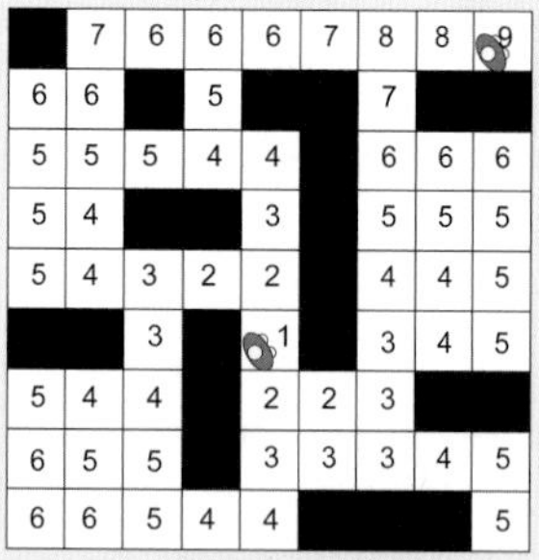

FIG 6.49 The running of a BFS to move from position 1 to the top right-hand corner.

The Depth-First Search (DFS) is simpler than the BFS and hence less effective. Instead of radiating out from the starting node, this algorithm simply follows one adjacent node to the next until it reaches the end of a path. Recursion works well for this algorithm and can be written as Listing 6.2.

Listing 6.2 A Depth-First Search Algorithm

```
DFS( a, vertex )
1. Let i = a;
2. Label node as i
```

For each adjacent node, n, to i, if n is labeled skip it,
if n is the end node then stop the search, else if n is not
labeled run this algorithm with DFS(a+1, n). An example of
the labeling process of a BFS is illustrated in Figure 6.50.

FIG 6.50 The running of a DFS to
move from position 1 to the top right-
hand corner.

The most popular algorithm used in games, for searching graphs, is called A*
(pronounced A-Star). What makes A* more efficient than BFS or DFS is that
instead of blindly picking the next adjacent node, the algorithm looks for one
that appears to be the most promising. From the starting node, the projected
cost of all adjacent nodes is calculated and the best node is chosen to be the
next on the path. From this next node the same calculations occur again and
the next best node is chosen. This algorithm ensures that all the best nodes
are examined first. If one path of nodes does not work out, the algorithm can
return to the next best in line and continue the search down a different path.

The algorithm determines the projected cost of taking paths based on the
cost of getting to the next node and an estimate of getting from that node
to the goal. The estimation is performed by a *heuristic* function. The term
"heuristic" seems to be one of those funny words in AI that is difficult to
define. Alan Newell first defined it in 1963 as a computation that performs
the opposite function to that of an algorithm. A more useful definition of
its meaning is given by Russell and Norvig, in *Artificial Intelligence*. They
define a heuristic as any technique that can be used to improve the average
performance of solving a problem that may not necessarily improve the
worse performance. In the case of *pathfinding*, if the heuristic offers a perfect
prediction, that is it can accurately calculate the cost from the current node
to the destination, then the best path will be found. However, in reality, the
heuristic is very rarely perfect and can only offer an approximation.

FIG 6.51 Creating a pathfinding object from the A* Pathfinding Project package.

Unity Hands-On
Pathfinding

Step 1: Open your completed project from the previous hands-on session or download a similar version called *AStar2* from the website. Open the *LineOfSight* scene. Rename the capsule bot constructed in the previous hands-on to "Bot" and make it into a prefab. If the enemy cube is still in the scene then delete it. Keep the ground plane.

This project includes the free version of the A* Pathfinding Project package (http://arongranberg.com/astar). We will use it to do all the pathfinding calculations for our bots.

Step 2: Create an empty game object and call it *A*. Select it in the Hierarchy and in the Inspector select Add Component and attach the Pathfinding > Pathfinder script to it as shown in Figure 6.51.

Step 3: On the *A* Path* panel that is now visible in the Inspector for the *A* game object, Select Add New Graph > Grid Graph. A new graph will be added to the panel and a small blue grid will appear over the plane in the scene as shown in Figure 6.52. Select the new grid graph in the Inspector to reveal its properties.

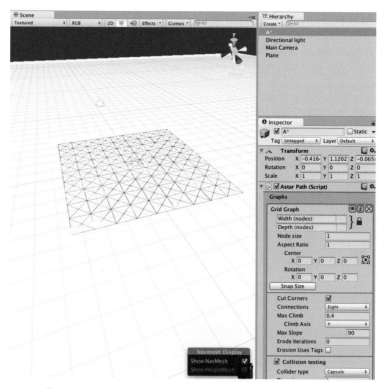

FIG 6.52 The grid graph component created by the pathfinding script.

Step 4: With the *A** game object selected press the R key. Side control cubes will appear on the grid graph as shown in Figure 6.53. Select one of the cubes on the side of the grid graph. It will change to yellow. You will then be able to drag the size of the grid graph out to fit the ground plane. Do this with all sides of the grid graph and make it slightly smaller than the ground. Each blue line on the grid graph represents a possible path that can be taken by an NPC.

The more paths, the greater the processing required for each NPC. If your environment does not require precise intricate movements from the bots or is not all that complex you can increase the node size of the graph as shown in Figure 6.54. Note however, when you change the node size, the

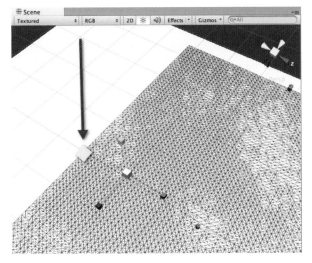

FIG 6.53 Resizing the grid graph.

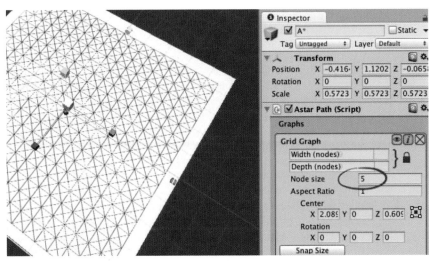

FIG 6.54 Making pathfinding nodes larger will make path calculates more efficient.

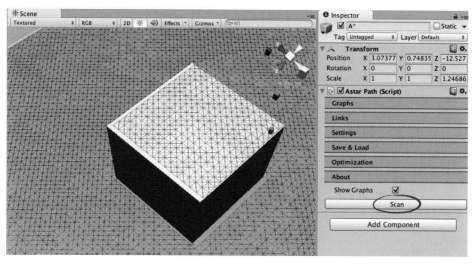

FIG 6.55 A grid graph displaying areas of an environment that are not traversable by an NPC.

grid graph will resize and you will have to scale it again. Therefore its best to set the node size before adjusting the grid graph to fit your map.

Step 5: Add a cube into the scene and sit it on the ground plane and intersecting such that the bottom goes slightly into the ground (e.g., there is definitely no gap under the cube). Resize it to about one-fifth the size of the ground plane. Select the *A** game object and in the Inspector click on the Scan button of the *A* Pathfinding* component. The grid graph will place red lines on top of the cube as shown in Figure 6.55. This area cannot be traversed by an NPC.

Step 6: Lower the cube so it is just protruding above the ground plane. Press the Scan button again. If the cube is low enough, blue grid lines will be drawn over the cube. If it is still red, it is too high. Try lowering it bit by bit and rescanning until it scans blue.

You can control the step height and slope in the A* grid graph settings. As shown in Figure 6.56 there are values for Max Climb and Max Slope you can set to control how the grid graph wraps itself over objects and how NPCs will behave when traversing the terrain. Its best to get your heights and slopes set to how you want before building up an entire game environment.

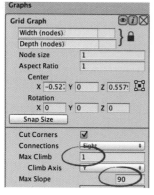

FIG 6.56 Setting the Max Climb distance and Max Slope angle.

Step 7: Using cubes, create a simple tower defense environment reminiscent of Cubemen. A simple version is shown in Figure 6.57. After adding each cube press the scan button to ensure you get the path calculations you desire. Place a Bot in the scene to check your scaling. Also add a sphere to act as the tower.

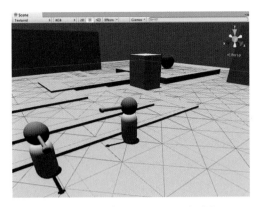

FIG 6.57 A simple tower defense world constructed with Unity primitives.

Step 8: Make the sphere the enemy in the *Bot's Attack* script (attached to its turret top). Attach a rigidbody to the bot (on its parent-most object). At this stage when you play the game the bot will turn toward the sphere and start shooting. It will not, however, move.

Step 9: Locate the *AIPath* script in the `AstarPathfindingProject/Core/AI` folder in the `Assets/Plugins`. Attach it to the Bot. It will automatically add a Seeker script as well. The only value that needs to be set is the Target as shown in Figure 6.58. Set the target to the sphere object.

FIG 6.58 Set the target to the sphere object.

Save and run. The bot will now seek out the target.

A few things to note. First, the Bot may not start moving straight away as it will still be calculating a path. Second, you might like to consider adding some drag to the Bot's rigidbody and/or change the friction on the world surfaces if it slides around too much. Sometimes the Bot can get enough speed up that the momentum will make it slide right off the edge of narrow paths.

Once you have one Bot set up you can make duplicates and add as many as you like.

You can find more information on the other settings for the AStar Pathfinding Project at http://arongranberg.com/astar.

6.5 Summary

In this chapter we have examined the use of the physics engine, procedural algorithms, and artificial intelligence for creating dynamic behavior within the game environment and in characters. When designing a mobile game, remember the functionality of the game engine isn't just there to carry out your commands that you give it in absolute precision. Some very interesting, challenging, and engaging game mechanics have been born as a result of letting go of the reins and letting the code do it for you.

CHAPTER 7

Multiplayer Experiences

Gaming as provided by mobile phone platforms is absorbing the growth that the new generation [of consoles] should have delivered.

Horace Dediu

7.1 Introduction

Multiplayer experiences are becoming more popular on mobile devices. In 2009, Zynga released *Words with Friends* (www.wordswithfriends.com). It is a Scrabble-like game available on most platforms in which players take turns spelling out words. The game sends a message to a player when it is their turn. The game is rarely played in real-time, with days and sometimes months going by before the next player plays. *Draw Something* by OMGPop later acquired by Zynga, is another popular social mobile game that works in a similar manner, where drawings are passed between players over the Internet and the player has to guess what the other player has drawn. It's like mobile Pictionary. Of course there are many more multiplayer games of these types available on mobile platforms.

Whether they are games with words or images being exchanged between players, the infrastructure that allows this type of communication between devices is not trivial. It is, however, relatively easy to implement as you will discover in this chapter. Thanks to the research and development that has gone into the Internet since the 1960s we can set up simple networked communications in a matter of moments. However, as the time between messages becomes faster and more people join in with the same game, the logistics of handling and synchronizing the data becomes more complex.

In this chapter, we will examine different types of multiplayer game experiences that you can create on mobile devices as well as explaining the underlying infrastructure and protocols of the Internet that make it all possible.

7.2 Playing Together on the Same Device

Before we delve into the setup for multiplayer games that take place on different devices, we will first turn our attention to players playing together on the same device. These are much easier to create, as we don't have to deal with message-sending over the Internet. In this section, we will examine both asynchronous and synchronous games.

7.2.1 Asynchronous Games

Asynchronous games—or turn-based games, as they are more readily known—are where players interact with the game environment one after the other, but not at the same time. Most board games operate in this manner. On the mobile platform we have *Trivial Pursuit*, based on the physical board game, and *Pathogen*, a strategy token-placing game similar to Reversi.

Technically the biggest challenge in developing such a game is to ensure the state of each player is recorded accurately. The game needs to remember each

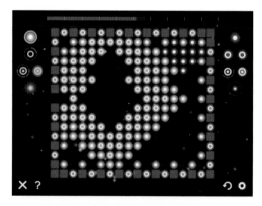

FIG 7.1 *Pathogen* on the iPad by Birnam Wood Games.

player's score, maybe other player details, and—most importantly—whose turn it is.

In the following hands-on session, the basic constructs for such a game will be developed, in which each player's data is stored in an array using a class to structure the individual data. The nice thing about turn-based games and using arrays is that the position of the array is relative to whose turn it is and therefore the turn can be used to index the data in the array for extraction and updating.

◉ Unity Hands-On
Multiplayer Die Rolling
In this hands-on we are going to modify the die rolling exercise from the previous chapter into a turn-based multiplayer game.

Step 1: Open the completed die rolling exercise from Chapter 6 or download a version from the website called *DiceRollingForMulti.zip*. In the Scene the game board will be set up with the green surface and the red die. When the game is run, the player's accumulated score and the last die roll will be displayed.

Step 2: The first thing we will do is create a data structure to hold each player's information including their name, an avatar picture, and score. For this we define a new class in the top of the scores script thus:

```
using UnityEngine;
using System.Collections;

public class Player
{
    public int avatar;
    public int score;
    public string name;

    public Player(int t, string n)
    {
        avatar = t;
        name = n;
    }
}
public class scores : MonoBehaviour {

    static Player[] players;
    static int totalScore = 0;
    static int diceValue = 0;
    ....
```

Notice this class is above the definition for the scores class. Inside the scores class a new array of players is created. Each position in the array holds the information for each player.

Step 3: Now a GUI needs to be written to allow for the entry of the number of players and their details. Before we do this though, we need some player avatar images. For this example four 64 × 64 icons have been taken from http://iconarchive.com. Download four of your own 64 × 64 images or make your own. Add them to Unity by dragging them onto the Assets folder in the Project.

To the scores script (attached to the Main Camera) add a new public property thus:

```
...
public class scores : MonoBehaviour {

    static Player[] players;
    public Texture2D[] avatarIcons;
    static int totalScore = 0;
    static int diceValue = 0;

...
```

Save and locate the newly exposed avatarIcons array in the Inspector (with the Main Camera selected in the Hierarchy), make the size of the array 4 and drag and drop each of the icons you just added into the array as shown in Figure 7.2.

Step 4: In this step we will construct a series of GUI configuration dialogs that create all the players and allow names and avatars to be set for each. This initialization of the game environment should happen when the game is first run. Therefore we will implement a Boolean value that is initially set to true and forces the configuration dialogs to appear. We will also create an integer value that keeps track of the configuration step that the player is on. In this case there are two steps. The first one is to select

FIG 7.2 Creating an array of avatar icons for a multiplayer game.

the number of players and the second is to set each player's name and avatar.

To prepare for this add the following properties and initial values to the *score* script thus:

```
...
public class scores : MonoBehaviour {

    static Player[] players;
    public Texture2D[] avatarIcons;
    static int totalScore = 0;
    static int diceValue = 0;
    public static bool gameStarted = false;
    bool initialised = false;
    int initStep = 0;

    private int playerSelectionGridInt = -1;
    private string[] playerSelectionStrings = {"1","2","3","4"};

    int playerDetails = 0;

    void Start()
    {
        initialised = false;
    }
    ...
```

Next, to the *OnGUI* function add:

```
void OnGUI()
{
    GUI.Label(new Rect(20,10,100,30),"Score: " +
    totalScore);
    GUI.Label(new Rect(20,30,1000,30),"Last Roll: " +
    diceValue);

    if(!initialised)
    {
    GUI.BeginGroup (new Rect (Screen.width / 2-100,
    Screen.height / 2-100, 200, 200));

        if(initStep == 0)
        {
                GUI.Box (new Rect (0,0,200,200), "How many
                players?");

            playerSelectionGridInt = GUI.SelectionGrid (
                    new Rect (20, 25, 160, 160),
                    playerSelectionGridInt,
                    playerSelectionStrings, 1);

            if(playerSelectionGridInt > = 0)
```

```
                        {
                            initStep++;
                            players = new Player[playerSelectionGridInt+1];

                            //create each empty player
                            for(int i = 0; i < players.Length; i++)
                            {
                            players[i] = new Player(0,"Player" + (i+1));
                            }
                        }
                    }
                    else if(initStep == 1)
                    {
            GUI.Box (new Rect (0,0,200,200), "Player" +
                (playerDetails+1) + " Details");

            GUI.Label(new Rect(20,25,100,30),"Name:");
            players[playerDetails].name = GUI.TextField (
                        new Rect (80, 25, 100, 30),
                        players[playerDetails].name);

            players[playerDetails].avatar = GUI.SelectionGrid (
                        new Rect (10, 60,130, 130),
                        players[playerDetails].avatar, avatarIcons, 2);

            if(GUI.Button(new Rect(145,100,50,30),"Next"))
            {
                        playerDetails++;
                if(playerDetails > = players.Length)
                        playerDetails = 0;
            }

            if(GUI.Button(new Rect(145,140,50,30),"Play"))
            {
                initStep++;
            }
                    }
                    GUI.EndGroup ();
                }
            }
```

Save and run. At the start of the game, a popup box will ask for the
number of players. Once this is selected, an array of this many players
is created and the next popup cycles through the players allowing
for the setting of avatars and names. Note that, after the last player, it
cycles back to the first and remembers previously entered details. The
Play button closes the configuration dialog. These dialogs are shown in
Figure 7.3.

FIG 7.3 Two dialog boxes for configuring our multiplayer game.

The preceding code uses Unity's `GUI.SelectionGrid`. For more details on its configuration see the GUI Controls section in the Unity Manual, http://docs.unity3d.com/Documentation/Components/gui-Controls.html

Step 5: You may have noticed while testing the configuration dialogs that the die gets in the way and it is even possible to throw it around. To fix this we will initially disable to the die and then, after the Play button is pressed, activate it. In the score script add a new public property thus:

```
public class scores : MonoBehaviour {

    static Player[] players;
    public Texture2D[] avatarIcons;
    public GameObject theDice;
    static int totalScore = 0;
    static int diceValue = 0;
...
```

Locate this new exposed property in the Inspector and drag and drop the die onto it as shown in Figure 7.4.

Step 6: In the `Start()` function, disable the die with this:

```
void Start()
{
    initialised = false;
    theDice.SetActive(false);
}
```

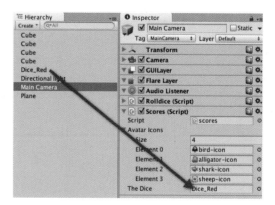

FIG 7.4 Making the die game object known to the scores script.

Make the die active again when the Play button is pressed thus:

```
if(GUI.Button(new Rect(145,140,50,30),"Play"))
{
    initStep++;
    theDice.SetActive(true);
}
```

Save and play. The die will only appear in the game after the *Play* button is pressed.

Step 7: We now need to attribute each die roll with a particular player and update their score. This will require a GUI element displaying the scores as well as informing the players whose turn it is. To keep track of this we will use an integer variable. Add one to the scores script thus:

```
public class scores : MonoBehaviour {

    static Player[] players;
    static int playerTurn = 0;
...
```

Step 8: The value of playerTurn can be used to update the score of the player in the players array. Instead of writing the score into diceValue and totalScore we should give the score to the player whose turn it is. To do this rewrite the UpdateScore() function in scores like this:

```
public static void UpdateScore(int value)
{
    players[playerTurn].score + = value;
    playerTurn++;
    if(playerTurn > = players.Length)
        playerTurn = 0;
}
```

Note at the end of the function the value of `playerTurn` is checked to see if it has exceeded the number of players. If it has it is set back to 0 indicating it is Player 1's turn again.

Step 9: To display these new scores for each player, a loop can be used to extract each score, player name, and avatar and draw it on the screen. Replace the GUI labels printing out `diceValue` and `totalScore` in the `OnGUI()` function of scores with:

```
void OnGUI()
{

    if(initStep == 2)
    {
        for(int i = 0; i < players.Length; i++)
        {
                GUI.Label(new Rect(20,64*i,64,64),
                    avatarIcons[players[i].avatar]);

                GUI.Label(new Rect(84,64*i,100,30),
                    players[i].name);

                GUI.Label(new Rect(84,64*i + 20,100,30),
                    ""+players[i].score);
        }
        return;
    }

    if(!initialised)
    {
...
```

Save and play to see the player turns and new GUI in action.

Step 10: Finally, we should display a message on the screen stating whose turn it is so the players don't get confused while playing. Add the following line to the `OnGUI()` function:

```
void OnGUI()
{
    if(initStep == 2)
    {
        GUI.Label(new Rect(Screen.width/2-75, 20, 150, 20),
                "Player " + players[playerTurn].name +
                " it's your turn!");

        for(int i = 0; i < players.Length; i++)
        {
...
```

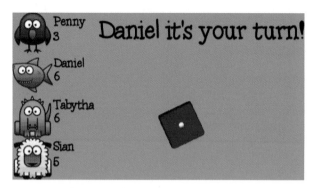

FIG 7.5 A completed version of the multiplayer die rolling game.

Save and play. With the addition of a font to style the GUI elements your final game could look like that in Figure 7.5.

7.2.2 Synchronous

Synchronous games, or games in which all players play at the same time, are quite popular, although sometimes difficult to design for, with so many fingers needing to touch the screen at the same time. These types of games lend themselves better to larger touch surfaces such as the Apple iPad or Samsung Galaxy Tab. Such games include Half Brick's *Fruit Ninja* multiplayer, Mass Developer's *Snowball Mania*, and Team 17 Digital Limited's *Worms 2: Armageddon*.

In the case of *Snowball Mania*, the game environment is divided into player sides by a river. The actual game landscape in this case creates the sides and players' characters interact with each other in the same world. In *Fruit Ninja*, the screen is split, players play in separate environments, and their final scores are compared.

While the player information and scoring system for a synchronous game is the same as asynchronous, the interactive component is different. When the game is turn-based, during each turn, any screen touches, tilts, or other interactions are all contributed to a single player. In a synchronous game, from the blind device's point of view, it cannot tell which player is taking which action. All that can be done is to determine which game pieces are being manipulated and attribute behavior to the player to whom they belong.

In the next hands-on section, a split-screen multiplayer game will be created that demonstrates the use of two cameras and dividing a single screen into two viewports for a split screen experience.

⚙ **Unity Hands-On**
Christmas Tap Challenge
In this hands-on session we will create a split-screen synchronous multiplayer game. The game will consist of a set of falling icons that each user must match to an icon presented in the corner of the screen by tapping

on them. If a player taps a falling icon that matches the one displayed in the corner they will get points, otherwise they will be penalized.

Step 1: Download the *ChristmasTap* project from the website. In the *maingame* Scene you will find a cube called spawner. There will be a number of icons and a prefab called Item in the Project. The Scene is setup for landscape viewing. The cube, which will spawn objects is placed in the centre of the window just above the camera's viewing volume.

Step 2: Create a C# script called *spawn* and add the following code:

```csharp
using UnityEngine;
using System.Collections;

public class spawn : MonoBehaviour {

    public GameObject itemPrefab;
    const int poolSize = 20;

    GameObject[] itemPool = new GameObject[poolSize];

    void Start ()
    {
        for(int i = 0; i < poolSize; i++)
        {
            itemPool[i] = (GameObject)
            Instantiate(itemPrefab,
                this.transform.position,
                itemPrefab.transform.rotation);

            itemPool[i].SetActive(false);
        }

        InvokeRepeating("SpawnItem",0.5f,0.5f);
    }

    void SpawnItem()
    {
        for(int i = 0; i < poolSize; i++)
        {
            if(!itemPool[i] .activeSelf)
            {
                itemPool[i].SetActive(true);
                itemPool[i].transform.position =
                    this.transform.position;

                this.transform.Rotate(
                        Vector3.forward,Random.
                        Range(0,360));

                itemPool[i].rigidbody2D.AddForce(
                    this.transform.right * 200);

                i = poolSize+1;
```

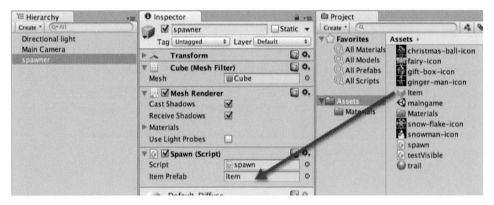

FIG 7.6 Setting the *spawn* script to use the Item prefab.

```
                                        }
                                     }
                                 }
                             }
```

Save and attach to the *spawner* game object. Locate the newly attached script on the *spawner* and set the Item Prefab property to Item from the Project as shown in Figure 7.6.

Examining the spawn script will reveal the use of a pool of game objects that are created at the start of the game. They are stored in an array and pulled, made active, pushed into the scene and then deactivated (thanks to the attached *testVisible* script). This method is similar to the platforms from the *Temple Run* recreation; however, in this case, the items are all instantiated in the $Start()$ function.

When play is pressed the *spawner* will push out quads with an angel icon on them.

Step 3: We will now make the quads falling down the screen take on random icon textures. To the top of the script we'll add an array to store all available textures and then just before pushing a quad out into the scene, assign a random texture thus:

```
public class spawn : MonoBehaviour {

    public GameObject itemPrefab;
    public Texture2D[] icons;
    const int poolSize = 20;

    ...

    void SpawnItem()
    {
        for(int i = 0; i < poolSize; i++)
        {
            if(!itemPool[i].activeSelf)
            {
```

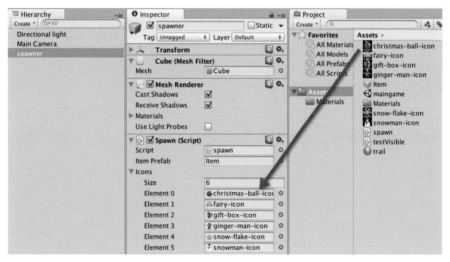

FIG 7.7 Assigning individual textures to a script array.

```
itemPool[i].renderer.material.SetTexture(
  "_MainTex",icons[Random.Range(0,
  icons.Length)]);

itemPool[i].SetActive(true);
...
```

Save the script. Again, locate it in the Inspector attached to the *spawner*. Set the size of the icons array to 6 and drag each texture from the Project into the empty element positions as shown in Figure 7.7.

Play. As the quads fall down the screen they will be assigned random textures.

Step 4: Add a new quad to the scene, call it *Matcher* and put one of the icon textures onto it. Position it in the upper left corner of the camera view as shown in Figure 7.8. This image will display to the player the falling quads that they should be tapping on.

Step 5: We will now add code to register a player tapping on an icon. Modify the *spawn* script thus:

```
public class spawn : MonoBehaviour {
    public GameObject itemPrefab;
    public GameObject matcher;
    public Texture2D[] icons;
    const int poolSize = 20;
    int score = 0;

    GameObject[] itemPool = new GameObject[poolSize];
```

```
...
void OnGUI()
{
    GUI.Label(new Rect(Screen.width-100,20,100,20),
    "Score: " + score);
}

void Update()
{

    if(Input.GetMouseButtonDown(0) ||
    (Input.touchCount > 0 &&
    Input.GetTouch(0).phase == TouchPhase.Began))
    {
        Ray ray = Camera.main.ScreenPointToRay
            (Input.mousePosition);
        RaycastHit2D hit =
            Physics2D.GetRayIntersection(ray,10000);
        if(!hit)
            return;
        if(hit.transform.gameObject.tag == "item")
        {
            if(hit.transform.gameObject.renderer.
                material.mainTexture ==
                matcher.renderer.material.mainTexture)
            {
                score + = 20;
            }
            else
            {
                score - = 20;
            }
        }
    }
}
}
```

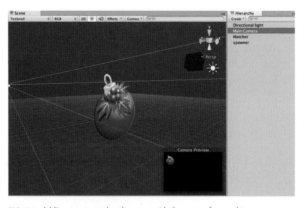

FIG 7.8 Adding a new quad to the scene with the texture for matching.

Save. A new exposed variable will show up in the Inspector called *Matcher*. Drag and drop the *Matcher* game object we just created from the Hierarchy onto this variable. This will allow the script to access its material. Also, set the tag of the Item prefab to "item" so it matches the hit testing code in the script.

Play. When an item is tapped on (or mouse-clicked) that matches the image shown in the left corner the score will increase by 20. In the case of an incorrect match, the score will decrease by 20.

In the script, when an item is touched, its texture is compared with the texture on the *Matcher*. This is the test that ascertains if the player has made a correct choice or not.

Step 6: To randomly change the image on the *Matcher* we can take advantage of the fact that the spawn code already has access to the *Matcher* and all the available textures. To the very top of the `Update()` function add:

```
void Update()
{
    if(Random.Range(0,1000)<10)
        matcher.renderer.material.SetTexture("_MainTex",
            icons[Random.Range(0,icons.Length)]);

    if(Input.GetMouseButtonDown(0) ||
...
```

Save and play. You now have a simple single-player matching game.

Step 7: To turn the game into a split-screen multiplayer game, we will use two cameras and rotate them so the tops of each scene meet down the center as shown in Figure 7.9.

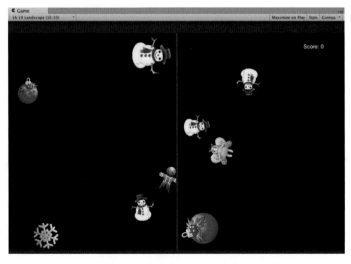

FIG 7.9 Using two cameras to create a split-screen game on one device.

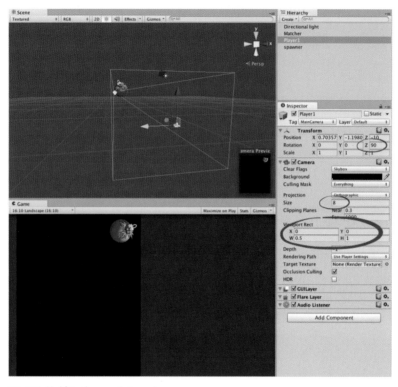

FIG 7.10 Modifying the camera's viewport.

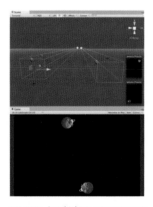

FIG 7.11 A multiplayer game setup on a single device with two cameras.

Rename the Main Camera to *Player 1*. Set its *z* rotation to 90, the size to 8 and its Viewport Rectangle to X = 0, Y = 0, W = 0.5, and H = 1. This will turn the camera on its side and restrict its rendering space to the left-hand side of the screen as shown in Figure 7.10. After you've changed the camera's settings adjust the positions and sizes of the *spawner* and *Matcher* so that you have a similar version of the game that you had before, but now half the size and on a 90 degree angle.

Step 8: Shift-select *Player 1*, *Matcher*, and *spawner*. Press CTRL+D (Win) or CMD+D (Mac) to duplicate all three. While they are still selected, drag all three in the *Scene* to another location in the 3D space. Rename each of the new items with a suffix of 2 so you can easily identify them. Set the *z* rotation of *Player 2* to 270 and the Viewport Rectangle to X = 0.5, Y = 0, W = 0.5, and H = 1. Delete the Audio Listener from *Player 2* (otherwise Unity will complain that you now have two in the scene). You will now have a split-screen setup with two sets of game as shown in Figure 7.11.

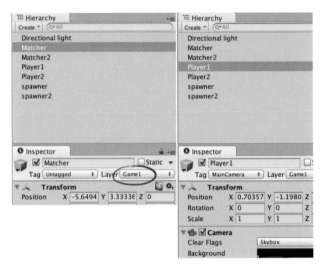

FIG 7.12 How to assign layers to objects and cameras.

Its important to keep the game environments far enough apart in 3D space that the cameras and objects in each don't overlap, otherwise you'll be able to see parts of one player's game in the other. An alternative to this is to use layers.

You don't have to do this now, but just be aware that you can have cameras set to render only certain layers. The layer seen by the camera is set in its Culling Mask. To play items in a layer, you create a new layer in the same way that you create tags and then assign them to the items.

With the new camera viewports setup, you'll be able to play the game and see two sets of *spawners* creating objects. As the cameras are rotated 90 degrees, they are actually looking at the scenes lying down. However, the scenes are still upright as you can see in the Scene.

● Viewports
In computer graphics, a viewport is the part of the screen used to display an image. The coordinate system used goes from 0 to 1 no matter what the size of the physical screen as shown in Figure 7.13 (a). In Figure 7.13 (b) the coordinate systems of several viewports are shown. Each viewport has a starting (x,y) coordinate and a width and height. Note the width and height are also expressed as a percentage of the screen resolution.

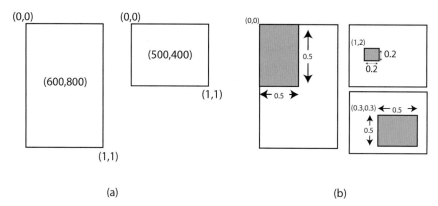

FIG 7.13 A variety of viewports; (a) illustrating how the viewport extends between coordinates 0 and 1 no matter what the screen resolution or orientation; (b) defining several different viewports using a starting (x,y) and width and height.

FIG 7.14 Ensuring the second game environment has its own Matcher and Item Prefabs.

Because of the way the viewport is defined, no matter what size the screen it will always be the same relative size (e.g., it resizes automatically with the resolution). For example if you have defined a viewport that is 0.5 wide or 50% of the screen, then it will always be 50% of the screen, no matter what the screen size.

Step 9: To ensure both game environments are independent of each other, create a duplicate of the *Item* prefab and name it *Item1*. Set the tag for *Item2* to *item2*. Select the *spawner2* game object and set the *Item* prefab to *Item1* and the *Matcher* to *Matcher2* of the spawn script as shown in Figure 7.14.

Once you've done this, ensure the original spawner object is linked to the first matcher and item prefab.

Step 10: This next part is a little tricky as it involves rotating the GUI coordinates to get the player scores in the correct location such that one player will see their score displayed at 180 degrees to the other player's score. To do this we manipulate the GUI coordinate system with rotations. Before we begin, it is important to get fixed in your mind that the GUI system sits over the entire device screen. It is not locked into the viewports. Therefore, we want to position it relative to how the viewports are positioned on the screen, but the inclusion of the viewports and two cameras makes no difference. All we will do is rotate the GUI system. Figure 7.15 illustrates the rotation of text that needs to take place.

The initial rotation taking place occurs from the default GUI rotation. That's how we are currently displaying the score. The easiest way to think about it is to look at the result you require and work backwards. Each rotation of the GUI compounds on top of the other therefore we should work with one score position at a time.

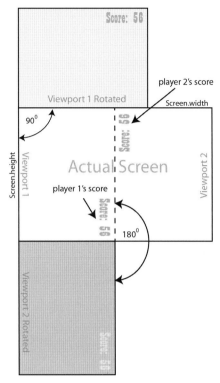

FIG 7.15 Conceptualization of rotating the GUI system to accommodate the scores for both players.

The final rotation of the scores is through a rotation of 90 degrees such that they are printed vertically. If we take the position we want Player 1's score in and rotate it back into the default GUI space (that is by −90 degrees) although it takes the text off the actual screen, it is where we must position the GUI Label. This label in the *Viewport 1 Rotated* section of Figure 7.15 has the score positioned at `x = Screen.height−100` and a `y = −Screen.width/2`. A GUI Label printed at this off-screen position, when rotated by 90 degrees will end up in the correct position for Player 1's score.

After rotating Player 1's score, because of the compounding nature of the rotations, the position of Player 2's score must be considered with respect to player 1's. Hence, rotating the desired location of Player 2's score back into player 1's GUI space, you'll see that the position is `x = Screen.height * 2−100` and `y = −Screen.width/2`.

For both of these rotations the pivot point differs. Player 1's score is pivoted around the screen origin whereas Player 2's score is pivoted around (`Screen.width/2, Screen.height`). The pivot point is always specified with respect to the actual screen.

To achieve this, create a new C# script called *scores* and add the following code:

```
using UnityEngine;
using System.Collections;

public class scores : MonoBehaviour {
    static public int[] playerScores = new int[2];
    float rotAngle;
    Vector2 pivotPoint;

    void OnGUI()
    {
        rotAngle = 90;
        pivotPoint = new Vector2(0,0);
        GUIUtility.RotateAroundPivot (rotAngle,
        pivotPoint);

        GUI.Label(new Rect(Screen.height 100,
        Screen.width/2.0f,100,20),
        "Score: " + playerScores[0]);

        rotAngle = 180;
        pivotPoint = new Vector2(Screen.width/2.0f,
        Screen.height);

        GUIUtility.RotateAroundPivot (rotAngle,
        pivotPoint);
        GUI.Label(new Rect(Screen.height*2-100,
        Screen.width/2.0f,100,20),
        "Score: " + playerScores[1]);
    }
}
```

Save and attach this code to a new empty game object added into the scene.

Delete the OnGUI function and score integer from the spawn script. Now there are two instances of this script in the scene (one on *spawner* and another on *spawner2*) we don't want any conflicts with the scoring system and it is best to put it in a single place.

Step 11: The spawn script is still performing raycasts as if there were only one camera in the scene for detecting taps on the game objects. This will not work now with two cameras and therefore we need to make a few adjustments. First add this new exposed property to the spawn script:

```
public class spawn : MonoBehaviour {

    public GameObject itemPrefab;
    public GameObject matcher;
    public Texture2D[] icons;
    const int poolSize = 20;
    int score = 0;
    public Camera cam;
```

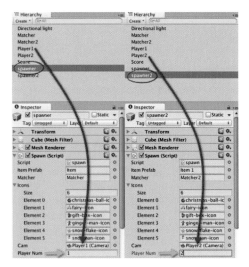

FIG 7.16 Setting up a script to use different cameras.

```
public int playerNum = 1;

GameObject[] itemPool = new GameObject[poolSize];
...
```

Save and locate the spawn code on each spawner game object. You'll find they have a *camera* property and a *player num* property. Set the camera for spawner to *Player1* and the camera for *spawner2* to *Player2* and the *player num* values as 1 and 2 respectively as shown in Figure 7.16.

Step 12: Now that the spawn script has access to different cameras, the code needs to be changed to cater for them. In addition the usual `ScreenPointToRay()` function will no longer work for casting a ray to hit an object as it only works when the screen space and camera viewport are the same. We therefore must convert the touch point or mouse position to a viewport position and then cast the ray into the 3D world. To do this, make these changes to the spawn script inside the `Update()` function:

```
void Update()
{
    if(Random.Range(0,1000)<10)
        matcher.renderer.material.SetTexture("_
        MainTex",
            icons[Random.Range(0,icons.Length)]);

    if(Input.GetMouseButtonDown(0) || (Input.touch-
    Count > 0 &&
        Input.GetTouch(0).phase == TouchPhase.Began))
```

```
                    {
        Vector3 touchPos =
            cam.ScreenToViewportPoint(Input.mousePosition);
        Ray ray = cam.ViewportPointToRay (touchPos);
        RaycastHit2D hit =
            Physics2D.GetRayIntersection(ray,10000);

        if(!hit)
                return;
        if(hit.transform.gameObject.tag == itemPrefab.tag)
        {
            if(hit.transform.gameObject.renderer.material.
            mainTexture
                == matcher.renderer.material.mainTexture)
            {
                scores.playerScores[playerNum-1] + = 20;
            }
            else
            {
                scores.playerScores[playerNum-1] - = 20;
            }
        }
    }
}
```

Save and play. If you build it to a device, you will be able to have a two-player game.

Step 13: The current version of the game only detects one touch at a time. If one player were to leave their finger down on the screen it would prevent detection of the other player's touches. We therefore need to record all touches that have begun since the last update and project rays from all to look for hits. Modify the Update() function of spawn thus:

```
void Update()
{
    if(Random.Range(0,1000)<10)
        matcher.renderer.material.SetTexture("_
        MainTex",
            icons[Random.Range(0,icons.Length)]);
    if(Input.GetMouseButtonDown(0))
    {

        ...

    }
    else if(Input.touchCount > 0)
    {
        for(int i = 0; i < Input.touchCount; i++)
        {
            if(Input.GetTouch(i).phase == TouchPhase.Began)
            {
```

```
            Vector3 touchPos = cam.ScreenToViewportPoint(
                Input.GetTouch(i).position);
            Ray ray = cam.ViewportPointToRay (touchPos);
            RaycastHit2D hit =
                Physics2D.GetRayIntersection(ray,10000);
        if(!hit)

                return;
    if(hit.transform.gameObject.tag == itemPrefab.tag)
    {

            if(hit.transform.gameObject.
                renderer.material.mainTexture ==
                matcher.renderer.material.mainTexture)
            {
                scores.playerScores[playerNum-1] + = 20;
            }
            else
            {
                scores.playerScores[playerNum-1] - = 20;
            }
        }
    }
}
```

Save. This code checks for all touches and tests them for raycasts and touches on world objects.

In order to see it in action you will have to build the game to a mobile device. In Player Settings set the Default Orientation to "Landscape Left" or the screen will be split incorrectly. Also, you may wish to slow down the spawning by changing the *Rigidbody Drag* on the two item prefabs.

Additional graphics, menus, fonts, and sound effects were added to this exercise and a published version called *Holiday Tap* was created. It is freely available in Apple's App Store and Google Play Store and a single-player version on Facebook.

7.3 Networking

Thus far we have explored multiplayer gaming on a single device. The advantage of presenting a multiplayer experience in this way is that it is much easier to have one instance of the game controlling and handling all user interactions. The moment the game becomes split over multiple devices, the developer has to start thinking about managing and sending messages between those devices for the purpose of ensuring each and every player on each and every device is seeing the same (or a very close) version of the game world. As a player makes a change to the game world, this needs to be updated to all other players' devices. These messages are sent among players using the Internet's communication protocols.

TCP/IP

Transmission Control Program/Internet Protocol or TCP/IP is the internal messaging standard for sending data. Data is sent in packages called *datagrams*, which contain messages from applications to other applications and communication information. The messages sent over the Internet between applications are called the *payload* of the datagram. The communication information (also known as the header) provides details of who sent the payload, its destination, size, and other details required for transmission.

Imagine a datagram to be a regular parcel that you send from the post office. The contents may be chocolates for your friend. These chocolates are the payload. Your friend's address on the front as the recipient, your address as the sender, the date of postage, the stamp showing the cost and weight of the parcel, and any other information (such as the "does not contain explosive or dangerous materials" sticker) is the header. The header information ensures the payload arrives safely to the destination. It also can tell your friend if the payload has been tampered with. If the final weight of the chocolates is much less than stated on the front, your friend will know they've been eaten in transit. He can then relay this information to you. Very similar checks and balances exist with datagrams to ensure they are delivered to the correct location and the contents have not been changed or damaged.

Part of the header specifies the IP address to which the datagram should be sent. This address uniquely identifies your computer when it is connected to the Internet. It is similar to the address you would write on a posted parcel to ensure it gets to the desired destination. At the time of writing, the most prolific format for an IP address is four decimal numbers (each between 0 and 255) separated by dots (called IPv4 address in dotted-decimal notation) for example 203.45.32.1. The address consists of two parts; a network part and a machine part. All machines connected to the same network will have the same first two numbers. The second two will vary with the number of machines connected to that network. For example, within your household you may have two computers connected to the same network and their IPs could be 192.168.3.1 and 192.168.3.2 as illustrated in Figure 7.17.

More often than not, if you are working in the same home or business with a single connection to the Internet, all the machines will share that connection via a router. Imagine this to be an apartment full of people sharing the same letter box. Each person has the same street address, just as every computer connected to the router has the same IP address. However, to distinguish each machine they will have a second internal IP address. So while the external address is 188.25.45.10 it could be shared by three machines each with internal IPs of 10.4.6.1, 10.4.6.2 and 10.4.6.3. These internal IPs are not visible externally and only used for internal purposes. These machines are considered to be behind a firewall and not accessible by their internal IP from outside.

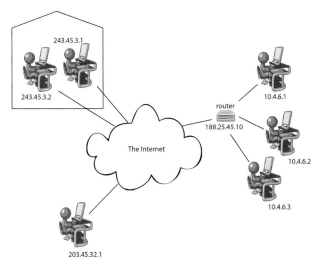

FIG 7.17 Computers connected to the Internet and example IP addresses.

So how do you get a message to a particular machine inside a shared Internet connection? The method is similar to putting an apartment number onto a parcel. Using what's called a network address translation (NAT) protocol, the router assigns each computer a unique number. Therefore a computer in the previous network may have the IP address 188.25.45.10 and a NAT ID of 346527. When trying to send messages between machines that are behind firewalls, the external IP address is used in conjunction with the NAT ID in a process called *NAT Punchthrough* to enable machines to uniquely identify one another.

Unity caters for the use of direct connections using machine IP addresses as well as NAT Punchthrough. If you are testing your game with machines connected to the same network, you'll find that NAT Punchthrough will not be required as all machines can essentially see each other. This is akin to the occupants of the previous analogized apartments being able to pass messages freely between each other while inside the building.

7.3.2 Clients and Servers

You may be wondering to yourself at this point how you find out the IP address and NAT ID for another device to which you are trying to connect. The plain and simple answer is that you must know what it is. In order to send a parcel to your friend, they must tell you their address. Unity provides methods to tell you the IP Address and NAT ID of the device. In order to send the messages, the unique address of at least one device on a server/client structure needs to be established. A server is an application that manages connections and messaging between all devices. It is run first and its IP Address broadcast. *Broadcast* in many cases can mean writing it down on a

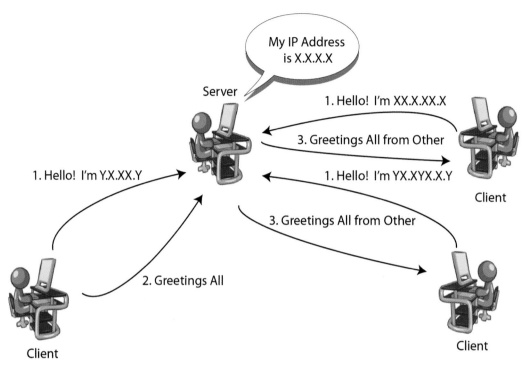

FIG 7.18 A client/server setup.

piece of paper and handing it to a player. When the server's address is known, another app can establish a connection to it by sending it a message. When the server receives the message it will immediately have the other device's IP address and back-and-forth communication can begin. The applications that connect to the server are called clients. Many clients may be allowed to connect to the server. The server facilitates all communication among them as shown in Figure 7.18. The clients need not know each other's IP addresses.

There are two types of game server; authoritative and non-authoritative. The authoritative server maintains the entire game world and runs all physics and interactive simulations. The clients merely interact with the world from afar by sending messages about how they would like to interact. The server processes the messages and then sends the new state of the world out to all clients. For example, if one player decides to blow up a building, they send this request to the server. The server carries out the action and then reports the world state of the game to everyone. The server is authoritative as it maintains the state of the entire game environment and dictates what happens and is allowed in that environment. It works by considering all requests from the clients to interact and then makes a final decision on what to do and how all the interactions should affect the game. Whenever the game environment is updated the server communicates its new state with all clients as shown in Figure 7.19.

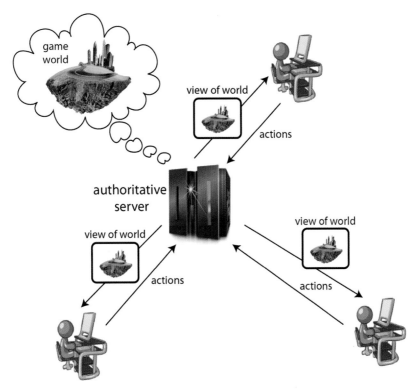

FIG 7.19 An authoritative server.

The advantages of an authoritative server are that there is only one version of the game world in existence and that all signals from the clients are processed together in order to determine how the world should change from the variety of player interactions. The client programs can then be much smaller as they don't need to remember or store the world nor hold all possible rules about how the world can be manipulated by players. This also makes cheating difficult, as the server, for validity, checks any data coming from a client before it is processed. For example, if a client were hacked to enable a player to alter the current health of their character to make it super strong in an instant, when the server received this information it would reject it as it wouldn't hold true with the information it knew about the game world.

The disadvantage with an authoritative server is the lag between networked message-sending. For example, if the player were in a racing game and put their foot on the brake, and that particular action message took a couple of tenths of a second to reach the server, be processed, and the player to get a response, the game would feel very unresponsive.

With a non-authoritative server, a copy of the game world and all physics simulations sit with each client. The server only acts as a conduit for communications between the clients as shown in Figure 7.20.

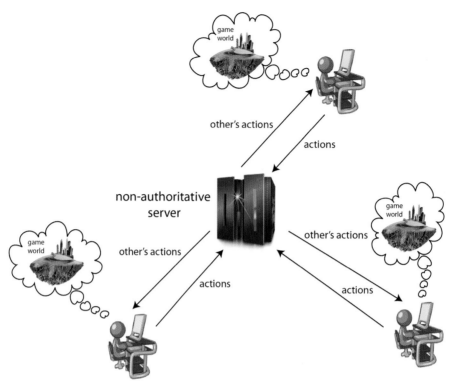

FIG 7.20 A non-authoritative server.

There are no lag issues between the player and their game with respect to controlling the character in the client's copy of the world, however lag will still occur with respect to messages coming from other clients. Lag is an inherent problem with networked games and will be discussed later.

It is also possible to establish a peer-to-peer network in which one client is connected directly to another. This format is not supported by Unity. However, in a game requiring all players to be present in order to play it is an acceptable format. For example, if you were playing a networked version of chess on two different devices both players would need to be connected for the game to continue. However in a more open world type game, such as *World of Warcraft* or *Minecraft Multiplayer*, if no clients are connected, the world ceases to exist. These types of virtual gaming environments are called persistent worlds meaning they continue to exist even when no one is playing. For these it is best to have a dedicated authoritative server.

There is no right or wrong configuration of the client/server relationship except the one that works best for your game. In a turn-based game an authoritative server works best as it is only dealing with messages from one player at a time. For something like a networked racing game a mixed approach may work with the client having a copy of the game world along with a backup one residing on the server. For the remainder of the chapter we will examine several different configurations.

In the next hands-on section we will use Unity to create a simple client and server application for sending chat messages.

Unity Hands-On
Sending Messages

In this hands-on session we are going to explore simple networking by building a chat program to pass text messages back and forth between devices. You can also test this code on the one development machine by running multiple copies of an app.

Step 1: Setup a new Unity Project called *Server*. Create a C# script called *server* and add the following:

```
using UnityEngine;
using System.Collections;

public class server : MonoBehaviour {

    int listenPort = 25000;
    bool useNat = false;
    private string connectionInfo = "";

    void OnGUI ()
    {
        if(GUI.Button(new Rect(10,10,100,30),
        "Start Server"))
        {
            Network.InitializeServer(32, listenPort,
            useNat);
        }

        GUI.Label(new Rect(10,40,200,30),
        connectionInfo);
        GUI.Label(new Rect(10,60,100,30), "Players: "
        + Network.connections.Length);
    }

    void OnServerInitialized()
    {
        connectionInfo = "IP: " + Network.player.
        ipAddress + " Port: " + Network.player.port;
    }
}
```

Attach the script to the Main Camera.

In order to pass networked messages, the object requires a Network View component. With the Main Camera selected in the Hierarchy select

Component > Miscellaneous > Network View. This will attach a Network View component to the camera.

Save and run. Press the Start Server button. The machine's IP address and port number on which the server is listening will be displayed. If everything is working as expected select File > Build & Run and then with the development platform set as PC, Mac & Linux Standalone, press the Build & Run button. Call the application *server*, and, when it runs, select it to be in Windowed mode and then press the Start Server button. You now have a server running on your desktop.

Step 2: Save the previous scene as *server* and create a new one called *client*. Create a new C# script called *client* and add the following code:

```csharp
using UnityEngine;
using System.Collections;

public class client : MonoBehaviour {

    string remoteIP = "127.0.0.1";
    int remotePort = 25000;
    int listenPort = 25000;
    string remoteGUID = "";
    bool useNat = false;
    private string connectionInfo = "";

    private string chatText = "Type Chat Message Here
    and Hit Send Button";

    private string allChat = "";

    void OnGUI ()
    {
        remoteIP = GUI.TextField(new Rect(10,10,100,30),
        remoteIP);

        remotePort = int.Parse(GUI.TextField(new
            Rect(120,10,100,30),""+remotePort));

        if(GUI.Button(new Rect(240,10,100,30),"
        Connect"))
        {
            if (useNat)
            {
                if (remoteGUID == "")
                    Debug.LogWarning("Invalid GUID
                    given.");
                else
                    Network.Connect(remoteGUID);
            }
            else
```

```
                {
                        Network.Connect(remoteIP, remotePort);
                }
        }
        chatText = GUI.TextField(new Rect(10,45,200,30),
            chatText);

        if(GUI.Button(new Rect(240,45,100,30),"Send"))
        {
                //send it to me by calling function directly
                ProcessChatText(chatText, 1);

                //send to everyone else
                networkView.RPC("ProcessChatText",
                    RPCMode.Others, chatText, 0);
        }

        allChat = GUI.TextArea(new Rect(10,80,300,300),
            allChat, 300);
    }

    void OnPlayerConnected(NetworkPlayer player)
    {
        allChat + = "\nPlayer " + " connected from " +
            player.ipAddress;
    }

    void OnConnectedToServer()
    {
            allChat + = "\nConnected To Server";
    }

    void OnDisconnectedFromServer ()
    {

    }
    [RPC]
    void ProcessChatText (string str, int mine)
        {
            if(mine == 1)
                allChat + = "\nMe: " + str;
            else
                allChat + = "\nThem: " + str;
        }
    }
```

Save. Attach the code and a Network View component to the Main Camera.

The preceding code includes a new type of function called a Remote Procedure Call (RPC). These special functions will be explored in depth in later sections. In short, these functions, preceded in code with the line [RPC], can be called from external programs. They allow one client to call functions in another client.

FIG 7.21 A simple chat server and two clients.

Step 3: Build & Run the client scene in Windowed mode. You will now be able to connect to the server. After hitting the Connect button on the client, click on the server window to bring it into focus. You will need to do this for the server to process the connection message. Try making a copy of the client executable file and run another copy. Connect this to the server too. You will now be able to send text messages back and forth between each client. Remember to click on each window in turn to bring it into focus to give it a chance to process the messages being sent. You should be seeing something similar to Figure 7.21.

You've just constructed a server and client application capable of passing messages. Messages don't just have to be written text. They can include information about player status, game environment status, and so on. In the next hands-on session we will extend our server and client to handle the beginnings of a networked racing game.

7.4 Synchronizing Worlds

Networked multiplayer games have and will always experience latency. This is the lag players notice between performing actions and when they actually occur within the game. As network speeds have increased, the lag has decreased somewhat; however, with the increase in available bandwidth, developers also take advantage to send more and more data between game clients, which in turn increases the lag.

With an authoritative server, what the player client sees is usually the game world as it was in the past. By the time the message gets from the server to the client about what the game world looks like, the information is old, especially in a fast-paced multiplayer game. Where you think an enemy is standing or a car is positioned on the track is where it was some tenths of a second ago.

In a way a networked multiplayer game must work a little time travel magic to bring all the client worlds into an acceptable alignment that makes the game playable. There are a couple of methods we can employ in our games to achieve this.

Entity extrapolation, also known as *dead reckoning*, is a predictive technique that originated in military applications. Given the last known position of an object, the acceleration, direction, and speed at which it is moving, and how long ago it was observed, its current location can be extrapolated. Of course this relies on the object not having changed acceleration, direction, or speed during this time. However, with networked messages only taking a relatively small amount of time to be relayed, it's an easy to implement and acceptable method for keeping game objects moving without having their exact position details.

The principle equation used in networked games is based on the linear physics of Equation 1, which states that the position now (P_t) equals the last known position (P_0) plus the last known velocity (V0) multiplied by the time delay (T) plus ½ the last known acceleration (A_0) multiplied by the time delay squared (T^2).

$$P_t = P_0 + V_0 T + \tfrac{1}{2} A_0 T^2 \qquad\qquad \textit{Equation 1}$$

The illustration in Figure 7.22 shows Equation 1 in action. Figure 7.22 (a) shows a vehicle with a last known velocity of one meter per second and no acceleration. After two seconds it will have travelled two meters in the same direction it was initially facing. Figure 7.22 (b) shows a vehicle traveling at 1 meter per second with an acceleration of one meter per second[2]. After one second the vehicle will have travelled 1.5 meters but due to acceleration will also be traveling at two meters per second. For each second a compounding effect takes place on the distance travelled.

Extrapolation can keep an object moving convincingly in the game environment until the next message arrives giving its next known location. At that point, the calculated position of the object and its actual location need to be reconciled.

Several techniques exist for resolving the positions of an object. One is to create a curve between the two positions and smoothly move the object along it. Another is to take the object's previous known velocity and the next known velocity and blend them while continuing to extrapolate.

In cases where players and game objects move erratically, dead reckoning cannot be applied as the predictive methods of linear physics cannot determine where a fast-moving and quick-turning object will be moment by

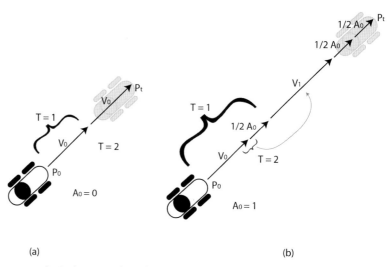

(a)   (b)

FIG 7.22 Dead reckoning using linear physics: (a) a vehicle traveling at one meter per second, with no acceleration after two seconds, (b) a vehicle traveling initially at one meter per second, accelerating at one meter per second² and traveling for two seconds.

moment. Instead *entity interpolation* is used. This method shows the player's character acting in the present and the other characters as they were in the past. This can only ever be the case because of network latency and the server's update cycle. The server continues to receive a stream of any player's actual position data. However, by the time this data gets to the server and is then relayed to all other clients the data is already old and only represents a snapshot of the past. Consider the illustration in Figure 7.23.

Position information from Player 1 may come in sporadically as the player moves. The server, working on an update cycle compiles this data and relays Player 1's position data to Player 2. It doesn't just send the last position of Player 1, but all the position changes that have taken place since the last update. The server has an authoritative set of the actual positions of Player 1 and replays these to Player 2 every 100 ms. By the time Player 2 gets this position data, the data is 100 ms old. For example, when Player 2 finds out that Player 1 is at position A, they are actually in the present at position D. However, Player 2 will not find this out for another 100 ms. Therefore, the state of the world that Player 2 sees is their own character in the present and all other characters 100 ms in the past. The nice thing about this is that Player 2 has perfect information about the position changes of Player 1 even if it is slightly old, and therefore the movement of Player 1 in Player 2's game world is smooth. Each position change send is marked with a timestamp allowing for a perfect reconstruction of past events when they happened.

If more accurate information is required, the server could be set to send updates every 10 ms instead. The server cannot send position details every

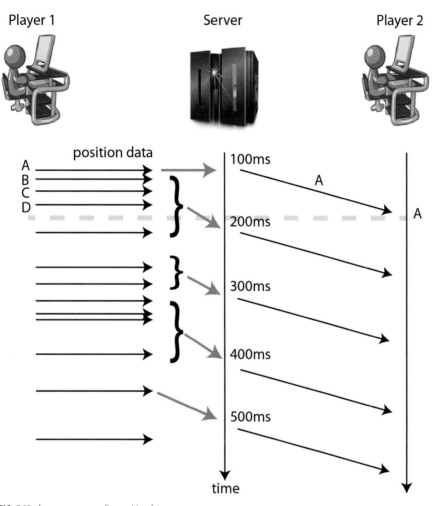

Player 1   Server   Player 2

position data

A
B
C
D

100ms

A

A

200ms

300ms

400ms

500ms

time

FIG 7.23 A games server sending position data.

time it gets them as 1) it operates on its own update cycle in the way it runs and 2) the more clients that connect the greater the load on the server and it could not possibly keep up a constant 100 ms cycle if forced to be constantly relaying messages immediately to the point that updates would become sporadic, unpredictable and in fact overload the message cycle far beyond 100 ms.

The important message to take away from network multiplayer message sending is that you will never have any player with perfect information as they only ever see a version of the game world in the past. In a fast-paced game in which position is critical, some problems do arise as items or players in your particular worldview may not actually be there anymore. If, for example, you were taking aim at an approaching enemy and had him perfectly in your sights and fired at him, as far as you are concerned it's a hit and he is dead. However in the split second it took for you to receive his past position he may have actually moved. This situation is not resolvable, because if you see the enemy get shot and he doesn't die it spoils the gameplay. As for the poor enemy that believes he's in a safe location and suddenly dies for no particular reason? Well that's unfortunately the payoff.

In the next hands-on section we will examine both extrapolation and interpolation for movement in networked games.

⦿ Unity Hands-On
Car Racing

This example is based on the networked car demo created by Unity back in version 2.6. A lot of the code is taken from it, as are the models. Thanks Unity!

Step 1: Download and open the *NetworkCarRacing* game from the website (*networkracing.zip*). In the Car Racing Scene you'll find a plane and a car as shown in Figure 7.24. If you play the scene you'll be able to drive the car with the arrow keys.

Step 2: Remove the car from the scene leaving just the plane. Make the plane much larger, scaling it by 5 in each dimension and place a seamless texture on it. Ensure the plane is positioned at (0,0,0).

Step 3: Unlike the previous hands-on exercise, the client and server code will exist as one in this application. This means any single instance of the game can act as the server and the others as clients. This is a common networking setup in peer-to-peer games where there is no main dedicated server.

Add an empty game object to the scene and call it *NetworkGUI* (GameObject > Create Empty). Create a new C# script called *connectGUI* and add the following code:

```
using UnityEngine;
using System.Collections;

public class connectGUI : MonoBehaviour {

    string remoteIP = "127.0.0.1";
    int remotePort = 25000;
    int listenPort = 25000;
    string remoteGUID = "";
    bool useNat = false;

    void OnGUI ()
    {
        if(Network.peerType == NetworkPeerType.
        Disconnected)
        {
            if(GUI.Button (new Rect(210,10,100,30),
            "Connect"))
```

FIG 7.24 The car in the starter project.

```
            {
                if(useNat)
                {
                    if(remoteGUID == "")
                        Debug.LogWarning("Invalid
                        GUID");
                    else
                        Network.Connect(remoteGUID);
                }
                else
                {
                        Network.Connect(remoteIP,
                        remotePort);
                }
            }
            if(GUI.Button(new Rect(Screen.
            width-110,10,100,30),
            "Start Server"))
            {
            Network.InitializeServer(32, listenPort,
            useNat);
            foreach (GameObject go in
                FindObjectsOfType(typeof(GameObject))as
                GameObject[])
            {
                go.SendMessage("OnNetworkLoaded
                Level",
                    SendMessageOptions.
                    DontRequireReceiver);
            }
        }
        remoteIP = GUI.TextField(new
            Rect(10,10,100,30),remoteIP);

        remotePort = int.Parse(GUI.TextField(
            new Rect(110,10,100,30),remotePort.
            ToString()));
    }
    else
    {
        GUI.Label(new Rect(10,50,200,30),"Local IP/
        Port: " +
            Network.player.ipAddress + "/" +
            Network.player.port);

        if(GUI.Button(new Rect(10,10,100,30),"Disconne
        ct"))
            Network.Disconnect(200);
    }
}

void OnServerInitialized()
```

```
    {
    if (useNat)
        Debug.Log("GUID is " + Network.player.guid +
        ". Use this on clients to connect with NAT.");

        Debug.Log("Local IP/port is " +
        Network.player.ipAddress
            + "/" + Network.player.port +
            ". Use this on clients to connect
            directly.");
    }

    void OnPlayerConnected(NetworkPlayer player)
    {
        Debug.Log("Player " + " connected from " +
            player.ipAddress);
    }

    void OnConnectedToServer()
    {
        Debug.Log("Connected To Server");

        foreach (GameObject go in
            FindObjectsOfType(typeof(GameObject))as
            GameObject[])
            go.SendMessage("OnNetworkLoadedLevel",
                SendMessageOptions.
                DontRequireReceiver);
    }

    void OnDisconnectedFromServer () {
    }
}
```

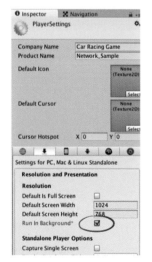

FIG 7.25 Project settings to set a
game to run in the background.

Attach this code to the *NetworkGUI* game object.

Play. You will get a GUI giving the player options to start a server or
connect to an existing one.

Step 4: A game server should run all the time even when its window
doesn't have focus. If the server is only running when active, it causes
issues with network communication. To ensure the server is always
running, select Edit > Project Settings > Player and in the settings for
the target platform tick the *Run In Background* tickbox as shown in
Figure 7.25.

Step 5: On starting a server or connecting to an existing one, a car needs
to be spawned. It needs to be spawned in the player's instance of the
game as well as all other connected clients. To achieve this, add an empty
game object to the scene called *Spawn*. Create a new C# script called
spawnPlayer and add the following code:

```
using UnityEngine;
using System.Collections;
public class spawnPlayer : MonoBehaviour {
    public GameObject playerPrefab;
    void OnNetworkLoadedLevel ()
    {
        // Randomize starting location
        Vector3 pos;

        //you might need to change these depending on
        where
        //your ground plane is located
        pos.x = 20 * Random.value;
        pos.y = 4;
        pos.z = 20 * Random.value;
        GameObject obj = Network.
        Instantiate(playerPrefab,
            pos, transform.rotation, 0) as GameObject;
    }
    void OnPlayerDisconnected (NetworkPlayer player)
    {
        Network.RemoveRPCs(player, 0);
        Network.DestroyPlayerObjects(player);
    }
}
```

The function `OnNetworkLoadedLevel()` is called from the *connectGUI* script. It is called for the player when the server is initialized or when they have connected to a server as a client. Note the method for calling the function is `SendMessage()`. This basically allows us to call functions in other *MonoBehaviour* classes via the parent game object.

Attach the *spawnPlayer* script to the *Spawn* game object. Set the exposed `playerPrefab` variable to the car prefab as shown in Figure 7.26.

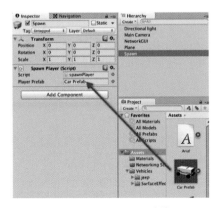

FIG 7.26 Setting the player character model for spawning.

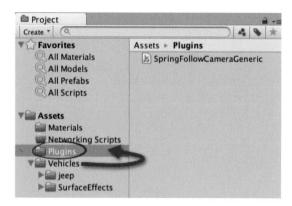

FIG 7.27 Creating a Plugins folder.

Play. The car is setup to spawn at a random location on top of the plane. If it doesn't spawn somewhere in front of the camera you may have to move the camera right out so you can see the entire scene.

Step 6: To have the camera attach and follow the player's car we will make use of the *SpringFollowCameraGeneric* script already attached to the Main Camera. This script is in JavaScript and accessing it to set the target property is a little tricky. We can't just set the target to the player's car in the Inspector because it doesn't exist until the player becomes a client or starts a server. Another problem is that, while it's straightforward to access JavaScript variables from C#, it's not so elementary the other way. The reason being that C# gets compiled before JavaScript by Unity. Therefore any C# referencing JavaScript will not think the JavaScript exists and it will throw an error. However, you can influence the compilation order by placing scripts that needs to be compiled first into a *Plugins* folder in the root of the project as shown in Figure 7.27.

Create a folder called Plugins (spelt and capitalized exactly like this) in the root of the Project. Locate the *SpringFollowCameraGeneric.js* file in the *Vehicles* folder and drag and drop it into the new *Plugins* one.

Now make the following change to *spawnPlayer.cs* to link the player's car to the camera:

```
void OnNetworkLoadedLevel ()
{
    ...
    GameObject obj = Network.Instantiate(playerPrefab,
        pos, transform.rotation, 0) as GameObject;
```

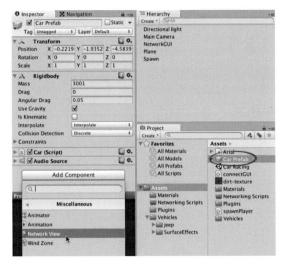

FIG 7.28 Adding a Network View component to the *Car* prefab.

```
Camera.main.GetComponent<SpringFollowCameraGeneric>().
target = obj.transform;
}
```

Save and play. After starting the server, the camera will now fly to the player's car and start following it.

Step 7: To send messages back and forth between clients a Network View component will need to be added. Add this component to the *Car* prefab in the project as shown in Figure 7.28.

Step 8: Create a new C# script called *initCarNetwork* and add the following:

```
using UnityEngine;
using System.Collections;

public class initCarNetwork : MonoBehaviour {

    void OnNetworkInstantiate (NetworkMessageInfo
    msg) {
        // This is our own player
        if (networkView.isMine)
        {
            Camera.main.SendMessage("SetTarget",
            transform);
            GetComponent<NetworkRigidbody>().enabled =
            false;
        }
        // This is just some remote controlled player
        // Turn off user control
```

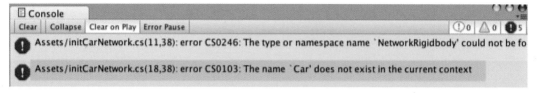

FIG 7.29 Errors obtained after creating <code>initCarNetwork<code>.

```
else
{
    name + = "Remote";
    GetComponent<Car>().
    SetEnableUserInput(false);
    GetComponent<NetworkRigidbody>().enabled =
    true;
}
}
}
```

Be warned. This code will give you errors like the ones shown in Figure 7.29. Even so, attach the code to the *Car* prefab.

The second error on the list about the *Car* not existing is the same issue we would have had before with respect to the camera following JavaScript as we had not put it into the Plugins directory.

Locate the *Car.js* script in the Vehicle folder and move it into Plugins. After this moves you'll get the same type of error for *SkidMarks.js*. Locate its original position and move it into Plugins as well.

The remaining error relates to `NetworkRigidBody`, a script we are yet to write.

Step 9: Create a new C# script called *NetworkRigidBody.cs*. Add the following code:

```
using UnityEngine;
using System.Collections;

public class NetworkRigidbody : MonoBehaviour
{
    void OnSerializeNetworkView(BitStream stream,
        NetworkMessageInfo info)
    {
    }
    void Update()
    {
    }
}
```

This code does not do anything yet, but it is required to make the *initCarNetwork* script happy and we will come back and fill it in soon. Save and attach to the *Car* Prefab. Don't play just yet.

Step 10: Earlier we set the Main Camera to follow the *Car* prefab. The problem now is that there will be more than one *Car* prefab racing around in the environment. We want to ensure the camera follows the current player's car only. To do this we make a small change to the *spawnPlayer* script thus:

```
void OnNetworkLoadedLevel ()
{

    ...
    GameObject obj = Network.Instantiate(playerPrefab,
        pos, transform.rotation, 0) as GameObject;

    if(obj.GetComponent<NetworkView>().isMine)
        Camera.main.GetComponent<SpringFollowCameraGen
        eric>
        ().target = obj.transform;
}
```

The new line of code will ensure the camera only follows the car representing the player in the current instance of the game.

Play. To test out the server connection, build out another version and run it alongside the Unity Editor version. You will need to start the server on one and then connect with the other.

The current version of *NetworkRigidbody* uses a brute force method of setting the position of the car. Each client sets the position of the other networked cars based on their state (transform, rigidbody, and animation data). The state data is sent around the network by the Network View component attached to the *Car* prefab. To make any object in the game world update in all clients, you just need to add a Network View component and it will do all the work for you.

⬤ **Network View Component**

For more information on the Network View Component see the Unity Reference Manual at http://docs.unity3d.com/Documentation/Components/net-NetworkView.html.

If a car moves enough in-between message updates, it will appear to be teleporting instantly from one place to another. It's not so noticeable when the server and client are on the same machine as the time between messages is quite small. In the next step, however, we will test the latency by building one client out onto a mobile device.

Step 11: Select Assets > Import Package > Standard Assets (Mobile) from the main menu. This will import a series of game objects including the *thumbstick controller*. Locate the *Single Joystick* prefab in the Assets/ Standard Assets (Mobile)/Prefabs folder of the project and drag into the scene. Find the *Joystick.js* script that belongs to the *Single Joystick* and move it into the Plugins directory. As the cars driving script will reference it, it needs to be compiled early on.

Step 12: Switch the Build Settings to Android or iOS. Ensure you add a *Bundle ID* as required. At this point you will encounter quite a few errors inherent in the old JavaScript code from the original Networking Unity project. To solve these, first locate *Skidmarks.js* in the Plugins folder and delete it. This will cause numerous errors in the *Car.js* script file. Replace your *Car.js* file with the one on the website. This new version will also automatically pick up the joystick you just added and use it for controlling the car (provided the joystick keeps its default name of *Single Joystick*). Another error will be thrown up by the contents of the Assets/Vehicles/ SurfaceEffects folder in the project. Just locate and delete the entire folder and contents. The project will now be free of errors. Build the project out to your mobile device. If the GUI buttons are too small you will have to update their sizes in *connectGUI.cs*.

Start the server first to reveal the IP address. Type this into your mobile and press Connect. Note this exercise assumes the server device and the client device are connected to the same network. The result of running the server in the Unity Editor and the client on an Android phone is shown in Figure 7.30.

If you want to try and connect to a server on a different network running behind a router you can attempt NAT Punchthrough. At the very top of the *connectGUI.cs* script you will find a Boolean value `useNat`. Set this to true and run the server. In the console a GUID (Globally Unique Identifier) will be displayed as shown in Figure 7.31. This can then be used in the client to connect instead of using the IP and port number.

Not all routers allow NAT Punchthrough and it might not work for you. Solving these issues is beyond the scope of this book and if you are interested in investigating Unity networking in more depth check out the networking manual at http://docs.unity3d.com/ Documentation/Components/NetworkReferenceGuide.html.

FIG 7.30 Running the client on a mobile and server in the editor.

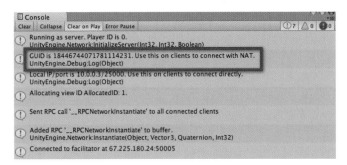

FIG 7.31 Server information provided in console for NAT Punchthrough.

Step 13: To integrate extrapolation and interpolation for the car movement we need to capture the transform data of each one and transmit it to all clients. With each piece of transform data a timestamp is recorded so a client on receiving the information can check for the movement of the car over time. The timestamp on the data received and the timestamp according to the client can be compared to determine where in the world the networked client should be positioned.

To begin we need to create a class for each client's transform data along with a timestamp. Add this to the top of the *NetworkRigidbody.cs* thus:

```
using UnityEngine;
using System.Collections;

class State
{

public double timestamp;
public Vector3 pos;
public Vector3 velocity;
public Quaternion rot;
public Vector3 angularVelocity;
public State(double t, Vector3 p, Vector3 v,
        Quaternion r, Vector3 a)
{
    timestamp = t;
    pos = p;
    velocity = v;
    rot = r;
    angularVelocity = a;
}
}
public class NetworkRigidbody : MonoBehaviour
{
...
```

All position, rotation, and movement data is encapsulated within this little State class.

Step 14: Each client will send a stream of *State* information to all other clients. As they are received they are stored in an array as shown in Figure 7.32.

The data is sent and received in the `OnSerializeNetworkView()` function. This function automatically determines if the data in use needs to be sent or received. Modify *NetworkRigidbody.cs* to handle this thus:

State[] bufferedStates = new State[20];

bufferedStates[0]	bufferedStates[1]	bufferedStates[2]	bufferedStates[3]	[4]	[5]
timestamp = 123456 pos = (10,0,50) veloctiy = (1,0,0) rot = 45 angularVelocity = (0,2,0)	timestamp = 123457 pos = (11,0,52) veloctiy = (1,0,0) rot = 45 angularVelocity = (0,2,0)	timestamp = 123458 pos = (12,0,53) veloctiy = (1.5,0,0) rot = 48 angularVelocity = (0,1,0)	timestamp = 123462 pos = (9,0,55) veloctiy = (3,0,0) rot = 47 angularVelocity = (0,0,0)	...	...

FIG 7.32 An array of the State data being streamed by clients.

```
public class NetworkRigidbody : MonoBehaviour
{
    int timestampCount;
    State[] bufferedStates = new State[20];

    void OnSerializeNetworkView(BitStream stream,
        NetworkMessageInfo info)
    {
// Send data to server
if (stream.isWriting)
{
            Vector3 pos = rigidbody.position;
            Quaternion rot = rigidbody.rotation;
            Vector3 velocity = rigidbody.velocity;
            Vector3 angularVelocity =
                rigidbody.angularVelocity;
            stream.Serialize(ref pos);
            stream.Serialize(ref velocity);
            stream.Serialize(ref rot);
            stream.Serialize(ref angularVelocity);
}
// Read data from remote client
else
{
            Vector3 pos = Vector3.zero;
            Vector3 velocity = Vector3.zero;
            Quaternion rot = Quaternion.identity;
            Vector3 angularVelocity = Vector3.zero;
            stream.Serialize(ref pos);
            stream.Serialize(ref velocity);
            stream.Serialize(ref rot);
            stream.Serialize(ref angularVelocity);

            //move all states in the array into
            //the next position
            //freeing up position [0] and causing the 20th to
            //drop off the end
            for(int i = bufferedStates.Length-1;i> = 1;i–)
            {
                bufferedStates[i] = bufferedStates[i-1];
            }

            //create new state from current data
                //and place in slot 0
            State state = new State(info.timestamp,
                    pos, velocity, rot, angularVelocity);
            bufferedStates[0] = state;

            //update clients own timestamp
            timestampCount = Mathf.Min( timestampCount + 1,
                    bufferedStates.Length);

            //check if states are in order
            for (int i = 0; i < timestampCount–1; i++)
```

```
                        {
                              if (bufferedStates[i].timestamp <
                                      bufferedStates[i+1].timestamp)
                                 Debug.Log("State inconsistent");
                        }
                  }
            }
```

Step 15: Thus far we've only created code to send and receive timestamped transform data. Now we need to use it. Within the Update() function of NetworkedRigidbody the code will use interpolation for the position of all networked players while there is data available and streaming in. When there is a large enough lag and no data is available extrapolation (dead reckoning) will kick in to keep the networked players moving. Add the following code to *NetworkedRigidbody.cs*:

```
public class NetworkRigidbody : MonoBehaviour
{
    int timestampCount;
    State[] bufferedStates = new State[20];

    public double interpolationBackTime = 0.1;
    public double extrapolationLimit = 0.5;

    ...

    void Update()
    {
            if(bufferedStates[0]   ==   null)
                 return;

        // Playback time of client in the past
        double interpolationTime = Network.time—
             interpolationBackTime;

        //if the latest timestamped data received
        //is newer than playback
        //time then use it
        if (bufferedStates[0].timestamp > interpolationTime)
        {
            //look through buffer for the
            //timestamp that matches the
            //start for the playback
            for (int i = 0; i < timestampCount; i++)
            {
                if (bufferedStates[i].timestamp < =
                interpolationTime ||
```

```
                i == timestampCount-1)
            {

            //Get playback data on either side of
            // the current timestamp
            State rhs = bufferedStates[Mathf.Max(i-1, 0)];
            State lhs = bufferedStates[i];

            //Get the elapsed time between the slots
            //And use it for interpolating
            //smooth movement between the states
            double length = rhs.timestamp-lhs.timestamp;
            float t = 0.0F;
            if (length > 0.0001)
                t = (float)((interpolationTime-lhs.
                timestamp) /
                length);

        transform.localPosition = Vector3.Lerp(lhs.pos,
            rhs.pos, t);

        transform.localRotation = Quaternion.Slerp(lhs.rot,

            rhs.rot, t);
                return;
        }
    }
}
// Use extrapolation
else
{

    State latest = bufferedStates[0];

    float extrapolationLength = (float)(interpolationTime-
        latest.timestamp);

    if (extrapolationLength < extrapolationLimit)
        {
            float axisLength = extrapolationLength *
                latest.angularVelocity.magnitude *
                Mathf.Rad2Deg;

            Quaternion angularRotation =
                Quaternion.AngleAxis(axisLength,
                latest.angularVelocity);

            rigidbody.position = latest.pos + latest.
            velocity *
                extrapolationLength;
```

```
                        rigidbody.rotation = angularRotation *
                        latest.rot;
                        rigidbody.velocity = latest.velocity;
                        rigidbody.angularVelocity = latest.
                        angularVelocity;
                        }
                }
            }
        }
```

The program now interpolates the transforms of networked players if the data in the received buffer is newer than 100 ms ago. This is the value of the `interpolationBackTime` variable. Otherwise extrapolation is used but only for 500ms (`extrapolationLimit`). Any longer than this and the actual position of the networked player and the predicted one could become too large and some funny movement behavior could evolve.

Step 16: Currently, the program, using the Network View, sends transform changes to each player via the server. So it automatically relays these changes and, on receiving the client's update, the position of the appropriate network players. This makes for quite jittery movement. To use the script we've just created for interpolation and extrapolation, it needs to be given to the Network View attached to the *Car* prefab.

To do this, select the *Car* prefab in the project. In the Inspector, locate its Network View and attached *NetworkRigidbody* script. Drag and drop the *NetworkRigidbody* script onto the Network View's `Observed` property as shown in Figure 7.33. To grab and drag the *NetworkRigidbody* script component you need to select it by its bolded heading circled in Figure 7.33.

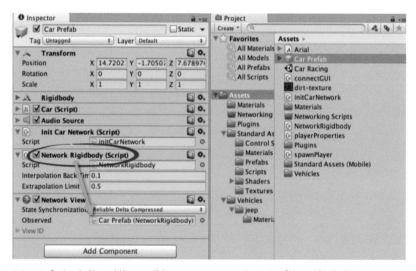

FIG 7.33 Setting the Network View to call the custom message sending script of *NetworkRigidbody*.

Now movement messages will be transmitted and handled by the *NetworkRigidbody* script.

Save, build out to your devices and try it out for smooth player movement.

7.5 Remote Procedure Calls

A remote procedure call (RPC) is a method of calling functions that reside in another program. This is handy in networked game development as you can get one client to call a function in another client. In Unity it allows us to extend the functionality of the *Networked View Component* and update states of networked players beyond their transform and animation data. For example, it can be used to set player names and change the physical parameters of their character.

In the next hands-on section we will use RPC to set the names of the players and colors of the cars.

☺ Unity Hands-On
Customizing Network Player Properties
Step 1: Open the completed project from the previous hands-on or download *NetworkCarRacingRPC* and open the *Car Racing* scene.
Step 2: Drag a copy of the *Car* prefab into the scene. Create a *3D Text Game Object* with Game Object > Create Other > 3D Text and rename it *PlayerName*. Attach it to the *Car* prefab and reposition and rotate as shown in Figure 7.34.
Step 3: Create a new C# script called *playerProperties* and add the following:

```
using UnityEngine;
using System.Collections;

public class playerProperties : MonoBehaviour {

    string myName = "unknown";

    void OnGUI()
    {
        //only display if this is the player's view
        if (networkView.isMine)
        {
            myName = GUI.TextField(new
                Rect(10,10,200,50),myName);

            if(GUI.Button(new Rect(220,10,50,50),"Set"))
            {
                SetName(myName);
            }
```

FIG 7.34 The *Car* prefab with 3D Text attached.

```
        }
    }
    void SetName(string newName)
    {
        this.GetComponent<TextMesh>().text = newName;
        networkView.RPC("OnReceiveName",
        RPCMode.Others, newName);
    }
    [RPC]
    void OnReceiveName(string newName)
    {
        this.GetComponent<TextMesh>().text = newName;
    }
}
```

Because this code is on all prefabs and all cars in the game are instantiated with the same code, you can control which parts of the code run only for the player themselves. In this case, the change name GUI is only drawn for the player. If you didn't put `networkView.isMine` around it, it would draw a text field for the name for each client that was connected to the game. When the name is set, it is updated locally and then the name is sent via a RPC to the player's avatar in all other connected games.

Save and attach this code and a Network View component to the *PlayerName* game object. Update the *Car* prefab and remove it from the scene.

On playing, click Start Server to create an instance of the *Car* prefab. It will now have the *PlayerName* attached. The GUI box on the screen in the

FIG 7.35 Player name being set and displayed on 3D text in the game world.

upper left corner can be used to set the name on the 3D text object as shown Figure 7.35.

Step 1: Having the 3D text facing away from the camera makes it difficult to read. We can force it to always face the camera by attaching a short script. Create a new C# script called *faceCamera* and add the following:;

```
using System.Collections;

public class faceCamera : MonoBehaviour {

    void Update ()
    {
        this.transform.LookAt(Camera.main.transform.
        position);
        this.transform.Rotate(new Vector3(0,180,0));
    }
}
```

Attach this script to the *PlayerName* game object that is attached to the *Car* prefab.

At this stage you might like to reposition the name label and resize it. The default anchor point for 3D text is the upper left corner of the mesh. This makes it a little awkward for revolving without it ending up hanging off the side of the car. Drag a copy of the *Car* prefab into the scene. Set the 3D text of the *PlayerName*'s anchor to middle center as shown in Figure 7.36. Update the prefab to save the changes and then remove it from the scene.

Step 5: Set the Network View of the *PlayerName*'s Observed property to none as shown in Figure 7.37. By default it will be observing the game object's transform, however we now have the *faceCamera* script to turn the *PlayerName* object and therefore don't want any conflicts. If you leave the Network View Observed property as it is, the *PlayerName* of any

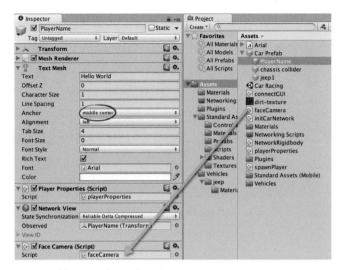

FIG 7.36 Adding camera facing script to the player's name.

FIG 7.37 Setting the *PlayerName*'s Network View to observe nothing.

networked players will flip around as it gets orientation details from the network and also from the *faceCamera* script.

Build to one or more mobile devices and test it out. The result is shown in Figure 7.38.

Step 6: We will now extend the RPC calls to allow players to change the color of their car. Modify *playerProperties* thus:

```
public class playerProperties : MonoBehaviour {

    string myName = "unknown";
    float colourSlider = 0.0f;
    float previousColour = 0.0f;
```

FIG 7.38 The networked car game with player names.

```
public Renderer carRenderer;

void OnGUI()
{
    //only display if this is the player's view
    if (networkView.isMine)
    {
        myName = GUI.TextField(new
        Rect(10,10,200,50),myName);
        if(GUI.Button(new Rect(220,10,50,50),"Set"))
        {
            SetName(myName);
        }
        colourSlider = GUI.HorizontalSlider
        (new Rect(280, 10,
            100, 30), colourSlider, 0.0f, 10.0f);

        if(colourSlider ! = previousColour)
        {
            SetColour(colourSlider);
            previousColour = colourSlider;
        }
    }
}
void SetName(string newName)
{
    ...
}

void SetColour(float colour)
{
    if(colour < 4)
        carRenderer.material.SetColor(" _Color", Color.red);
    else if (colour < 7)
```

```
                carRenderer.material.SetColor(" Color", Color.green);
            else if (colour < = 10)
                carRenderer.material.SetColor(" Color", Color.blue);
            networkView.RPC("OnReceiveColour", RPCMode.Others,
            colour);
}
[RPC]
void OnReceiveName(string newName)
{
...
}
[RPC]
void OnReceiveColour(float colour)
{
    if(colour < 4)
        carRenderer.material.SetColor(" Color",
        Color.red);
    else if (colour < 7)
        carRenderer.material.SetColor(" Color",
        Color.green);
    else if (colour < = 10)
        carRenderer.material.SetColor(" Color",
        Color.blue);
}
}
```

Save. Once again, place a copy of the *Car* prefab in the scene. Select its *PlayerName* child object that has the *playerProperty* script attached. In the Inspector you will find a new exposed variable called carRenderer. This will be set to point to the renderer of the *Car* prefab to make it easy to change its color.

Within the *Car* prefab there is a child called main. Drag and drop it onto the exposed carRenderer property of the *playerProperty* script as shown in Figure 7.39.

FIG 7.39 Adding access to the car renderer component for the *playerProperty* script.

The OnGUI part of the script now includes a slider for changing the color of the car. Try it out. It will change from red to green to blue. The SetColor() function takes care of the actual color change. Note there is also an equivalent RPC call that allows the color message to be sent around to all clients for updating the color of the players' cars.

To send more data using RPC, follow the same rules of creating one function to change the property of the current client and an RPC version to do the same for all networked instances. The property changing function must make a call to the RPC version to ensure the message is sent to all connected clients.

7.6 Interacting with the Web

Slow turn-based multiplayer experiences can be achieved without the need for a constantly running, dedicated server application like the one previously created. In the case of a game such as *Words with Friends* or *Civilization* for mobile, when the time between turns is inconsequential, a Web server can act as mediator and message sender. Player details are stored in an online database and the game code calls a Web server to access this data and update it as needed. To send out push notifications (to be examined in Chapter 8) to your players requires the storage of a token ID that uniquely identifies a mobile device, and a Web server and database are paramount for this.

Unity provides the necessary functionality to send and receive data from the web. With its WWW class, developers are able to download the HTML of webpages and submit Web forms. In this section we will examine the writing of data to a Web server for storage and the retrieving of this data. In addition, the same WWW class will then be used to demonstrate how dynamic content could be added into your game where an image on a website can be used to texture the surface of a game object.

In the next hands-on session we will explore the reading and writing of data by pairing a Unity application with a server side PHP script.

◉ Unity Hands-On
Reading and Writing with PHP
For this exercise you will need access to a webserver with PHP in order to create your own PHP script. However, if you don't possess the capability to run PHP, the identical code is running on the Holistic website and you are welcome to send your queries to that instead.

Step 1: Create a new Unity Project. This project will work either in the Editor or built out to a mobile device. Create a new C# script called *saveToken*. Add the following code:

```
using UnityEngine;
using System.Collections;

public class saveToken : MonoBehaviour {

    string token = "";
    string result = "";

    void Start()
    {

    }

    void OnGUI()
    {
        GUI.Label(new Rect(10,10,100,30),"Token:");
```

```
            token = GUI.TextArea(new Rect(10,40,200,60),
            token);

            if(GUI.Button(new Rect(220,40,100,60),"Save"))
            {
            result = "Sending . . . ";
            StartCoroutine(SaveTokenToWeb());
            }

        if(GUI.Button(new Rect(330,40,100,60),"Get All"))
        {
            result = "Retrieving Tokens . . . ";
            StartCoroutine(GetAllTokens());
        }

        GUI.Label(new Rect(10,160,100,30),"Result:");
        result = GUI.TextArea(new Rect(10,190,400,200),
        result);
    }
    IEnumerator SaveTokenToWeb()
    {
        string url =
            "http://www.holistic3d.com/mobilefiles/server/
            SaveToken.php";

        WWWForm form = new WWWForm();
        form.AddField("token", token);

        WWW www = new WWW(url,form);

        yield return www;

        Debug.Log(www.text);
        result = www.text;
    }
    IEnumerator GetAllTokens()
    {
        string url =
            "http://www.holistic3d.com/mobilefiles/server/
            SaveToken.php";

        WWWForm form = new WWWForm();
        form.AddField("gettoken", "1");

        WWW www = new WWW(url,form);

        yield return www;
        result = www.text;
        }
    }
```

Save and attach it to the main camera. This code creates a simple GUI
that allows you to send data to the web server as well as get data back.

If you have your own web server you can replace the address in the `url` string with your own after creating the PHP in the next step.

At this stage you can press play and test the sending of a token to the server as well as retrieving all tokens stored there. If you click on the Get All button, the results will appear as shown in Figure 7.40. Be patient as the server might be busy.

Step 2: The PHP server side code for this example is:

```php
<?php
$tokenfile = "tokens.txt";

if($_REQUEST['token'])
{

    //add tokens into a text file
    if(!file_exists($tokenfile))
    {

        file_put_contents($tokenfile,"");
    }

$fh = fopen($tokenfile, 'a') or
    die("can't open file ".$tokenfile);

$stringData = $_REQUEST['token']."\n";
fwrite($fh, $stringData);
fclose($fh);
echo "<?xml version = '1.0' encoding = 'UTF-8'?>".
    "<html><body>Token Saved in File</body></
    html>";
}
else if ($_REQUEST['gettoken'])
{
    //read all tokens out of the text file and report
    $fileContents = "<?xml version = '1.0' encoding =
    'UTF-8'?>".

        "<html><body>Token List:<br>";

$handle = @fopen($tokenfile, "r");
    if ($handle)
    {
        while (($buffer = fgets($handle, 4096)) ! ==
        false)
        {
            $fileContents = $fileContents.$buffer."<br>";
        }
        fclose($handle);

    }
    $fileContents = $fileContents."</body></html>";
```

FIG 7.40 The result of performing a Get All.

```
        echo $fileContents;
    }
    else
    {
        echo "<?xml version = '1.0' encoding = 'UTF-8'?>".
            "<html><body>Invalid Request</body></html>";
        exit;
    }

    ?>
```

Save this file as *SaveToken.php* on your webserver and direct the Unity C# script to your own `url` for testing.

For more details see the WWW namespace at http://docs.unity3d. com/Documentation/ScriptReference/WWW.html.

Through extension of this exercise and the introduction of a server-side SQL database, along with PHP and the Unity client side code, you can create some very powerful multiplayer turn-based games.

Pulling data from the Web, as we have just done, is another method for updating content in your game without releasing an update for the entire app. Besides text, you can also grab image, movies, models, and audio clips from a Web server at run time. For example, in a multiplayer game, a player could change their character's skin by uploading a new texture to a website that would then in turn be download by all clients. All players would be able to see the character's changed appearance.

Unity Pro offers the ability to create Asset Bundles that can contain all of the before mentioned items and have them loaded from the Web. As this functionality is restricted to Pro, it won't be covered here. However, the interested reader is encouraged to read more about it in the Unity Manual at http://docs.unity3d.com/Documentation/Manual/AssetBundlesIntro.html.

It is possible in all versions of Unity to pull text and images from the Web. In the next hands-on we will explore this functionality.

◉ Unity Hands-On
Unity Web Textures
Step 1: Create a new Unity Android or iOS Project that contains a single Sphere. Position the camera to be pointing directly at the Sphere such that it takes up most of the window. This sphere will have planetary

texture maps from *Nasa* placed on its surface so you might like to rotate it by attaching a C# script called *spin* with the following:

```
using UnityEngine;
using System.Collections;

public class spin : MonoBehaviour {

    void Update () {
        this.transform.Rotate(new Vector3(0,1,0),0.1f);
    }
}
```

Step 2: Create a new C# script called *downloadTexture* and add the following code:

```
using UnityEngine;
using System.Collections;

public class downloadTexture : MonoBehaviour
{
    void Start()
    {
        string url =
        "http://laps.noaa.gov/albers/sos/mercury/
        mercury/mercury_rgb_cyl_thumb.jpg";

        StartCoroutine(LoadTexture(url));
    }

    IEnumerator LoadTexture(string url)
    {
        WWW www = new WWW(url);
        yield return www;
        renderer.material.mainTexture = www.texture;
    }
}
```

Save and attach both scripts to the Sphere. Play to see the texture loaded on the Sphere.

The `LoadTexture()` function is written as a coroutine so that the call to the Web and the lag that may follow doesn't freeze the program. This means any other actions going on in the game can continue without the consequence of a missing texture or downed website.

Try putting in other planetary texture maps from the same website to change the surface of the sphere.

7.7 Summary

In this chapter we have examined numerous methods for establishing multiplayer gaming environments on mobile devices. While multiple players on one device are easy to implement, the small nature of the screens can make gameplay difficult with all the fingers jostling for space. Moving to a multiplayer configuration with multiple devices introduces many new issues that require the developer to have a solid understanding of message sending via the Internet. When a dedicated game server is not available or required, pulling updated data from the Web is an efficient means of managing the multiplayer experience.

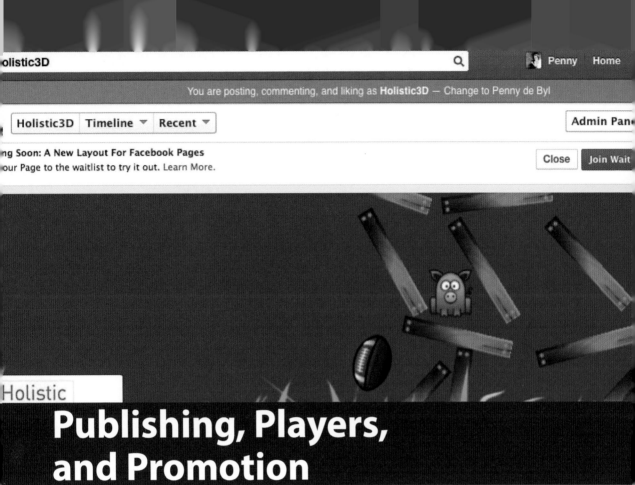

Holistic

Publishing, Players, and Promotion

The little games that make so much money these days are like magazines—like
People *magazine. It's great, you read the gossip, but after a while it's done.*

Patrice Desilets (former Ubisoft and THQ creative director)

8.1 Introduction

According to Super Monitoring, statistics-gathers for digital media, in 2013, 91% of all people on the Earth had a mobile phone, with 56% having a smartphone. In fact there are more mobile devices on Earth than there are people. People with smartphones spend 80% of their phone-time using apps, with games accounting for almost half of this.

In the beginning, the mobile device wasn't taken all that seriously as a gaming platform. Many young indie gaming companies had their initial success in the newly unpopulated app stores. Nowadays the story is very different. With more than one million apps in the Apple App Store and the same in Google Play, it's very difficult as a new developer to get instantly noticed. In fact a

491

whole industry of mobile publishing and mobile marketing companies has sprung up in recent years to accommodate the advertising needs of the developers.

Monetizing mobile apps has also become a strategic affair. Word of mouth and mass downloads are something of the past and developers have had to think more in terms of economics when designing their games. To many game designers, thinking of maximizing revenue with in-game advertising and in-app purchases is somewhat like selling your soul. However, it's a sad fact of this mobile industry that if you want to stay in the game, so to speak, you must compete with a plethora of freely available games.

In this chapter, tools for monetization and publishing mobile games are presented. Plugins that allows for social networking with Twitter and Facebook are explored along with in-app purchasing and banner advertising. Targeting game genre to mobile player demographics and designing to be noticed will also be discussed. We begin with a discussion of the mechanics of app publishing in Google Play and the Apple App Store. The reason being that knowledge of the settings that will be required during the publishing process is required to set up the third-party plugins discussed in later sections.

8.2 Publishing

You've finished your game and now its time to get it into an app store. Where do you start? If you've started with an iOS app you'll already be familiar with "paperwork" Apple requires. Android development, on the other hand, hasn't required any interactions with Google Play.

8.2.1 The Rise of the Mobile Marketplace

One of the most surprising and powerful side-effects of the proliferation of mobile applications and technologies, is the rise of the now immensely wealthy mobile marketplace: a unified, reliable, developer-independent store where seasoned and amateur developers are able to distribute and sell their digital wares to a completely captivated market. The mobile marketplace is continually growing, with hundreds of apps (and updates) being reviewed and added to the stores daily, providing a portable point of sale, where consumers can easily access millions of relatively inexpensive applications and games (compared to console and desktop games). In 2011, after three years of operation, the Apple App Store reached half a million apps, 15% of which were games.

These online marketplaces that deliver software directly to consumer hardware via the Internet are called *digital application distribution platforms*. The first online store of this *one-click-install* type, with direct-to-consumer applications, was the Advanced Packaging Tool (APT) released in 1998 for

Debian GNU/Linux systems. Released in 2008, also on the Linux platform was CNR (one-click and run), another software delivery system. Since the launches of CNR and the Apple App Store, a plethora of other app stores for a variety of platforms have come to be including:

- The Google Apps Marketplace (www.google.com/enterprise/ marketplace): Established in 2010, this online store provides business app plugins for online use to perform enterprise-level tasks from project management to accounting.
- Amazon Appstore for Android (www.amazon.com/gp/mas/get/android): Opened in 2011, this store operates as a software client on Google Android devices allowing users to purchase and download software directly to their devices.
- The Windows 8 Store: This component of Microsoft Windows was announced in early 2012. It replaced the Windows Marketplace, an online software distribution system.
- Google Play (formerly the Android Market before it merged with Google Music[1]): Released in 2008, this app distribution system is Google Android's equivalent of Apple's iOS App Store.

● Note

Google, Apple, and Microsoft all take a 30% cut of the sales price for apps sold through their online stores. Microsoft does however reduce this percentage down to 20% after $25,000 in sales has been reached. The word *app*, short for application, was voted word of the year by the Associated Press in 2011.

This ever-expanding and new digital marketplace presented a variety of new challenges, including unique advertising and marketing possibilities, as well as debates regarding content pricing and sales.

8.2.2 Publishing to the Apple App Store

The procedures for releasing a game in the App Store are as regulated as the process for provisioning devices for development as examined in Chapter 1. Here are the basic steps required. Note, these steps are correct at the time of writing. Although they haven't changed dramatically over the years, it's best to check with the Apple Developer Portal documentation if you find these to be different in practice.

---

[1] Another digital distribution system.

Step 1: Publishing to the App Store requires your game have its own App ID and be built against a distribution provisioning profile. Until now you will have been using a development profile and possibly a wildcard App ID. If your game doesn't have its own App ID in the store (e.g., an App ID associated with the exact Bundle ID you are using) you need to create one. Create an App ID for your game with an Explicit App ID as shown in Figure 8.1.

Step 2: You also need to follow the steps to create a distribution provisioning profile for your game, in the Developer Center, as shown in Figure 8.2.

Step 3: If you've included Push Notification with your game, you will also need to create a new Push Production Certificate within the App ID settings as shown in Figure 8.3. This is just below where you would have created the development one.

Step 4: Submitting a game for the App Store occurs on a different website to the developer center; iTunes Connect (http://itunesconnect. apple.com). Only the admin account on the Apple Dev Center account can log into iTunes Connect with the exact same login details. All other developers need to be added by the administrator from within iTunes Connect via the Manage Users section as shown in Figure 8.4.

FIG 8.1 Creating an Explicit App ID for your game.

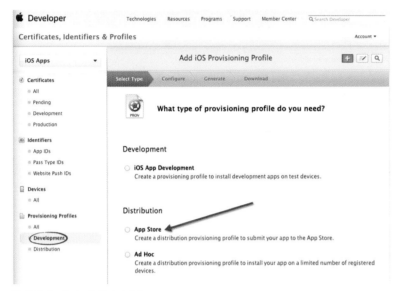

FIG 8.2 Creating a Developer Provisioning Profile for your game.

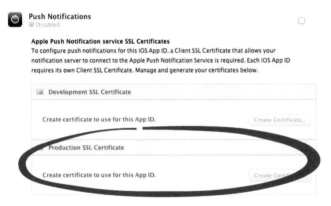

FIG 8.3 Creating a production certificate for push notification.

To submit a game for publishing, click on the Manage Your Apps link shown in Figure 8.4. On the Manage Your Apps page, a new app can be added via the Add New App button as shown in Figure 8.5. You can also edit the information on your other apps in this location.

While following the process to add a new app you will be required to select the Bundle ID. In the provided dropdown box, the Bundle ID previously entered into the Apple Dev Center in Step 1 will appear. Continue following through the steps and entering the required information. Note, you do not have to upload the final game at this stage. You can come back and upload at a later stage.

FIG 8.4 The homepage in iTunes Connect when logged in.

FIG 8.5 Managing and adding iOS Apps in iTunes Connect.

Step 5: When you are ready to upload the game to the App Store, you'll find a Ready to Upload Binary button in iTunes Connect when viewing the details you previously entered about your game as shown in Figure 8.6.

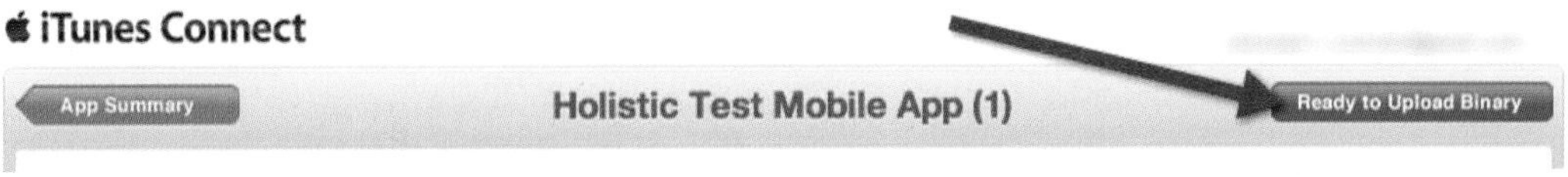

FIG 8.6 Ready to upload binary.

FIG 8.7 Obtaining a Production Certificate from Apple.

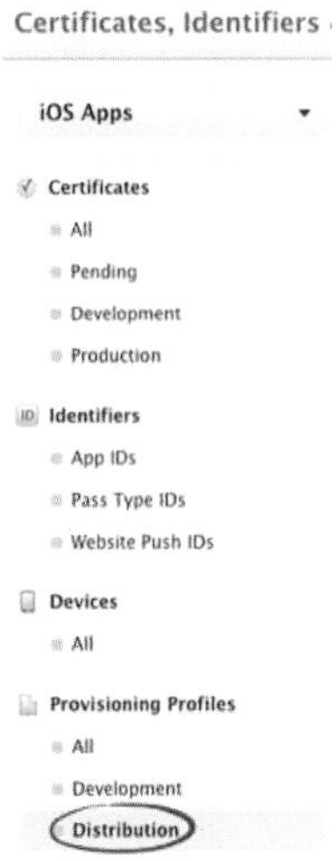

FIG 8.8 Creating a Distribution Profile.

⬤ Note

If you are yet to integrate third-party plugins, the Game Center or In-App Purchases with your game you should do this now, *before* proceeding. These items will be explored later in this chapter.

Step 6: To begin the upload process of your game to the App Store, first you need a Production Certificate. This is created in the Apple Developer Center. Under Certifications, select Production, and add a new certificate as shown in Figure 8.7. The certificate belongs to you as a developer. It is not specific to an app. A single certificate can be used across multiple apps. Therefore you only need to create one. Once created, download the new certificate file and double-click to install.

Step 7: Obtain a distribution profile for you game from the Developer Center for the App Store under the menu item shown in Figure 8.8. Download the provisioning profile when created and double-click to install.

Step 8: Build your game out from Unity using the exact Bundle ID registered in Step 1. Ensure you are not using a wildcard. At this time build and run the game on a mobile device to check it is all working correctly.

Step 9: Locate the Xcode file that was created from the build. It will be in a folder named as you entered it into Unity as shown in Figure 8.9.

FIG 8.9 The Xcode file created by Unity.

FIG 8.10 Signing your game with the distribution certificates.

Step 10: Open this file to open in Xcode. Ensure you have the latest version of Xcode.

Step 11: In the Build Settings for your game in Xcode, locate the Code Signing section and set the Release to *iOS Distribution* and for *Any iOS SDK* to the production certification you just created as shown in Figure 8.10.

Step 12: In Xcode select Product > Clean Build Folder from the main menu. This will remove all other builds and associated files.

Step 13: Next select Product > Archive. This will open the Organizer and present your game for validation as shown in Figure 8.11. Click the validate button to check the archived game has been signed correctly and is ready for upload. After validation, provided you don't have any errors or warnings, the Distribute button will upload your game to the App Store for review. Don't click this until you are absolutely certain you are ready for your game to be released.

FIG **8.11** Validating and distributing a game.

On submission of your files to iTunes Connect you will receive an email confirming that your game is under review, you can also keep track of your app's status including sales using Apples iTC mobile App. This process can take up to two weeks. If there is something wrong with your game and it needs further work, there will be another two weeks' delay after resubmitting. Be prepared for this cycle to occur. To minimize the risk of rejection by Apple, consider the following checklist of information and items you must have ready.

☑ A unique name for your game not already used in the App Store. If you want to release your game in Google Play you'll need to check it doesn't exist in there either.

☑ A description for the game. Make it exciting. Point out the features. Do not use the word "beta" anywhere as Apple will reject it.

☑ A price for your game, otherwise called a tier. E.g., At the time of writing Tier 1 is $USD 0.99, Tier 2 is $USD 1.99.

☑ The primary and secondary categories under which the game falls. The categories include Book, Business, Catalog, Medical, etc., and of course Game.

☑ Copyright information. E.g., the name of the person or company who owns the exclusive rights to the game.

☑ The contents description by which Apple sets the game's rating. E.g., suitable for children, adults only, etc. Apple determines this as you answer questions in iTunes Connect regarding the nature of the content in your game.

☑ A list of keywords that describe the content as well as the type of game. For example if it is a simulation farm game, include the words *simulation* and *farm*. This will be the information that will bring your game up when players do a search in the App Store. If the game is like *Farmville*, then say it!

☑ A SKU number. This is a random sequence of letters and numbers that make up a unique identifier that you will use for your game. SKU comes from the old book keeping term Stock Keeping Unit.

- ☑ A working application website URL.
- ☑ A large version of the app icon. It should be a jpg, png, or tif file with at least 72 DPI and must be 1024 × 1024 pixels. This is the high quality image that will display in the App Store.
- ☑ A series of screenshots in differing resolutions depending on your target device. iTunes Connect requires at least images for one device. For 3.5-inch retina display images it requires a 960 × 640 or 960 × 600, for 4-inch retina it requires 1,136 × 640 or 1,136 × 600 and for iPad 1,024 × 768, 2,048 × 1536, or 2,048 × 1496. The portrait versions of all these images are also acceptable. All should be in jpg, png, or tif format.
- ☑ The support website URL. Your support website should resolve at the URL you supply. If it isn't available, your app is likely to be rejected.
- ☑ A support email address.
- ☑ An End User License Agreement, if required.
- ☑ A date for App Store release. This should be at least two weeks into the future to allow for the review process to take place.
- ☑ The game without an Application Quit button. A Quit button might be useful while testing for being able to quickly restart your game, however Apple will reject it outright if you keep it in and you will be asked to remove it.
- ☑ The game without a Donate button of any kind. Apple will reject these.
- ☑ The game compiled with an Apple Distribution Certificate and a Distribution App Store Provisioning profile.
- ☑ The game's IPA file correctly compiled and tested on all your target iOS devices.

If you have all the items in the previous list prepared before starting the upload and procedure in iTunes Connect, the review process should be smooth sailing.

For more information on the App Store publishing and review process see https://developer.apple.com/appstore/resources/approval/guidelines.html (Apple Developer login required).

8.2.3 Publishing to Google Play

Publishing your game to Google Play is a far easier process than submitting to Apple. The process is fully automated and you should be ready to have your game in the store within a couple of hours of upload. This means you'll want all ancillary items prepared such as support websites and other materials related to the game.

Here are the steps to publish into Google Play. As with the same steps for Apple, they are correct at the time of writing. Check with the Google Developer Portal if you find these to be different in practice.

Step 1: Visit the Google Play Developers Console at https://play.google.com/apps/publish/signup and sign in with your Google account. If you don't have one you will need to set one up. Follow the steps presented on the page to become a Google Developer.

Step 2: In the Developer Console select the Add New Application button as shown in Figure 8.12.

Step 3: Follow the steps presented to you by Google to complete a store listing. When you have completed all sections of the listing you can upload the binary file containing your game in the APK section as shown in Figure 8.13.

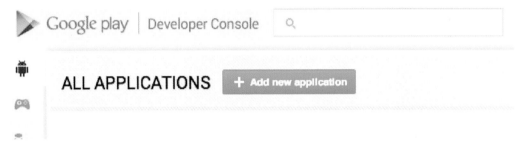

FIG 8.12 Add a new app into the Developer Console.

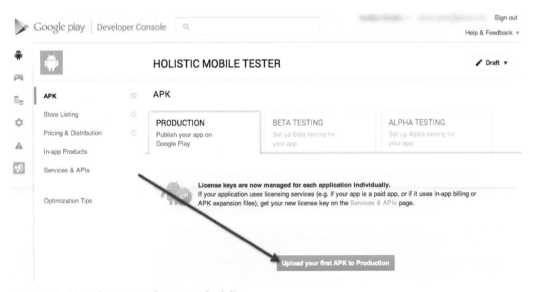

FIG 8.13 Upload the production version of your game to Google Play.

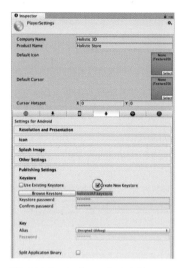

FIG 8.14 Creating Keystore for Android.

FIG 8.15 Creating an Alias Key.

The APK file is the file that Unity creates each time you do a build of the project. By default, this APK is in debug mode. You are required to make a release version of the APK before uploading. To do this select Player Settings from the Build & Run popup. In the Inspector, locate the Publishing Settings as shown in Figure 8.14.

Tick the Create New Keystore box and then click on the Browse Keystore button. The popup folder dialog will ask for a location and name for the new keystore file. Put it in a location that is convenient and give it a password.

In the next part of the publishing settings section, drop down the box next to the Alias of Key and select *Create a new key* as shown in Figure 8.15.

Next a popup window will ask for details about the key. Fill it out with as many details as possible. Some are optional, but you will definitely need an alias and password. When you return to the Publishing Settings section, yet again, drop down the box next to Alias and the key you just created will appear. Select it.

Build the project as usual. The APK produced will be signed for release.

Step 4: Go to the Google Play Developer Console > Your APP > APK and select the production tab. Click the Upload New APK button to upload your signed APK to production.

As previously mentioned, the Google Play game submission process is far more relaxed than Apple's publishing process. Even so, there are a number of things you should have ready before beginning to ensure submission goes smoothly. Here is a checklist:

- ☑ A game title.
- ☑ A description of your game. Make it exciting and mention features and unique elements.
- ☑ At least two screenshots up to a maximum of eight.
- ☑ A high-resolution version of your game icon (512 × 512), a feature graphic (1,024 × 500) and a promotion graphic (180 × 120). The images should be in jpg or png without transparency.
- ☑ The URL to a promotional video (optional).
- ☑ The content rating.
- ☑ An application type (application or game) and category.
- ☑ Pricing information.
- ☑ Distribution locations.
- ☑ A support website URL.
- ☑ The game APK file compiled and working on Android devices.

For more information on the publishing process in Google Play see http://developer.android.com/distribute/googleplay/publish/preparing.html.

8.3 Players

The ultimate aim of creating an awesome mobile game, besides the creative and artistic satisfaction, is getting it into the hands of players. Nowadays simply getting a game into the app store doesn't guarantee anyone will play it and keep playing it. First they have to find the game in among the hundreds of thousands of others and then it must be something they want to download and play.

In addition, although you may be creating games for the love of it, this in the end won't pay the bills and you'll have to consider how to monetize your app to create an income stream.

Delivering what the players want in a mobile game at an acceptable price is paramount if you want to stay in the business. In this section we will examine the genres of games that get downloaded and played the most as well as strategies for earning money.

8.3.1 Pick your Audience

If you are serious about making money from making mobile games you should consider what the audience is buying. The grand idea of creating a AAA third-person shooter for massive multiplayer action is not the best place to focus your initial efforts. Overnight success in the industry is a myth with *Angry Birds* having been *Rovio's* 52nd attempt at releasing a money-making app; their last attempt before giving up the industry. If you are looking at starting out as a mobile game developer it might be worth considering creating a few popular types of games before putting your efforts into the game of your dreams. The following list is the top ten game genres in the top 300 grossing games in the Apple App Store in December 2013.

10. **3D Car racing:** First- and third-person 3D car racing games make up 4% of the mobile games in the App Store. Examples include *Real Racing* and *Need for Speed*.
9. **Sports (golf, soccer, snooker, etc.):** With traditional sporting games such as golf, soccer, and snooker making up 7% of the App Store games, this genre is certainly not contained to console and desktop play. Examples include *Tiger Woods PGA Tour 12* and *FIFA 14*.
8. **Virtual pets and buddies:** The nurturing game mechanic in which players interact and look after virtual humans or animals is still very popular and ideally suited to the small size of the mobile device screen—7% of the top 300 grossing games fit into this genre. Some examples include *My Talking Tom*, *The Sims Free Play*, and *Hatchi*.
7. **Social role-playing games:** As mobile devices lend themselves nicely to networked multiplayer games that can be played anywhere and anytime, playing against someone else at your leisure in a turn-based game is appealing. The multitude of role-playing games that make up 9% of the top grossing games indeed fit this bill. This genre is usually flooded with fantastical tales of medieval times where the players explore and defend kingdoms as royalty, peasants, or wizards. Examples include *Reign of Dragons*, *Kingdom Age*, and *Kingdoms of Camelot*.
6. **Sort and match:** With *Candy Crush Saga* sitting at the top of the App Store charts it's no wonder that 9% of the top games implement the most basic sort and match game mechanics. In fact two-thirds of the games in this category are grid-based tile sliding games that include *Bejeweled*, *Bubble Witch Saga*, and *Pet Rescue Saga*.

5. **Endless runner:** When you think of endless runners, the first game that probably comes to mind is *Temple Run*. This game, released in 2011 spawned many similar type games including *Minion Rush* and *Subway Surfer*. Along with their 2D side-scrolling endless environments (e.g., *Ski Safari*), this group makes up 9% of the top grossing games.

4. **First- and third-person combat:** In 2011 Flurry Analytics (www.flurry.com) reported "gamer games" (those more traditionally thought of as video games) the fifth most popular genre. In this category they included racing games, shooters, battle, and sports; the traditional games a *gamer* would play. In this top ten, combining these genres would place the "gamer" genre at number 1 with 20%. However we consider these combined game types to have their own distinct game mechanics and therefore they are reported separately here. It is interesting to note the growth in the years since the Flurry report. This will have been fueled by the growth in technology with the mobile devices allowing for more platform-type games and the fact that gamers will simply spend more money on games. First- and third-person combat games alone account for 11% of the top grossing games. Examples include *Tomb Raider*, *Call of Duty*, and *Fight Back*.

3. **Building and simulation:** Games in which cities are built and destroyed—12% of the top games fall into this category. These games include *Minecraft*, *Megapolis*, and *Village Life*. In these games the player builds houses, villages, and cities in which simulated citizens live. They are mostly god-type games, where the player plays a god or the mayor. Citizens must collect natural resources to craft the buildings of the game world. These games lend themselves perfectly to IAP as players who want to get ahead and build more quickly can swap real money for virtual building materials instead of waiting for their citizens to come up with the goods.

2. **Casual, quick fire:** There are so many games that fit into this genre with numerous mechanics that separately they are hardly noticeable as their own genre. However, collectively these pick-up and put-down games make up 15%. Games in this category include *Angry Birds*, *Cut-the-Rope*, and *Fruit Ninja*. What brings them together in this category is their perfect balance of art and design with novel and highly interactive game mechanics. They are also perfect for casual gaming as episodes of the game are short. If a level is not completed in one sitting, while waiting for a bus for example, it's not difficult for the player to pick up where they left off and replay the short level they didn't previously finish.

1. **Poker and casino:** Gambling games, such as *Slotomania*, *Poker by Zynga*, and *Double-Down Casino* are the biggest group of top grossing mobile games being 17% of the total. By 2015 it is estimated the revenue from these games will be in excess of

$USD 48 billion.[2] The highly addictive nature of gambling is well-documented and it's no wonder that this category of games has reached the number one position, making poker, slot machines, and other casino games so readily available and perfect for exploiting IAP.

Today there is enough variation in the types of games mobile owners are playing to give the game designer quite a lot of scope. To get noticed though, you need to have a unique product, solid game mechanics, and a professional polished finish. However, to make a living as a mobile game developer you'll have to also consider how you're going to monetize your app.

8.3.2 Pick your Approach

With the introduction of free-to-play game formats, players have become less willing to pay for games before playing them. In 2012, Gartner (www.gartner.com) reported 89% of all mobile app downloads were free and predicts that by 2016 this percentage will have increased to 93%. While free games enjoy many more downloads than paid ones, as a business model giving away your product is not sustainable. Two strategies to gain revenue from the free-to-play model that have become quite successful are in-game advertising and in-app purchasing.

8.3.3 In-Game Advertising

Spending on in-game advertising is expected to reach $USD 1 billion in 2014.[3] The formats for promotion in the medium range from static product placement to interactivity with products and advertising banners. Companies who see the potential in merging advertising with mobile games have begun to pop up, their business model being to use in-house developed mobile games rebranding them by replacing textures in the environment with logos from their customers. For example a *Temple Run*-style game could be reworked as a pizza delivery game and, by simply replacing a texture or two, remade for *Dominoes* or *Pizza Hut* in a matter of moments. However, these types of games are being specifically used as vehicles to deliver advertising and brand interactivity.

One such marketing company offering product placement in mobile games is Mobile Media Placement. Check out their offering for

---

[2] Source: www.juniperresearch.com/viewpressrelease.php?pr=204.
[3] Source: www.brandrepublic.com/News/908125/Screen-Digest-forecasts-1bn-boom-in-game-advertising.

pizza brands at www.youtube.com/watch?v=41RYyQaZoWk&feature=youtu be_gdata_player.

For developers who are seeking to release a free game and receive an income from adverting, banner ads are the easiest to deploy. Banner ads popup in-game and the developer receives an income on each click from the player.

Services are available that have the ads prepared and ready to go. The developer signs up for an account with these services and then pulls the ad content into their game. For each click-through from a player, the developer can receive around $US0.05 to $US0.10. Some services pay per 1,000 clicks (as is the case with banner advertising on YouTube). One such service is Ad Mob by Google that we will examine in the next hands-on session.

◉ Unity Hands-On
Ad Banner Advertising with Ad Mob
In this hands-on session we will build an Android app that displays ads from Ad Mob.

Step 1: Go to http://apps.admob.com and sign up for an account. You will not need bank account details at this early stage.
Step 2: When signed into Ad Mob there will be a red Monetize button. Click on this and add the details about your app as shown in Figure 8.16.

FIG 8.16 The setup page for registering an app with Ad Mob.

When registering your app, as it doesn't exist, choose to add it manually and pick a suitable name.

You will have two options for ad type; banner and interstitial. A banner ad takes up a small part of the screen and is placed over or to the side of gameplay. An interstitial ad is a full page advertisement that can show as the game is loading or in-between loading scenes. For this exercise select banner.

On submission of the form you will receive an Ad Unit ID and an Ad Unit name. Note these down.

Step 3: Download the *Admob* Unity Project from the website. Open the Test Scene. This freely available project is available courtesy of *MicroEyes* on the Unity Forums at http://forum.unity3d.com/threads/173292-Admob-Unity-Package-that-work-with-Unity-3–2-amp-above and from the advice of *vARDAmir* and *Totalshaden* in the same thread the project has been updated to work with the latest Ad Mob SDK.

In the scene you have opened there will be the Main Camera and an object called AdvertisementManager. This is a prefab you can use in other projects available in the Assets/Prefabs folder.

Step 4: Select the *AdvertisementManager* and locate the attached script in the *Inspector*. The setting here will link the ads back to your *AdMob Ad Unit Id*. In the exposed *Publisher Id* property for the script type in the *Ad Unit Id* created in Step 2. The rest of the settings you can leave as they are or you can set according to those in Figure 8.17.

Step 5: Save and build the app out to an Android Device. There are some scripted buttons in the GUI of *AdvertisementManager.cs* script that show you how to call some of the functionality of the plugin. The results of your efforts should look like those in Figure 8.18.

FIG 8.18 An Android App displaying a banner ad.

Apples own advertising service is iAd. Like Ad Mob, iAd has a large network of high (and low) profile individuals and businesses advertising their services and goods through banner ads placed in mobile and desktop applications. Integrating iAds into your Unity game is far simpler than for Ad Mob at the current time as Unity has a built in wrapper for the Apple iAd framework.

⊙ Unity Hands-On

Creating an iAd Banner

Step 1: Create a new Unity iOS project.

Step 2: Create a new C# script called *bannerAd* and add the following:

```
using UnityEngine;
using System.Collections;

public class bannerAd : MonoBehaviour {

    private ADBannerView banner = null;

    void OnGUI()
    {
        if(GUI.Button(new Rect(10,100,80,80),"Show/
        Hide"))
        {
            if(banner.loaded)
            {
                banner.visible = !banner.visible;
            }
        }
    }
    void Start()
    {
        banner = new ADBannerView(ADBannerView.Type.
        Banner,
            ADBannerView.Layout.Bottom);
```

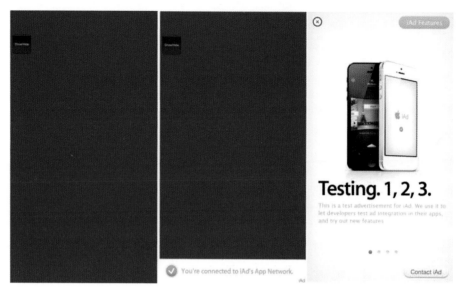

FIG 8.19 The iAd framework in action.

```
ADBannerView.onBannerWasClicked + =
OnBannerClicked;
ADBannerView.onBannerWasLoaded + =
OnBannerLoaded;
}
void OnBannerClicked()
{
    Debug.Log("Clicked!\n");
}

void OnBannerLoaded()
{
    Debug.Log("Loaded!\n");
}
}
```

Attach the script to the Main Camera. Save and build to your iOS device. A button will appear on the screen that you can use to turn the banner view on and off. The iAd framework is very nicely integrated, as you will discover when you touch the ad as shown in Figure 8.19.

⦿ Note (iPad only)

If you are programming for iOS 6 and above for the iPad, the ad can also be presented as a rectangle. To see this modify the code thus:

```
void Start()
{
    banner = new ADBannerView(ADBannerView.Type.
    MediumRect,
        ADBannerView.Layout.Bottom);
    ADBannerView.onBannerWasClicked + = OnBanner-
    Clicked;
    ADBannerView.onBannerWasLoaded + = OnBanner-
    Loaded;
}
```

The result will have the iAd show up as a 300 × 250 rectangle (there is no way to change the size at this time) as shown in Figure 8.20. Note it will cause an exception if run on an iPhone so you will need to test the device type if building to both.

FIG 8.20 A rectangular banner ad displayed on the iPad.

Step 3: Real ads will not show up on the iAd banner until the app has been published via iTunes Connect. The steps for publishing will be covered later in this chapter, however, if you wish to integrate iAds into your game you will need to complete an iAd App Network contract before you publish your game.

Revenue from banner ads is pay-per-click. This means you want players to click on the ad. At the same time you don't want the ad to be so annoying that players don't want to play your game anymore, while ads that stop the gameplay or restrict the player's view are just down right infuriating. To maximize the revenue from in-app advertising consider:

- Placing the ad at the end of a gaming challenge, not the beginning. Research shows there is a higher volume of click-throughs on banner ads when the player has finished a level.[4] Ads placed at the beginning of the game on a loading screen when the player is anticipating the challenge, simply don't work.
- Using the same ad for consistency and exposure. The more a player sees the same ad, the more they will be compelled to investigate it. However, don't overdo it, and make it possible to turn the ads off with an in-app purchase. The price you charge for this should be relative to the income obtained from advertising. This could be as high as $5.99.[5]
- The size of the ad with respect to the screen it will be viewed on. Tablet players click-through more ads than phone players because ads on tablets are far more readable given the relative sizing.[6] Consider using banner ads on tablet devices and full-page ads on smaller screens.
- Going global. You game, when in the app stores will be available almost everywhere on the Earth. Therefore you'll want to consider using multiple ad provision services and integrating location-based marketing to best target the consumer and make the ad relevant to them. That way you can expect more revenue from click-throughs.

If, and hopefully when, you find yourself with a really compelling game, in-app purchasing may be another avenue to explore for monetization. The longer a player spends in your game the more likely they are to make an in-app purchase.

8.3.4 In-App Purchasing

In mid-2013 King, the developers of the *Candy Crush Saga*, removed all in-game advertising in favor of in-app purchasing (IAP). The game that, as of July

---

[4] Source: www.gamasutra.com/blogs/BryanAtwood/20111220/9127.
[5] Source: www.placeplay.com/remove-in-app-advertising-with-iap.
[6] http://blog.inner-active.com/2011/12/6-mobile-advertising-lessons-we-learned-in-2011-that-will-maximize-app-revenue-in-2012.

2013, had more than 6.7 million active users and was earning $633,000 per day in the US iOS App Store purely from IAP.

Of course, if you don't have the volume of users you won't get the same volume of IAP; however, with free apps taking up to 93% of apps being downloaded, you are giving your game a far better chance of being picked up and played if it is free initially and then IAP offers the player an enhanced gaming experience.

The types of things that can be offered as IAP include digital content, functionality, and in-app services. Digital content covers a range of merchandise and subscriptions including consumable products, non-consumable products, and subscriptions. Consumable IAPs in games include any items that are continually purchased and traded in. For example, buying coins in *Clash of Clans* allows players to finish city buildings quicker. Any in-game currency purchased with real world coin and then used up in the virtual game world to acquire temporary items or status is consumable. Non-consumable IAPs in a game include unlocking levels or downloadable content. These items are purchased once and continue to be available to the player for the life of the game. IAP subscriptions may be episodic or one-off. Episodic subscriptions are auto-renewed. While the subscription is active the player has access to game functionality and content. In 2011, Big Fish Games released the first subscription-based mobile app service for games. For a monthly price players can access a multitude of Big Fish-produced games from inside Instantly Play (available on iOS and Android). At the end of each subscription period, usually a month, the subscription is auto-renewed. Single subscriptions are one-off payments made to access content for a limited amount of time. They are not automatically renewed; however, a player is free to purchase another subscription.

Rules with respect to including IAP in games are carefully monitored by Apple. They do not allow IAPs for the purchase of real-world goods or services and will not approve any IAPs for unsuitable content including pornography or defamatory materials. While Google have similar restrictions on IAP (or what Google call IAB—In-App Billing) with respect to offensive content, their policy does not restrict the sale of physical goods or real-world services.

There are numerous paid plugins for Unity that help you set up your game for IAP. The more notable and popular of these being Prime 31's Storekit and Unibill; both available in the Unity Asset Store. The transactions themselves are setup in iTunes Connect and Google Play. In iTunes Connect, where App IDs are managed, after an app has been registered, when editing an app the option to add IAPs appears as a blue button. For this option to be available you will have had to register with Apple as a paid developer, which will require you to give them your bank account details. Each IAP is added to the app through reference to the Bundle ID and the items Product ID shown in Figure 8.21.

In Google Play, In-App Billing is configured in a similar way. First you require a merchant wallet to be set up with Google that can only be applied for by the

FIG 8.21 An IAP configured for an app in iTunes Connect.

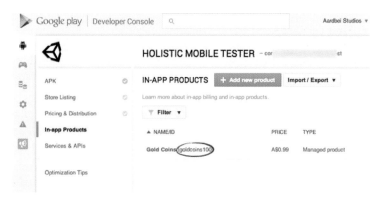

FIG 8.22 The Google Play In-App Billing Store Setup.

administrator of your Google Play account. Next, a signed version of your APK file is uploaded. Once the file is uploaded you will be allowed to create an in-app store as shown in Figure 8.22.

Each item created in the Google Play system is identified by an ID. This ID is used to link the items back into the Unity code. In addition, for Unity, you will also require an app license key as shown in Figure 8.23.

The Bundle ID, Product ID, and Keys (Android Only) link the game with the In-App purchasing system. The structure of the store from the viewpoint of the player still needs to be written. This can be as complicated or as simple as you

FIG 8.23 The license key for accessing in app functionality.

like. However the connection between your game in Unity and the App Stores needs to be performed by a Unity plugin as the functionality is not in built.

The good news is that there is an excellent open-source project that does all the work for you. The project is Soomla (www.soom.la). The Web front to the project steps you through the creation of a store, allows you to make it look like you want, links back to the app stores, and creates a Unity project for you. In the next hands-on session we will investigate IAP with Soomla for iOS.

◉ Unity Hands-On
Setting up IAP

While this exercise mostly examines Apple IAP, the process also works for Google Play. Soomla is compatible with both platforms. To follow this exercise through for Android, the process is identical with the exception that the Google In-App Billing and item purchases need to be set up in Google Play for your app.

Step 1: Create an App ID in the Apple Dev Center for this new App. If you have a testing Bundle ID setup you can use that for now. Visit iTunes Connect, edit your app and add In-App Purchasing. Work through the steps for adding purchasable items. Keep track of all the Project IDs that you create as shown in Figure 8.24.

Step 2: Visit http://soom.la and create a new account (it's free). Once logged in go to the My Games link at the top and then select the Add Storefront button.

Step 3: Select a template you would like to use. You can fully customize the images and text as your proceed.

Step 4: The template you selected with all default items will be displayed. There are two types of purchases in a Store Front; Coins and Market Purchase. Coins are the currency you can use inside your game. Market Purchases are in-app payments and link to the IAP system. As shown in Figure 8.25, the Product ID from iTunes Connect is used to identify market purchases in Soomla.

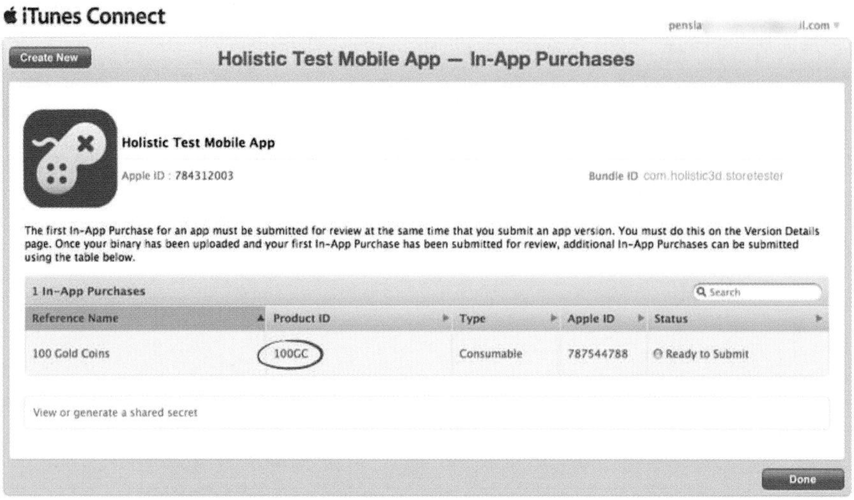

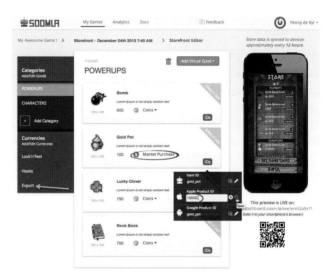

iTunes Connect
Create New
Holistic Test Mobile App — In-App Purchases
Holistic Test Mobile App
Apple ID : 784312003
Bundle ID com.holistic3d.storetester
The first In-App Purchase for an app must be submitted for review at the same time that you submit an app version. You must do this on the Version Details page. Once your binary has been uploaded and your first In-App Purchase has been submitted for review, additional In-App Purchases can be submitted using the table below.
1 In-App Purchases
Search
Reference Name
Product ID
Type
Apple ID
Status
100 Gold Coins
100GC
Consumable
787544788
Ready to Submit
View or generate a shared secret
Done

FIG 8.24 Creating purchasable items in iTunes Connect.

SOOMLA
My Games
Analytics
Docs
Feedback
Penny de Byl
My Awesome Game !
Storefront - December 24th 2013 7:40 AM
Storefront Editor
Store data is synced to devices approximately every 12 hours.
Categories
Add/Edit Goods
POWERUPS
CHARACTERS
Add Category
Currencies
Add/Edit Currencies
Look'n'Feel
Hooks
Export
4 Goods
POWERUPS
Add Virtual Good
Bomb
500
Coins
Gold Pot
100
Market Purchase
Lucky Clover
750
Coins
Rock Book
750
Coins
IDs
Item ID
gold_pot
Apple Product ID
100GC
Google Product ID
gold_pot
Save
This preview is LIVE on:

FIG 8.25 A default Soomla storefront and setting up purchase IDs.

Note

With Android, the purchase IDs are made up in Soomla first and added into the Google Play Console *after* the app has been built to a signed APK file.

Step 5: When you are finished editing the storefront, select the Export option. On the next page ensure you select the Unity 3D option and fill

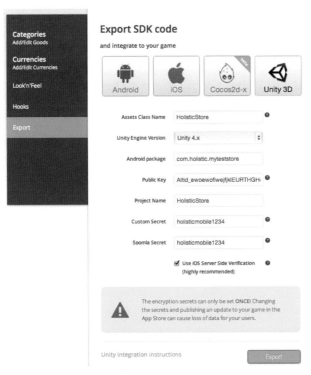

FIG 8.26 Exporting the Soomla package for Unity.

out the form, shown in Figure 8.26, using your own details. Enter the correct Bundle ID and if you've used the Google Play store, add the key given in the Google Play Console for your game. The custom and secret keys are ones made up but remember them for later. Press the Export button when you are ready to download the package.

Step 6: Unzip the Soomla package and open the project in Unity. Open the scene called *scene*. In the Hierarchy select the Soomla game object. In the Inspector the values for Soomla show. You will need to set the custom and secret keys (Soom Sec) as you entered them into the Soomla system. If you've used Android enter the license key (as shown in Figure 8.27) here as well. Remember to setup the Bundle ID for your game and then build and run.

When testing out the storefront on your device, a default home page will appear. On pressing the button, the store will come up as shown in Figure 8.28. Any items that were set as market purchases will ask the player to login to the iTunes Store to complete the transaction. The purchase of the item can be made and then the amounts are updated in your game store.

To test the purchasing system, in iTunes Connect where the IAPs are setup you can also add test user accounts. By putting in the Apple IDs of anyone testing the game, they will be able to make fake purchases.

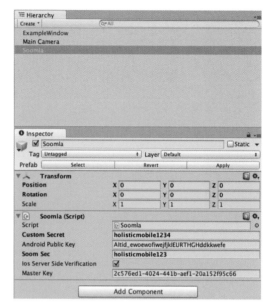

FIG 8.27 Settings for the Soomla object in Unity.

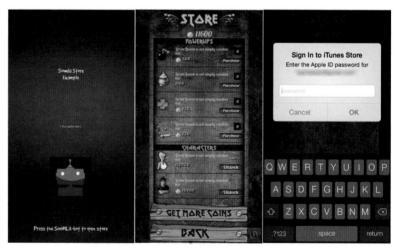

FIG 8.28 Soomla in action.

For more details on the use of Soomla visit http://soom.la/docs/#unity-getting-started

For more details on the Android IAP process see http://developer.
android.com/google/play/billing/index.html.

For more details on the iOS IAP process see https://developer.apple.
com/in-app-purchase.

8.3.5 Record their progress

Leaderboards and badges are as old as games themselves and you'll find
these constructs used not only in computer games, but also in board games,
card games, sports, and the classroom. They act as a sign of recognition
for player achievements to a broader community and are a way to entice
motivation in other players to play and achieve even in single-player games.
Adding this extra meta-game to a single-player game makes it multiplayer as
players can challenge each other to beat their scores.

The Apple Game Center, introduced in 2010, is a social gaming network
in which players can invite friends to play games, challenge high scores,
matchmake for multiplayer games, and track achievements. In 2013, Google
released their own social gaming network called Google Play Games.

In Unity, a Social API has been implemented to provide easy access to all
Apple Game Center functionality. On the Apple side, setting up the Game
Center is very similar to IAP. From within iTunes Connect, leaderboards and
achievements are setup. The Social API in Unity can access this information
and store results and achievements for each player using their Apple ID. In the
following hands-on exercise we will create a simple leaderboard and set of
achievements in the Game Center and create an iOS application to access and
record information in it.

☉ Unity Hands-On
Implementing the Apple Game Center
Step 1: Log into iTunes Connect and select Manage Your Apps. If you
haven't already, add a new app for this exercise. If you have another app
that you use for testing this can also be used. The same Bundle ID must be

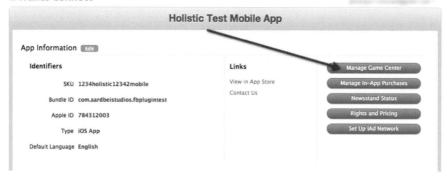

FIG 8.29 How to begin setting up the Apple Game Center for an app.

used in Unity to link the Unity game with the iTunes settings. Select the app as if to edit it. Click on the Manage Game Center button as shown in Figure 8.29.

Step 2: In the Game Center setup you can add both *leaderboards* and *achievements*. Leaderboards receive and rank scores separately to achievements. The overall score accumulated by players can be recorded in a leaderboard and used to rank players. Achievements represent the accomplishment of challenges. For example, if a player were to kill ten vampires in 30 seconds then they might receive the "Buffy" achievement, whereas another player in the same game could blow up five vehicles with one bazooka shot and gain the "Bruce Willis" achievement. These achievements are irrespective of the players score in the game.

In the Game Center for the app you are testing here, add at least one leaderboard and three achievements as shown in Figure 8.30.

Be sure to record the IDs for the leaderboards and achievements, as you will require them in your code later.

Step 3: Create a new iOS Unity Project and set the bundle ID to the one for the app for which you just setup the Game Center. Create a new C# script called *gameCenter* and add the following code:

```
using UnityEngine;
using System.Collections;
using UnityEngine.SocialPlatforms;

public class gameCenter : MonoBehaviour
{
    string messages = "";

    void Start ()
    {
        Social.localUser.Authenticate
        (ProcessAuthentication);
```

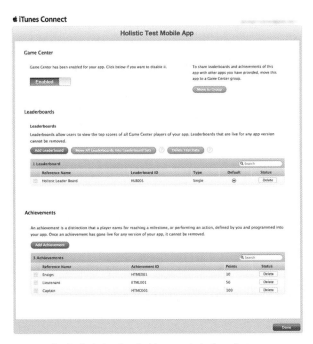

FIG 8.30 Creating leaderboards and achievements in the Game Center setup.

```
    }

    void ProcessAuthentication (bool success)
    {
        if (success) {
            messages + = "Authenticated, checking
            achievements.\n";
            Social.LoadAchievements
            (ProcessLoadedAchievements);
        }
        else
            messages + = "Failed to authenticate.\n";
    }

    void ProcessLoadedAchievements (IAchievement[]
    achievements)
    {
        if (achievements.Length == 0)
            messages + = "Error: no achievements
            found.\n";
        else
            messages + = achievements.Length + "
            achievements.\n";

        Social.ReportProgress ("Achievement01", 100.0,
        result = > {
            if (result)
```

```
                        messages + = "Reported achievement
                        progress.\n";
                   else
                        messages + = "Failed to report
                        achievement.\n";
              });
         }
    }
```

Save and attach it to the Main Camera.

The `Social.localUser.Authenticate()` function attempts to connect the user to the Game Center with their Apple ID. Once this process completes then the `ProcessAuthentication()` function runs and reports on the outcome. When this runs on an iOS device it calls up the Game Center login as shown in Figure 8.31 (a). If you run the game again the authentication will return a "Welcome back" popup as shown in Figure 8.31. **Step 4:** The Game Center can be queried for the achievements that are listed within. To do this add the following `OnGUI()` function to the code:

```
void OnGUI()
{
    if(GUI.Button(new Rect(10,10,100,60),"List"))
```

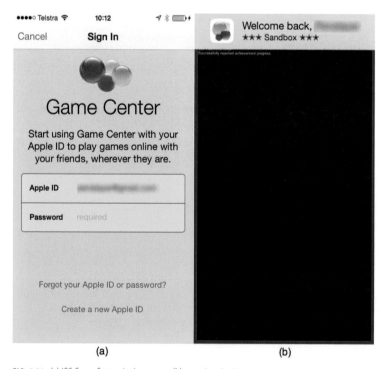

(a)   (b)

FIG 8.31 (a) iOS Game Center signing screen, (b) returning sign in popup.

```
{
    Social.LoadAchievementDescriptions
    (achievmentList = >
    {
        if (achievmentList.Length > 0)
        {
            messages + = "There are " +
            achievment List.Length +
                " achievement descriptions.\n";
            string achievementDescriptions =
            "Achievement
                Descriptions ========== \n";
            foreach (IAchievementDescription
            ad in achievmentList)
            {
                achievementDescriptions += "\t" +
                    ad.id + " " +
                    ad.title + " " +
                    ad.unachievedDescription + "\n";
            }
            messages += achievementDescriptions +
                "\n" + " ================= \n";
        }
        else
            messages += "Failed to load achievement
                descriptions.\n";
        });
    }
    messages = GUI.TextArea(new Rect(10,100,Screen.
    width-20,
        Screen.height-110), messages);
}
```

Save and build out to your device for testing. You can run this code in the editor to receive test messages; however, building it to an iOS device will test the connection with the Game Center you set up for the app. When the "List" button is pressed you will receive a list of the achievements in the Game Center.

Step 5: To explore more functionality of the Social API add the following code into the bottom of the OnGUI() function:

```
if(GUI.Button(new Rect(120,10,100,60),"Score"))
{
    Social.ReportScore (150, "HLB001", success => {
        messages + = success ? "Reported score
        successfully.\n":
```

FIG 8.32 The Game Center user interface.

```
                              "Failed to report score.\n";
                    });
          }

          if(GUI.Button(new Rect(230,10,100,60),
          "Achievements"))
          {
              Social.ShowAchievementsUI();
          }

          if(GUI.Button(new Rect(340,10,100,60),"Unlock"))
          {
              Social.ReportProgress("HTMC001", 100.0, success
              = > {
                  messages + = success ? "Reported achievement
                  successfully.\n" : "Failed to report
                  achievement.\n";
              });
          }
```

Save, build, and run. The first button sends a score value to the leaderboard as identified by the string "HLB001." You will need to put your own leaderboard ID in there. The second button reveals the Game Center user interface as shown in Figure 8.32. The Game Center user interface reveals the player's achievements and score in the leaderboard. The third button reports achievement progress to the Game Center. You will need to replace the achievement id of "HTMC001" with your own achievement ID as you entered it into the Game Center.

This hands-on has revealed only a small part of the Game Center hooks available in Unity as the full implementation is beyond the scope of this book. For more information on the Unity Social API see http://docs.unity3d.com/Documentation/Components/net-SocialAPI.html.

8.4 Getting Pushy

Alerting a player when it's their turn is often achieved in mobile games through the use of push notification. It can also be used to remind people to play your game. Both Apple and Google provide notification services that forward messages from third-party applications via their servers to registered mobile devices through a constantly open IP connection.

8.4.1 Apple Push Notification Service

The Apple Push Notification Service (APNS) was released in 2009 with iOS 3.0. It allows for messages to be sent directly to the mobile device using a unique device token that is allocated upon registration. The device token is not the same as the device identifier seen in Xcode. It is used in the process of provisioning a device for development. The device token is given out to any service that wants to send push notifications to it.

Before you, as a developer, can send messages directly to a device via your app you must set the app up to enable push notification. This is done in the Apple Developer Center where you obtain a certificate with which to sign your app. The certificate is associated with the Bundle ID. This is built into your app, which is then placed on a mobile device. On running the app, a message pops up asking for permission to accept push notifications. This is the iOS checking that the owner of the device allows such messages to be received. When the device owner allows push notifications to be turned on, the device is registered with the APNS and given a device token. The device token is in turn given back to the app's developer so they can push out messages from their own server.

When a developer wants to push out a message, the message, Bundle ID, and device token are sent to APNS, which validates the message and then sends it onto the device. This process is illustrated step-by-step in Figure 8.33.

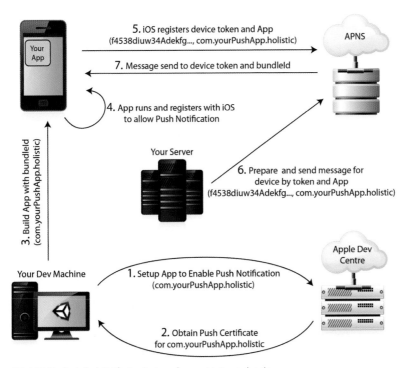

FIG 8.33 The Apple Push Notification Device and app registration push cycle.

In the next hands-on section we will examine the setup and sending of a simple push notification to a Unity-made app for iOS. As you will see the entire push functionality is controlled by the Bundle ID and there is very little to prepare in the Unity environment to enable push notification.

◉ Unity Hands-On
Getting Pushy with iOS

This hands-on session will show you how to get set up for sending push notifications to iOS devices. It should go without saying that you will need to be developing on a Mac to continue. If you are working in Windows, the next hands-on will work for you and repeats the process in this exercise for pushing to Android devices.

Step 1: Download the *iOSPush* project from the website. Open the main scene. It will be empty. However in the Assets folder you will find the third-party push notification code from *App42 Cloud API* (http://api. shephertz.com). The entire project and sample code is also available on *Github* at https://github.com/shephertz/App42iOSUnity3DPushPlugin. But for now you only need the *iOSPush* project.

Step 2: Setup the Bundle ID that you will use for this app in the Player Settings as shown in Figure 8.34. It must be one that you as an Apple developer will be able to create.

Step 3: Open Keychain Access. From the menu select Certificate Assistant > Request a Certificate from a Certificate Authority as shown in Figure 8.35.

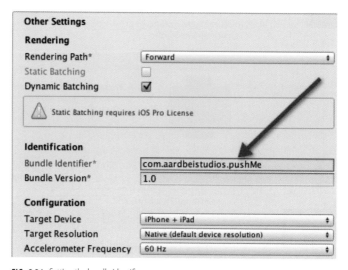

FIG 8.34 Setting the bundle identifier.

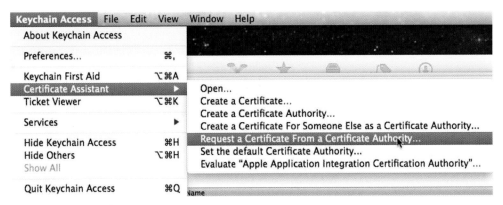

FIG 8.35 Requesting a certificate.

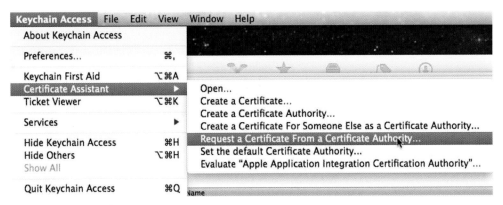

FIG 8.36 Certificate information

Step 4: Fill in the certificate information as shown in Figure 8.36, select Saved to Disk and press Continue. Save the certificate request file to your desktop.

Step 5: Return to the Keychain Access and the Keys area. In it you will find newly created keys named after the Common Name you put in the certificate request; one public and one private as shown in Figure 8.37. Right-click on the private key and select Export. Save the *.p12* file. It will ask for a passphrase to protect the file. Enter something you will remember keeping in mind the password will be used later in a .php script.

Step 6: Sign into the Apple Developer website. Click on iOS Apps Identifiers. Click on the + sign to add a new iOS App ID. Fill out the "Registering an App ID" form that comes up with a description, App ID Prefix (select one from the given list), enter an Explicit App ID and use the exact same Bundle ID that was used in your Unity project, and right

FIG 8.37 Newly created public and private keys for the certificate.

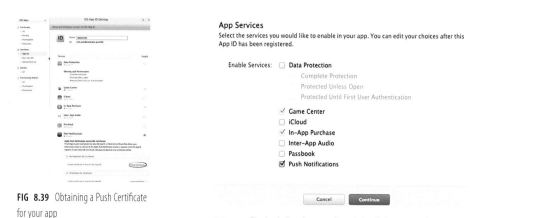

FIG 8.39 Obtaining a Push Certificate for your app

FIG 8.38 The Apple Development Centre's App ID Registration form.

at the bottom of the form tick the Push Notifications tickbox as shown in Figure 8.38. Press the Continue button at the bottom.

Step 7: The next form that comes up confirms the options you have selected. Ensure Push Notification is turned on and click on the Submit button.

Step 8: In the list of App IDs locate the newly created app and select it. An Edit button will become available. Click on it.

Step 9: In the page that appears as shown in Figure 8.39, scroll down and click on Create Certificate in the Development SSL Certificate area.

● Note

When you're ready to submit your App to the App Store you will need to repeat this process and obtain a *Production* version of the certificate.

Step 10: The next webpage that appears will step you through the creation of the certificate. You already did this in Step 4. Upload this file on the next page. In the end you will be given a push services certificate to download especially for your app as shown in Figure 8.40.

Step 11: Double-click on the certificate and it will install as shown in Figure 8.41. In Keychain Access you will see this certificate paired with the previously generated key. Save the downloaded *.cer* file with the *.p12* and the certificate request file. Later you will be typing in the names of these files and it would be pertinent at this point to give them short distinct names with no spaces for example *aps_cert.cer* and *push_key.p12*

Step 12: Return to the Apple Dev Centre and select Development under Provisioning Profiles. Add a new one for your app as shown in Figure 8.42. Configure it to the App ID you previously created especially for this exercise. Follow the steps through to the end. Download the Provisioning Profile and double-click on the file to add to Xcode.

Step 13: Return to the Unity project and create a new C# script called *PushScript*. Add the following code:

```
using UnityEngine;
using System.Collections;
using com.shephertz.app42.paas.sdk.csharp;
using com.shephertz.app42.paas.sdk.csharp.
pushNotification;
using System;
```

Name:	Apple Development iOS Push Services: com.aardbeistudios.pushMe
Type:	APNs Development iOS
Identifier ID:	Holistic Push
Expires:	Dec 14, 2014

Download

FIG 8.40 The push certificate created specifically for your app.

FIG 8.41 The certificate installed on your machine. Note the Bundle ID.

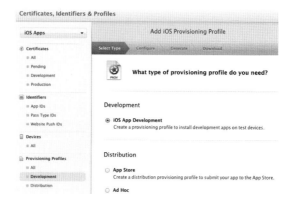

FIG 8.42 Creating a new provisioning profile for the app

```
using System.Runtime.InteropServices;

public class PushScript : MonoBehaviour
{
    [System.Runtime.InteropServices.DllImport
    ("__Internal")]
    extern static public void registerForRemoteNotifica-
    tions();

    [System.Runtime.InteropServices.DllImport
    ("__Internal")]
    extern static public void setListenerGameObject(
        string listenerName);

    string dT = "unknown";

    // Use this for initialization
    void Start ()
    {
        Debug.Log("Start called");
        setListenerGameObject(this.gameObject.name);
    }

    void OnGUI()
    {
        GUI.Label(new Rect(10,10,600,60), dT);
    }

    //Sent when the application successfully
    //registered with Apple Push Notification
    Service (APNS).
    void onDidRegisterForRemoteNotificationsWith
    DeviceToken(
        string deviceToken)
    {
        if (deviceToken != null && deviceToken.
        Length! =0)
```

```
            {
                Debug.Log("Device Token is " + deviceToken);
                dT = deviceToken;
            }
        }

        //Sent when the application failed to be regis-
        tered
        //with Apple Push Notification Service (APNS).
        void onDidFailToRegisterForRemoteNotificationsWith-
        Error(
            string error)
        {
                Debug.Log(error);
        }

        //Sent when the application Receives a push notifi-
        cation
        void onPushNotificationsReceived(string
        pushMessageString)
        {
                Debug.Log(pushMessageString);
        }
    }
```

Save and attach to the Main Camera.

This code taps into the precompiled code provided by *App42* that is
written for Xcode. It is beyond the scope of this book to explain the
intricacies of dealing with plugins except to present this code that will
get a Push Notification example working for you. The code imports two
functions from the API; `registerForRemoteNotifications()` and
`setListenerGameObject()`. When run, these functions register the
app and obtain a device token for push notifications and sit in wait for
any incoming messages.

Save. Build and run the app on your mobile device.

Step 14: When the app runs for the first time the device will ask for
permission to allow push notifications as shown in Figure 8.43.

Select OK. After push registration occurs, the GUI label on the screen will
display the device token. Remember this, as you will need it for sending
a push message to the app. If you do not receive a request to allow push
notification, ensure you have followed the certificate and provisioning
steps exactly.

You can also find the device token for this particular program in the
Xcode output window shown in Figure 8.44. And `Debug.Log()`
functions that run inside your Unity project will print out to this area
when the application has been built and run from the Unity Editor. It's

FIG 8.43 A standard iOS message asking for permission to turn on push notification.

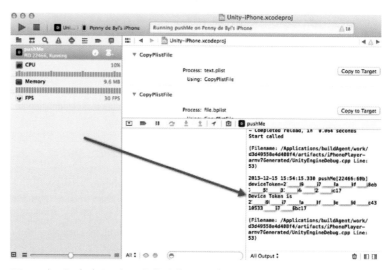

FIG 8.44 Locating the device token in the Xcode Output window.

a great trick for debugging other variables in Unity while testing on the phone. Once the device token is located in the output window in Xcode it is easy to copy and paste it for use later.

Step 15: Sending a push notification requires a server to connect to the APNS. There are third-party operators such as App42, Push IO (www.push.io), and Urban Airship (www.urbanairship.com) to name a few but for now we are going to use the services that come with Mac OS.

Recall the certificate and *.p12* files created earlier. You are now going to use them. Open a Terminal Window and navigate to the folder with your certificate and *.p12* files. Create a *.pem* file from the certificate by typing in:

```
openssl x509 -in aps_cert.cer -inform der -out PushCert.pem
```

Next create a .pem file from the .p12 key with:

```
openssl pkcs12 -nocerts -out PushKey.pem -in push_key.p12
```

This step will ask for the original password you placed on the key as well as a new password to place on the *.pem* file.

The *.pem* file format places the certificate and key into a format that the server code we will create in a moment can better deal with. Interestingly, the name stands for Privacy Enhanced Email, an old failed project for email security. Only the *.pem* file extension lived on.

To use both of these *.pem* files we join them into one with:

```
cat PushCert.pem PushKey.pem > ck.pem
```

Step 16: In the same folder as the *ck.pem* file create a new text file with a plain text editor such as Unitron, Monodevelop, or Textpad called simplepush.php. Add the following code:

```php
<?php

//code care of http://www.raywenderlich.com/32960/
apple-push-//notification-//services-in-ios-6-tutorial-
part-1

$deviceToken = 'YOUR_DEVICE_TOKEN_HERE';
$passphrase = 'holistic';
$message = 'My first push notification!';
$ctx = stream_context_create();
stream_context_set_option($ctx, 'ssl', 'local_cert',
'ck.pem');
stream_context_set_option($ctx, 'ssl', 'passphrase',
$passphrase);

// Open a connection to the APNS server
$fp = stream_socket_client(
    'ssl://gateway.sandbox.push.apple.com:2195', $err,
    $errstr, 60,
    STREAM_CLIENT_CONNECT|STREAM_CLIENT_PERSISTENT, $ctx);

if (!$fp)

    exit("Failed to connect: $err $errstr" . PHP_EOL);

echo 'Connected to APNS' . PHP_EOL;

// Create the payload body
$body['aps'] = array(
    'alert' = > $message,
    'sound' = > 'default'
    );
```

```
// Encode the payload as JSON
$payload = json_encode($body);

// Build the binary notification
$msg = chr(0) . pack('n', 32) . pack('H*',
$deviceToken) . pack('n', strlen($payload)) . $payload;

// Send it to the server
$result = fwrite($fp, $msg, strlen($msg));

if (!$result)
    echo 'Message not delivered' . PHP_EOL;
else
    echo 'Message successfully delivered' . PHP_EOL;

// Close the connection to the server
fclose($fp);
?>
```

Be sure to replace the `deviceToken` and `passphrase` with the one you recorded earlier. The code makes a connection with the APNS server and then delivers a payload.

For more information on the contents of an APNS payload see https://developer.apple.com/library/ios/documentation/ NetworkingInternet/Conceptual/RemoteNotificationsPG/ Chapters/ApplePushService.html#//apple_ref/doc/uid/ TP40008194-CH100-SW1.

Step 17: In the terminal window navigate to the folder with this php code and the *ck.pem* file. To execute a push notification type:

```
php simplepush.php
```

If a successful connection is made you will receive a message back from the APNS on the command line and a push notification should pop up on your phone as shown in Figure 8.45.

For another take on the use of APNS see the excellent tutorial at www.raywenderlich.com/32960/apple-push-notification-services-in-ios-6-tutorial-part-1.

FIG 8.45 A push notification arriving.

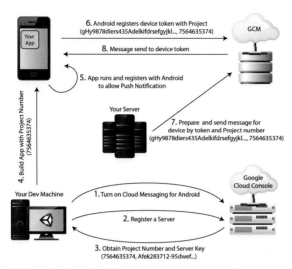

FIG 8.46 The Google Cloud Messaging device registration and push cycle.

8.4.2 Google Cloud Messaging for Android

The Google Cloud Messaging for Android (GCM) is a service run by Google that allows you to send push messages to mobile devices running your game. To use the service you need to run your own server (or use a third party's) to send messages to the Google HTTP or the GCM Cloud Connection (CCS) servers that push out the message to registered devices. Conceptually and structurally it's very much like APNS as shown in Figure 8.46. However, rather than the bundle ID tying all certificates and keys together, a project number (set up in the Google Cloud Console) is used to join all the processes.

In the hands-on session that follows we will investigate the GCM push process to the same extent as we did with the APNS.

⊙ **Unity Hands-On**
Getting Pushy with Android
The Unity side plugins used in this exercise are taken from Unity-GCM project in Github found here https://github.com/kskkbys/unity-gcm. You do not require this project to complete this hands-on session; however, it is provided should you wish to explore the functionality further and keep up-to-date with code changes in the future.

Download the *AndroidPush* project from the website. Setup your own Bundle ID. Create a new C# script called *GCMTest* and add the following code:

```
using UnityEngine;
using System.Collections;
using System.Collections.Generic;
```

```csharp
public class GCMTest : MonoBehaviour
{

    private string[] project_ids =
    {"YOUR_PROJECT_ID_HERE"};
    private string msgtext = "(null)";

    void Start ()
    {

        GCM.Initialize ();

        // Set callbacks
        GCM.SetErrorCallback ((string errorId) => {
            Debug.Log ("Error!!! " + errorId);
            GCM.ShowToast ("Error!!!");
            msgtext = "Error: " + errorId;
        });

        GCM.SetMessageCallback ((Dictionary<string,
        object>
            table) => {
                Debug.Log ("Message!!!");
                GCM.ShowToast ("Message!!!");
                msgtext = "Message: " + System.
                Environment.NewLine;
                foreach (var key in table.Keys) {
                    msgtext += key + " = " +
                    table[key] +
                    System.Environment.NewLine;
                }
        });

        GCM.SetRegisteredCallback ((string
        registrationId) => {
                Debug.Log ("Registered!!! " +
                registrationId);
                GCM.ShowToast ("Registered!!!");
                msgtext = "Register: " +
                registrationId;
        });

        GCM.SetUnregisteredCallback ((string
        registrationId) = > {
                Debug.Log ("Unregistered!!! " +
                registrationId);
                GCM.ShowToast ("Unregistered!!!");
                msgtext = "Unregister: " +
                registrationId;
        });

        GCM.SetDeleteMessagesCallback ((int total) => {
                Debug.Log ("DeleteMessages!!! " +
                total);
```

```
                GCM.ShowToast ("DeleteMessaged!!!");
                msgtext = "DeleteMessages: " + total;
        });
    }
    void OnGUI()
    {
        if (GUI.Button (new Rect(10, 10, 100, 60),
        "Register")) {
                GCM.Register (project_ids);
        }
        GUI.TextArea (new Rect(10, 80, 500, 100),
        msgtext);
    }
    void Update () {
    }
}
```

Save and attach the code to the Main Camera.

When you press play in the Editor you will see a register button and a textbox. The push functionality will not work in the editor.

Open *AndroidManifest.xml* in the Assets/Plugins/Android folder and replace the Bundle ID with your Bundle ID. It appears in three places. If you create a push application for Android from scratch you'll need to copy and use this *AndroidManifest.xml* file in your new project to ensure push is allowed by the app when installed.

Sign up with the Google Cloud Platform at https://cloud.google.com. Once this process is completed sign in and go to the console.

In the console create a new project by clicking on the big red button as shown in Figure 8.47. Give the project a name and select a project ID. Neither of the values entered here are significant so pick your own.

On completing the project creation you will be presented with a Project Number as shown in Figure 8.48. Take this number and retype exactly into the *GCMTest* script in place of YOUR_PROJECT_ID_HERE.

FIG 8.47 Creating a new Google Cloud Project.

In the Google Cloud Console under APIs turn on the Google Cloud Messaging for Android as shown in Figure 8.49.

In the left-hand menu click on Credentials and then the Public API access Create New Key, then Server Key, then Create. This is creating an authority for you to push messages from a Web service (as we did previously with the PHP for testing the APNS). The new app you are creating will be a Web service so be sure to select that option.

After the app has been registered, click on it in the Credentials to see the settings. The value you need to note is the Server API Key shown in Figure 8.50.

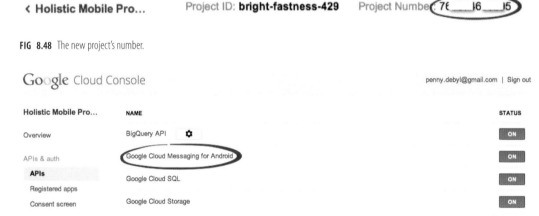

FIG 8.48 The new project's number.

FIG 8.49 Turning on Google Cloud Messaging for Android.

FIG 8.50 The API Key provided by Google for your push service.

Build the Unity app to an Android device. When running, press the Register button on the GUI and note the text that appears in the textbox after registration. It will be a very long string of letters and numbers. This is the Android device token. Take a copy of it.

Create a new text file on your computer called *androidpush.php* and add the following code:

```php
<?php
$apiKey = "YOUR_SERVER_KEY";
$registrationIDs =
array( "YOUR_VERY_LONG_DEVICE_TOKEN");

$message = "Pushing to Holistic Android Push";
$url = 'https://android.googleapis.com/gcm/send';

$fields = array('registration_ids' =>
$registrationIDs,
    'data' > array( "message" => $message,
    "ticker" => "Holistic Push",
    "content_title" => "Push Test",
    "content_text" => $message ),
    );

$headers = array('Authorization: key = ' . $apiKey,
    'Content-Type: application/json');

$ch = curl_init();

curl_setopt( $ch, CURLOPT_URL, $url );

curl_setopt( $ch, CURLOPT_POST, true );
curl_setopt( $ch, CURLOPT_HTTPHEADER, $headers);
curl_setopt( $ch, CURLOPT_RETURNTRANSFER, true );

curl_setopt( $ch, CURLOPT_POSTFIELDS, json_encode(
$fields ) );

$result = curl_exec($ch);

curl_close($ch);

echo $result;
?>
```

Replace the `apiKey` value with the one you obtained for your server from the Google Cloud Console and the `registrationIDs` with your device token. Note that this is an array and can send the push message out to more than one device at a time.

Open a Terminal window. Navigate to the location of the php script and enter:

```
php androidpush.php
```

All going well you will receive a push message on your Android device as shown in Figure 8.51.

FIG 8.51 A message pushed to an Android device.

For detailed information on GCM visit the developers guide at http://developer.android.com/google/gcm/index.html.

Both solutions for deploying APNS and GCM with Unity result in the all-important device token being reported inside the game. As you have seen, when the server sends a push notification to either APNS or GCM, the device token is required to identify the recipient of the message. The examples thus far have required us to manually copy and paste this token from the games into PHP server code. The ideal situation would be for the device token to be reported directly from the game to the server where it could be stored in a database for future use using similar methods as shown in Chapter 7.

After all the functionality has been added to your game and it has been thoroughly tested, it is ready to publish. However, a word to the wise—don't expect overnight success. The app stores are crowded places and your strategies for being noticed should begin as the same time that development does.

8.5 Promotion

It doesn't matter how good your game is if players never see it. Ben Cousins, executive producer at EA believes that in four to five years it will be near impossible for new entrants to become noticed.[7] Nevertheless, there are a number of approaches you can take to maximize your chance of success. They are outlined in this section.

8.5.1 Icon Design

One way to get noticed in the stores is to create a standout icon for your app. With so many icons competing for space on the device screen, it's the ones that are different that will attract the player's eye. In the example of two iOS screens, shown in Figure 8.52, a lot of icons are vying for attention.

The black background works well to bring any lighter colored images to the front. The whitest ones are indeed the standout. If you look at the image from far away and squint to make it out of focus, the icons that stand out the most are TV, eBay, and Reminders. However, with the white background, the darker ones stand out the most, with goMoney, Kindle, Bond Mobile, and

[7] Source: www.gamasutra.com/view/news/205515/Charting_the_future_of_the_mobile_games_space.php.

FIG 8.52 iOS icons displayed on a iPhone 5 with contrasting backgrounds.

Find iPhone being the standouts. Of course you can't control the color of the background on anyone's phone nor do users spend their time squinting at the screen. So the best you can hope for is to design a simple standout icon by following a few simple design rules.

Here are the top five rules you should adhere to when creating an app icon.

1. **You can't go past a good metaphor:** As discussed in Chapter 3, metaphors are universally recognized symbols that communicate a common meaning among viewers. For example the triangle play button. In Figure 8.52 several common metaphors are used on the in-built apps icons of the iOS including the camera, phone, messages, and mail. Over the years the logos of popular services such as Twitter and Facebook have also become metaphors.

Metaphors work well when they are presented with minimal colors; two contrasting colors work well. Most metaphors are silhouettes, symbolic of the items they represent. The shape you use must be immediately recognizable.

Google takes a reductive approach to designing icons. Their designers take everyday objects and well-known shapes and reduce them to recognizable silhouettes. In addition they restrict the color palette used to their internationally recognized red, green, blue, and yellow in addition to values of grey. This design standard is the template by which Google's designers work to ensure consistency in their icon designs.

2. **Use bold contrasting colors:** One of the most important thing people tend to dismiss when deciding on color is the relationship the projected color has with the human eye. It is the active light being projected from the mobile device screen that is perceived by the eye. White is therefore an active color that hits the retina. Black is the absence of light. The eye does not perceive black, but rather the colors around it. Of the two iOS screens shown in Figure 8.52, it is the dark background on the left that is far easier to view on an active screen as the background is not competing for attention with the information on the screen. The image on the right, however, projects nearly all of the background white onto the eye and the brain must pick out amongst all this noise the grey text.

Again, you have no control over the background color and text color shown with your icon but for the best display you want to create an icon with a good even balance of contrasting colors. If the background of the icon is dark, the images within should be light and vice versa.

3. **Get the right balance and proportions:** Apple's iOS 7 icons are created to a strict formula that fits within a grid on a rounded cornered square. Many templates are available to you for creating a conforming icon. Of course, you don't have to adhere to this type of design, but if you want your icon to look like an iOS icon or just need some direction with respect to good design layout then consider starting with the template. An example of the grid and an icon designed around it is shown in Figure 8.53.

   Get Photoshop templates for Apples iOS7 grid designs at www. eazytiger.net/blog/the-first-ios-7-icon-grid-photoshop-template and http://savvyapps.com/blog/ios-7-app-icon-template-obsessive-designers.

FIG 8.53 An icon created using the iOS 7 grid template.

4. **Great at all sizes:** An icon needs to be recognizable at 1,024 × 1,024 pixels and 57 × 57 pixels, where the first is the size of the icon in the App Store and the latter the icon on the screen of an iPhone 3. Simplicity of design, reduction of colors, and use of metaphors will greatly assist the process. When the icon is created it should also be pixel perfect. This means aligning each shape and color area in the icon to the pixel grid. When using a vector drawing tool for creating icons, if a shape overlaps the pixel grid then when rasterized anti-aliasing occurs, the edges of the shape are spread across two pixels instead of one and grey values are introduced removing any crisp borders. These fuzzy borders are exacerbated as the image is enlarged as shown in Figure 8.54.

FIG 8.54 An icon that is not pixel perfect (left) and the same that is pixel aligned (right).

For detailed instructions on aligning images to the pixel grid in Adobe Illustrator visit http://medialoot.com/blog/3-valuable-pixel-perfect-illustrator-techniques.

5. **Don't include text:** If you hadn't noticed already, on the mobile screen right under each icon is text. This is added by the operating system and tells the user exactly what each icon does (in as fewer characters as possible). Therefore, you don't need to integrate text into your icon design as, when it is at small icon size, users won't be able to read it anyway. The only exception to the rule is if your icon is only a single character like the one Facebook uses. But then again, unless you are as big and recognizable as Facebook, chances are slim that you will make a metaphor for yourself from the use of an alphabetical character.

Google's design standards can be examined at www.behance.net/gallery/Google-Visual-Assets-Guidelines-Part-1/9028077.

8.5.2 Getting Noticed

With some 2,000-plus apps being released daily, it's easy for your game to be overlooked. Apple does provide an option to sort by release date that may help generate some initial interest. Unfortunately, Google do not, and your game becomes a drop in the ocean, undiscoverable by all but those who know the exact name of your game and type it into the search surrounded by double-quotes. It really is very difficult to get discovered by chance in any app store.

There is a plethora of advice available on the Web on promoting mobile apps. Following are the top five suggestions for mobile game promotion that you can achieve with a very small or no budget.

1. **Create a webpage:** Even before the game is released you should create a webpage. On the page you should include full details about the game, the back story, a developer's journal, video trailers, video gameplay, screenshots, and any other assets to make the website a companion to the game. Creating the page beforehand means you will know the URL and can link to it from the game's description in the app store and inside the game itself. The webpage should also include direct download links to the app stores.

2. **Create a press kit:** Even before the game is released you'll want to start drumming up some interest. Putting together a collection of multimedia that describes and shows off your game in the best light is not something that you can just throw together at the last minute. It is best that the press kit be available online and the URL emailed to as many influential mobile game journalists as you can find email addresses for. Some journalists' email addresses are available in the magazine, on the magazine's website, or on personal blogs. The press kit should include details about you, a description of the game, a list of the key unique features of the game, a walk-through of the gameplay, screenshots, a trailer video, and gameplay video.

3. **Pay someone else to do it:** If you have the budget and you really aren't into self-promotion then you should get someone else to promote the game for you. There are a number of online services that can do this including Appency (www.appency.com), Appular (http://appular.com), and App Promo (http://app-promo.com).

   In addition, you might consider joining a publishing network such as Chillingo (publishers of *Angry Birds* and *Cut the Rope*). They will take a percentage of your profits, but if you currently don't have any profits then it has to be a better deal.

   Unity also has its own publishing arm Unity Games (www.unitygames. com) through which you can get development and promotional support for your game.

4. **Release it for free initially:** Free mobile games enjoy a 9:1 download rate compared to paid games. If you are to have a paid game, instead of including IAP, why not release the game for free initially, build up some

hype and players, and then revert to a flat download rate? Apps going free for short periods of time can get picked up by promotional services such as Apps Gone Free (http://appadvice.com/appnn/tag/appsgonefree) and Free App a Day (http://freeappaday.com).

5. **Promote on social media:** It goes without saying that you should be telling all your friends and followers on Facebook and Twitter about your game, even though this will only have limited reach. You will also want to ensure that the players of the game also tell their friends and the best way to do this is to integrate Facebook and Twitter functionality into the game itself. You should also create a page in Facebook for the game and promote it if you have the finances. Page promotion starts at $US6 per day.

There are also people on Fiverr (www.fiverr.com) and Craigslist (www. craigslist.org) that you can pay to promote your game on their social networks. For $5 you could have someone else promote your game to 120,000 people in their social network.

Accessing the player's social network requires the use of plugins for Unity. In the next sections we will investigate the integration of Facebook and Twitter with your game.

8.5.3 Facebook Integration

Facebook is a popular place to post messages about game use and status. The system itself has also become a widespread method for user authentication. Many third-party applications and games are now using Facebook profiles of their users to populate their data. For example, Web services such as Vimeo (www.vimeo.com) and Prezi (www.prezi.com) and online games providers Reign of Blood (http://reignofblood.net) and MindJolt (www.mindjolt.com) have integrated Facebook logins.

Since mid-2013, Facebook integration with Unity has become a lot easier. Facebook released the free Unity Facebook SDK that is now available in the Unity Asset Store and will be used in the next hands-on session.

⦾ **Unity Hands-On**
Posting to Facebook
Step 1: Create a new Unity Android or iOS project. If you have a choice, setting up Facebook for Android is a simpler process, however both will be covered here. Setup the Bundle ID in the player preferences of the build settings.
Step 2: Select Window > Asset Store
Step 3: In the store locate the Facebook SDK for Unity plugin as shown in Figure 8.55. Import it into your project.

Step 4: Visit http://developers.facebook.com and login with your Facebook details. Select App > Create New App from the top menu bar as shown in Figure 8.56. Give the app a name and select a category. Submit.

Step 5: The next page that opens will display the Dashboard and the details of this new Facebook app. At the top of the page you will see an App ID and App Secret as shown in Figure 8.57. You will need these to integrate your app with Facebook, so keep them handy.

Step 6: Select the Settings Link from the Dashboard menu. Click on the Add Platform button and add iOS, Android or both.

Step 7: In Unity, with the Facebook SDK imported, there will be a new option for Facebook in the top main menu. Select Facebook > Edit Settings to bring up the settings panel in the Inspector. In it, place your Facebook App ID as shown in Figure 8.59.

FIG 8.55 The Facebook SDK for Unity in the Asset Store.

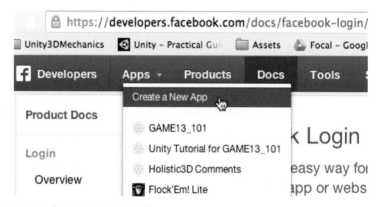

FIG 8.56 Create a new app in Facebook.

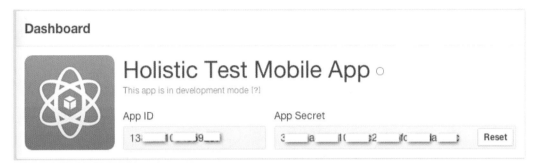

FIG 8.57 The App ID and App Secret for your Facebook app.

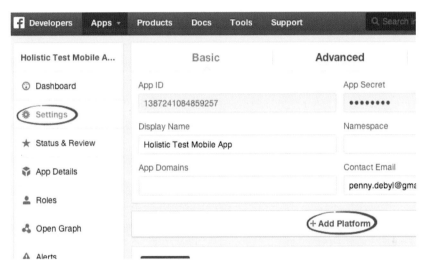

FIG 8.58 Adding platform support to a Facebook app.

This panel also shows you the details you need to transcript over to the Facebook app's settings page in the Dashboard if you are building for Android. Several of these values are based on the Bundle ID and that is why it is important to do it first. Transfer the values for Package Name, Class Name, and Debug Android Key Hash as they appear in your Unity across into the Android Settings. Turn Single-Sign On to On if you want this ability in your app.

Step 8: If you are building for iOS, the information required in the Facebook settings must come from iTunes Connect. And the Bundle ID chosen must be the same as the one you are using in Unity. To get this new Bundle ID to show up in the list given by iTunes Connect as shown in Figure 8.41, the app must be registered in the Apple Dev Center first. If you haven't registered the App ID you can use the link to get a new Bundle ID as shown in Figure 8.60.

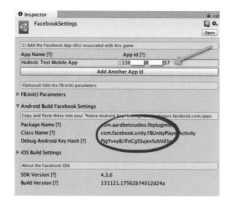

FIG 8.59 The Facebook Settings panel in Unity.

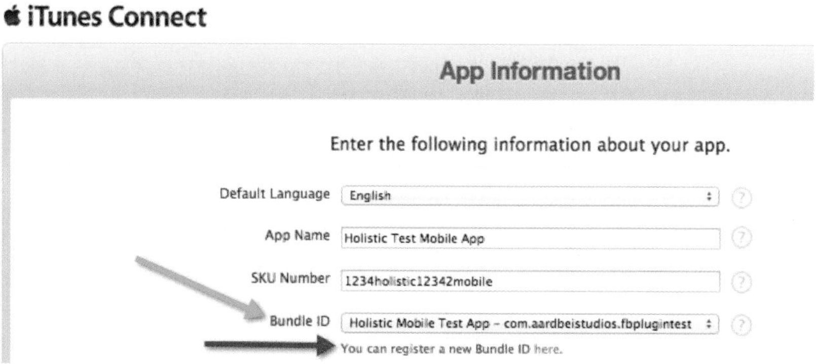

iTunes Connect

App Information

Enter the following information about your app.

Default Language   English

App Name   Holistic Test Mobile App

SKU Number   1234holistic12342mobile

Bundle ID   Holistic Mobile Test App – com.aardbeistudios.fbplugintest
You can register a new Bundle ID here.

FIG 8.60 Setting up an App in iTunes Connect.

After going through the App creation process in iTunes Connect you will be presented with an App ID. If you want the Facebook compatibility on both iPhone and iPad then be sure to include screen images for both sizes when asked.

Take the App ID and put it into the Facebook Settings page in the Dashboard as shown in Figure 8.61.

Save the changes in the Facebook Dashboard.

● Note

If you have only just created the Apple ID for the app and gone straight to adding it into the Facebook settings, you will receive a warning on saving. Facebook will not be able to find your new Apple ID if the app has not been released in the stores. You can use another released app ID in its place for testing purposes. This is not ideal. However, without having an app ID registered with Facebook you can still test the code in this exercise.

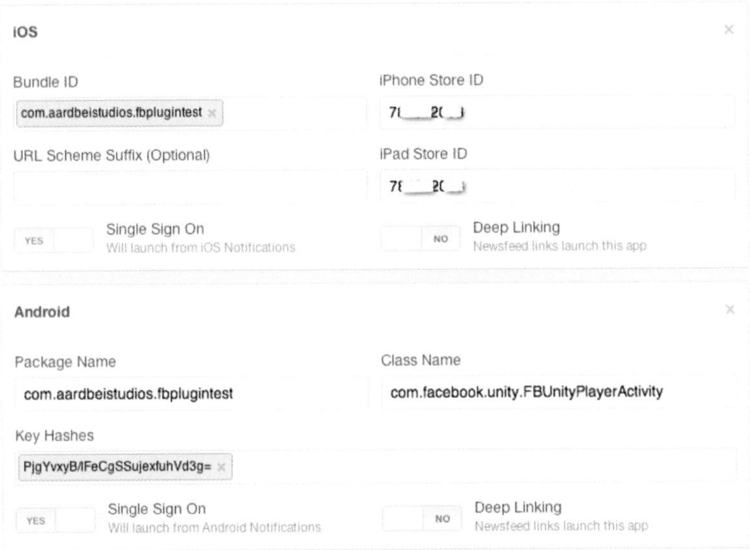

FIG 8.61 Setting up IDs to link your app to Facebook.

Step 9: In Unity, create a new Scene. Add a new C# script called *FacebookTester* and add the following code:

```
using UnityEngine;
using System.Collections;

public class FacebookTester : MonoBehaviour
{
    private bool isInit = false;
    string messages = "";
    public Vector2 scrollPosition = Vector2.zero;

    private void CallFBInit()
    {
        messages += "Initialising. . . . \n";
        FB.Init(OnInitComplete, OnHideUnity);
    }

    private void OnInitComplete()
    {
        messages += "FB.Init successful.\n";
        messages += "Logged in? " +
        FB.IsLoggedIn + "\n";
        isInit = true;
    }

    private void CallFBLogin()
    {
```

```
                FB.Login("email,publish_actions",
                LoginCallback);
        }
        void LoginCallback(FBResult result)
        {
                if (result.Error ! = null)
                    messages += "Error Response:" +
                    result.Error +
                        "\n";
                else if (!FB.IsLoggedIn) {
                    messages + =
                    "Login cancelled by Player\n";
                }
                else
                {
                    messages + = "Logged in.\n";
                }
        }

        private void OnHideUnity(bool isGameShown)
        {
                messages += "Game Visible? " +
                isGameShown + "\n";
        }
        void OnGUI()
        {
            if(GUI.Button(new Rect(10,10,100,60),"Initialise
            FB"))
            {
                    CallFBInit();
            }

        if(GUI.Button(new Rect(10,80,100,60),"Login"))
        {
                    if(FB.IsLoggedIn)
                        messages +=
                        "Already Logged In.\n";
                    else
                        CallFBLogin();
        }

        if(GUI.Button(new Rect(10,150,100,60),"Logout"))
        {
                    FB.Logout();
                    messages += "Logged out.\n";
        }

        scrollPosition = GUI.BeginScrollView(
            new Rect(10, Screen.height - 200, Screen.
            width-20,
            190), scrollPosition, new Rect(0,0,Screen.
            width-20, 600));
```

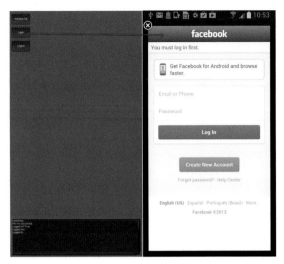

FIG 8.62 Logging into Facebook on Android.

```
GUI.TextArea(new Rect(10, 10, Screen.width-20,
    600), messages);

GUI.EndScrollView();
}
}
```

Attach the script to the Main Camera, save and run in the Editor. You'll be able to try initializing and logging in. Try also building out to your mobile device. Press the Initialize button first. If you are already logged in, press the Logout button and then try logging in. The device will switch to a Facebook login page as shown in Figure 8.62.

The code for this functionality is split into a set of calls to functions made by button presses and a series of callback functions. The callback functions are run by the Facebook SDK when certain events happen. For example after you press the Log In button, the functionality is given over to the Facebook SDK which does its thing and when finished reports back to your code via the LoginCallback() function.

In a game setting you wouldn't have such an elaborate series of buttons for the user to press through just to connect to Facebook. You could do it automatically or on a single button press for example:

```
...
void Start()
{
    FB.Init(OnInitComplete, OnHideUnity);
}
```

```
private void OnInitComplete()
{
    FB.Login("email,publish_actions",
    LoginCallback);
}

void LoginCallback(FBResult result)
{
    if (result.Error != null)
        messages += "Error Response: " + result.Error +
        "\n";
    else if (!FB.IsLoggedIn) {
        messages += "Login cancelled by Player\n";
    }
    else
    {
        messages += "Logged in.\n";
    }
}
...
```

The string given to the FB.Login() function is a comma delimited list of permissions you are asking from your player. For details on these see https://developers.facebook.com/docs/reference/login.

Step 10: Once the player is logged into Facebook your game will be able to post to their wall. To do this, first add a new button into the OnGUI() code thus:

```
if(GUI.Button(new Rect(10,220,100,60),"Post"))
{
    StartCoroutine(PostMessage());
    messages += "Posting Message.\n";
}
```

Next you need to create a new function to perform the post and a callback method for it. Place the following just above the OnGUI() function:

```
void GenericCallback(FBResult result)
{
    if (result.Error != null)
        messages += "Error Response:\n" + result.Error
        + "\n";
    else
    {
        messages += "Success Response\n";
    }
}

private IEnumerator PostMessage()
{
    yield return new WaitForEndOfFrame();
```

```
    var wwwForm = new WWWForm();
    wwwForm.AddField("message",
        "Testing my Unity game Facebook functionality " +
        "I learned about in Holistic Mobile Game
        Development");

    FB.API("me/feed", Facebook.HttpMethod.POST,
    GenericCallback, wwwForm);
}
```

Save, build and test on your device. All having gone to plan you will get a post come up on your Facebook feed as shown in Figure 8.63.

The function doing all the work here is `FB.API()`. The first parameter tells Facebook where to put the post, the second to expect a post, the third is the callback function to run after the post occurs, and the fourth is the data for the post. Note the data is in the form of a `WWWForm` that we examined in Chapter 7.

The first parameter, in this case "me/feed" is the location in the Facebook Graph where you want to post information to or get information from. The Graph is a large tree of nodes containing all the data stored in Facebook. Of course you can only get out the data you have permission to access.

Step 11: To request information from Facebook about the player, instead of using a `Facebook.HttpMethod.POST` we use a `Facebook.HttpMethod.GET`. Try this out by getting the player's profile picture and displaying it in Facebook with the following changes to your code:

```
using UnityEngine;
using System.Collections;

public class FacebookTester : MonoBehaviour
{
    private bool isInit = false;
    string messages = "";
    public Vector2 scrollPosition = Vector2.zero;

    private Texture2D playerPicture;

    void TextureCallback(FBResult result)
    {
```

Penny de Byl
Testing my Unity game Facebook functionality I learned about in Holistic Mobile Game Development

Like · Comment · Share · 20 seconds ago via Holistic Test Mobile App · 🔧 ▼

FIG 8.63 How the post from Unity will appear in Facebook.

```
        playerPicture = null;
        if (result.Error ! = null)
            messages += "Error:\n" + result.Error + "\n";
        else
        {
            playerPicture = result.Texture;
            messages += "Success!\n";
        }
    }

    void OnGUI()
    {

        if(GUI.Button(new Rect(10,290,100,60),"Get Picture"))
        {
            FB.API("me/picture", Facebook.HttpMethod.GET,
                TextureCallback);
            messages += "Requesting User Picture.\n";
        }
        if(playerPicture != null)
        {
            GUI.DrawTexture(new Rect(Screen.width - 210, 10,
                200,200), playerPicture, ScaleMode.ScaleToFit);
        }
        ...
```

Save and build out to your device. After initializing Facebook and ensuring the player is logged in, pressing the Get Picture button will return the player's profile picture and place it in the upper right of the screen as shown in Figure 8.64.

The FB.API() function makes calls to the Facebook interface using the strings "me/feed" or "me/picture" and others. These are analogous to the direct calls as shown at https://developers.facebook.com/docs/reference/api/examples. The full call has the format: https://graph.facebook.com/ followed by a specific request string and an access token. The access token is required to access user information to which your app has been given access. The FB.API() call in Unity takes care of the https prefix and the access token suffix such that you end up giving it just the part that requests the information you desire.

Step 12: To post a screenshot to Facebook, we first capture the image on the device and save it to a 2D Texture. Next the form posting data to Facebook is modified to include a binary field into which the texture is copied. Modify your code to include this functionality thus:

```
    ...

    private IEnumerator PostScreenshot()
    {
        yield return new WaitForEndOfFrame();
```

FIG 8.64 Displaying the Facebook profile picture of a player.

```
    var width = Screen.width;
    var height = Screen.height;
    var image = new Texture2D(width, height,
        TextureFormat.RGB24, false);

    image.ReadPixels(new Rect(0, 0, width, height), 0, 0);
    image.Apply();
    byte[] screenshot = image.EncodeToPNG();

    var wwwForm = new WWWForm();
    wwwForm.AddBinaryData("image", screenshot,
        "HolisticFacebook.png");

    wwwForm.AddField("message", "Posting Screenshot from
        Holistic Mobile Dev Tutorial.");

    FB.API("me/photos", Facebook.HttpMethod.POST,
        GenericCallback, wwwForm);
}
void OnGUI()
{
    ...
    if(GUI.Button(new Rect(10,360,100,60),"Screenshot"))
    {
        StartCoroutine(PostScreenshot());
        messages += "Posting Screenshot.\n";
    }
    ...
```

Save, build to your device, and test. An image of the current screen will be taken and posted to your Facebook feed as shown in Figure 8.65.

Step 13: It is also possible to call up native Facebook dialog boxes from within Unity. To pull up a friend's list to which you can send a request about your app try adding this button into the OnGUI()

```
    ...
    if(GUI.Button(new Rect(10,430,100,60),"Friends"))
    {
        FB.AppRequest(
            message: "Check out Holistic Mobile Game
            Development!",
            callback: GenericCallback);
        messages += "Getting Friends.\n";
    }
    ...
```

Note, requests will not be sent when the app is in sandbox mode. You must make it live in the Facebook Dashboard's Status and Review section. When a friend receives a request it looks like that in Figure 8.66.

FIG 8.65 A screen shot posted to Facebook.

Holistic Test Mobile App
1 request – Ignore all

Daniel De Byl
Check out Holistic Mobile Game Development!
10 minutes ago

Accept ✕

FIG 8.66 A Facebook request sent from your app.

A prefilled feed dialog can also be called up by adding:

```
if(GUI.Button(new Rect(10,500,100,60),
"Feed Dialog"))
{
FB.Feed(link: "http://www.holistic3d.com",
    linkName: "Holistic Game Development",
    linkCaption: "An Awesome Website",
    linkDescription: "Everything you ever wanted to
    know about game development.",
    picture: "http://holistic3d.com/wp-
    content/uploads/2011/11/frontCover.jpg",
    callback: GenericCallback
);
}
```

FIG 8.67 The Facebook feed dialog called up from the code.

Save and build to your mobile for testing. The feed dialog will appear as in Figure 8.67.

For all the details on integrating Unity with Facebook see the reference guide at https://developers.facebook.com/docs/unity. In addition, the Facebook SDK downloaded at the start of the hands-on session has example code you can explore to broaden your understanding of its functionality.

8.5.4 Twitter (Twitter iOS plugin)

While, at the time of writing, Twitter hasn't released its own Unity plugin like Facebook, there are a number of third-party options available in the Unity Asset Store. In this section we will examine a freely available one for iOS called Twitter iOS Plugin by GenITeam. It links directly with the built in iOS Twitter functionality and is a snap to implement. Note, publishing to Twitter via Android will not be covered, as at the time of writing there were no freely available Unity plugins; however, the principle is much the same. Check the Unity asset store to see what is available.

Twitter Integration

Step 1: Create a new iOS Unity project. Download and import the *Twitter iOS Plugin* from the Asset Store. Create a new C# script called *TwitterTester* and add the following code:

```
using UnityEngine;
using System.Collections;

public class TwitterTester : MonoBehaviour {

    string tweet = "";
    public static string tweetPhoto = "screenShot.png";

    void GetImage()
    {
        Application.CaptureScreenshot( tweetPhoto );
    }

    void OnGUI()
    {
        GUI.Label(new Rect(10,10,200,30),
        "Tweet Text");

        tweet = GUI.TextArea(new Rect(10,40,300,60),
        tweet);
        if(GUI.Button(new Rect(10,110,100,60),"Tweet"))
        {
            TwitterSDK.postStatusUpdate(tweet);
        }

        if(GUI.Button(new Rect(10,170,100,60),
        "Tweet Photo"))
        {
            GetImage();
            TwitterSDK.postStatusUpdateWithImage
            (tweet,
                Application.persistentDataPath + "/"
                + tweetPhoto);
        }
    }
}
```

Attach the script to the Main Camera, save, and build to your iOS device. This code includes a text area and two buttons. One button will tweet just the text to Twitter and the other will include a screen capture photo. If the user is not logged into Twitter, the iOS takes over and asks the user to login. In addition, all message-posting dialogs that appear belong to the iOS.

For more expert information on indie game marketing see www.pixelprospector.com/the-big-list-of-indie-game-marketing.

It would seem that promoting your mobile game and making it stand out from the crowd involves as much work as creating the game in the first place. And it does. You've created an awesome game and put a lot of your heart and soul into its production and now you need to show just as much enthusiasm telling everyone about it. It's not easy and as Appency's catchphrase states, you have to *make a big noise* about it.

8.6 Summary

The creative process of design and developing a great mobile game seems contradictory to the strategic and sometimes political landscape of publicity and monetizing. Many game designers live in hope that, like great artists and actors, they will be *discovered*. The reality is that it is a long road to success and you will need help. Make a big noise about your game. Tell as many people as possible and get those people to tell as many people as possible. Hire experts who know what they are doing to get your game seen and downloaded by as many players as possible. Furthermore, listen to the advice of those who've come before you. You are no longer creating just a mobile game, but building up a supporting narrative and network around it that will entice and engage new players.

Index